INSTRUCTOR'S RESOURCE MANUAL WITH CHAPTER TESTS

RICHARD N. AUFMANN

VERNON C. BARKER

JOANNE S. LOCKWOOD

MARIA H. ANDERSEN

INTERMEDIATE ALGEBRA: AN APPLIED APPROACH

SEVENTH EDITION

Richard N. Aufmann
Palomar College

Vernon C. Barker
Palomar College

Joanne S. Lockwood
Plymouth State College

HOUGHTON MIFFLIN COMPANY   BOSTON NEW YORK

Senior Sponsoring Editor: Lynn Cox
Associate Editor: Melissa Parkin
Senior Project Editor: Nancy Blodget
Manufacturing Coordinator: Karmen Chong
Marketing Manager: Ben Rivera

Printed in the U.S.A.

ISBN: 0-618-520384

1 2 3 4 5 6 7 8 9-EB-09 08 07 06 05

PREFACE

The Instructor's Resource Manual for Aufmann/Barker/Lockwood's Intermediate Algebra: An Applied Approach contains suggested Course Sequences, Chapter Tests, Answers to the Chapter Tests, and AIM for Success Slide Show printouts.

The Chapter Tests contain four multiple-choice and four free-response tests per chapter as well as assorted cumulative tests. These ready-to-use tests may be photocopied and are designed to take one hour. Answers are provided in a separate section.

A PowerPoint® Slide Show, which presents a lesson plan for the AIM for Success student preface in the text, is available on the instructor's Class Prep CD as well as the text website. Full printouts of the ten slides (which may be used as transparency masters) as well as a smaller printout of each slide with its accompanying instructor notes are provided in this resource manual.

Contents

COURSE SEQUENCES

Basic Course Sequence

Week	Suggested Assignment
1	Sections 1.1, 1.2, and 1.3
2	Section 1.4 Test, Chapter 1 Section 2.1
3	Sections 2.3, 2.4, and 2.5
4	Test, Chapter 2 Sections 3.1, 3.2, and 3.3
5	Sections 3.4 and 3.5 Test, Chapter 3
6	Sections 4.1, 4.2, and 4.3
7	Section 4.4 Test, Chapter 4 Sections 5.1 and 5.2
8	Sections 5.3, 5.4, 5.5, and 5.6
9	Test, Chapter 5 Sections 6.1, 6.2, and 6.4
10	Section 6.5 Test, Chapter 6 Section 7.1
11	Sections 7.2, 7.3, and 7.4
12	Test, Chapter 7 Sections 8.1, 8.3, and 8.4
13	Section 8.6 Test, Chapter 8 Section 9.1
14	Sections 9.2, 9.3, and 9.4 Test, Chapter 9
15	Sections 10.1, 10.2, and 10.3
16	Sections 10.4 and 10.5 Test, Chapter 10

Average Course Sequence

Week	Suggested Assignment
1	Sections 1.1, 1.2, 1.3, and 1.4
2	Sections 2.1, 2.2, 2.3, and 2.4
3	Section 2.5 Test, Chapters 1–2 Sections 3.1 and 3.2
4	Sections 3.3, 3.4, 3.5, and 3.7
5	Sections 4.1, 4.2, 4.3, and 4.4
6	Test, Chapters 3–4 Sections 5.1, 5.2, and 5.3
7	Sections 5.4, 5.5, and 5.6 Section 6.1
8	Sections 6.2, 6.3, 6.4, and 6.5
9	Section 6.6 Test, Chapters 5–6 Sections 7.1 and 7.2
10	Sections 7.3 and 7.4 Sections 8.1 and 8.2
11	Sections 8.3, 8.4, and 8.6
12	Test, Chapters 7–8 Sections 9.1 and 9.2
13	Sections 9.3 and 9.4 Sections 10.1 and 10.2
14	Sections 10.3, 10.4, and 10.5 Test, Chapters 9–10
15	Sections 11.1, 11.2, and 11.3
16	Sections 12.1 and 12.4 Test, Chapters 11–12

Comprehensive Course Sequence

Week	Suggested Assignment
1	Sections 1.1, 1.2, 1.3, and 1.4
2	Sections 2.1, 2.2, 2.3, 2.4, and 2.5
3	Sections 3.1, 3.2, 3.3, and 3.4
4	Sections 3.5, 3.6, and 3.7 Test, Chapters 1–3
5	Sections 4.1, 4.2, 4.3, and 4.4
6	Section 4.5 Sections 5.1, 5.2, and 5.3
7	Sections 5.4, 5.5, and 5.6 Section 6.1
8	Sections 6.2, 6.3, 6.4, and 6.5
9	Section 6.6 Test, Chapters 4–6 Sections 7.1 and 7.2
10	Sections 7.3 and 7.4 Sections 8.1 and 8.2
11	Sections 8.3, 8.4, 8.5, and 8.6
12	Sections 9.1, 9.2, 9.3, and 9.4
13	Test, Chapters 7–9 Sections 10.1, 10.2, and 10.3
14	Sections 10.4 and 10.5 Sections 11.1 and 11.2
15	Sections 11.3, 11.4, and 11.5 Section 12.1
16	Sections 12.2, 12.3, and 12.4 Test, Chapters 10–12

CHAPTER TESTS

Form A Tests

Free Response

Name: _____

Date: _____

1. Solve by factoring: $3x^2 - 10x - 8 = 0$

2. Solve by factoring: $4x(x+2) = 16x - 3$

3. Write a quadratic equation that has integer coefficients and has solutions $-2/3$ and 3.

4. Solve by taking square roots: $x^2 - 288 = 0$

5. Solve by taking square roots: $2(x-2)^2 - 18 = 0$

6. Solve by completing the square: $x^2 + 8x - 2 = 0$

7. Solve by completing the square: $x^2 - 6x - 10 = 0$

8. Solve by using the quadratic formula: $x^2 + 5x - 2 = 0$

9. Solve by using the quadratic formula: $9x^2 - 18x + 2 = 0$

10. Use the discriminant to determine whether $3x^2 - 4x = -2$ has one real number solution, two real number solutions, or two complex number solutions.

11. Solve: $x^4 - 81 = 0$

12. Solve: $x - 8x^{1/2} + 15 = 0$

13. Solve: $\sqrt{x-4} = 6 - x$

14. Solve: $\sqrt{12x-7} = 3x - 1$

15. Solve: $\dfrac{x+3}{x-3} - x = 3$

16. Solve: $\dfrac{3}{x-1} - \dfrac{2}{x+2} = 1$

17. Solve and graph the solution set of $2x^2 + 5x - 12 < 0$.

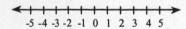

18. Solve and graph the solution set of $\dfrac{x}{x-3} < -2$.

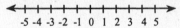

19. One car travels 200 mi. A second car, traveling 10 mi/h faster than the first car, makes the same trip in 1 hour less time. Find the speed of the slower car.

20. The length of a rectangle is 1 m more than three times the width. The area of the rectangle is 200 m². Find the length of the rectangle.

1. Find the vertex and axis of symmetry of the parabola given by $y = 2x^2 - 5x + 3$.

2. State the domain and range of the function $f(x) = x^2 - 4x + 1$.

3. Graph: $f(x) = -x^2 - 2x + 3$

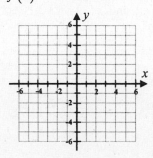

4. Graph: $f(x) = |x| - 1$

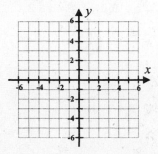

5. Find the x-intercepts of $y = 3x^2 - 11x + 6$.

6. Find the zeros of $f(x) = x^2 + 6x + 2$.

7. Use the discriminant to determine the number of x-intercepts of the graph of $y = 3x^2 + 5x + 2$.

8. Find the minimum value of the function $f(x) = x^2 - 4x - 7$.

9. Find two numbers whose sum is 40 and whose product is a maximum.

10. A rectangle has a perimeter of 40 ft. Find the maximum area of the rectangle.

Name: _____

11. Determine whether the graph represents the graph of a function.

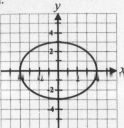

12. Determine whether the graph represents the graph of a 1-1 function.

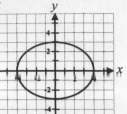

13. For $f(x) = x^2 + 1$ and $g(x) = x - 2$, find $f(1) - g(1)$.

14. For $f(x) = 2x - 1$ and $g(x) = x + 3$, find $(f \cdot g)(2)$.

15. For $f(x) = 3x - 2$ and $g(x) = x^2 - 2x + 4$, find $\left(\dfrac{f}{g}\right)(-2)$.

16. Given $f(x) = 4x + 1$ and $g(x) = 5x - 2$, find $f[g(2)]$.

17. Given $g(x) = x^2 + 1$ and $h(x) = x - 2$, find $g[h(x)]$.

18. Let $f(x) = \dfrac{x+1}{3}$. Find $f^{-1}(x)$.

19. Are the functions $f(x) = x - 2$ and $g(x) = 2 - x$ inverses of each other?

20. Find the inverse of the function $\{(1,3), (2,5), (6,7)\}$.

Chapters 7-9 Cumulative Test A

Name: ______________________
Date: ______________________

1. Simplify: $\left(4a^6b^2\right)^{1/2}\left(8a^3b^9\right)^{1/3}$

2. Write $\left(2x^2+7\right)^{1/2}$ as a radical expression.

3. Simplify: $\sqrt{16y}-\sqrt{20x^2y}$

4. Simplify: $\left(\sqrt{12}+\sqrt{-27}\right)-\left(\sqrt{3}-\sqrt{-48}\right)$

5. Solve: $\sqrt[5]{8x}+4=6$

6. Write a quadratic equation that has integer coefficients and has solutions $\frac{1}{3}$ and -2.

7. Solve by taking square roots: $3x^2-12=0$

8. Solve by completing the square: $x^2-6x+4=0$

9. Solve: $x^4-x^2-6=0$

10. Solve: $\sqrt{3x+10}=x+4$

11. Solve: $x^2 - 5x - 14 > 0$

12. The length of a rectangle is 5 ft more than twice the width. The area of the rectangle is 250 ft^2. Find the length of the rectangle.

13. State the domain and range of the function $f(x) = -x^2 - 3x + 1$.

14. Find the minimum value of $f(x) = x^2 - 2x + 9$.

15. Graph: $y = x^2 + 6x + 3$

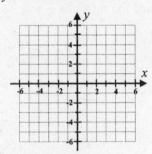

16. Graph: $f(x) = |x + 2|$

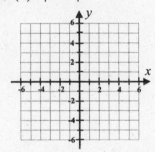

17. Let $f(x) = 3x - 9$. Find $f^{-1}(x)$.

18. Given $f(x) = x^2 - 4$ and $g(x) = 3 - x$, find $\left(\dfrac{f}{g}\right)(-1)$.

19. Given $f(x) = 1 - x$ and $g(x) = x^2 + 3$, find $(f \cdot g)(2)$.

20. Given $f(x) = 3x - 1$ and $g(x) = 2x + 1$, find $g[f(4)]$.

1. Given the function $f(x) = e^{3x}$, evaluate $f(-1)$. Round to the nearest ten-thousandth.

2. Given $P(x) = \left(\dfrac{1}{2}\right)^{2x}$, evaluate $P\left(-\dfrac{1}{2}\right)$.

3. Graph: $f(x) = 2^{x-2}$

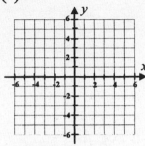

4. Evaluate: $\log_5 625$

5. Solve for x: $\log_3 x = 4$

6. Write $2^3 = 8$ in logarithmic form.

7. Write $\log_5 125 = 3$ in exponential form.

8. Write $\log_3 \dfrac{x^2 y z^4}{\sqrt{y}}$ in expanded form.

9. Write $2\log_2 x - 5\log_2 y - \log_2 z$ as a single logarithm with a coefficient of 1.

10. Evaluate: $\log_2 3$
    Round to the nearest ten-thousandth.

11. Write $\ln\left(\dfrac{\sqrt{x}}{2y}\right)$ in expanded form.

12. Write $2\ln y - \ln x - \dfrac{1}{3}\ln z$ as a single logarithm with a coefficient of 1.

13. Evaluate: $\log_2 15$
Round to the nearest ten-thousandth.

14. Graph: $f(x) = \log_3(x-4)$

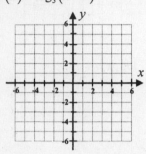

15. Solve for x: $5^x = 20$
Round to the nearest ten-thousandth.

16. Solve for x: $4^{3x-1} = 16^{x+3}$

17. Solve for x: $27^{2x-1} = 81^{x+2}$

18. Solve for x: $\log_5(3x) - \log_5(x^2 - 1) = \log_5 2$

19. Solve for x: $\log_5(3x+2) = 3$

20. An investment of \$10,000 is placed into an account that earns 12% interest compounded quarterly. In approximately how many years will the investment be worth twice the original amount? Use the compound interest formula $P = A(1+I)^n$, where A is the original value of the investment, I is the interest rate per compounding period, n is the total number of compounding periods, and P is the value of the investment after n periods.

Name: _____

Date: _____

1. Graph: $x = 2y^2 - 4y + 1$

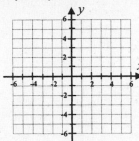

2. Graph: $y = x^2 - 4x - 1$

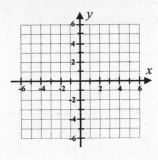

3. Find the vertex and axis of symmetry of the parabola given by $y = 3x^2 - 2x + 1$.

4. Find the equation of the circle (in standard form) with radius 5 and center $(3, -2)$.

5. Find the equation of the circle (in standard form) that passes through the point $(2, -1)$ and whose center is $(-1, 4)$.

6. Write the equation $x^2 + y^2 + 2y - 24 = 0$ in standard form and then sketch its graph.

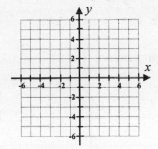

7. Write the equation $x^2 + y^2 - 6x + 4y + 4 = 0$ in standard form and then sketch its graph.

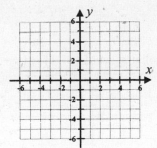

8. Sketch a graph of $\dfrac{x^2}{9} + \dfrac{y^2}{4} = 1$.

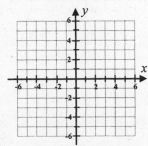

9. Sketch a graph of $\dfrac{x^2}{9} + \dfrac{y^2}{36} = 1$.

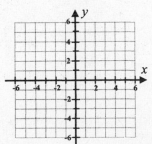

Name: _____

10. Sketch a graph of $\dfrac{x^2}{25} - \dfrac{y^2}{4} = 1$.

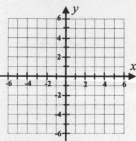

11. Sketch a graph of $\dfrac{y^2}{4} - \dfrac{x^2}{9} = 1$.

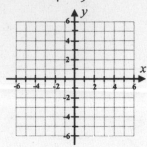

12. Solve: $y = x^2 - 3x + 2$

$y = -x^2 + 4x + 6$

13. Solve: $2x^2 + y^2 = 18$

$x^2 - y^2 = 6$

14. Graph the solution set of $(x-1)^2 + (y-3)^2 \le 9$.

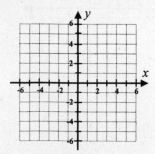

15. Graph the solution set: $(x+1)^2 + y^2 \le 25$

$x - 2y \le -2$

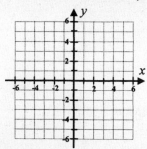

Name: _____

Date: _____

1. Write the 5th term of the sequence whose nth term is given by the formula $a_n = \dfrac{n+1}{2n}$.

2. Write the 5th and 12th terms of the sequence whose nth term is given by the formula $a_n = \dfrac{n-1}{n+3}$.

3. Evaluate: $\displaystyle\sum_{n=1}^{5}(n-2)$

4. Write $\displaystyle\sum_{n=1}^{4}\frac{n}{2}x^n$ in expanded form.

5. Find the 21st term of the arithmetic sequence $-7, -3, 1, \ldots$

6. Find the formula for the nth term of the arithmetic sequence $2, 7, 12, \ldots$

7. Find the number of terms in the finite arithmetic sequence $2, 6, 10, \ldots, 170$.

8. Find the sum of the first 24 terms of the arithmetic sequence $16, 14, 12, \ldots$

9. Find the sum of the first 24 terms of the arithmetic sequence whose first term is 12 and whose common difference is 3.

10. Find the 6th term of the geometric sequence $3, \sqrt{3}, 1, \ldots$

11. Find the 6th term of the geometric sequence whose first term is 3 and whose common ratio is 2.

12. Find the sum of the first seven terms of the geometric sequence $-8,\ 4,\ -2, \ldots$

13. Find the sum of the first five terms of the geometric sequence whose first term is 4 and whose common ratio is $1/2$.

14. Find the sum of the infinite geometric sequence

$$4,\ 1,\ \frac{1}{4}, \ldots$$

15. Find an equivalent fraction for $0.4\overline{3}$.

16. Find the 3rd term in the expansion of $\left(x^2 + y^2\right)^6$.

17. Evaluate: $\dfrac{9!}{7!}$

18. Evaluate: $\dbinom{12}{4}$

19. A contest offers 12 prizes. The first prize is $8000, and each successive prize is $600 less than the preceding prize. What is the total amount of prize money that is being awarded?

20. A real estate broker estimates that a piece of land will increase in value at a rate of 10% each year. If the original price of the land is $50,000, what will be its value in 10 years?

Name: _____

Date: _____

1. Given $f(x) = 3^{-2x}$, evaluate $f(-1)$.

2. Solve for x: $\log_3 x = -2$

3. Graph: $f(x) = 3^x - 2$

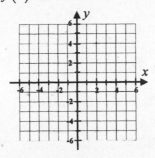

4. Graph: $y = x^2 + 6x + 2$

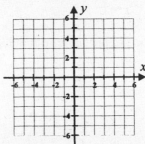

5. Evaluate: $\log_2 32$

6. Write $\log_2 \dfrac{x^3}{yz^4}$ in expanded form.

7. Solve for x: $4^{2x-1} = 8^x$

8. Solve for x: $\log_3 (5x - 3) = 3$

9. The percent of correct responses that a student can give on a vocabulary test increases with practice and can be approximated by the equation $P = 100(1 - 0.8^t)$, where P is the percent of correct responses and t is the number of days of practice. Find the percent of correct responses a student will make after six days of practice.

10. Boxes are stacked in a warehouse so that there are 32 boxes in the bottom row, 28 boxes in the next row, and so on in an arithmetic sequence. There are 4 boxes in the top row. How many boxes are in the stack?

Name: _____

11. Sketch the graph of $\dfrac{x^2}{1} + \dfrac{y^2}{16} = 1$.

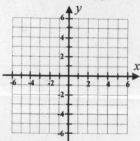

12. Graph the solution set of $y > x^2 - 2x - 3$.

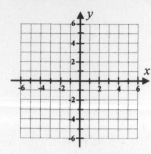

13. Find the equation of the circle with radius 4 and center $(-1, 0)$.

14. Solve:
$$y = x^2 - 3x + 2$$
$$2x + y = 4$$

15. Find the sum of the series $\displaystyle\sum_{n=1}^{4} \dfrac{3}{2n+1}$.

16. Find the sum of the first 25 terms of the arithmetic sequence $-15, -11, -7, \ldots$

17. Write the 14th term of the sequence whose nth term is given by the formula $a_n = \dfrac{5}{2n-3}$.

18. Find the 5th term of the geometric sequence $3, 9, 27, \ldots$

19. Find the sum of the infinite geometric sequence $1, \dfrac{3}{4}, \dfrac{9}{16}, \ldots$

20. Find the 5th term in the expansion of $(x - 2y)^7$.

Name: _____

Date: _____

1. Simplify: $-4^2(-3)(7)^2$

2. Evaluate $a^2 - b(ac - b)$ when $a = -3$, $b = -2$, and $c = 4$.

3. Simplify: $5y + 4(x - 2y) - 4(2y - x)$

4. Translate and simplify "five less than the sum of three consecutive integers."

5. Solve: $3x - 2(x - 4) = 2(3 - 2x)$

6. Solve: $\dfrac{4}{5}x - 2 = 6$

7. A postal-clerk sold some 20-cent stamps and some 28-cent stamps. Altogether 160 stamps were sold for a total of $40.80. How many 28-cent stamps were sold?

8. A goldsmith mixed 40 g of a 50% gold alloy with 100 g of a 15% gold alloy. What is the percent concentration of the resulting alloy?

9. Simplify: $\left(4ab^2\right)^2 \left(-3ab^3\right)^3$

10. Simplify: $x^{n+3}\left(x^{2n} - 3x - 5\right)$

11. Factor: $x^2 - 7x - 30$

12. Factor: $2x^4 y^4 + 5x^2 y^2 - 12$

13. Solve by factoring: $4x^2 = -12x$

14. Simplify: $\dfrac{8x^3 - y^3}{20x^3y + 10x^2y^2 + 5xy^3}$

15. Simplify: $\dfrac{6x^2 - 5x - 4}{6x^2 + 5x + 1} \cdot \dfrac{3x^2 + 7x + 2}{3x^2 - 10x + 8}$

16. Simplify: $\dfrac{4}{x+3} - \dfrac{6}{x-2}$

17. Simplify: $\dfrac{4 - \frac{2x}{x-3}}{x - \frac{18}{x-3}}$

18. Solve $Ft = mV_1 - mV_2$ for V_1.

19. Simplify: $\sqrt{50a^4b^7}$

20. Simplify: $\sqrt{27x^4y} - 2x\sqrt{48x^2y}$

21. Simplify: $\dfrac{4}{2+\sqrt{5}}$

22. Simplify: $\sqrt{52} + \sqrt{-125}$

23. Graph: $y = -\dfrac{4}{3}x + 2$

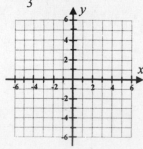

24. Graph the solution set of $2x - 3y \geq 6$.

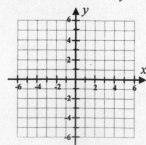

25. Find the slope of the line containing the points $(2,3)$ and $(-4,5)$.

26. Find the equation of the line that contains the point $(-3,1)$ and has slope $\dfrac{3}{8}$.

27. Simplify: $(4-3i)(1+i)$

28. Solve: $(x-3)^2 = 54$

29. Solve: $x^2 + 6x + 13 = 0$

30. Solve: $\dfrac{2}{x} - \dfrac{1}{x-3} = 2$

31. For the function $g(x) = 9 - x^2$, find $g(1+h)$.

32. Find the length of the line segment with endpoints $(2,-1)$ and $(3,-5)$.

33. Given $f(x) = 2x^2 + 1$ and $g(x) = 3x$, find $g\left[f(2)\right]$.

34. A rectangle has a perimeter of 32 ft. Find the maximum area of the rectangle.

35. Graph: $x = -y^2 + 4y$

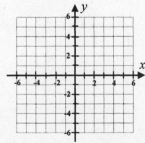

36. Sketch a graph of $\dfrac{x^2}{25} + \dfrac{y^2}{4} = 1$.

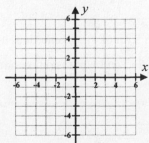

37. Find the equation of the circle (in standard form) with radius 7 and center $(0, -4)$.

38. Write $\log_2 \sqrt[3]{\dfrac{x}{y^2 z}}$ in expanded form.

39. Solve: $\begin{aligned} 3x - 2y &= -10 \\ x &= 4y - 10 \end{aligned}$

40. Solve: $\begin{aligned} 2x - 2y - 3z &= 11 \\ 3x - 2y &= 10 \\ y - z &= -1 \end{aligned}$

41. Evaluate the determinant: $\begin{vmatrix} 3 & -4 \\ 0 & -2 \end{vmatrix}$

42. Solve: $\begin{aligned} x^2 + y^2 &= 5 \\ x^2 &= 4y \end{aligned}$

43. Evaluate: $\log_7 343$

44. Solve for x: $\log_3 x = 4$

45. Solve for x: $2^{6x+3} = 8^{x-5}$

46. Solve for x: $\log_2 (3x - 4) = 3$

47. Write the 9th term of the sequence whose nth term is given by the formula $a_n = \dfrac{10}{n+1}$.

48. Find the sum of the first 30 terms of the arithmetic sequence $8, 13, 18, \ldots$

49. Find the 7th term of the geometric sequence whose first term is 243 and whose common ratio is $\dfrac{1}{3}$.

50. Write $(x + 2)^5$ in expanded form.

Form B Tests

Free Response

Name: _____

Date: _____

1. Solve by factoring: $15x^2 - x = 2$

2. Solve by factoring: $x(x+6) = 5 + 2x$

3. Write a quadratic equation that has integer coefficients and has solutions 3 and −3.

4. Solve by taking square roots: $36x^2 = 25$

5. Solve by taking square roots: $(x-1)^2 - 12 = 0$

6. Solve by completing the square: $x^2 - 8x - 2 = 0$

7. Solve by completing the square: $2x^2 + 2x - 4 = 0$

8. Solve by using the quadratic formula:
    $2x^2 + 5x + 2 = 0$

9. Solve by using the quadratic formula:
    $3x^2 - 2x + 4 = 0$

10. Use the discriminant to determine whether $x^2 - 6x = -15$ has one real number solution, two real number solutions, or two complex number solutions.

11. Solve: $3x^4 - 28x^2 + 9 = 0$

12. Solve: $2x + \sqrt{x} - 15 = 0$

13. Solve: $\sqrt{3x-2} + 4 = x$

14. Solve: $\sqrt{x-1} + 1 = \sqrt{x}$

15. Solve: $\dfrac{1}{y} - \dfrac{1}{y-4} = \dfrac{4}{3}$

16. Solve: $\dfrac{x}{x-2} - \dfrac{3}{x-1} = 2$

17. Solve and graph the solution set of $\dfrac{2}{x-4} \geq 2$.

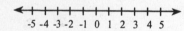
-5 -4 -3 -2 -1 0 1 2 3 4 5

18. Solve and graph the solution set of $\dfrac{(x-3)(x+2)}{x-2} < 0$.

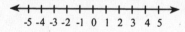
-5 -4 -3 -2 -1 0 1 2 3 4 5

19. The sum of the squares of the first and third of three consecutive positive odd integers is 250. Find the two integers.

20. A car travels 180 mi. A second car, traveling 15 mi/h faster than the first car, makes the same trip in 1 h less time. Find the speed of each car.

Name: _____
Date: _____

1. Find the vertex and axis of symmetry of the parabola whose equation is $y = x^2 - 6x + 3$.

2. State the domain and range of the function $f(x) = x^2 + 5$.

3. Graph: $f(x) = \dfrac{1}{2}x^2 + 1$

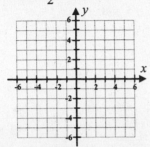

4. Graph: $f(x) = -\sqrt{4 - x}$

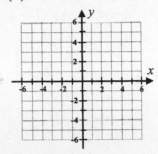

5. Find the x-intercepts of $y = 3x^2 + 9x$.

6. Find the zeros of the function $f(x) = 2x^2 - 15x + 28$.

7. Use the discriminant to determine the number of x-intercepts of the graph of $y = 3x^2 - 5x + 6$.

8. Find the maximum value of the function $f(x) = -x^2 + 8x - 2$.

9. The perimeter of a rectangular window is 32 ft. Find the dimensions of the window that will enclose the largest area.

10. Find the maximum product of two numbers whose sum is 84.

Name: _____

11. Determine whether the graph represents the graph of a function.

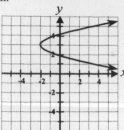

12. Determine whether the graph represents the graph of a 1-1 function.

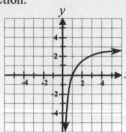

13. For $g(x) = 3x - 5$ and $f(x) = -2x + 3$, find $g(2) - f(2)$.

14. For $f(x) = 2x - 5$ and $g(x) = 3 - x$, find $(f \cdot g)(-2)$.

15. For $f(x) = x^2 - 3x$ and $g(x) = x^2 - 2x + 7$, find $\left(\dfrac{f}{g}\right)(-1)$.

16. Given $f(x) = x^2 - 2$ and $g(x) = 3x + 1$, find $f[g(0)]$.

17. Given $f(x) = 2x^2 - 3$ and $g(x) = x + 2$, find $f[g(x)]$.

18. Let $f(x) = 4x - 6$. Find $f^{-1}(x)$.

19. Are the functions $f(x) = 3x - 2$ and $g(x) = \dfrac{1}{3}x + 2$ inverses of each other?

20. Find the inverse of the function $\{(-1,3), (2,5), (7,11)\}$.

Chapters 7-9 Cumulative Test B

Name: __________
Date: __________

1. Simplify: $\left(64m^3n^{-9}\right)^{1/3}\left(m^{-1/3}n^{5/6}\right)^6$

2. Write $\left(5-x^2\right)^{1/2}$ as a radical expression.

3. Simplify: $\left(\sqrt{x}+3\right)^2$

4. Simplify: $\left(\sqrt{8}+\sqrt{-18}\right)-\left(\sqrt{32}-\sqrt{-50}\right)$

5. Solve: $\sqrt{3x}=\sqrt{3x-5}+1$

6. Write a quadratic equation that has integer coefficients and has solutions 3 and $-\dfrac{2}{3}$.

7. Solve by taking square roots: $(x-4)^2-25=0$

8. Solve by completing the square: $2x^2+2x-3=0$

9. Solve: $x-8x^{1/2}+15=0$

10. Solve: $\dfrac{x}{x-4}-\dfrac{8}{x+3}=4$

11. Solve: $x^2 - 4 > 0$

12. A car travels 120 mi. A second car, traveling 10 mi/h faster than the first car, makes the same trip in 1 h less time. Find the speed of each car.

13. Graph: $y = x^2 + 4x + 1$

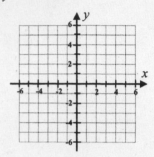

14. Graph: $f(x) = 3|x| - 1$

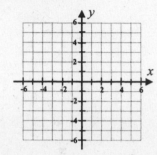

15. Find the zeros of the function $f(x) = -x^2 + 2x + 24$.

16. Find the maximum value of the function $f(x) = -3x^2 + 6x - 2$.

17. Given $f(x) = 4x + 1$ and $g(x) = x^2 - 2$, find $(f \cdot g)(3)$.

18. Given $f(x) = x^2$ and $g(x) = 7x - 4$, find $f[g(-2)]$.

19. Determine whether the graph represents the graph of a 1-1 function.

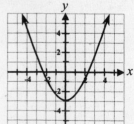

20. Let $f(x) = 2x + 3$. Find $f^{-1}(x)$.

Name: _____
Date: _____

1. Given $R(t) = e^{-t} + 1$, evaluate $R(-1)$. Round to the nearest ten-thousandth.

2. Given $f(x) = 2^{x-1}$, evaluate $f(-3)$.

3. Evaluate: $\log_3 27$

4. Graph: $f(x) = 2^x - 5$

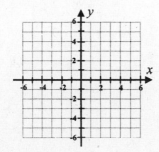

5. Graph: $f(x) = \left(\dfrac{1}{2}\right)^{-x}$

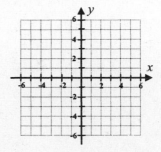

6. Write $2^{-3} = \dfrac{1}{8}$ in logarithmic form.

7. Write $\log_8 \dfrac{1}{8} = -1$ in exponential form.

8. Solve for x: $\log_6 x = -2$
    Round to the nearest ten-thousandth.

9. Write $\ln\left(\dfrac{x^2}{yz^3}\right)$ in expanded form.

10. Express $\dfrac{1}{2}(\ln x - 2\ln y)$ as a single logarithm with a coefficient of 1.

11. Write $3\log_5 x - \dfrac{1}{2}\log_5 y + 2\log_5 z$ as a single logarithm with a coefficient of 1.

Name: _____

12. Write $\log_4 (xy)^3$ in expanded form.

13. Evaluate: $\log_4 20$
Round to the nearest ten-thousandth.

14. Graph: $f(x) = \log_5 (x+1)$

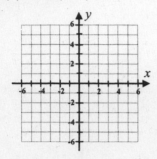

15. Graph: $f(x) = \log_2 (x-2)$

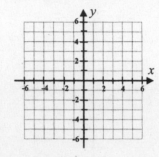

16. Solve for x: $2^{x+1} = 8^{3x-5}$

17. Solve for x: $5^x = 45$
Round to the nearest ten-thousandth.

18. Solve for x: $\log_6 2x = \log_6 2 + \log_6 (3x-4)$

19. Find the hydrogen ion concentration, H^+, of lemon juice, which has a pH of 2.1. Use the equation $pH = -\log(H^+)$. Round to the nearest thousandth.

20. The percent of correct data entries a computer operator can make increases with practice and can be approximated by the equation $P = 100(1 - 0.8^t)$, where P is the percent of correct entries and t is the number of weeks of practice. How many weeks of practice are required before an operator can make 95% of the entries correctly?

1. Graph: $x = y^2 - 2y - 4$

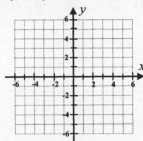

2. Graph: $y = -2x^2 - x + 2$

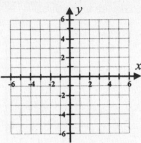

3. Find the vertex and axis of symmetry of the parabola given by $x = -y^2 + 2y - 2$.

4. Find the equation of the circle (in standard form) with radius 5 and center $(-1, 4)$.

5. Find the equation of the circle (in standard form) that passes through the point $(-4, 2)$ and whose center is $(1, -2)$.

6. Write the equation $x^2 + y^2 - 6x - 6y = -14$ in standard form and then sketch its graph.

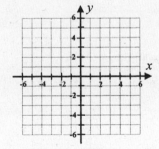

7. Write the equation $x^2 + y^2 - 6x = 0$ in standard form and then sketch its graph.

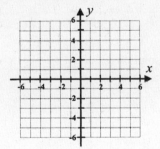

8. Sketch a graph of $\dfrac{x^2}{4} + \dfrac{y^2}{36} = 1$.

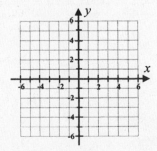

9. Sketch a graph of $\dfrac{x^2}{9} + \dfrac{y^2}{25} = 1$.

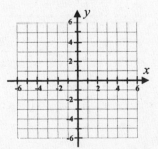

Name: _____

10. Sketch a graph of $\dfrac{x^2}{9} - \dfrac{y^2}{36} = 1$.

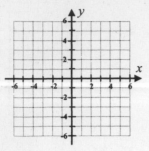

11. Sketch a graph of $\dfrac{y^2}{9} - \dfrac{x^2}{16} = 1$.

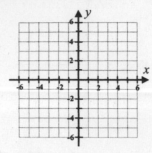

12. Solve: $y = x^2 - 3x - 6$
$\quad\quad\quad\ y = 3x + 1$

13. Solve: $x^2 + y^2 = 25$
$\quad\quad\quad\ x - 2y = 2$

14. Graph the solution set of $\dfrac{x^2}{4} + \dfrac{y^2}{25} < 1$.

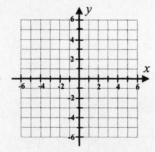

15. Graph the solution set: $x^2 + y^2 < 25$
$\quad\quad\quad\quad\quad\quad\quad\quad\ x - 2y < 2$

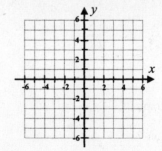

Name: _____

Date: _____

1. Write the 8th term of the sequence whose nth term is given by the formula $a_n = (-1)^{n+1} n$.

2. Write the 7th terms of the sequence whose nth term is given by the formula $a_n = \dfrac{n^2 + 1}{n + 2}$.

3. Evaluate: $\displaystyle\sum_{n=1}^{4} \dfrac{n}{n+1}$

4. Write $\displaystyle\sum_{n=1}^{5} \dfrac{x^{n-1}}{n^2}$ in expanded form.

5. Find the 7th term of the arithmetic sequence $1, \dfrac{3}{4}, \dfrac{1}{2}, \ldots$

6. Find the formula for the nth term of the arithmetic sequence $6, 13, 20, \ldots$

7. Find the number of terms in the finite arithmetic sequence $8, 11, 14, \ldots, 155$.

8. Find the sum of the first 25 terms of the arithmetic sequence $-5, -\dfrac{5}{2}, 0, \ldots$

9. Find the sum of the arithmetic series: $\displaystyle\sum_{n=1}^{20} \left(\tfrac{1}{2}n + 2\right)$

10. Find the 6th term of the geometric sequence $-2, 8, -32, \ldots$

11. Find the 10th term of the geometric sequence
$$-\frac{1}{27}, \frac{1}{9}, -\frac{1}{3}, \ldots$$

12. Find the sum of the first eight terms of the geometric sequence $-3, 9, -27, \ldots$

13. Find the 6th term of the geometric sequence whose first term is 3 and whose common ratio is -2.

14. Find the sum of the infinite geometric sequence
$$1, -\frac{2}{3}, \frac{4}{9}, \ldots$$

15. Find an equivalent fraction for $0.3\overline{2}$.

16. Find the 4th term in the expansion of $(2x-3)^4$.

17. Evaluate: $\dfrac{14!}{12!}$

18. Evaluate: $\begin{pmatrix} 9 \\ 5 \end{pmatrix}$

19. A contest offers 10 prizes. The first prize is $5000, and each successive prize is $350 less than the preceding prize. What is the value of the 8th-place prize?

20. A rubber ball is dropped from a height of 20 ft. The ball bounces to $4/5$ of its previous height with each bounce. How high does the ball bounce on the fifth bounce?

Name: _____

Date: _____

1. Given $f(x) = 3^{-x}$, evaluate $f(-2)$.

2. Graph: $f(x) = 2^x - 4$
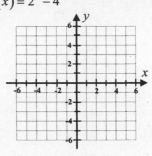

3. Evaluate: $\log_2 16$

4. Write $3\log_5 x - 2\log_5 y - \dfrac{1}{2}\log_5 z$ as a single logarithm with a coefficient of 1.

5. Evaluate: $\log_6 4.2$
    Round to the nearest ten-thousandth.

6. Solve for x: $\ln x = 6$
    Round to the nearest ten-thousandth.

7. Solve for x: $6^{5x-2} = 6^{3x+4}$

8. Solve for x: $\log_5 x + \log_5 (5x - 3) = \log_5 2$

9. Graph: $y = 2x^2 - x - 3$
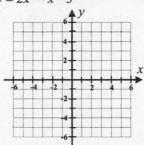

10. Find the equation (in standard form) of the circle with radius 8 and center $(-1, 4)$.

11. Sketch the graph of $\dfrac{x^2}{25} + \dfrac{y^2}{36} = 1$.

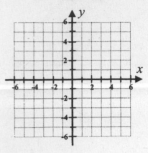

12. Sketch the graph of $\dfrac{y^2}{4} - \dfrac{x^2}{36} = 1$.

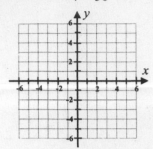

13. Solve: $y = x - 4$
$y = 2x^2 - 4x - 2$

14. Graph the solution set of $\dfrac{x^2}{4} + \dfrac{y^2}{25} < 1$.

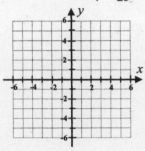

15. Write the 26th term of the sequence whose *n*th term is given by the formula $a_n = \dfrac{3n}{n+1}$.

16. Evaluate: $\displaystyle\sum_{n=1}^{4} (n^2 - 3)$

17. Find the sum of the first 35 terms of the arithmetic sequence whose first term is 27 and whose common difference is −2.

18. Find the sum of the infinite geometric sequence
$3, -1, \dfrac{1}{3}, \ldots$

19. Find an equivalent fraction for $0.2\overline{4}$.

20. Find the 8th term in the expansion of $(x + 2y)^{10}$.

1. Simplify: $(-2)^2 (-3)^3$

2. Evaluate $b^2 - 4ac$ when $a = 2$, $b = -3$, and $c = -5$.

3. Simplify: $3x - 2[3 - 2(x - y) - x]$

4. Translate and simplify "two times the sum of the first and third of three consecutive even integers."

5. Solve: $\dfrac{3}{5}x - 1 = 6$

6. Solve: $2[3 - 2(2x - 5)] = 2(3 - x)$

7. A stamp collection consisting of 23 stamps includes 4¢ stamps and 9¢ stamps. The total value of the stamps is $1.27. Find the number of each type of stamp in the collection.

8. A commuter plane flies to a small town from a major airport. The average speed flying to the small town was 220 mph, and the average speed returning was 180 mph. The total flying time was 5 h. Find the distance between the two airports.

9. Simplify: $(-2xy^2)(-4xy)^2$

10. Simplify: $(a - 2)(a^2 + 4a - 1)$

11. Factor: $8x^3 - 27$

12. Factor: $2x^2 - 9x - 18$

13. Factor: $6x^3 + 15x^2 - 9x$

14. Simplify: $\dfrac{3x^2 - 15x + 18}{3x^2 - 12}$

15. Simplify: $\dfrac{x^2-5}{x^2+2x-15} \cdot \dfrac{x^2-3x}{3x^2-15}$

16. Simplify: $\dfrac{2x-1}{2x-3} - \dfrac{11}{2x^2+5x-12}$

17. Simplify: $\dfrac{\frac{3}{2a+5}-3}{\frac{2}{2a+5}+2}$

18. Solve: $x - \dfrac{2x}{x-4} = \dfrac{2x-15}{x-4}$

19. Simplify: $3a\sqrt{27ab^2} - 5b\sqrt{12a^3}$

20. Simplify: $\dfrac{2\sqrt{x}}{\sqrt{x}-\sqrt{y}}$

21. Simplify: $\sqrt{-2}\left(\sqrt{8}-\sqrt{-9}\right)$

22. Simplify: $\sqrt[4]{3x-5}=2$

23. Graph: $3x-2y=-6$

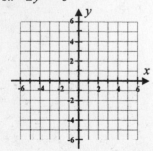

24. Graph the solution set of $2x+y \geq 2$.

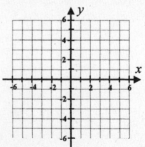

25. Find the slope of the line containing the points $(6,-1)$ and $(-4,-1)$.

26. Find the equation of the line containing the points $(-2,-5)$ and $(1,-3)$.

Final Exam Form B (*continued*)

Name: _____

27. Solve: $3x^2 - 2x + 1 = 0$

28. Solve: $x^2 - 11x + 12 = 0$

29. Solve: $\sqrt{x-3} + \sqrt{x} = 3$

30. Given $f(x) = 3 - 2x + x^2$, evaluate $f(-3)$.

31. Find the length of the line segment with endpoints $(2,5)$ and $(4,-1)$.

32. Given $f(x) = \dfrac{2}{3}x - 4$, find $f^{-1}(x)$.

33. A 13-ft ladder is leaning against a building. How high on the building will the ladder reach when the bottom of the ladder is 5 ft from the building?

34. Graph: $y = x^2 + 3x - 2$

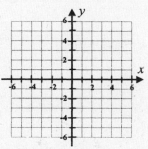

35. Find the x-intercepts of the parabola $y = 2x^2 - 7x - 4$.

36. Find the equation of the circle that passes through the point $(2,1)$ and whose center is $(-2,3)$.

37. Sketch a graph of $\dfrac{x^2}{16} - \dfrac{y^2}{4} = 1$.

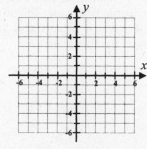

38. Solve: $4x + y = -1$
$8x - 2y = 10$

39. Solve: $2x - 3y + z = 7$
$$x + 2y - 2z = -1$$
$$3x - y + z = 4$$

40. Solve: $y = x^2 + 2x - 2$
$$y = -x^2 - 3x + 1$$

41. Solve for x: $\log_2 x = -5$

42. Solve for x: $\log_2 x + \log_2 (2x - 3) = 1$

43. Given $f(x) = 2^{-x} + 3$, evaluate $f(-1)$.

44. Write $\log_5 \sqrt{\dfrac{xz^3}{y^4}}$ in expanded form.

45. Solve for x: $2^{x+4} = 16^{x-2}$

46. Find the 3rd term in the expansion of $(3x + y)^4$.

47. Find the 15th term of the sequence whose nth term is given by the formula $a_n = \dfrac{2n+1}{n}$.

48. Find the sum of the first 40 terms of the arithmetic sequence $-2, 3, 8, ...$

49. A jet plane flying with the wind flew 1950 mi in 3 hours. Against the wind, the plane could fly only 1200 mi in the same amount of time. Find the rate of the plane in calm air.

50. A laboratory ore sample contains 500 mg of radioactive material with a half-life of 1 hour. Find the amount of radioactive material in the sample at the beginning of the fifth hour.

Form C Tests

Free Response

Name: _____

Date: _____

1. Solve by factoring: $3x^2 - 14x + 8 = 0$

2. Solve by factoring: $x(x-5) = 14$

3. Write a quadratic equation that has integer coefficients and has solutions $-5/2$ and 3.

4. Solve by taking square roots: $4(x-1)^2 = 36$

5. Solve by taking square roots: $4(x-1)^2 - 8 = 0$

6. Solve by completing the square: $x^2 - 4x - 7 = 0$

7. Solve by completing the square: $x^2 - 2x + 9 = 0$

8. Solve by using the quadratic formula:
   $2n^2$ n 1 0

9. Solve by using the quadratic formula:
   $2x^2 - 5x - 18 - 0$

10. Use the discriminant to determine whether $5x^2 - 3x = -6$ has one real number solution, two real number solutions, or two complex number solutions.

Name: _____

11. Solve: $x^4 - 256 = 0$

12. Solve: $x - 3x^{1/2} - 40 = 0$

13. Solve: $\sqrt{x+8} = 4 - \sqrt{x}$

14. Solve: $\sqrt{7x-3} = 2x-3$

15. Solve: $\dfrac{2}{3} - \dfrac{3}{x} = \dfrac{1}{x-6}$

16. Solve: $\dfrac{1}{x-1} + \dfrac{2}{x+1} = 1$

17. Solve and graph the solution set of
$(x+4)(x-2) > 0$.

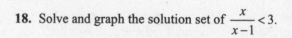

-5 -4 -3 -2 -1 0 1 2 3 4 5

18. Solve and graph the solution set of $\dfrac{x}{x-1} < 3$.

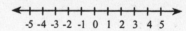

-5 -4 -3 -2 -1 0 1 2 3 4 5

19. The sum of the squares of two consecutive odd integers is 202. Find the two integers.

20. The length of a rectangle is 5 m more than the width. The area is 176 m². Find the length of the rectangle.

1. State the domain and range of the function $f(x) = 4 + x^2$.

2. Find the vertex and axis of symmetry of the parabola given by $y = x^2 - 4x + 2$.

3. Graph: $f(x) = 2x^2 - 3x + 1$

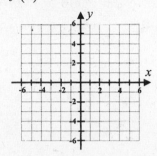

4. Graph: $f(x) = -\sqrt{x - 2}$

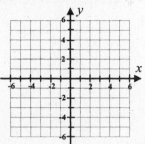

5. Find the x-intercepts of the graph of $y = x^2 + 5x - 24$.

6. Find the zeros of $f(x) = 2x^2 + 5x - 3$.

7. Use the discriminant to determine the number of x-intercepts of the graph of $y = -x^2 - 5x + 1$.

8. Find the maximum value of the function $f(x) = -2x^2 - 4x + 1$.

9. Find the minimum product of two numbers whose difference is 24.

10. A rectangle has a perimeter of 60 ft. Find the dimensions of the rectangle that will have the maximum area.

Name: _____

11. Determine whether the graph represents the graph of a function.

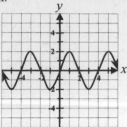

12. Determine whether the graph represents the graph of a 1-1 function.

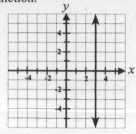

13. For $f(x) = x^2$ and $g(x) = x + 4$, find $f(1) + g(1)$.

14. For $f(x) = x^2 - 1$ and $g(x) = 2x + 3$, find $(f \cdot g)(-2)$.

15. For $f(x) = 3 - x^2$ and $g(x) = x + 7$, find $\left(\dfrac{f}{g}\right)(2)$.

16. Given $f(x) = 5x - 1$ and $g(x) = -3x$, find $f[g(2)]$.

17. Given $f(x) = x + 1$ and $g(x) = x^2$, find $f[g(x)]$.

18. Let $f(x) = 5x - 2$. Find $f^{-1}(x)$.

19. Let $f(x) = \dfrac{1}{2}x + 3$. Find $f^{-1}(x)$.

20. Are the functions $f(x) = 3x$ and $g(x) = \dfrac{x}{3}$.

1. Given $f(x) = e^{-2x} + 1$, evaluate $f(2)$.
   Round to the nearest ten-thousandth.

2. Given $g(x) = 2^{x+2}$, evaluate $g(-4)$.

3. Graph: $f(x) = 3^x + 1$

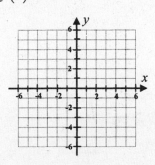

4. Solve for x: $\ln x = 1.2$
   Round to the nearest ten-thousandth.

5. Write $5^{-3} = \dfrac{1}{125}$ in logarithmic form.

6. Write $\log_{10} 1 = 0$ in exponential form.

7. Evaluate: $\log 100,000,000$

8. Write $\log_b \left(xy^2 \sqrt{z} \right)$ in expanded form.

9. Write $\ln \left(x^5 y^2 z \right)$ in expanded form.

10. Write $2 \ln x - 5 \ln y$ as a single logarithm with a coefficient of 1.

11. Write $3\log_a x - 2\log_a y - \log_a z$ as a single logarithm with a coefficient of 1.

12. Evaluate: $\ln\dfrac{2}{3}$

  Round to the nearest ten-thousandth.

13. Evaluate: $\log_3 9.9$

  Round to the nearest ten-thousandth.

14. Solve for x: $125^{x+1} = 25^{x-2}$

15. Graph: $f(x) = \log_2(x-1)$

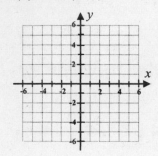

16. Graph: $f(x) = \log_5(2x)$

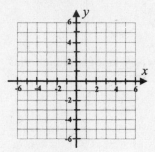

17. Solve for x: $3^{2x-1} = 3^{7x-11}$

18. Solve for x: $\log_3\left(\dfrac{3x-6}{x+2}\right) = 2$

19. A sample of Iron-59 contains 50 mg. One hundred days later, the sample contains 10.75 mg. What is the half-life of iron-59, in days? Round to the nearest tenth.

20. Find the number of decibels of sound in a factory in which the power of the sound is approximately 4.5×10^{-8} watts. Use the equation $D = 10(\log L + 16)$, where D is the number of decibels of sound and L is the power of the sound measured in watts.

Name: _____

Date: _____

1. Graph: $x = -\dfrac{1}{2}y^2 + 3$

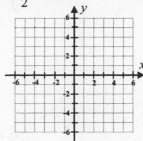

2. Graph: $y = -2x^2 + 16x - 34$

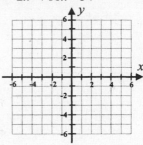

3. Find the vertex and axis of symmetry of the parabola given by $x = y^2 - 4y + 10$.

4. Find the equation of the circle (in standard form) with radius $\sqrt{5}$ and center $(-1, 2)$.

5. Find the equation of the circle (in standard form) that passes through the point $(2,1)$ and whose center is $(-1,1)$.

6. Write the equation $x^2 + y^2 - 6x - 4y + 4 = 0$ in standard form and then sketch its graph.

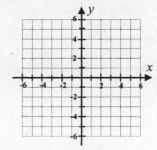

7. Write the equation $x^2 + y^2 - 2x - 4y + 1 = 0$ in standard form and then sketch its graph.

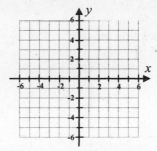

8. Sketch a graph of $\dfrac{x^2}{1} + \dfrac{y^2}{9} = 1$.

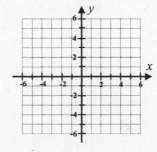

9. Sketch a graph of $\dfrac{x^2}{16} + \dfrac{y^2}{4} = 1$.

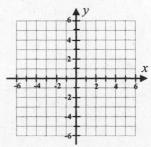

Name: _____

10. Sketch a graph of $\dfrac{x^2}{25} - \dfrac{y^2}{4} = 1$.

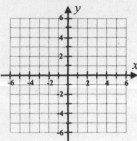

11. Sketch a graph of $\dfrac{y^2}{9} - \dfrac{x^2}{4} = 1$.

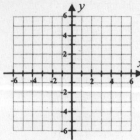

12. Solve: $3x^2 + y^2 = 20$

$\quad\quad\quad 5x^2 - y^2 = 12$

13. Solve: $x^2 + y^2 = 34$

$\quad\quad\quad y = x + 2$

14. Graph the solution set of $x^2 + y^2 \le 9$.

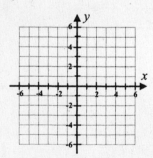

15. Graph the solution set: $x^2 + y^2 \ge 4$

$\quad\quad\quad \dfrac{x^2}{9} + \dfrac{y^2}{25} < 1$

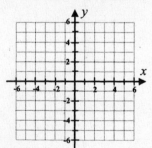

Name: _____
Date: _____

1. Write the 8th term of the sequence whose nth term is given by the formula $a_n = (-1)^{n-1} n$.

2. Write the 7th and 10th terms of the sequence whose nth term is given by the formula $a_n = \dfrac{1}{n(n+1)}$.

3. Evaluate: $\displaystyle\sum_{n=1}^{4} (-1)^n (n+1)^2$

4. Write $\displaystyle\sum_{n=1}^{5} \dfrac{x^n}{n}$ in expanded form.

5. Find the 28th term of the arithmetic sequence $-5, -1, 3, \ldots$

6. Find the 9th term of the arithmetic sequence whose first term is 3 and whose common difference is -5.

7. Find the formula for the nth term of the arithmetic sequence $1, 6, 11, \ldots$

8. Find the number of terms in the finite arithmetic sequence $5, 9, 13, \ldots, 73$.

9. Find the sum of the first 30 terms of the arithmetic sequence $2, 6, 10, \ldots$

10. Find the 6th term of the geometric sequence $2, -4, 8, \ldots$

11. Find the 7th term of the geometric sequence whose first term is 9 and whose common ratio is $1/3$.

12. Find the sum of the first five terms of the geometric sequence $5, 15, 45, \ldots$

13. Find the sum of the first eight terms of the geometric sequence whose first term is 2 and whose common ratio is $-1/2$.

14. Find the sum of the infinite geometric sequence
$5, \; 2, \; \dfrac{4}{5}, \ldots$

15. Find an equivalent fraction for $0.\overline{12}$.

16. Find the 4th term in the expansion of $(2x - 3)^5$.

17. Evaluate: $\dfrac{10!}{3!7!}$

18. Evaluate: $\begin{pmatrix} 9 \\ 2 \end{pmatrix}$

19. The distance a ball rolls down a ramp each second is given by an arithmetic sequence. The distance, in feet, traveled by the ball during the nth second is given by $2n - 1$. Find the total distance the ball will travel in 5 seconds.

20. A tennis ball is dropped from a height of 12 ft. The ball bounces to 80% of its previous height with each bounce. How high does the ball bounce on the fifth bounce? Round to the nearest tenth.

Name: _____

Date: _____

1. Given $f(x) = 3^{x^2}$, evaluate $f(-1)$.

2. Graph: $f(x) = 3^{-x} + 1$

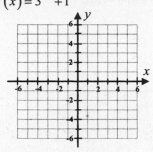

3. Evaluate: $\log_5 125$

4. Solve for x: $\log_3 x = 4$

5. Write $\log_3 x^2 y$ in expanded form.

6. Graph: $f(x) = -\log_2 x$

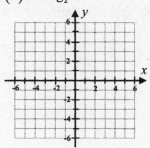

7. Solve for x: $2^{2x-1} = 8^{3x+9}$

8. Solve for x: $\log_2 x + \log_2(x+1) = \log_2 2$

9. Graph: $y = x^2 - 2x - 2$

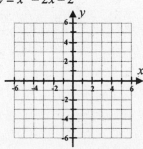

10. Find the equation of the circle with radius 9 and center $(0, -4)$.

11. Sketch the graph of $\dfrac{y^2}{25} - \dfrac{x^2}{4} = 1$

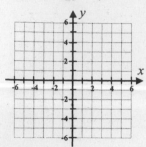

12. Solve: $x^2 + y^2 = 16$
$$y^2 = 4x + 4$$

13. Graph the solution set of $\dfrac{x^2}{4} + \dfrac{y^2}{16} > 1$.

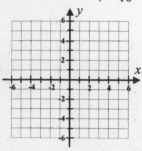

14. Evaluate: $\displaystyle\sum_{n=1}^{4} \left(n^2 - 3\right)$

15. Find the 20th term of the arithmetic sequence $-4, -1, 2, \ldots$

16. Write the 10th term of the sequence whose nth term is given by the formula $a_n = \dfrac{4n}{n-2}$.

17. Find the 9th term of the geometric sequence $4, 2, 1, \ldots$

18. Find an equivalent fraction for $0.3\overline{4}$.

19. A display of cans in a grocery store consists of 30 cans in the bottom row, 27 cans in the next row, and so on in an arithmetic sequence. The top row has 3 cans. Find the total number of cans in the display.

20. Find the 5th term in the expansion of $(2x - 1)^8$.

1. Simplify: $-2(-1)^3(-2)^2$

2. Evaluate $(a+3b)^2 \div (-ab)$ when $a = 3$ and $b = -2$.

3. Simplify: $3x - 2(y - 4x) - 3(x - y)$

4. Translate and simplify "six less than the sum of two consecutive integers."

5. Solve: $2x - 9 = 6x - 25$

6. Solve: $\dfrac{3x-2}{5} - \dfrac{x+1}{2} = \dfrac{4x+3}{10}$

7. A coin collection consists of nickels and quarters. The number of quarters is two less than two times the number of nickels. The total value is $3.90. Find the number of each type of coin.

8. How many millimeters of pure acid must be added to 60 ml of a 28% acid solution to make a 60% solution?

9. Simplify: $\left(2^{-3}x^2y^{-1}\right)\left(2^{-1}xy^2\right)^{-2}$

10. Simplify: $(x - 3y)(2x + y)$

11. Factor: $2x^2y - xy - 21y^2$

12. Factor: $8 - 7x - x^2$

13. Factor: $64x^4 - x$

14. Simplify: $\dfrac{a^4 + ab^3}{a^3 - a^2b + ab^2}$

15. Simplify: $\dfrac{x^2+2x-8}{x^2+6x+8} \div \dfrac{x^2-5x+6}{5x+10}$

16. Simplify: $\dfrac{5x}{x^2-9} - \dfrac{2x}{x^2+3x}$

17. Simplify: $\dfrac{\frac{5}{3x-2}-10}{\frac{4}{3x-2}+4}$

18. Solve $V = \pi r(r+h)$ for h.

19. Simplify: $\sqrt[5]{32x^8y^{10}}$

20. Simplify: $\sqrt{81x^3} - 3x\sqrt{16x}$

21. Simplify: $\dfrac{\sqrt{x}}{\sqrt{x}-\sqrt{5}}$

22. Simplify: $(-5i)(-4i)$

23. Simplify: $\sqrt{-3}\left(\sqrt{-12}+\sqrt{3}\right)$

24. Given $f(x) = \dfrac{2x^2}{x-2}$, evaluate $f(-2)$.

25. Graph: $x - 2y = 5$

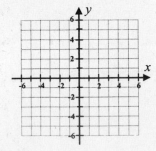

26. Graph the solution set of $y \ge \dfrac{2}{3}x + 2$.

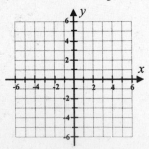

Final Exam Form C (*continued*)

Name: _____

27. Find the slope of the line containing the points $(-1, 3)$ and $(-4, -2)$.

28. Find the equation of the line that contains the point $(-1, 4)$ and has slope $\frac{2}{3}$.

29. Solve: $3x^2 + 3x - 6 = 0$

30. Solve: $8x^2 + 45x - 18 = 0$

31. The length of a rectangle is 5 cm less than twice the width. The area of the rectangle is 375 cm^2. Find the length and width of the rectangle.

32. Graph: $y = x^2 - x - 2$

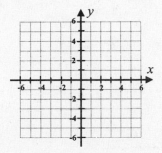

33. Is the set of ordered pairs a function?
$$\{(0,0), (1,1), (1,-1), (2,4), (2,-4)\}$$

34. Given $f(x) = 3x - 2$, find $f^{-1}(x)$.

35. Find the x-intercepts of the parabola given by $y = x^2 - 3x - 18$.

36. Find the equation of the circle (in standard form) with radius 8 and whose center is $(-2, 4)$.

37. Solve: $x + 4y = 8$
$3x + 5y = 3$

38. Solve: $x^2 - y^2 = -5$
$2x^2 + 3y^2 = 35$

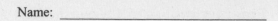

Name: _____

39. Sketch a graph of $\dfrac{y^2}{9} - \dfrac{x^2}{16} = 1$.

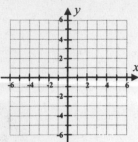

40. Solve: $\begin{aligned} 2x - y + 3z &= 9 \\ -x + 2y + 2z &= 9 \\ x + y + z &= 6 \end{aligned}$

41. Evaluate the determinant: $\begin{vmatrix} 0 & -2 & -3 \\ 5 & 3 & 1 \\ -1 & 2 & 4 \end{vmatrix}$

42. Given $f(x) = 3^{-x+1}$, evaluate $f(-3)$.

43. Solve for x: $\log_4 x = -2$

44. Evaluate: $\log 5260$
Round to the nearest ten-thousandth.

45. Solve for x: $9^{x+3} = 27^{x-1}$

46. Solve for x: $\log_6 x + \log_6 (x+1) = 1$

47. Find the sum of the series: $\displaystyle\sum_{n=4}^{7} (-1)^n (2n+1)$

48. Find the number of terms in the finite arithmetic sequence $-11, -5, 1, \ldots, 55$.

49. Find the sum of the infinite geometric sequence $1, -\dfrac{1}{3}, \dfrac{1}{9}, \ldots$

50. Find the 3rd term in the expansion of $(x+3)^4$.

Form D Tests

Free Response

1. Graph the ordered pairs $(-1, 2)$ and $(-3, -3)$.

2. Graph the ordered-pair solutions of $y = x^2 - 3$ when $x = -2, -1, 0, 1,$ and 2.

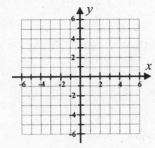

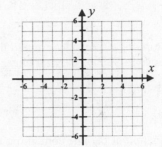

3. Find the midpoint and length (to the nearest hundredth) of the line segment between the points $P_1(2, -3)$ and $P_2(5, 4)$.

4. Graph: $y = \dfrac{1}{3}x + 1$

5. Graph: $x + 2y = 4$

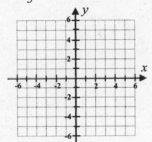

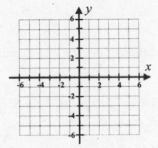

6. Find the slope of the line containing the points $P_1(-3, 1)$ and $P_2(2, 2)$.

7. Given $r(t) = \dfrac{3t}{t+3}$, evaluate $r(-1)$.

8. Find the x-intercept of the line $4x - 2y = 12$.

9. Find the y-intercept of the line $4 - 5x = 6y$.

10. Graph the line that passes through $(2, 0)$ and has slope -1.

11. Graph the solution set of $y \geq -2x + 3$.

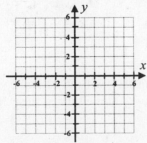

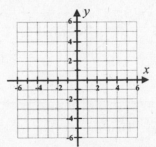

12. Find the equation of the line that contains the point $(-3, 2)$ and has slope $-\dfrac{3}{2}$.

13. A manufacturer of staplers determined that the cost to produce 1000 staplers was $3600. The cost to produce 2000 staplers was $6800. Write a linear equation for the cost, y, of producing x staplers.

14. Find the equation of the line containing the points $P_1(2, -1)$ and $P_2(-1, -4)$.

15. Find the equation of the line that contains the point $(-2, 3)$ and has slope 0.

16. Find the equation of the line that contains the point $(2, -4)$ and is parallel to the line $2x - 3y = 6$.

17. Find the domain and range of the function $\{(1, 2), (-1, 2), (3, 2), (-7, 2)\}$.

18. What values of x are excluded from the domain of $f(x) = \dfrac{3x - 4}{2}$?

Problems 19 and 20 refer to the graph below.

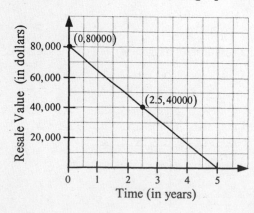

19. The graph to the left shows the resale value of a printing press and the time since it was purchased. Write a sentence that describes the meaning of the ordered pair, $(2.5, 40000)$.

20. Find when the printing press will have a resale value of $20,000.

1. Simplify: $-3-4+11-(-5)$

2. Simplify: $9(-2)^3$

3. Simplify: $\dfrac{5}{18} \div \left(-\dfrac{10}{21}\right)$

4. Simplify: $\dfrac{2}{3} - \dfrac{2-\frac{5}{6}}{2^3-1} \div \dfrac{1}{2}$

5. Evaluate $\dfrac{b^2-4ac}{2a}$ when $a=-1$, $b=-2$, and $c=1$.

6. Identify the property that justifies the statement:
$$a(b+c)=ab+ac$$

7. Simplify: $3\big[4x-(5+6x)\big]-(3x-1)$

8. Find $A \cup B$, given $A=\{1,3,5\}$ and $B=\{2,4,6\}$.

9. Solve: $-\dfrac{5}{9}x = \dfrac{10}{27}$

10. Solve: $\dfrac{3}{4}t - \dfrac{7}{10}t = 3$

11. Solve: $2x-9 \geq -1$ or $7-3x \leq 5$
   Write the solution set in interval notation.

12. Solve: $|2x-1| = 3$

13. Solve: $|4x-3| > 9$
   Write the solution set in set-builder notation.

14. The sum of the first and second of three consecutive odd integers is three more than three times the third integer. Find the third integer.

Name: _____

15. A jogger runs a distance at a speed of 8 mph and returns the same distance running at a speed of 6 mph. Find the total distance that the jogger ran if the total time running was $1\frac{3}{4}$ hour.

16. How many ounces of pure water must be added to 64 oz of a 12% salt solution to make an 8% salt solution?

17. Solve $A = \dfrac{b+h}{2}$ for h.

18. Given $f(x) = 5x^2 + 2x - 1$, evaluate $f(-2)$.

19. Find the slope of the line containing the points $P_1(3,-2)$ and $P_2(-1,-2)$.

20. Find the y-intercept of the line $3x - 5y = 15$.

21. Find the equation of the line that contains the point $(5,1)$ and has slope -3.

22. Find the equation of the line containing the points $P_1(3,2)$ and $P_2(-1,4)$.

23. Find the equation of the line that contains the point $(4,-1)$ and is perpendicular to the line $3x + 4y = 4$.

24. Graph: $2x - y = 4$

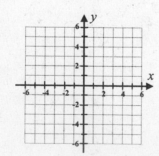

25. Graph the solution set of $-2x + 5y \geq 10$.

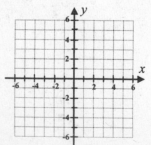

Name: _____

Date: _____

1. Solve by factoring: $4x^2 + 11x = -6$

2. Solve by factoring: $2x^2 - x - 1 = 0$

3. Write a quadratic equation that has integer coefficients and has solutions $-1/2$ and 3.

4. Solve by taking square roots: $4(x-2)^2 = 64$

5. Solve by taking square roots: $3x^2 = 27$

6. Solve by completing the square: $2x^2 - 3x - 2 = 0$

7. Solve by completing the square: $2x^2 + 5x - 12 = 0$

8. Solve by using the quadratic formula:
$x^2 - 6x + 3 = 0$

9. Solve by using the quadratic formula:
$x^2 - 7x + 3 = 0$

10. Use the discriminant to determine whether $2x^2 - 4x = -2$ has one real number solution, two real number solutions, or two complex number solutions.

11. Solve: $x^4 - 64 = 0$

12. Solve: $x - 9x^{1/2} + 18 = 0$

13. Solve: $\sqrt{2x-4} + 4 = x$

14. Solve: $\sqrt{4x+3} = 2x - 1$

15. Solve: $\dfrac{x+2}{x-2} - x = 2$

16. Solve: $\dfrac{2}{x+5} - \dfrac{3}{x-5} = 1$

17. Solve and graph the solution set of $x^2 + 2x - 8 \geq 0$.

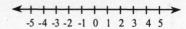

-5 -4 -3 -2 -1 0 1 2 3 4 5

18. Solve and graph the solution set of $\dfrac{2x-3}{(x+5)(x+2)} > 0$.

-5 -4 -3 -2 -1 0 1 2 3 4 5

19. The length of a rectangle is 6 m more than the width. The area is 432 m^2. Find the length of the rectangle.

20. The sum of the squares of two consecutive positive odd integers is 290. Find the smaller integer.

Chapter 9 Test Form D

Name: _____

Date: _____

1. State the domain and range of the function $f(x) = x^2 - 8x + 16$.

2. Find the vertex and axis of symmetry of the parabola given by $y = x^2 - 10x + 2$.

3. Graph: $f(x) = 3 - x^2$

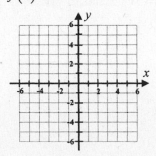

4. Graph: $f(x) = |2x - 3|$

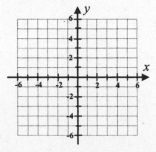

5. Find the x-intercepts of the graph of $y = 2x^2 - 3x + 1$.

6. Find the zeros of $f(x) = 4x^2 + 4x - 35$.

7. Use the discriminant to determine the number of x-intercepts of the graph of $y = x^2 + 2x + 5$.

8. Find the minimum value of the function $f(x) = 3x^2 - 6x + 8$.

9. Find two numbers whose difference is 32 and whose product is a minimum.

10. A rectangle has a perimeter of 60 ft. Find the maximum area of the rectangle.

11. For $f(x) = x^2 + 1$ and $g(x) = 3x - 2$, find $f(-1) - g(-1)$.

12. For $f(x) = x^2 - 2x$ and $g(x) = x - 5$, find $(f \cdot g)(3)$.

13. For $f(x) = x^2 - 3x$ and $g(x) = x^2 - 2x + 5$, find $\left(\dfrac{f}{g}\right)(-1)$.

14. Given $f(x) = 3x + 2$ and $g(x) = 3x - 2$, find $f[g(-2)]$.

15. Given $g(x) = x^2 - 1$ and $h(x) = x + 3$, find $g[h(x)]$.

16. Let $f(x) = 6 - 2x$. Find $f^{-1}(x)$.

17. Determine whether the graph represents the graph of a 1-1 function.

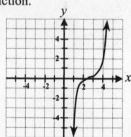

18. Determine whether the graph represents the graph of a function.

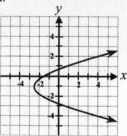

19. Let $f(x) = 5x + 1$. Find $f^{-1}(x)$.

20. Are the functions $f(x) = -2x$ and $g(x) = \dfrac{x}{2}$ inverses of each other?

Chapters 7-9 Cumulative Test D

Name: ______________________

Date: ______________________

1. Simplify: $x^{1/2}\left(x^{3/2}-x^{1/4}\right)$

2. Write $\sqrt[3]{(x-1)^4}$ as an exponential expression.

3. Simplify: $(4+7i)-(-3-i)$

4. Simplify: $\sqrt{3}\left(\sqrt{6}-\sqrt{-3}\right)$

5. Solve: $\sqrt{2x+5}-3=4$

6. Write a quadratic equation that has integer coefficients and has solutions $-3/2$ and 4.

7. Solve by taking square roots: $(x-2)^2-24=0$

8. Solve by completing the square: $x^2-8x+6=0$

9. Solve: $x^4-5x^2+4=0$

10. Solve: $\sqrt{2x-1}=x-4$

11. Solve: $\dfrac{x}{x-4} - \dfrac{1}{x+3} = 2$

12. Solve: $\dfrac{2x}{x-4} > 1$

13. The length of a rectangle is 5 ft more than twice the width. The area of the rectangle is $900\ \text{ft}^2$. Find the length of the rectangle.

14. Find the *x*-intercepts of the parabola given by $y = x^2 - x - 20$.

15. Graph: $y = -x^2 + 3x - 5$

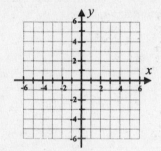

16. Graph: $f(x) = |x+2|$

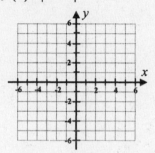

17. Find the maximum value of the function $f(x) = -x^2 + 1$.

18. Given $f(x) = 3 - x$ and $g(x) = x^2 - 2$, find $(f \cdot g)(-1)$.

19. Given $f(x) = x^2$ and $g(x) = 5 - x$, find $f\big[g(-2)\big]$.

20. Let $f(x) = 2x + 3$. Find $f^{-1}(x)$.

Name: _____
Date: _____

1. Given $f(x) = e^{x-1}$, evaluate $f(3)$.
   Round to the nearest ten-thousandth.

2. Given $f(x) = 2^{x-1}$, evaluate $f(5)$.

3. Graph: $f(x) = \left(\dfrac{1}{2}\right)^{-x}$

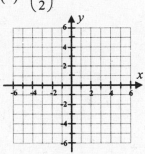

4. Graph: $f(x) = 3^x - 1$

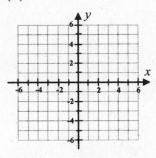

5. Write $5^{-2} = \dfrac{1}{25}$ in logarithmic form.

6. Write $\log_7 \dfrac{1}{49} = -2$ in exponential form.

7. Evaluate: $\log 0.000001$

8. Solve for x: $\log_5 x = 2.5$
   Round to the nearest ten-thousandth.

9. Write $\log \sqrt[3]{x^2 y^4}$ in expanded form.

10. Write $\dfrac{1}{2}\log_2 x - (\log_2 y + \log_2 z)$ as a single logarithm with a coefficient of 1.

11. Write $\ln \dfrac{x^3}{\sqrt{y}}$ in expanded form.

12. Write $2\ln x - \frac{1}{2}\ln y + 3\ln z$ as a single logarithm with a coefficient of 1.

13. Evaluate: $\ln \dfrac{3}{4}$

Round to the nearest ten-thousandth.

14. Evaluate: $\log_5 1.2$

Round to the nearest ten-thousandth.

15. Graph: $f(x) = \log_3 (x-2)$

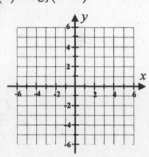

16. Graph: $f(x) = \log_5 (x+1)$

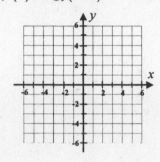

17. Solve for x: $2^{2x+1} = 8^{x-2}$

18. Solve for x: $2^x = 8^{3x-1}$

19. Solve for x: $\log_4 15 - \log_4 x = \log_4 (x-2)$

20. A deposit of $4000 is made into an account that earns 9% annual interest compounded semiannually. What is the value of the investment after 10 years?

Use the compound interest formula $P = A(1+I)^n$, where A is the original value of the investment, I is the interest rate per compounding period, n is the total number of compounding periods, and P is the value of the investment after n periods.

Chapter 11 Test Form D

Name: _____
Date: _____

1. Graph: $y = \dfrac{1}{2}x^2 + 2x - 1$

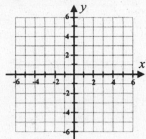

2. Graph: $x = y^2 - 4y + 5$

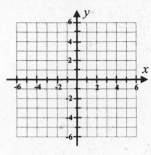

3. Find the vertex and axis of symmetry of the parabola given by $y = x^2 - 4x + 1$.

4. Find the equation of the circle (in standard form) with radius 3 and center $(0, -2)$.

5. Find the equation of the circle (in standard form) that passes through the point $(2, 4)$ and whose center is $(-3, 4)$.

6. Sketch a graph of $(x+2)^2 + (y-1)^2 = 4$.

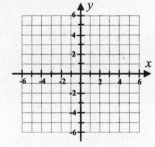

7. Write the equation $x^2 + y^2 + 6x - 4y + 4 = 0$ in standard form and then sketch its graph.

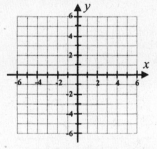

8. Sketch a graph of $\dfrac{x^2}{1} + \dfrac{y^2}{4} = 1$.

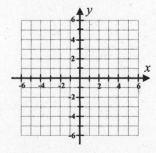

9. Sketch a graph of $\dfrac{x^2}{16} + \dfrac{y^2}{9} = 1$.

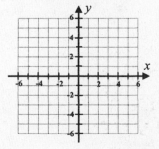

Name: _____

10. Sketch a graph of $\dfrac{y^2}{9} - \dfrac{x^2}{4} = 1$.

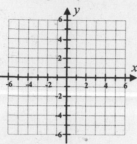

11. Sketch a graph of $\dfrac{x^2}{9} - \dfrac{y^2}{36} = 1$.

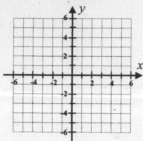

12. Solve: $x^2 + y^2 = 18$

$x + y = 6$

13. Solve: $y = 2x^2 + x - 8$

$y = x^2 - 2x + 20$

14. Graph the solution set of $\dfrac{x^2}{4} - \dfrac{y^2}{9} > 1$.

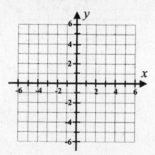

15. Graph the solution set: $x^2 + y^2 > 9$

$y < 2x + 1$

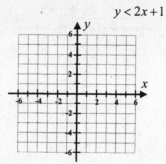

Name: _____

Date: _____

1. Write the 8th term of the sequence whose nth term is given by the formula $a_n = \dfrac{n-1}{n+2}$.

2. Write the 5th and 9th terms of the sequence whose nth term is given by the formula $a_n = \dfrac{n}{n+1}$.

3. Evaluate: $\displaystyle\sum_{n=1}^{5} n^3$

4. Write $\displaystyle\sum_{n=1}^{4} 2x^{-n}$ in expanded form.

5. Find the 12th term of the arithmetic sequence $-15, -4, 7, \ldots$

6. Find the formula for the nth term of the arithmetic sequence $2, 6, 10, \ldots$

7. Find the number of terms in the finite arithmetic sequence $-6, -1, 4, \ldots, 124$

8. Find the sum of the first 12 terms of the arithmetic sequence $16, 12, 8, \ldots$

9. Find the sum of the first 22 terms of the arithmetic sequence $12, 18, 24, \ldots$

10. Find the 5th term of the geometric sequence $3, 12, 48, \ldots$

11. Find the 4th term of the geometric sequence whose first term is $3/8$ and whose common ratio is 2.

12. Find the sum of the first seven terms of the geometric sequence $4, -12, 36, \ldots$

13. Find the sum of the first six terms of the geometric sequence whose first term is 24 and whose common ratio is $1/2$.

14. Find the sum of the infinite geometric sequence $9, 3, 1, \ldots$

15. Find an equivalent fraction for $0.6\overline{3}$.

16. Find the 3rd term in the expansion of $(2x-3)^4$.

17. Evaluate: $\dfrac{18!}{15!}$

18. Evaluate: $\begin{pmatrix} 8 \\ 3 \end{pmatrix}$

19. A "theater in the round" has 50 seats in the first row, 60 seats in the second row, 70 seats in the third row, and so on in an arithmetic sequence. Find the number of seats in the theater if there are 24 rows of seats.

20. The temperature of a hot water spa is $70°F$. Each minute the temperature is 1.5% higher than during the previous minute. Find the temperature of the spa after 20 minutes. Round to the nearest tenth.

Name: _____

Date: _____

1. Given $f(x) = 3^{x+4}$, evaluate $f(-3)$.

2. Graph: $f(x) = 2^{-x} - 1$

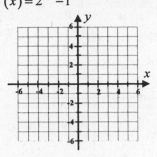

3. Evaluate: $\log_6 36$

4. Solve for x: $\log_3 x = -2$

5. Write $3\log_2 x - 4\log_2 y + 2\log_2 z$ as a single logarithm with a coefficient of 1.

6. Graph: $f(x) = \log_3 (x - 2)$

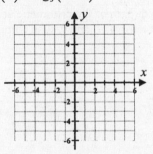

7. Solve for x: $2^{5x+1} = 2^{2x-2}$

8. Solve for x: $\log_3 (x^2 - 8x) = 2$

9. Graph: $y = -x^2 + 4x - 2$

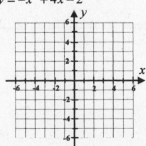

10. Find the equation of the circle (in standard form) with radius 7 and center $(-3, 3)$.

11. Sketch the graph of $\dfrac{x^2}{36}+\dfrac{y^2}{9}=1$.

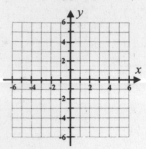

12. Solve: $x-2y=-5$
$x^2+y^2=25$

13. Graph the solution set of $y\le\dfrac{3}{2}x^2-\dfrac{3}{2}x+1$.

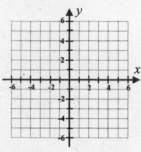

14. Evaluate: $\displaystyle\sum_{n=3}^{5}(-1)^n(2n-3)$

15. Find the 12th term of the arithmetic sequence whose first term is 10 and whose common difference is -4.

16. Find the number of terms in the finite arithmetic sequence -3, 0, 3, $\dots$, 39.

17. Find the sum of the first 40 terms of the arithmetic sequence 1, 4, 7, ...

18. Find the 6th term of the geometric sequence whose first term is -6 and whose common ratio is $\dfrac{1}{2}$.

19. Find the sum of the infinite geometric sequence
$6,-3,\dfrac{3}{2},\dots$

20. Find the 4th term in the expansion of $(2x+3)^5$.

1. Simplify: $5 - 2(3 - 4 \cdot 2^2)$

2. Evaluate $a^3 b^2 + 2c$ when $a = -2$, $b = 3$, and $c = -1$.

3. Simplify: $5x - 4[2x - 4(3x - 4y) + 2y]$

4. Find $A \cap B$, given $A = \{1, 2, 3, 4, 5, 6\}$ and $B = \{2, 3, 4\}$.

5. Solve: $\dfrac{4}{5}x - 2 = 6$

6. Solve: $3[5 - 2(4x - 3)] = 3(2x + 1)$

7. A rare coin collection consisting of 42 coins includes 2¢ coins and 3¢ coins. The total value of the coins is $1.16. Find the number of each type of coin in the collection.

8. Two planes are 1200 mi apart and traveling toward each other. One plane is traveling 100 mi/h faster than the other. The planes pass each other in 3 hours. Find the speed of the faster plane.

9. Simplify: $(3x^2 y)(-2xy)^3$

10. Simplify: $(a + 3)(a^2 - a - 1)$

11. Factor: $12x^2 - 5x - 2$

12. Factor: $y^3 - 27$

13. Factor: $5x^4 - 10x^3 - 120x^2$

14. Simplify: $\dfrac{3x^2 - 5x - 12}{x^2 + x - 12}$

15. Simplify: $\dfrac{3x^2 - x - 2}{x^2 + 4x - 5} \cdot \dfrac{x^2 - 25}{12x + 8}$

16. Simplify: $\dfrac{1 + \frac{3}{x} - \frac{10}{x^2}}{1 - \frac{7}{x} + \frac{10}{x^2}}$

17. The real estate tax for a house that is valued at $72,000 is $2520. At this rate, what is the value of a house for which the real estate tax is $6300?

18. A 25-ft ladder is leaning against a building. How high on the building will the ladder reach when the bottom of the ladder is 7 ft from the building?

19. Solve: $\dfrac{5}{3x+1} + 2 = \dfrac{16}{3x+1}$

20. Simplify: $3y\sqrt{32x^2} - x\sqrt{128y^2}$

21. Simplify: $\dfrac{\sqrt{4}}{\sqrt{4} - \sqrt{2}}$

22. Simplify: $\sqrt{-4}\left(\sqrt{12} + \sqrt{-1}\right)$

23. Solve: $\sqrt[4]{2x-6} = 2$

24. Solve: $3x^2 - 10x = 8$

25. Graph: $2x + 3y = 6$

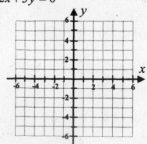

26. Graph the solution set of $x - 3y \le 4$.

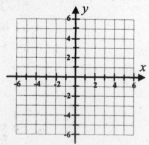

27. Find the equation of the line that contains the point $(5,0)$ and has a slope of $-\dfrac{3}{4}$.

28. Find the equation of the line that contains the point $(-2,-1)$ and is parallel to the line $2x - y = 3$.

29. Solve: $x^2 - 3x - 7 = 0$

30. Solve: $\dfrac{2}{x-2} + \dfrac{3}{x+2} = 2$

31. Given $f(x) = 2x^2 + 3x + 7$, find $f(1+h)$.

32. Is the set of ordered pairs a function?
$$\{(5,-15),(6,-18),(7,-21),(8,-24)\}$$

33. Graph: $y = -x^2 + x + 3$

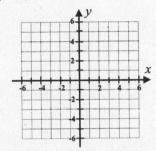

34. Sketch a graph of $\dfrac{x^2}{9} + \dfrac{y^2}{4} = 1$

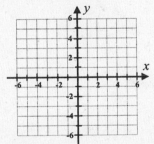

35. Find the x-intercepts of the parabola given by $y = x^2 - 7x + 12$.

36. Find the equation of the circle with radius 5 and whose center is $(3,-2)$.

37. Given $f(x) = -2x^2 + 5$ and $g(x) = -3x$, find $g[f(-2)]$.

38. Solve: $7x - 2y = -4$
$3x - y = -6$

Name: _____

39. Solve: $3x + y - 2z = 6$
$\qquad 2x - 3y - z = 7$
$\qquad x - 2y + 3z = -3$

40. Solve: $x^2 + y^2 = 12$
$\qquad 3x^2 + 4y^2 = 36$

41. Evaluate the determinant: $\begin{vmatrix} 4 & 3 & 0 \\ -2 & 1 & 1 \\ 3 & -1 & 2 \end{vmatrix}$

42. Evaluate: $\log_2 243$

43. Solve for x: $\log_4 x = 3$

44. Write $\log_2 \sqrt{x^5 y^3}$ in expanded form.

45. Solve for x: $3^{2x+3} = 27^{x+1}$

46. Solve for x: $\log_2 x + \log_2 (x - 1) = 1$

47. Find the 28th term of the arithmetic sequence whose first term is 40 and whose common difference is −4.

48. Find the sum of the first 40 terms of the arithmetic sequence 1, 6, 11, ...

49. Find the sum of the first 6 terms of the geometric sequence 25, 5, 1, ...

50. Find the 2nd term in the expansion of $(2x - 5)^3$.

Form E Tests

Multiple Choice

1. Find the additive inverse of 2.48.

   a. $\dfrac{1}{2.48}$
   b. 2.48
   c. −2.48
   d. 8.42

2. Write the set of real numbers between −3 and 4 using set-builder notation.

   a. $\{x \mid -3 < x < 4\}$
   b. $\{x \mid -3 \leq x \leq 4\}$
   c. $\{x \mid -3 \leq x < 4\}$
   d. $\{x \mid [-3, 4)\}$

3. Simplify: $-12 + 5 - (-4) - 6$

   a. 9
   b. −9
   c. −10
   d. −17

4. Simplify: $\left| -48 \div 6 \right|$

   a. −7
   b. −48
   c. −8
   d. 8

5. Simplify: $102 \div (-17)$

   a. 6
   b. −6
   c. 9
   d. −3

6. Simplify: $\left| 2(-3) \right|$

   a. 1
   b. −1
   c. −6
   d. 6

7. Simplify: $-2^2 (-3)^2 (5)$

   a. −180
   b. 180
   c. 36
   d. −36

8. Write $\{x \mid x \geq -4\}$ in interval notation.

   a. $(-\infty, 4)$
   b. $(-4, \infty)$
   c. $[-4, \infty)$
   d. $[4, \infty)$

9. Simplify: $\dfrac{5}{6} - \dfrac{2}{3} - \dfrac{8}{9}$

   a. $\dfrac{13}{18}$
   b. $-\dfrac{13}{18}$
   c. $\dfrac{19}{18}$
   d. $\dfrac{11}{18}$

10. Simplify: $-\dfrac{13}{24} \div \left(\dfrac{3}{8} \right)$

    a. $-\dfrac{3}{4}$
    b. $-\dfrac{13}{9}$
    c. $\dfrac{13}{9}$
    d. $\dfrac{4}{9}$

11. Simplify: $31.24 - 8.12 + 1.07$

    a. 24.19
    b. 23.12
    c. −22.05
    d. 22.05

12. Simplify: $(0.8)(-2.4)(-3.8)$

    a. 0.7296
    b. −72.96
    c. 7.296
    d. −7.296

13. Simplify: $24 - 6\left[4 - 3(16 - 4) \div 8\right]$

   a. -18 **b.** 27 **c.** 18 **d.** 24

14. Simplify: $\dfrac{3}{8} - \left(\dfrac{3^2 - 4}{3 - 9}\right) \div \dfrac{2}{9}$

   a. $\dfrac{33}{8}$ **b.** $\dfrac{27}{8}$ **c.** $\dfrac{63}{8}$ **d.** $\dfrac{31}{8}$

15. Evaluate $(a - b) \div (c - b)^2$ when $a = -5$, $b = 3$, and $c = -1$.

   a. $\dfrac{1}{2}$ **b.** $-\dfrac{1}{2}$ **c.** 2 **d.** -2

16. Evaluate $a - \dfrac{b^2 - 5c}{2c^2 + a} + c$ when $a = 5$, $b = -3$, and $c = -1$.

   a. 2 **b.** 7 **c.** 6 **d.** 3

17. Identify the property that justifies the statement: $z + (-z) = 0$

   a.   The Inverse Property of Addition
   b.   The Addition Property of Zero
   c.   The Associative Property of Addition
   d.   The Distributive Property

18. Identify the property that justifies the statement: $(a + b) + c = c + (a + b)$

   a.   The Commutative Property of Addition
   b.   The Inverse Property of Addition
   c.   The Associative Property of Addition
   d.   The Distributive Property

19. Simplify: $5a - 2\left[3a - 6(a + 1)\right]$

   a. $-a + 12$ **b.** $11a + 12$ **c.** $11a - 12$ **d.** $-a - 12$

20. Simplify: $5b - 2\left[3a - 2(b - 5a)\right]$

   a. $9b - 26a$ **b.** $9b - 14a$ **c.** $9b + 14a$ **d.** $4b - 21a$

21. Translate and simplify "one-third of the total of nine times a number and twenty-seven."

   a. $3n + 27$ **b.** $\dfrac{1}{3}n + 9$ **c.** $9n + 9$ **d.** $3n + 9$

22. Tom is four years older than Sue. If Sue's age is x, express Tom's age in terms of x.

   a. $4 - x$ **b.** $x - 4$ **c.** $x + 4$ **d.** $4x$

23. Find $A \cup B$, given $A = \{-3, -2, -1\}$ and $B = \{1, 2, 3\}$.

   a. $\{-3, -2, -1, 1, 2, 3\}$ **b.** $\{0\}$ **c.** $\{-3, 1, 2, 3\}$ **d.** $\varnothing$

24. Find $A \cap B$, given $A = \{-3, -2, -1, 0\}$ and $B = \{0, 1, 2, 3, 4\}$.

   a. $\{-1, 0, 1\}$ **b.** $\{-3, -2, -1, 0, 1, 2, 3, 4\}$
   c. $\varnothing$ **d.** $\{0\}$

1. Solve: $-4 = x - 11$

   a. -15 **b.** 7 **c.** 15 **d.** -7

2. Solve: $\dfrac{8}{15} = x + \dfrac{2}{5}$

   a. $\dfrac{2}{15}$ **b.** $\dfrac{3}{5}$ **c.** $-\dfrac{2}{15}$ **d.** $\dfrac{1}{5}$

3. Solve: $-\dfrac{4}{3}y = \dfrac{16}{27}$

   a. $-\dfrac{9}{4}$ **b.** $\dfrac{4}{9}$ **c.** $\dfrac{64}{81}$ **d.** $-\dfrac{4}{9}$

4. Solve: $2x - 4 = 5x + 3$

   a. $-\dfrac{7}{3}$ **b.** $-\dfrac{5}{9}$ **c.** $-\dfrac{1}{5}$ **d.** 1

5. Solve: $3x + 5 = 7x - 3$

   a. $\dfrac{1}{2}$ **b.** $-\dfrac{1}{2}$ **c.** 2 **d.** -2

6. Solve: $\dfrac{3}{4}x - 2 = -8$

   a. -8 **b.** $-\dfrac{40}{3}$ **c.** $-\dfrac{9}{2}$ **d.** $-\dfrac{16}{3}$

7. Solve: $7x - 3(2x - 4) = 4(2 - x)$

   a. $\dfrac{9}{2}$ **b.** 3 **c.** $-\dfrac{4}{5}$ **d.** -2

8. Solve $P = 2\ell + 2w$ for ℓ.

   a. $\ell = \dfrac{P - 2w}{2}$ **b.** $\ell = \dfrac{2w - P}{2}$ **c.** $\ell = \dfrac{P}{2} - 2w$ **d.** $\ell = \dfrac{2w - 2}{P}$

9. Solve: $\dfrac{x+2}{5} - \dfrac{x-1}{2} = 1$

   a. -3 **b.** $-\dfrac{11}{3}$ **c.** $-\dfrac{1}{3}$ **d.** 3

Chapter 2 Test Form E (*continued*)

Name: _____

10. Solve $3x - 2 > 6x + 7$ and write the solution set in interval notation.

    a. $\left(-\infty, \dfrac{5}{3}\right)$ **b.** $(-3, \infty)$ **c.** $(-\infty, 3)$ **d.** $(-\infty, -3)$

11. Choose the graph that shows the solution set of $-3 + 5(x - 2) < 3x + 1$.

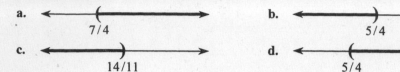

    a. $7/4$ **b.** $5/4$ **c.** $14/11$ **d.** $5/4$

12. Solve $3x - 2 > -14$ and $5 - 4x > 11$ and write the solution set in set-builder notation.

    a. $\left\{x \mid x < -4 \text{ and } x < -\dfrac{3}{2}\right\}$ **b.** $\left\{x \mid -4 < x < -\dfrac{3}{2}\right\}$

    c. $\left\{x \mid x > -4 \text{ and } x > -\dfrac{3}{2}\right\}$ **d.** $\left\{x \mid -\dfrac{3}{2} < x < 4\right\}$

13. Solve $4x - 5 > 3$ or $2 - 3x < -4$ and write the solution set in interval notation.

    a. $(-2, 2)$ **b.** $(2, \infty) \cup (-\infty, -2)$ **c.** $(-\infty, 2) \cup (-2, \infty)$ **d.** $(2, \infty)$

14. Two times the difference between a number and eight is less than or equal to three times the sum of the number and six. Find the smallest number that will satisfy the inequality.

    a. 34   **b.** −33   **c.** −34   **d.** −22

15. Solve: $|5x - 4| = 1$

    a. 1 and $\dfrac{3}{5}$ **b.** −1 and $-\dfrac{3}{5}$ **c.** −1 and $\dfrac{3}{5}$ **d.** 1 and $-\dfrac{3}{5}$

16. Solve: $|7x - 1| + 5 = 2$

    a. $-\dfrac{2}{7}$ and $\dfrac{4}{7}$ **b.** $\dfrac{4}{7}$ **c.** $-\dfrac{4}{7}$ and $\dfrac{2}{7}$ **d.** no solution

17. Solve $|5 - 2x| < 7$ and write the solution set in interval notation.

    a. $(-1, 6)$ **b.** $(1, 6)$ **c.** $(-\infty, -1) \cup (6, \infty)$ **d.** $\varnothing$

6. Find the slope of the line containing the points $P_1(-2,3)$ and $P_2(1,-4)$.

    a. undefined   **b.** $-\dfrac{7}{3}$ **c.** 0   **d.** $-\dfrac{3}{7}$

7. Given: $f(x) = 3x^2 - 5x$, evaluate $f(-2)$.

    a. 2   **b.** -2 **c.** 22   **d.** -22

8. Find the *y*-intercept of the line $3x + 2y = -6$.

    a. $(0,3)$ **b.** $\left(0,-\dfrac{1}{2}\right)$ **c.** $(0,-3)$ **d.** $(-3,0)$

9. Which is the graph of the line that passes through the point $(-1,4)$ and has slope $-\dfrac{2}{3}$?

  a.   **b.**   **c.**   **d.**

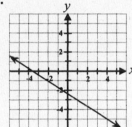 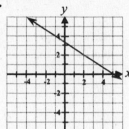 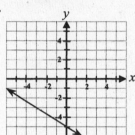 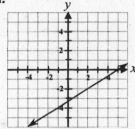

10. Find the equation of the line that contains the point $(-1,4)$ and has slope -2.

    a. $y = -2x + 4$ **b.** $y = -2x - 2$ **c.** $y = -2x - 6$ **d.** $y = -2x + 2$

11. Find the equation of the line that contains the point $(-1,-2)$ and has an undefined slope.

    a. $x = -1$ **b.** $x = -2$ **c.** $y = -1$ **d.** $y = -2$

12. Find the equation of the line containing the points $P_1(5,0)$ and $P_2(2,-3)$.

    a. $y = x + 5$ **b.** $y = -x + 5$ **c.** $y = x - 5$ **d.** $y = -x - 5$

13. A manufacturer of backpacks determines that the cost to produce 100 backpacks is $1500. The cost to produce 500 backpacks is $7000. Write a linear equation for the cost, *y*, of producing *x* backpacks.

    a. $y = 13.75x$ **b.** $y = 13.75x + 125$ **c.** $y = 0.073x$ **d.** $y = 0.073x + 250$

14. Find the equation of the line that contains the point $(5,-3)$ and is perpendicular to the line $y = \frac{4}{3}x + 8$.

    a. $y = -\frac{3}{5}x + 6$ **b.** $y = -\frac{3}{4}x + 8$ **c.** $y = -\frac{3}{4}x + \frac{3}{4}$ **d.** $y = -\frac{3}{4}x + 2$

15. Find the range of the function $f(x) = 2 - x$ for the domain $\{-1, 0, 2\}$.

    a. $\{x \mid x \in \mathbb{R}\}$ **b.** $\{1, 2, 0\}$ **c.** $\{0\}$ **d.** $\{3, 2, 0\}$

16. Which is the graph of the solution set of $2x - y \le 3$?

    a.   **b.**   **c.**   **d.**

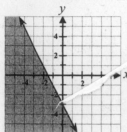 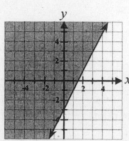 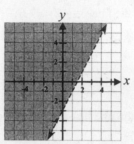 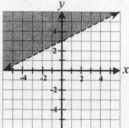

17. Find the length of the line segment between $P_1(2,-1)$ and $P_2(3,5)$.

    a. $\sqrt{37}$ **b.** $\sqrt{35}$ **c.** $\sqrt{41}$ **d.** 3

18. What values of x are excluded from the domain of $f(x) = \frac{x+2}{x+3}$?

    a. 0 **b.** -3 **c.** -2 **d.** 3

Problems 19 and 20 both refer to the graph below.

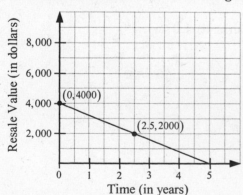

19. The graph to the left shows the relationship between the resale value of a computer system and the time since it was purchased. Which of the following statements describes the meaning of the ordered pair $(2.5, 2000)$?

    a. 2.5 computers were purchased for $2,000.
    b. 2.5 computers were purchased for $2,000 each.
    c. After 2.5 years, the computer was purchased for $2,000.
    d. After 2.5 years, the resale value of the computer was $2,000.

20. Estimate how much value the computer loses each year.

    a. $800   **b.** $1,000   **c.** $4,000   **d.** $600

Name: _____

Date: _____

1. Simplify: $-20(36)(4)(-3)$

   a. -8640 b. 8640 c. -7200 d. 7200

2. Simplify: $-1(-2)^3(-3)$

   a. 24 b. 12 c. -24 d. -12

3. Simplify: $\dfrac{5}{6} - \dfrac{7}{9} + \dfrac{1}{2}$

   a. $\dfrac{5}{9}$ b. $\dfrac{4}{9}$ c. $\dfrac{1}{3}$ d. $-\dfrac{23}{54}$

4. Simplify: $\left(\dfrac{3}{2}\right)^2 - \left(\dfrac{2}{3} - \dfrac{5}{6}\right) - 2$

   a. $-\dfrac{1}{12}$ b. $\dfrac{5}{12}$ c. $\dfrac{1}{12}$ d. $\dfrac{53}{12}$

5. Evaluate $\dfrac{ab-c}{c^2-a} \div \dfrac{a}{c}$ when $a = 4$, $b = -2$, and $c = -3$.

   a. $-\dfrac{4}{3}$ b. -1 c. $\dfrac{4}{3}$ d. $\dfrac{3}{4}$

6. Find $A \cap B$, given $A = \{-4,-2,0\}$ and $B = \{0,2,4\}$.

   a. $\{-4,-3,-2,1,2,3,4\}$ b. $\{0\}$ c. $\varnothing$ d. $\{-4,-2,0,2,4\}$

7. Simplify: $3x - 2\big[x - 2(x-3y) - 4y\big]$

   a. $5x - 20y$ b. $-3x - 4y$ c. $-3x - 20y$ d. $5x - 4y$

8. Translate and simplify "a number plus the product of the number minus ten and five."

   a. $6n - 50$ b. $-4n + 50$ c. $2n - 10$ d. $n - 5$

9. Solve: $y + 1.6 = 5.2$

   a. -6.8 b. -3.6 c. 6.8 d. 3.6

10. Solve: $4-(2-x)=3\left[4-2(1-3x)\right]$

    a. $-\dfrac{8}{5}$ **b.** 4 **c.** $-\dfrac{4}{17}$ **d.** $\dfrac{2}{5}$

11. Solve $2x+7\le 4x+9$ and write the solution set in set-builder notation.

    a. $\left\{x \mid x \le -1\right\}$ **b.** $\left\{x \mid x \ge 1\right\}$ **c.** $\left\{x \mid x \ge -1\right\}$ **d.** $\left\{x \mid x \ge 8\right\}$

12. Solve: $\left|3-2x\right|-1=4$

    a. -1 and 4 **b.** 1 and -4 **c.** -1 and -4 **d.** no solution

13. Solve $\left|2x-1\right|\ge 0$ and write the solution set in interval notation.

    a. $\varnothing$ **b.** $(-\infty,\infty)$ **c.** $\left(-\infty,\dfrac{1}{2}\right]$ **d.** $\left[\dfrac{1}{2},\infty\right)$

14. A child's piggy bank contains nickels, dimes, and quarters. There are twice as many nickels as dimes and five more dimes than quarters. The total value of all the coins is $6.40. How many quarters are in the bank?

    a. 12   **b.** 16   **c.** 15   **d.** 8

15. A jogger runs a distance at a speed of 8 mi/h and returns the same distance running at a speed of 6 mi/h. Find the total distance that the jogger runs if the total time running was one hour forty-five minutes.

    a. 6 mi   **b.** 12 mi   **c.** 10 mi   **d.** 7 mi

16. A 3% salt solution is mixed with a 9% salt solution. How many grams of the 9% salt solution were used to make 150 g of a 4% salt solution?

    a. 125 g   **b.** 40 g   **c.** 25 g   **d.** 20 g

17. Given $R(x)=x^2+3x$, evaluate $R(-2)$.

    a. -10 **b.** -2 **c.** 2 **d.** 10

18. Which is the graph of $3x+2y=6$?

    a. 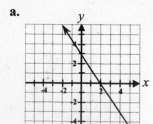   **b.** 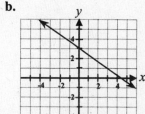   **c.** 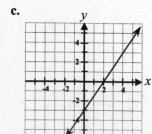   **d.**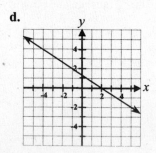

19. Find the slope of the line containing the points $P_1(3,-1)$ and $P_2(-2,4)$.

   a. 5   **b.** -1 **c.** 1   **d.** -3

20. Find the y-intercept of the line $7x - 2y = -5$.

   a. $\left(0, \dfrac{5}{2}\right)$ **b.** $\left(\dfrac{5}{2}, 0\right)$ **c.** $\left(0, -\dfrac{5}{2}\right)$ **d.** $\left(0, \dfrac{2}{5}\right)$

21. Find the equation of the line that contains the point $(2,-5)$ and has slope $\dfrac{3}{2}$.

   a. $y = \dfrac{3}{2}x - 7$ **b.** $y = \dfrac{3}{2}x - 8$ **c.** $y = \dfrac{3}{2}x - 2$ **d.** $y = \dfrac{3}{2}x - 7$

22. Find the equation of the line that contains the points $P_1(1,4)$ and $P_2(-3,0)$.

   a. $y = 2x + 2$ **b.** $y = 2x + 6$ **c.** $y = x - 2$ **d.** $y = x + 3$

23. Find the equation of the line that contains the point $(2,-3)$ and is perpendicular to the line $y = \dfrac{3}{2}x + 8$.

   a. $y = \dfrac{3}{2}x - 6$ **b.** $y = -\dfrac{2}{3}x + \dfrac{13}{3}$ **c.** $y = -\dfrac{2}{3}x - \dfrac{5}{3}$ **d.** $y = \dfrac{2}{3}x - \dfrac{13}{3}$

24. The graph below shows the relationship between the cost for new farm machinery and the depreciation allowed for income tax purposes. Write the equation that represents the depreciated value of the machinery.

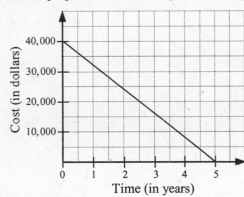

   a. $y = -800x + 40$

   b. $y = -\dfrac{1}{8000}x$

   c. $y = -8000x + 40000$

   d. $y = 80x - 40$

25. Which is the graph of the solution set of $x + y < -2$?

   a.
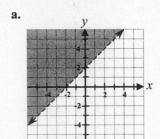

   b.
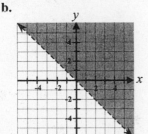

   c.
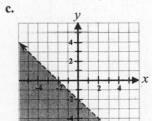

   d.
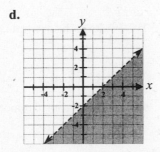

1. Choose the graph that shows the solution to the following system of equations: $2x + 3y = -2$
$$-x + y = 4$$

a.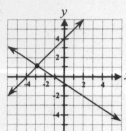

b.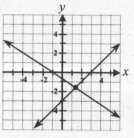

c.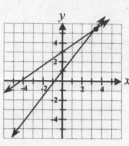

d.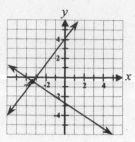

2. Solve by substitution: $x - 2y = -6$
$$y = 3x - 2$$

   a. $\left(\dfrac{1}{2}, -\dfrac{1}{2}\right)$ b. $(2, 4)$ c. $(4, 2)$ d. $(2, 2)$

3. An investment advisor deposited $50,000 into two simple interest accounts. On the tax-free account the annual simple interest rate is 7.5% and on the money market fund the annual simple interest rate is 12.5%. How much should be invested in the money market account so that both accounts earn the same amount of interest?

   a. $31,250   b. $22,000   c. $25,000   d. $18,750

4. Solve by the addition method: $4x - 5y = -2$
$$-3x + 2y = 5$$

   a. $\left(2, \dfrac{11}{5}\right)$ b. $(2, 5)$ c. $\left(1, \dfrac{7}{2}\right)$ d. $(-3, -2)$

5. Solve by the addition method: $x - 2y + z = 5$
$$2x - 2y - 3z = 3$$
$$-x + y + 2z = -1$$

   a. $(-3, 1, 2)$ b. $(2, -1, 1)$ c. $(-2, 1, 2)$ d. $(2, 2, -1)$

6. Evaluate the determinant: $\begin{vmatrix} 8 & -3 \\ 4 & -2 \end{vmatrix}$

   a. 28 b. 4 c. -28 d. -4

7. Evaluate the determinant: $\begin{vmatrix} 3 & -2 & 1 \\ 0 & -3 & 4 \\ 2 & -1 & 2 \end{vmatrix}$

   a. -52 b. 16 c. -16 d. 8

8. Solve by using Cramer's Rule: $2x + 5y = -6$
$$x + 4y = 0$$

   a. $(-4, 2)$ b. $\left(1, -\dfrac{1}{2}\right)$ c. $(-8, 2)$ d. $(-6, 2)$

9. Solve by using Cramer's Rule: $2x - 3y + z = 0$
    $$x + 2y - 3z = -7$$
    $$3x + y - 2z = -7$$

    a. $(0, 3, 2)$ b. $(-1, 1, 0)$ c. $(-1, 1, 2)$ d. $(-1, 0, 2)$

10. A crew rowing with the current rowed 11 mi in 2 hours. Against the current, the crew rowed 5 mi in 2 hours. Find the rate of the current.

    a. 2 mph   b. 1 mph   c. 1.5 mph   d. 3 mph

11. Flying with the wind, a plane flew 420 mi in 3 hours. Against the wind, the plane could fly only 270 mi in the same amount of time. Find the rate of the wind.

    a. 115 mph   b. 15 mph   c. 30 mph   d. 25 mph

12. A coin bank contains only dimes and quarters. The total value of the coins in the bank is $3.70. If the dimes were quarters and the quarters were dimes, the total value of the coins would be $2.95. Find the number of quarters in the bank.

    a. 7 quarters   b. 9 quarters   c. 10 quarters   d. 12 quarters

13. A restaurant manager buys 80 lb of hamburger and 30 lb of steak for a total cost of $163. A second purchase, at the same prices, includes 150 lb of hamburger and 50 lb of steak and costs $310. Find the price of 1 lb of hamburger.

    a. $1.25   b. $0.90   c. $2.30   d. $2.50

14. Choose the graph that shows the solution set for the system of inequalities: $x \le 0$
    $$x + 2y + 4 \ge 0$$

    a. 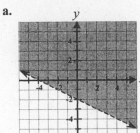   b. 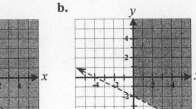   c. 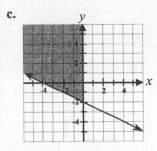   d.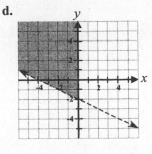

15. Choose the graph that shows the solution set for the system of inequalities: $y > -2x + 1$
    $$3y - x \le 3$$

    a. 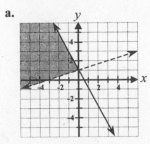   b. 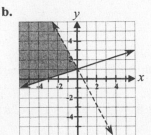   c. 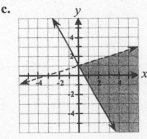   d.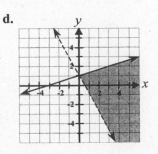

1. Simplify: $\left(5x^2 - 3x - 3\right) - \left(3x^3 - 2x^2 + 5x - 7\right)$

   a. $8x^3 + 7x^2 + x + 5$ b. $-3x^3 + 7x^2 - 8x + 4$ c. $-3x^3 + 3x^2 - 8x + 4$ d. $-3x^3 + 7x^2 + x - 4$

2. Simplify: $x^{2n+3} \cdot x^{3-n}$

   a. x^{n+6} b. x^n c. x^{3n} d. x^{3n+6}

3. Simplify: $\left(\dfrac{2a^2b}{3x^2y}\right)^3 \left(\dfrac{-6xy^2}{a^3b}\right)^2$

   a. $\dfrac{16by}{3ax^4}$ b. $\dfrac{32a^2y}{3bx^2}$ c. $\dfrac{16x^4}{3y}$ d. $\dfrac{32by}{3x^4}$

4. Given $P(x) = -5x^2 - 3x + 3$, evaluate $P(-3)$.

   a. 109 b. 29 c. -23 d. -33

5. Write $456,000,000,000$ in scientific notation.

   a. 4.56×10^{-11} b. 4.56×10^9 c. 4.56×10^{11} d. 4.56×10^{12}

6. The distance around the earth is $25,000$ mi. How long does it take for light to travel around the earth? Light travels 1.86×10^5 mi/s. Round to the nearest hundredth of a second.

   a. 0.13 s b. 0.14 s c. 1.3 s d. $46,000$ s

7. Simplify: $\left(-3x^2 + 4x - 6\right)\left(-4x^2\right)$

   a. $-3x^2 + 4x + 24x^2$ b. $12x^4 - 16x^3 + 24x^2$ c. $12x^4 - 16x^2 + 24x^2$ d. $-7x^2 + 4x - 6$

8. Simplify: $\left(4b^2 - 2b - 5\right)\left(2b - 2\right)$

   a. $8b^3 - 12b^2 - 6b + 10$ b. $8b^3 - 10b^2 - 7b + 10$ c. $8b^3 + 10b^2 - 13b + 10$ d. $8b^3 + 12b^2 - 6b - 10$

9. Simplify: $\left(1 - xy\right)\left(1 + xy\right)$

   a. $2 - x^2y^2$ b. $1 + x^2y^2$ c. $2 + x^2y^2$ d. $1 - x^2y^2$

10. The length of a rectangle is $(3x + 4)$ ft and the width is $(2x - 6)$ ft. Find the area of the rectangle in terms of the variable x.

    a. $\left(6x^2 - 10x - 24\right)$ ft^2 b. $\left(6x^2 - 29x - 28\right)$ ft^2 c. $\left(6x^2 + 13x - 28\right)$ ft^2 d. $\left(6x^2 - 29x + 28\right)$ ft^2

11. Factor: $6x^2y^2 - 3xy^2 + 21y^2$

    a. $3y^2(2x^2 - 3x + 21)$ b. $3y^2(2x^2 - x + 7)$ c. $3y(2x^2y - xy + 3y)$ d. $3y^2(6x^2 - x + 14)$

12. Factor: $x(2a + 3) - y(2a + 3)$

    a. $(x - y)(2a - 3)$ b. $(x - y)(2a + 3)$ c. $2ax + 3x - 2ay - 3y$ d.   Nonfactorable

13. Factor: $x^2 - x - 20$

    a. $(x + 4)(x + 5)$ b. $(x + 5)(x - 4)$ c. $(x - 5)(x + 4)$ d. $(x - 4)(x - 5)$

14. Factor: $9x^2 + 9x - 10$

    a. $(3x - 2)(3x - 5)$ b. $(3x + 2)(3x + 5)$ c. $(3x + 2)(3x - 5)$ d. $(3x - 2)(3x + 5)$

15. Divide: $\dfrac{3x^2y^3 - 9x^3y}{3x^2y}$

    a. $3xy^2 - 3xy$ b. $y^2 - 3x$ c. $xy^2 - 3x$ d. $y^2 - 9x$

16. Divide by using long division: $\dfrac{x^3 - x^2 - 10x + 4}{x + 3}$

    a. $x^2 - 4x + 2$ b. $x^2 - 4x + 2 + \dfrac{2}{x + 3}$ c. $x^2 - 4x + 2 - \dfrac{2}{x + 3}$ d. $x^2 + 2x - 4 - \dfrac{8}{2x + 3}$

17. Factor: $9x^2 - 64$

    a. $(3x + 8)^2$ b. $(3x - 8)(3x + 8)$ c. $(3x - 8)^2$ d.   Nonfactorable

18. Factor: $27a^3 - 1$

    a. $(3a - 1)(9a^2 + 3a + 1)$ b. $(3a - 1)(9a^2 + 9a + 1)$

    c. $(3a + 1)(9a^2 + 3a + 1)$ d.   Nonfactorable

19. Factor: $3x^{2n} + 11x^n - 4$

    a. $(3x^n - 1)(x^n - 4)$ b. $(3x^n + 1)(x^n - 4)$ c. $(3x^n - 1)(x^n + 4)$ d. $(3x^n + 1)(x^n + 4)$

20. Solve: $4x^2 = 1$

    a. $\dfrac{1}{4}$ and $-\dfrac{1}{4}$ b. $\dfrac{1}{2}$ and $-\dfrac{1}{2}$ c. $\dfrac{1}{2}$ d. $\dfrac{1}{4}$

Name: _____

Date: _____

1. Simplify: $\dfrac{12-x-x^2}{5x^2+30x+40}$

   a. $\dfrac{3-x}{5x+2}$　　　b. $\dfrac{x-3}{5(x+2)}$　　　c. $\dfrac{3-x}{5(x+2)}$　　　d. $\dfrac{x-3}{5x+2}$

2. Simplify: $\dfrac{3x^3+7x^2-6x}{6x^2+14x-12}$

   a. $\dfrac{x(3x-2)}{2(3x+2)}$　　　b. $\dfrac{x}{2}$　　　c. $\dfrac{3x-2}{2(3x+2)}$　　　d. $-\dfrac{x}{2}$

3. Simplify: $\dfrac{15x^2+10x}{2x^2-13x+20}\cdot\dfrac{2x^2-3x-5}{30x^3+20x^2}$

   a. $\dfrac{x+1}{2(x-4)}$　　　b. $\dfrac{2x-5}{x(2x+5)}$　　　c. $\dfrac{x-1}{2x(x+4)}$　　　d. $\dfrac{x+1}{2x(x-4)}$

4. Simplify: $\dfrac{12x^3-6x^2}{6x^2-5x+1}\div\dfrac{24x^3-12x^2}{12x^2-7x+1}$

   a. $\dfrac{4x-1}{2(2x-1)}$　　　b. 1　　　c. $\dfrac{2x-1}{2x+1}$　　　d. $\dfrac{4x+1}{4x-1}$

5. Given $P(x)=\dfrac{2x^2+1}{x^2-5x+1}$, find $P(-1)$.

   a. -1　　　b. $\dfrac{3}{7}$　　　c. $\dfrac{1}{7}$　　　d. $-\dfrac{1}{7}$

6. Find the domain of $f(x)=\dfrac{x-1}{x^2+1}$.

   a. $\{x\,|\,x\neq1\}$　　　b. $\{x\,|\,x\neq0,1\}$　　　c. $\{x\,|\,x\neq-1,1\}$　　　d. $\{x\,|\,x\in\text{real numbers}\}$

7. Find the missing numerator: $\dfrac{x-2}{3x+6}=\dfrac{?}{3x^2-6x-24}$

   a. x^2-6x-8　　　b. $3x^2-12$　　　c. x^2-6x+8　　　d. x^2+6x+8

8. Simplify: $\dfrac{x-4}{2x^2-3x-2}-\dfrac{3}{2x+1}$

   a. $-\dfrac{2(x-1)}{(2x+1)(x-2)}$　　　b. $-\dfrac{2x-8}{2x^2-3x-2}$　　　c. $-\dfrac{1}{x-1}$　　　d. $-\dfrac{2(x+1)}{2x^2-3x-2}$

9. Simplify: $\dfrac{4x+4}{4x^2-1}+\dfrac{3}{1-2x}$

   a. $-\dfrac{2x-3}{4x^2-1}$　　　b. $\dfrac{1}{2x+1}$　　　c. $-\dfrac{1}{2x+1}$　　　d. $-\dfrac{1}{1-2x}$

10. Simplify: $\dfrac{x-1+\frac{4}{x+3}}{x+3+\frac{4x}{x+3}}$

   a. $\dfrac{1}{9}$　　　b. $\dfrac{x-3}{x+9}$　　　c. $\dfrac{x+1}{x-9}$　　　d. $\dfrac{x+1}{x+9}$

11. Simplify: $\dfrac{\frac{1}{2b}+\frac{1}{4}}{\frac{4}{b^2}-1}$

    a. $\dfrac{b}{4(2-b)}$ **b.** $\dfrac{2+b^2}{1+b}$ **c.** $\dfrac{4}{b(2+b)}$ **d.** $\dfrac{b}{2(1-b)}$

12. Solve: $\dfrac{3}{x-1}=\dfrac{8}{3x}$

    a. $-\dfrac{8}{17}$ **b.** -8 **c.** 8 **d.** 1

13. Solve: $\dfrac{15}{2x-3}=\dfrac{6}{x}$

    a. 6 **b.** $-\dfrac{2}{3}$ **c.** -6 **d.** -2

14. The license fee for a car that costs $8500 is $102. At the same rate, what is the license fee for a car that costs $5000?

    a. $60   **b.** $55   **c.** $70   **d.** $75

15. Solve: $\dfrac{x}{3}-\dfrac{5}{8}=\dfrac{x}{12}$

    a. $-\dfrac{5}{2}$ **b.** $\dfrac{15}{8}$ **c.** $\dfrac{8}{15}$ **d.** $\dfrac{5}{2}$

16. Solve: $\dfrac{2}{x^2-1}=\dfrac{3}{x-1}-\dfrac{5}{x+1}$

    a. -3 **b.** $-\dfrac{3}{4}$ **c.** -5 **d.** 3

17. The income, I, of a website designer varies directly as the number of hours worked, h. If the designer earns $208 in 8 hours, how much will the designer earn by working 38 hours?

    a. $832   **b.** $922   **c.** $988   **d.** $1024

18. Solve $E=\dfrac{kQ}{d^2}$ for Q.

    a. $Q=\dfrac{Ed^2}{k}$ **b.** $Q=\dfrac{Ek}{d^2}$ **c.** $Q=\dfrac{Ed}{k}$ **d.** $Q=\dfrac{d^2}{Ek}$

19. One water pipe can fill a large tank with water in 16 hours. Another pipe can fill the tank in 24 hours. How long will it take to fill the tank if both pipes are open?

    a. 10 h   **b.** 9.5 h   **c.** 9.6 h   **d.** 18 h

20. A motorcycle travels 208 mi in the same amount of time as a car travels 180 mi. The rate of the motorcycle is 7 mi/h greater than the rate of the car. Find the rate of the car.

    a. 52 mi/h   **b.** 50 mi/h   **c.** 45 mi/h   **d.** 55 mi/h

Name: _____

Date: _____

1. Simplify: $\left(-4x^2y^3\right)^2\left(-3x^2y\right)^3$

   a. $-432x^{10}y^9$

   b. $-144x^8y^9$

   c. $432x^{10}y^9$

   d. $432x^{10}y^{10}$

2. Simplify: $\left(\dfrac{-5xy}{3a^2b}\right)^3\left(\dfrac{6ab}{10x^2y}\right)^2$

   a. $-\dfrac{5y}{3a^4bx}$

   b. $-\dfrac{5xy}{3a^2b}$

   c. $\dfrac{25xy}{3a^4b}$

   d. $-\dfrac{5b}{9a^2bx}$

3. Write 0.00024 in scientific notation.

   a. 2.4×10^4

   b. 2.4×10^{-3}

   c. 2.4×10^{-4}

   d. 2.4×10^{-5}

4. Simplify: $\left(4a^2-1\right)\left(5a^2+3\right)$

   a. $20a^4-17a^2+3$

   b. $20a^4-7a^2-3$

   c. $20a^4-17a^2-3$

   d. $20a^4+7a^2-3$

5. Simplify: $\left(a^n-2b^n\right)\left(a^n+2b^n\right)$

   a. $a^{2n}+4b^{2n}$

   b. $a^{2n}-4b^{2n}$

   c. $a^{2n}-4a^nb^n+4b^{2n}$

   d. $a^{2n}+4a^nb^n+4b^{2n}$

6. Factor: $x^2+13x+12$

   a. $(x-12)(x-1)$

   b. $(x+12)(x+1)$

   c. $(x+12)(x-1)$

   d. $(x-12)(x+1)$

7. Factor: $12a^2+35ab+25b^2$

   a. $(4a+5b)(3a-5b)$

   b. $(4a-5b)(3a-5b)$

   c. $(4a+5b)(3a+5b)$

   d. $(4a-5b)(3a+5b)$

8. Factor: $6x^3-51x^2+108x$

   a. $-3x(2x-9)(x-4)$

   b. $3x(2x+9)(x-4)$

   c. $3x(2x-9)(x+4)$

   d. $3x(2x-9)(x-4)$

9. Solve by factoring: $8x^2-5x=3$

   a. $\dfrac{3}{8}$ and 1

   b. $-\dfrac{3}{8}$ and 1

   c. -1 and $\dfrac{3}{8}$

   d. $-\dfrac{3}{8}$ and -1

10. Simplify: $\dfrac{2x^2+9x-5}{2x^2+5x-3}$

   a. $\dfrac{x+3}{x+5}$

   b. $2x-1$

   c. $\dfrac{x+5}{x+3}$

   d. $\dfrac{x-5}{2x-1}$

11. Simplify: $\dfrac{3}{x-2}-\dfrac{5}{2x-1}$

   a. $\dfrac{x+7}{(x-2)(2x-1)}$

   b. $\dfrac{x-1}{(x-2)(2x-1)}$

   c. $\dfrac{x-13}{(x-2)(2x-1)}$

   d. $\dfrac{7}{2x-1}$

12. Solve: $\dfrac{6}{x-5} = \dfrac{4}{x}$

     a. -5 **b.** -6 **c.** -10 **d.** 2

13. Simplify: $\dfrac{1-\frac{9}{x^2}}{1+\frac{1}{x}-\frac{12}{x^2}}$

     a. $\dfrac{x+2}{x+3}$ **b.** $\dfrac{x+3}{x+4}$ **c.** $x+3$ **d.** $\dfrac{x+3}{x-4}$

14. Solve: $3-\dfrac{x}{x-4} = \dfrac{4}{4-x}$

     a. 4 **b.** -4 **c.** 1 **d.**   No solution

15. Four computers can print out a file in 10 min, 20 min, 30 min, and 60 min respectively. How long would it take to print the file with all four computers working together?

     a.   5 min   **b.**   10 min   **c.**   30 min   **d.**   15 min

16. A passenger train travels 240 mi in the same amount of time as it takes a freight train to travel 180 mi. The rate of the passenger train is 20 mph faster than the rate of the freight train. Find the rate of the passenger train.

     a.   60 mph   **b.**   80 mph   **c.**   70 mph   **d.**   50 mph

17. The profit, P, realized by a company varies directly as the number of products it sells, s. If a company makes a profit of \$6500 on the sale of 260 products, what is the profit when the company sells 5000 products?

     a.   \$125,000   **b.**   \$20,000   **c.**   \$120,000   **d.**   \$80,000

18. Solve by substitution: $3x-5y=-4$
                          $y=3x-4$

     a. $(-2,-10)$ **b.** $(2,2)$ **c.** $\left(2,-\dfrac{2}{5}\right)$ **d.** $\left(\dfrac{4}{3},0\right)$

19. Solve by the addition method: $2x+3y=3$
                              $5x+2y=-9$

     a. $(3,-12)$ **b.** $(3,-1)$ **c.** $(-3,3)$ **d.** $(1,-7)$

20. Solve by using Cramer's Rule: $x-2y-4z=2$
                                $2x+y-z=7$
                                $x-3y+3z=-7$

     a. $(1,2,0)$ **b.** $(2,2,-1)$ **c.** $(1,-1,2)$ **d.** $(2,-2,1)$

Name: _____
Date: _____

1. Simplify: $\left(a^{3/8} \cdot a^{1/4}\right)^4$

   a. $a^{9/8}$

   b. $a^{5/2}$

   c. $a^{9/4}$

   d. $2a^{5/2}$

2. Simplify: $x^{-1/3}\left(x^{7/3} + x^{1/3}\right)$

   a. $x^2 + 1$

   b. $x + 1$

   c. $x^2 + x$

   d. x^2

3. Write $(4-x)^{1/2}$ as a radical expression.

   a. $2 - \sqrt{x}$

   b. $4 - x$

   c. $4^{1/2} - x^{1/2}$

   d. $\sqrt{4-x}$

4. Write $-\sqrt[3]{4x^2 y}$ as an exponential expression.

   a. $\left(-4x^2 y\right)^{1/3}$

   b. $-\left(4xy\right)^{2/3}$

   c. $-\left(4x^2 y\right)^{1/3}$

   d. $-4\left(xy\right)^{2/3}$

5. Simplify: $-\sqrt{64a^4 b^{12}}$

   a. $-8ab^{20}$

   b. $16a^2 b^6$

   c. $-8a^2 b^3$

   d. $-8a^2 b^6$

6. Simplify: $\sqrt{50a^6 b^9}$

   a. $5a^3 b^5 \sqrt{2}$

   b. $5a^3 b^4 \sqrt{2b}$

   c. $5a^3 b^4 \sqrt{2}$

   d. $2a^3 b^4 \sqrt{5b}$

7. Simplify: $\sqrt[3]{-27a^8 b^{12}}$

   a. $-3a^2 b^4 \sqrt[3]{a^2}$

   b. $3a^2 b^4 \sqrt[3]{a^2}$

   c. Not a real number

   d. $-3a^2 b^4 \sqrt[3]{ab}$

8. Simplify: $3\sqrt{18x^4 y^2} - 3x\sqrt{2x^2 y^2}$

   a. $-x\sqrt{16x^2}$

   b. $24x^2 y\sqrt{2}$

   c. $-6x^2 y\sqrt{2}$

   d. $6x^2 y$

9. Simplify: $3\sqrt[3]{81a^3 b^4} - 2a\sqrt[3]{24b^4}$

   a. $13ab\sqrt[3]{3b}$

   b. $5ab^2 \sqrt[3]{3}$

   c. $-5ab\sqrt[3]{3ab}$

   d. $5ab\sqrt[3]{3b}$

10. Simplify: $\sqrt[3]{16x^4 y^3} \cdot \sqrt[3]{12x^2 y^4}$

    a. $4x^2 y^2 \sqrt[3]{3y}$

    b. $4x^2 \sqrt[3]{6y}$

    c. $4xy\sqrt[3]{3y}$

    d. $4x^2 y\sqrt[3]{3xy}$

Chapter 8 Test Form E (continued)   Name: _____

11. Solve: $x - x^{1/2} - 6 = 0$

    a. 9 and 4   **b.** 9 and $2i$ **c.** 3, -3, $2i$, and $-2i$ **d.** 9

12. Solve: $x^4 - 16 = 0$

    a. 2 and $2i$ **b.** 4 and $4i$ **c.** 2, -2, $2i$, and $-2i$ **d.** 4, -4, $4i$, and $-4i$

13. Solve: $\sqrt{3x-2} + 4 = x$

    a. 9   **b.** 2   **c.** 2 and 9   **d.** -2

14. Solve: $\sqrt{3x+2} - 1 = 1$

    a. $\dfrac{1}{3}$ **b.** $\dfrac{2}{3}$ **c.** $\dfrac{3}{2}$ **d.** $\varnothing$

15. Solve: $\dfrac{3}{2x-3} - \dfrac{5}{x} = 1$

    a. $-1 + \dfrac{\sqrt{34}}{2}$ and $-1 - \dfrac{\sqrt{34}}{2}$ **b.** $1 + \dfrac{\sqrt{26}}{2}i$ and $1 - \dfrac{\sqrt{26}}{2}i$

    c. $\dfrac{3}{2}$ and -5 **d.** $4 + 2\sqrt{34}$ and $4 - 2\sqrt{34}$

16. Solve: $\dfrac{x}{2x-3} - \dfrac{2}{x-1} = 1$

    a. $i\sqrt{3}$ and $-i\sqrt{3}$ **b.** 3 and -3 **c.** 1 and -3 **d.** $\sqrt{3}$ and $-\sqrt{3}$

17. Solve: $2x^2 - 11x + 5 < 0$

    a. $\left\{x \mid -\dfrac{1}{2} < x < 5\right\}$ **b.** $\left\{x \mid \dfrac{1}{2} < x < 5\right\}$ **c.** $\left\{x \mid x < -5 \text{ or } x > \dfrac{1}{2}\right\}$ **d.** $\varnothing$

18. Solve: $\dfrac{1}{x+4} > 2$

    a. $\left\{x \mid \dfrac{7}{2} < x < 4\right\}$ **b.** $\left\{x \mid x > -\dfrac{7}{2} \text{ or } x < -4\right\}$

    c. $\left\{x \mid -4 < x < -\dfrac{7}{2}\right\}$ **d.** $\varnothing$

19. The rate of a plane in calm air is 140 mph. Flying with the wind, the plane can fly 450 mi in 2 h less time than is required to make the return trip against the wind. Find the rate of the wind.

    a. 20 mph   **b.** 25 mph   **c.** 40 mph   **d.** 30 mph

20. The height of a triangle is one-half the length of the base. The area of the triangle is 81 in^2. Find the height of the triangle.

    a. 12 in.   **b.** 18 in.   **c.** 36 in.   **d.** 9 in.

Name: _____

Date: _____

1. Find the axis of symmetry of the parabola given by $y = x^2 - 10x + 4$.

   a. $y = -5$ **b.** $y = 5$ **c.** $x = -5$ **d.** $x = 5$

2. Find the zeros of the function $f(x) = x^2 + 4$.

   a. $-2, 2$ **b.** $2i, -2i$ **c.** $-\sqrt{2}, \sqrt{2}$ **d.** $-2+i, -2-i$

3. Find the minimum value of the function $f(x) = x^2 - 18x + 65$.

   a. 65 **b.** -16 **c.** 9 **d.** -9

4. Find two numbers whose sum is 10 and whose product is a maximum.

   a. 0 and 10 **b.** 2 and 8 **c.** 5 and 5 **d.** -12 and 2

5. Which is the graph of the function $f(x) = |x| - 3$?

   a. 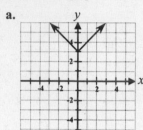 **b.** 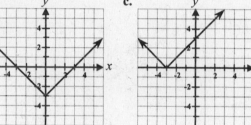 **c.**   **d.**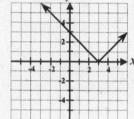

6. Determine which graph represents the graph of a function.

   a. 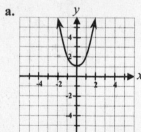 **b.** 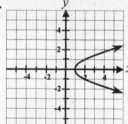 **c.** 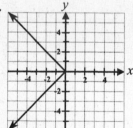 **d.**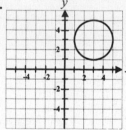

7. For $f(x) = x^2 - 8x + 3$ and $g(x) = 2x - 5$, find $f(0) - g(0)$.

   a. 0 **b.** -2 **c.** 2 **d.** 8

8. For $f(x) = 2x - 3$ and $g(x) = x^3$, find $(f \cdot g)(4)$.

   a. -60 **b.** 60 **c.** 320 **d.** -59

9. For $f(x) = 2x^2 - 3$ and $g(x) = x - 4$, find $\left(\dfrac{f}{g}\right)(5)$.

    a. 22   **b.** 97   **c.** 47   **d.** 235

10. Given $f(x) = x^2 + 2x - 1$ and $g(x) = 4x$, find $f\big[g(-1)\big]$.

    a. 25   **b.** 7   **c.** 23   **d.** 9

11. Given $f(x) = 3x - 2$ and $g(x) = 2x + 7$, find $f\big[g(x)\big]$.

    a. $6x + 3$ **b.** $6x + 23$ **c.** $6x - 19$ **d.** $6x + 19$

12. Determine which graph represents the graph of a one-to-one function.

    a. 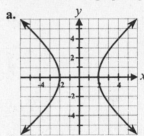   **b.** 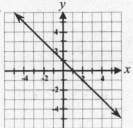   **c.** 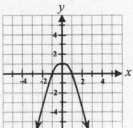   **d.**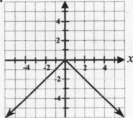

13. Let $f(x) = 3x - 7$. Find $f^{-1}(x)$.

    a. $f^{-1}(x) = -3x + 7$ **b.** $f^{-1}(x) = -\dfrac{1}{3}x + \dfrac{7}{3}$ **c.** $f^{-1}(x) = \dfrac{1}{3}x + \dfrac{7}{3}$ **d.** $f^{-1}(x) = \dfrac{1}{3}x - \dfrac{7}{3}$

14. Which of the functions are inverses of each other?

    a. $f(x) = 3x,\ g(x) = \dfrac{1}{3}x$ **b.** $f(x) = 2x - 1,\ g(x) = \dfrac{1}{2}x + \dfrac{1}{2}$

    c. $f(x) = -2x,\ g(x) = -\dfrac{1}{2}x$ **d.** All of the above

15. Find the inverse of the function $\{(1,2),(8,-1),(6,3)\}$.

    a. $\left\{\left(1,\dfrac{1}{2}\right),\left(\dfrac{1}{8},-1\right),\left(\dfrac{1}{6},\dfrac{1}{3}\right)\right\}$ **b.** $\{(1,2),(8,-1),(6,3)\}$

    c. $\{(-1,-2),(-8,1),(-6,-3)\}$ **d.** $\{(2,1),(-1,8),(3,6)\}$

1. Simplify: $x^{-2/3} \cdot x^{5/4}$

   a. $x^{5/6}$

   b. $x^{7/12}$

   c. $x^{-1/12}$

   d. $x^{3/4}$

2. Simplify: $\sqrt{32xy^6z^8}$

   a. $8y^3z^4\sqrt{x}$

   b. $4x^2y^3z^4$

   c. $2xy^3z^4$

   d. $4y^3z^4\sqrt{2x}$

3. Simplify: $\sqrt{-9}\left(2-\sqrt{-1}\right)$

   a. $3+6i$

   b. $3-6i$

   c. $-3+6i$

   d. $-3-6i$

4. Solve: $\sqrt{2x+3}-\sqrt{2x}=1$

   a. $\dfrac{1}{2}$

   b. 2

   c. 1

   d. 4

5. Write a quadratic equation that has integer coefficients and has solutions -3 and $\dfrac{1}{5}$.

   a. $5x^2+16x-3=0$

   b. $5x^2+14x-3=0$

   c. $x^2+2x-15=0$

   d. $x^2-2x-15=0$

6. Solve by taking square roots: $(2x-3)^2-8=0$

   a. $\dfrac{3+2\sqrt{2}}{2}$ and $\dfrac{3-2\sqrt{2}}{2}$

   b. 3 and -2

   c. $-3+2\sqrt{2}$ and $-3-2\sqrt{2}$

   d. $\dfrac{-3+2\sqrt{2}}{2}$ and $\dfrac{-3-2\sqrt{2}}{2}$

7. Solve: $\sqrt{4x-2}=2x-1$

   a. $-\dfrac{1}{2}$ and $\dfrac{3}{2}$

   b. $-\dfrac{1}{2}$

   c. $\dfrac{1}{2}$ and $\dfrac{3}{2}$

   d. $\dfrac{3}{2}$

8. Solve: $\dfrac{4}{x+1}+\dfrac{2}{x-1}=2$

   a. -4 and 2

   b. -1 and 2

   c. 0 and 3

   d. $\dfrac{5}{2}$

9. Solve: $3x^2+13x+12>0$

   a. $\left\{x\,|\,x>-\dfrac{4}{3} \text{ or } x<-3\right\}$

   b. $\left\{x\,|\,-3<x<-\dfrac{4}{3}\right\}$

   c. $\left\{x\,|\,-\dfrac{4}{3}<x<3\right\}$

   d. $\left\{x\,|\,x<-\dfrac{4}{3} \text{ or } x<-3\right\}$

10. A boat traveled 36 mi down a river and then returned the same distance. The total time for the round trip was 5 h, and the rate of the river's current was 3 mi/h. Find the rate of the boat in still water.

   a. 12 mi/h   **b.** 15 mi/h   **c.** 18 mi/h   **d.** 9 mi/h

11. Which is the graph of $y = -x^2 - 1$?

   a. 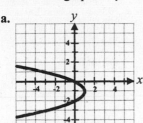   **b.** 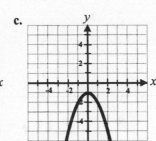   **c.**   **d.**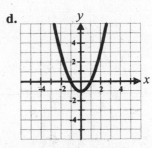

12. Which is the graph of $f(x) = |x + 1|$?

   a. 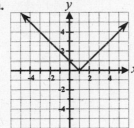   **b.** 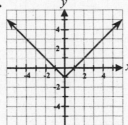   **c.** 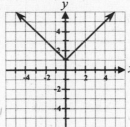   **d.**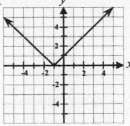

13. Given $f(x) = 3x + 1$ and $g(x) = x - 4$, find $(f \cdot g)(1)$.

   a. 0   **b.** -8 **c.** 8   **d.** 10

14. Given $f(x) = 4x + 1$ and $g(x) = -2x + 2$, find $f[g(1)]$.

   a. 1   **b.** -15 **c.** 17   **d.** -17

15. Let $f(x) = 2x + 6$. Find $f^{-1}(x)$.

   a. $f^{-1}(x) = \dfrac{1}{2}x - 3$ **b.** $f^{-1}(x) = \dfrac{1}{2x + 6}$ **c.** $f^{-1}(x) = \dfrac{1}{2}x - \dfrac{3}{2}$ **d.** $f^{-1}(x) = 2x - \dfrac{3}{2}$

Name: _____

Date: _____

1. Given $f(x) = e^{-2x}$, evaluate $f(2)$. Round to the nearest ten-thousandth.

   a. 0.2707
   b. 0.0183
   c. 0.27067
   d. 0.01832

2. Given $f(x) = 2^{x-3}$, evaluate $f(5)$.

   a. 16
   b. $\frac{1}{4}$
   c. 8
   d. 4

3. Which is the graph of $f(x) = 2^x - 2$?

   a.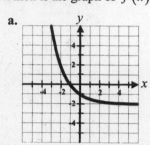
   b.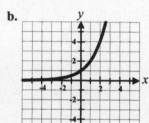
   c.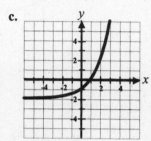
   d.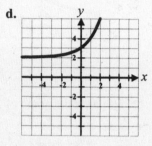

4. Evaluate: $\ln e^3$

   a. 1.3029
   b. 20.0855
   c. 3
   d. $\frac{1}{3}$

5. Solve for x: $\log_2 x = -5$

   a. $\frac{1}{32}$
   b. 32
   c. $\frac{1}{25}$
   d. $\frac{2}{5}$

6. Write $25^0 = 1$ in logarithmic form.

   a. $\log_1 0 = 25$
   b. $\log_{25} 1 = 0$
   c. $\log_0 1 = 25$
   d. $\log_1 25 = 0$

7. Write $\log_8 64 = 2$ in exponential form.

   a. $64^{1/2} = 8$
   b. $64^{-2} = 8$
   c. $2^8 = 64$
   d. $8^2 = 64$

8. Write $\frac{1}{3}\log_4 x + \frac{2}{3}\log_4 y - 2\log_4 z$ as a single logarithm with a coefficient of 1.

   a. $\log_4 \frac{\sqrt[3]{xy}}{z}$
   b. $\log_4 \frac{\sqrt[3]{xy^2}}{z^2}$
   c. $\sqrt[3]{\log_4 \frac{xy^2}{z^2}}$
   d. $\log_4 \frac{\sqrt[3]{xy^2}}{z}$

9. Write $\log_5 \dfrac{x^3}{y\sqrt{z}}$ in expanded form.

    a. $3\log_5 x + \log_5 y - \dfrac{1}{2}\log_5 z$ **b.** $3\log_5 x - \log_5 y + \dfrac{1}{2}\log_5 z$

    c. $3\log_5 x - \dfrac{1}{2}\log_5 yz$ **d.** $3\log_5 x - \log_5 y - \dfrac{1}{2}\log_5 z$

10. Write $\dfrac{1}{2}\ln x - 3\ln y - 2\ln z$ as a single logarithm with a coefficient of 1.

    a. $\ln x^2 y^3 z^2$ **b.** $\ln \dfrac{\sqrt{xy^3}}{z^2}$ **c.** $\ln \dfrac{\sqrt{x}}{y^3 z^2}$ **d.** $\ln \dfrac{x^2}{y^3 z^2}$

11. Write $\log_4 x \sqrt[4]{\dfrac{y}{z}}$ in expanded form.

    a. $\sqrt[4]{\log_4 \dfrac{xy}{z}}$ **b.** $\log_4 x + 4\log_4 y - 4\log_4 z$

    c. $\dfrac{(\log_4 x)(4\log_4 y)}{4\log_4 z}$ **d.** $\log_4 x + \dfrac{1}{4}\log_4 y - \dfrac{1}{4}\log_4 z$

12. Evaluate: $\ln 6$
Round to the nearest ten-thousandth.

    a. 1.7918   **b.** 0.7782   **c.** 1.792   **d.** 0.778

13. Evaluate: $\log_9 40$
Round to the nearest ten-thousandth.

    a. 1.6021   **b.** 0.1780   **c.** 1.6789   **d.** 1.6788

14. Which is the graph of $f(x) = \log_2(x-1)$?

    a. 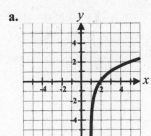   **b.** 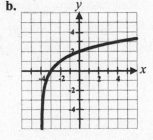   **c.** 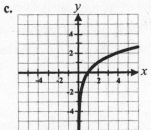   **d.**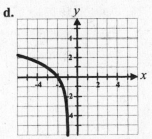

Name: _____

15. Solve for x: $2^x = 11$
    Round to the nearest ten-thousandth.

    a. 3.4594   b. 0.2891   c. 0.3135   d. 0.7404

16. Solve for x: $4^{3x-5} = 16^{x+3}$

    a. 2   b. 12   c. 7   d. 11

17. Solve for x: $5^{4x-1} = 125$

    a. -2 b. $\dfrac{3}{2}$ c. 1   d. $\dfrac{5}{2}$

18. Solve for x: $\log(x+3) - \log(x-1) = \log x$

    a. 3   b. -3 or 1 c. 3 or -1 d. 1

19. Solve for x: $\log_3\left(\dfrac{2x+5}{x}\right) = 3$

    a. $\dfrac{5}{7}$ b. $\dfrac{1}{5}$ c. $-\dfrac{1}{5}$ d. -5

20. An isotope has a half-life of approximately 80 days. How many days are required for a 20-milligram sample of this isotope to decay to 5 mg? Use the exponential decay equation $A = A_0\left(\frac{1}{2}\right)^{t/k}$, where A is the amount of radioactive material present after time t, k is the half-life, and A_0 is the original amount of radioactive material.

    a. 140 days   b. 200 days   c. 160 days   d. 120 days

Name: _____

Date: _____

1. Which is the graph of $x = y^2 + 2y$?

a. 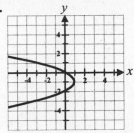   b. 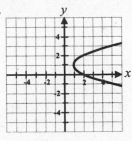   c. 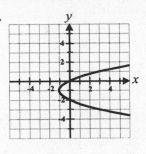   d.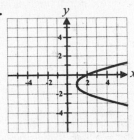

2. Find the axis of symmetry of the parabola $y = 2x^2 - 4x - 3$.

   a. $x = 2$ b. $x = 1$ c. $x = -2$ d. $x = -1$

3. Find the vertex of the parabola given by $y = -3x^2 + 6x - 5$.

   a. $(-2, -29)$ b. $(-2, 1)$ c. $(1, 2)$ d. $(1, -2)$

4. Find the equation of the circle with radius 5 and center $(3, 1)$.

   a. $(x+3)^2 + (y+1)^2 = 25$ b. $(x-3)^2 + (y-1)^2 = 25$

   c. $(x+3)^2 + (y+1)^2 = 5$ d. $(x-2)^2 + (y-3)^2 = 5$

5. Find the equation of the circle with radius 4 and center $(3, 0)$.

   a. $(x-3)^2 + y^2 = 4$ b. $x^2 + (y-3)^2 = 4$

   c. $(x-3)^2 + y^2 = 16$ d. $(x+3)^2 + y^2 = 16$

6. Which is the graph of $x^2 + y^2 + 4x + 6y + 4 - 0$?

a.   b. 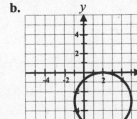   c. 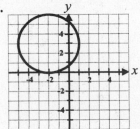   d.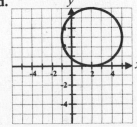

Name: _____

7. Write $x^2 + y^2 - 2x + 6y + 6 = 0$ in standard form.

    a. $(x-1)^2 + (y+3)^2 = 9$ **b.** $(x+1)^2 + (y-3)^2 = 9$

    c. $(x-1)^2 + (y+3)^2 = 4$ **d.** $(x+1)^2 + (y-3)^2 = 4$

8. Which is the graph of $\dfrac{x^2}{36} + \dfrac{y^2}{4} = 1$?

  a. 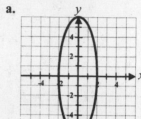   **b.** 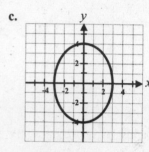   **c.**   **d.**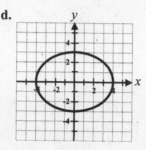

9. Which is the graph of $\dfrac{y^2}{16} - \dfrac{x^2}{4} = 1$?

  a. 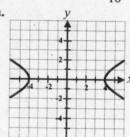   **b.** 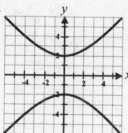   **c.** 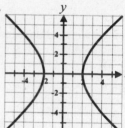   **d.**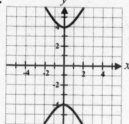

10. Solve: $x^2 + y^2 = 4$
             $3x^2 - y^2 = 12$

    a. $(0,2)$ and $(0,-2)$ **b.** $(2,0)$ and $(-2,0)$

    c. $\left(1,\sqrt{3}\right)$ and $\left(-1,-\sqrt{3}\right)$ **d.** $\left(\sqrt{5},3\right)$ and $(5,-3)$

11. Solve: $y = x^2 - 3x + 2$
             $y = -x^2 + 2x + 5$

    a. $(3,2)$ and $(0,1)$ **b.** $(6,1)$ and $(2,-1)$

    c. $(0,1)$ and $(7,-1)$ **d.** $\left(-\dfrac{1}{2},\dfrac{15}{4}\right)$ and $(3,2)$

Name: _____

12. Which is the graph of the solution set of $x \geq -y^2 - 4y - 1$?

a.
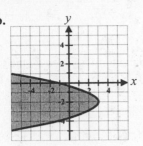

b.

c.

d.
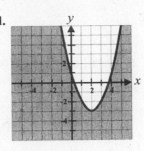

13. Which is the graph of the solution set of $\dfrac{x^2}{16} + \dfrac{y^2}{4} < 1$?

a.
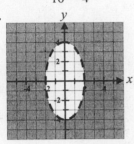

b.
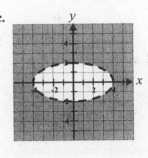

c.
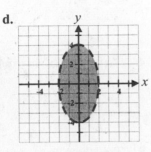

d.

14. Choose the graph that shows the solution set for: $\dfrac{x^2}{4} + \dfrac{y^2}{25} \leq 1$

$$2x - y > -4$$

a.
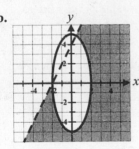

b.
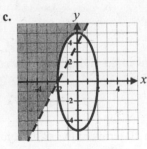

c.
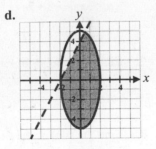

d.

15. Choose the graph that shows the solution set for: $y < -x^2 - 4x + 1$

$$x + 2y + 4 > 0$$

a.
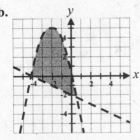

b.
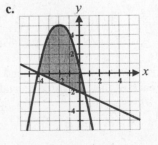

c.

d.

1. Write the 9th term of the sequence whose nth term is given by the formula $a_n = (-1)^n (n-4)$.

   a. -13 **b.** 13 **c.** -5 **d.** 5

2. Write the 9th and 10th terms of the sequence whose nth term is given by the formula $a_n = \dfrac{n}{n^2+1}$.

   a. $\dfrac{9}{82}, \dfrac{10}{83}$ **b.** $\dfrac{9}{19}, \dfrac{10}{21}$ **c.** $\dfrac{9}{82}, \dfrac{10}{101}$ **d.** $82, 101$

3. Evaluate: $\displaystyle\sum_{n=1}^{4} (-1)^n (n^2 - 1)$

   a. -10 **b.** 10 **c.** 12 **d.** 26

4. Write $\displaystyle\sum_{n=1}^{3} 2^n x^n$ in expanded form.

   a. $2x + 4x^2 + 8x^3$ **b.** $2x + 2x^2 + 2x^3$ **c.** $2x + 4x^4 + 8x^8$ **d.** $2x - 4x^2 + 8x^3$

5. Find the 40th term of the arithmetic sequence $-2, 4, 10, \ldots$

   a. 244 **b.** 226 **c.** 238 **d.** 232

6. Find the formula for the nth term of the arithmetic sequence $-8, -5, -2, \ldots$

   a. $a_n = -8 + 3n$ **b.** $a_n = 3n - 11$ **c.** $a_n = 3n - 5$ **d.** $a_n = n + 3$

7. Find the number of terms in the finite arithmetic sequence $1, 8, 15, \ldots, 190$.

   a. 32 **b.** 28 **c.** 24 **d.** 30

8. Find the sum of the first 20 terms of the arithmetic sequence $7, 10, 13, \ldots$

   a. 880 **b.** 860 **c.** 710 **d.** 740

9. Find the sum of the first 22 terms of the arithmetic sequence whose first term is -15 and whose common difference is 3.

   a. 363 **b.** 726 **c.** 396 **d.** 792

10. The distance a ball rolls down a ramp each second is given by an arithmetic sequence. The distance in feet traveled by the ball in each of the first three seconds is given by the sequence 4, 12, 20. Find the distance the ball travels during the 10th second.

    a. 82 ft   **b.** 72 ft   **c.** 76 ft   **d.** 60 ft

11. Find the 6th term of the geometric sequence 2, $2\sqrt{2}$, 4, ...

    a. 16   b. $\dfrac{\sqrt{2}}{8}$ c. $8\sqrt{2}$ d. $4\sqrt{2}$

12. Find the 8th term of the geometric sequence whose first term is 64 and whose common ratio is $\dfrac{1}{2}$.

    a. 4   b. $\dfrac{1}{8}$ c. 2   d. $\dfrac{1}{2}$

13. Find the sum of the first six terms of the geometric sequence 12, 6, 3, ...

    a. 21   b. $\dfrac{63}{8}$ c. $\dfrac{189}{16}$ d. $\dfrac{189}{8}$

14. Find the sum of the first five terms of the geometric sequence whose first term is 4 and whose common ratio is 2.

    a. 124   b. 252   c. 62   d. 104

15. Find the sum of the infinite geometric sequence 10, 2, $\dfrac{2}{5}$, ...

    a. 8   b. 25   c. $12\dfrac{1}{2}$ d. 18

16. Find an equivalent fraction for $0.\overline{185}$.

    a. $\dfrac{5}{12}$ b. $\dfrac{5}{27}$ c. $\dfrac{4}{63}$ d. $\dfrac{4}{33}$

17. A laboratory ore sample contains 1000 mg of a radioactive material with a half-life of 1 hour. Find the amount of radioactive material in the sample at the beginning of the sixth hour.

    a. 125 mg   b. 15.625 mg   c. 31.25 mg   d. 62.5 mg

18. Evaluate: $\dfrac{20!}{17!}$

    a. 6840   b. 380   c. 342   d. 116,280

19. Evaluate: $\dbinom{13}{4}$

    a. 143   b. 17,160   c. 1430   d. 715

20. Find the 4th term in the expansion of $(x^2 - 2)^6$.

    a. $-160x^6$ b. $80x$ c. $-120x^6$ d. $160x^3$

1. Given $f(x) = 3^{2x} - 1$, evaluate $f(-1)$.

   a. $\dfrac{8}{9}$
   b. $\dfrac{10}{9}$
   c. $-\dfrac{8}{9}$
   d. $-\dfrac{10}{9}$

2. Solve for x: $\ln x = -1.5$
   Round to the nearest ten-thousandth.

   a. 0.2231
   b. −0.4055
   c. 0.03162
   d. −4.4817

3. Write $\log_{10} x^3 \sqrt{y^3}$ in expanded form.

   a. $3\log_{10} x + \dfrac{3}{2}\log_{10} y$
   b. $\dfrac{1}{3}\log_{10} x + \dfrac{2}{3}\log_{10} y$
   c. $3\log_{10} x - \dfrac{3}{2}\log_{10} y$
   d. $\sqrt{\log_{10} x^3 y^3}$

4. Solve for x: $\log_5 x + \log_5 (2x - 1) = \log_5 6$

   a. 2 and $-\dfrac{3}{2}$
   b. -2 and $\dfrac{3}{2}$
   c. -2
   d. 2

5. Find the pH of a sulfuric acid solution for which the hydrogen ion concentration is 3.16×10^{-3}. Use the pH equation, $\text{pH} = -\log(\text{H}^+)$, where H^+ is the hydrogen ion concentration of the solution. Round to the nearest tenth.

   a. 2.5
   b. 2.0
   c. 3.0
   d. 3.5

6. Which is the graph of $y = -x^2 + 3$?

   a.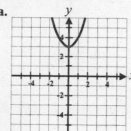
   b.
   c.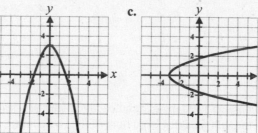
   d.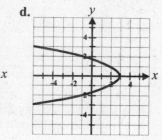

7. Find the equation of the circle with radius 7 and center $(-1, 5)$.

   a. $(x-1)^2 + (y+5)^2 = 49$
   b. $(x-5)^2 + (y+1)^2 = 49$
   c. $(x+1)^2 + (y-5)^2 = 7$
   d. $(x+1)^2 + (y-5)^2 = 49$

8. Which is the graph of $\dfrac{y^2}{16} - \dfrac{x^2}{36} = 1$?

   a.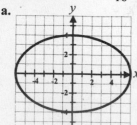
   b.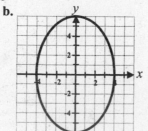
   c.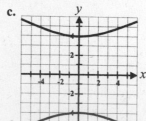
   d.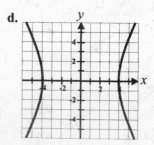

9. Solve: $2x^2 + y^2 = 12$

$\qquad x^2 = 2y$

   a. $(-2,2)$ and $(2,2)$
         b. $(-2,2)$, $(2,2)$, $\left(-6,2\sqrt{3}\right)$, and $\left(-6,-2\sqrt{3}\right)$

   c. $\left(1,\sqrt{10}\right)$ and $\left(-1,\sqrt{10}\right)$
         d. $(2,2)$ and $(2,-2)$

10. Which is the graph of the solution set of $\dfrac{x^2}{9} + \dfrac{y^2}{25} \le 1$?

  a.   **b.**   **c.**   **d.**

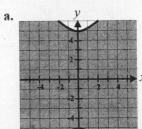 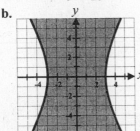 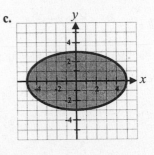 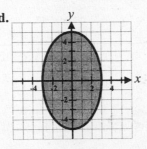

11. Write the 9th term of the sequence whose *n*th term is given by the formula $a_n = \dfrac{3}{n(n+1)}$.

   a. $\dfrac{1}{24}$
         b. $\dfrac{1}{30}$
         c. $\dfrac{3}{82}$
         d. $\dfrac{3}{65}$

12. Find the 12th term of the arithmetic sequence whose first term is 3 and whose common difference is -5.

   a. -63
         b. 52
         c. -52
         d. -57

13. Find the sum of the infinite geometric sequence 4, -2, 1, ...

   a. 6
         b. $\dfrac{3}{8}$
         c. 12
         d. $\dfrac{8}{3}$

14. A contest offers 8 prizes. The first prize is $25,000 and each successive prize is $2000 less than the preceding prize. What is the value of the 8th-place prize?

   a. $13,000
         b. $16,000
         c. $14,000
         d. $11,000

15. Find the 7th term in the expansion of $\left(2x^2 - y^2\right)^7$.

   a. $-28x^2y^{10}$
         b. $14x^2y^{12}$
         c. $14y^{12}$
         d. $28x^2y^{12}$

1. Simplify: $-10(-2)^3(3)^2$

   a. -720 b. 720 c. 360 d. -360

2. Evaluate $\dfrac{c^2+b}{a-bc} \div \dfrac{2c}{a}$ when $a=-3$, $b=-3$, and $c=5$.

   a. $-\dfrac{2}{3}$ b. $-\dfrac{11}{20}$ c. $\dfrac{8}{21}$ d. $\dfrac{2}{7}$

3. Simplify: $30y-2\big[3y-4(x-5y)+6x\big]$

   a. $-4y-4x$ b. $-16y+20x$ c. $-16y-4x$ d. $-4y+20x$

4. Translate and simplify "a number increased by four-sevenths of the number."

   a. $\dfrac{4}{7}n$ b. $\dfrac{7}{11}n$ c. $\dfrac{4}{11}n$ d. $\dfrac{11}{7}n$

5. Solve: $9x-4=5-3x$

   a. $\dfrac{1}{12}$ b. $\dfrac{3}{4}$ c. $\dfrac{4}{3}$ d. $-\dfrac{3}{4}$

6. Solve: $\dfrac{2-2a}{3}-2a=14$

   a. -5 b. $-\dfrac{14}{3}$ c. 10 d. -6

7. The sum of two numbers is thirty-two. Six times the smaller number is twelve more than three times the larger number. Find the larger number.

   a. 18 b. 20 c. 24 d. 12

8. Two cars are 206 mi apart and traveling toward each other. One car travels 7 mph faster than the other car. The cars meet in 2 hours. Find the speed of the faster car.

   a. 47 mph   b. 52 mph   c. 55 mph   d. 57 mph

9. Simplify: $\left(3a^2b^{-1}\right)^{-3}\left(6a^3b^{-2}\right)^2$

   a. $\dfrac{4}{3b}$ b. $\dfrac{2a}{b}$ c. $\dfrac{4a^{12}}{3b^7}$ d. $\dfrac{4a^5}{3b}$

10. Simplify: $\left(3-x^2\right)\left(4+3x^2\right)$

    a. $12-13x^2+3x^4$ b. $12+5x^2-3x^4$ c. $12-5x^2-3x^4$ d. $12+13x^2-3x^4$

11. Factor: $a^{n+3}+a^3$

    a. $a^{3n}(a+1)$ b. $a^3\left(a^n+1\right)$ c. $a^n\left(a^3+a\right)$ d. $a^3\left(a^n+a\right)$

12. Factor: $4x^2-11xy+6y^2$

    a. $(4x-3y)(x+2y)$ b. $(4x+3y)(x-2y)$ c. $(4x-3y)(x-2y)$ d. $(4x+3y)(x+2y)$

13. Solve by factoring: $4x^2 + 11x - 20 = 0$

    a.   2 and $-\dfrac{5}{2}$ **b.** -2 and $\dfrac{5}{2}$ **c.** $-\dfrac{5}{4}$ and 4   **d.** $\dfrac{5}{4}$ and -4

14. Simplify: $\left(4x^3 + 5x^2 - 12x + 2\right) \div \left(4x + 5\right)$

    a. $x^2 - 3 + \dfrac{17}{4x+5}$ **b.** $x^2 + 3 + \dfrac{17}{4x+5}$ **c.** $x^2 - 3 + \dfrac{13}{4x+5}$ **d.** $x^2 - 3 - \dfrac{17}{4x+5}$

15. Simplify: $\dfrac{49 - x^2}{3x^2 + 20x - 7} \div \dfrac{x^2 - 5x - 14}{6x^2 + x - 1}$

    a. $-\dfrac{2x-1}{x+2}$ **b.** $-\dfrac{3x-1}{3x+1}$ **c.** $\dfrac{2x+1}{x+2}$ **d.** $-\dfrac{2x+1}{x+2}$

16. Simplify: $\dfrac{x}{x^2+2} - 2 + \dfrac{3}{2x+2}$

    a. $-\dfrac{4x^3 - x^2 + 6x + 2}{2(x+1)(x^2+2)}$ **b.** $\dfrac{4x-1}{2(x+1)}$ **c.** $-\dfrac{4x^2-x}{2(x+1)}$ **d.** $\dfrac{1-4x}{2(x+1)}$

17. Simplify: $\dfrac{\frac{1}{a} - \frac{1}{a+1}}{\frac{1}{a} + \frac{3}{a+1}}$

    a. $\dfrac{1}{a+1}$ **b.** $\dfrac{1}{4a+1}$ **c.** $\dfrac{2a+1}{4a+1}$ **d.** $\dfrac{2a+1}{3a+1}$

18. Solve: $\dfrac{3}{x-2} - 4 = \dfrac{6}{x-2}$

    a. $\dfrac{5}{4}$ **b.**   2   **c.** $-\dfrac{5}{4}$ **d.** $\dfrac{4}{5}$

19. Simplify: $\sqrt[5]{32x^5 y^{25}}$

    a. $2x^2 y^{10}$ **b.** $2xy^5$ **c.** $4xy^5$ **d.** $2xy^{20}$

20. Simplify: $\sqrt{125x^4 y^2} - x\sqrt{45x^2 y^2}$

    a. $8x^2 y\sqrt{5}$ **b.** $2xy\sqrt{5}$ **c.** $2x^2 y\sqrt{5}$ **d.** $2x^2 y\sqrt{5x}$

21. Simplify: $\left(\sqrt{x} + 3\right)^2$

    a. $x + 6\sqrt{x} + 9$ **b.** $x + 9$ **c.** $x^2 + 3x + 9$ **d.** $x + 3\sqrt{x} + 9$

22. Simplify: $\left(\sqrt{27} - \sqrt{-9}\right) + \left(\sqrt{3} + \sqrt{-100}\right)$

    a. $4\sqrt{3} + 13i$ **b.** $6\sqrt{3} - 13i$ **c.** $6\sqrt{3} + 13i$ **d.** $4\sqrt{3} + 7i$

23. Simplify: $\dfrac{-3i}{3+i}$

    a. $-\dfrac{3}{8} - \dfrac{9}{8}i$ **b.** $-\dfrac{3}{10} - \dfrac{9}{10}i$ **c.** $-\dfrac{3}{10} + \dfrac{9}{10}i$ **d.** $\dfrac{3}{10} + \dfrac{9}{10}i$

24. Which is the graph of $y = -\dfrac{3}{2}x + 1$?

  a. 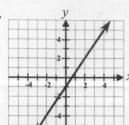   **b.** 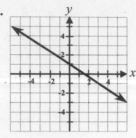   **c.** 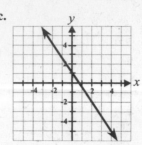   **d.**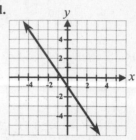

25. Find the slope of the line containing the points $(-2,2)$ and $(5,1)$.

  a. $\dfrac{1}{7}$ **b.** $-\dfrac{1}{7}$ **c.** -7 **d.** 7

26. Find the equation of the line containing the points $(2,-2)$ and $(1,3)$.

  a. $y = \dfrac{5}{3}x + \dfrac{4}{3}$ **b.** $y = -\dfrac{5}{3}x + \dfrac{14}{3}$ **c.** $y = -5x + 8$ **d.** $y = \dfrac{5}{3}x - \dfrac{14}{3}$

27. Which is the graph of the solution set of $3x + y \geq 3$?

  a. 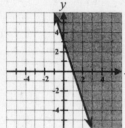   **b.** 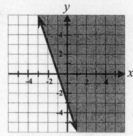   **c.** 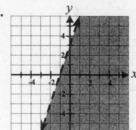   **d.**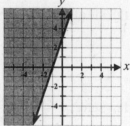

28. Solve: $x^2 + 4x + 8 = 0$

  a. $-2 + 2i$ and $-2 - 2i$ **b.** $2 + 2i$ and $2 - 2i$

  c. $2 + i\sqrt{2}$ and $2 - i\sqrt{2}$ **d.** $2 + \sqrt{2}$ and $2 - \sqrt{2}$

29. Solve: $x^4 - 5x^2 - 36 = 0$

  a. $3, -3, i\sqrt{2}$, and $-i\sqrt{2}$ **b.** $3i, -3i, \sqrt{2}$, and $-\sqrt{2}$

  c. 2 and -3 **d.** $3, -3, 2i$, and $-2i$

30. Solve: $\sqrt{6 - x} - 2x = 9$

  a. -3 and $-\dfrac{25}{4}$ **b.** -3 **c.** $-\dfrac{25}{4}$ **d.** -3 and $\dfrac{25}{4}$

31. Given $f(x) = -x^2 - 3x + 5$, evaluate $f(2)$.

  a. 5 **b.** -13 **c.** -5 **d.** 13

32. Which of the set of ordered pairs is a function?

  a. $\{(7,-2),(8,-3),(9,-2),(7,4)\}$ **b.** $\{(1,1),(1,4),(1,5)\}$

  c. $\{(0,0),(-1,1),(-2,2),(-3,3)\}$ **d.** All of the above

33. Given $f(x) = x^2 - 1$ and $g(x) = 2x$, find $f[g(-2)]$.

    a. -15 **b.** 15 **c.** 17 **d.** -17

34. Which is the graph of $x = y^2 + 2y - 4$?

    a. 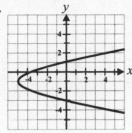   **b.** 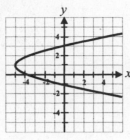   **c.** 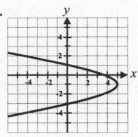   **d.**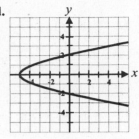

35. Find the minimum value of the function $f(x) = x^2 - x + 2$.

    a. $\dfrac{7}{4}$ **b.** 2 **c.** $\dfrac{9}{4}$ **d.** 1

36. Find the distance between the points $(6,1)$ and $(-3,4)$.

    a. $7\sqrt{2}$ **b.** $2\sqrt{7}$ **c.** $3\sqrt{10}$ **d.** $10\sqrt{3}$

37. Which is the graph of $x^2 + y^2 - 4x + 4y - 8 = 0$?

    a. 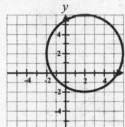   **b.** 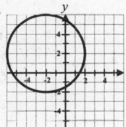   **c.** 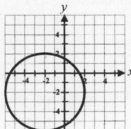   **d.**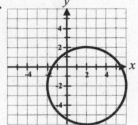

38. Solve: $4x + 3y = -21$
                $-x + 2y = -3$

    a. $(-6,1)$ **b.** $\left(\dfrac{9}{2}, -1\right)$ **c.** $(-3,-3)$ **d.** $(1,-1)$

39. Solve: $2y - 3z = 1$
                $x - 3y = 4$
                $x + z = 0$

    a. $(1,-1,-1)$ **b.** $(2,-1,1)$ **c.** $(2,2,-1)$ **d.** $(1,-2,2)$

40. Evaluate the determinant: $\begin{vmatrix} 1 & -1 & 3 \\ 4 & -2 & -2 \\ 3 & 1 & -2 \end{vmatrix}$

    a. 24 **b.** 10 **c.** -8 **d.** 34

41. Flying with the wind, a pilot flew 960 miles between two cities in 3 hours. The return trip against the wind took 4 hours. Find the rate of the wind.
    a. 30 mph
    b. 50 mph
    c. 40 mph
    d. 280 mph

42. Given $f(x) = 3^{1-2x}$, evaluate $f(-2)$.
    a. $\dfrac{1}{27}$
    b. 243
    c. 27
    d. 9

43. Solve for x: $\log_4 x = -\dfrac{1}{2}$
    a. $\dfrac{1}{4}$
    b. $\dfrac{1}{2}$
    c. 16
    d. $\dfrac{1}{16}$

44. Write $3\log_3 x + 4\log_3 y - 2\log_3 z$ as a single logarithm with a coefficient of 1.
    a. $\log_3 \dfrac{x^3 y^4}{z^2}$
    b. $\log_3 \dfrac{\sqrt[3]{x}\sqrt[4]{y}}{z}$
    c. $\log_3 \dfrac{\sqrt[3]{x^3 y^4}}{\sqrt{z}}$
    d. $\dfrac{\log_3 x^3 y^4}{\log_3 z^2}$

45. Solve for x: $5^{2x} = 40$
    Round to the nearest ten-thousandth.
    a. 1.4460
    b. 2.2920
    c. 1.1460
    d. 1.866

46. Solve for x: $\log_5 (7x^2 - 30x) = 2$
    a. $\dfrac{5}{7}$
    b. $\dfrac{5}{7}$ and -5
    c. $-\dfrac{5}{7}$ and 5
    d. 5

47. Evaluate: $\displaystyle\sum_{n=1}^{3} (n+1)^2$
    a. 9
    b. 17
    c. 23
    d. 29

48. Find the formula for the nth term of the arithmetic sequence 14, 11, 8, ...
    a. $a_n = 17 - 3n$
    b. $a_n = 14 - 3n$
    c. $a_n = 17 + 3n$
    d. $a_n = 11 - 3n$

49. Find the sum of the first six terms of the geometric sequence 3, 6, 12, ...
    a. -189
    b. 63
    c. $\dfrac{63}{2}$
    d. 189

50. Find the 4th term of the expansion of $(x^2 - 3)^5$.
    a. $-270x^4$
    b. $-135x^4$
    c. $270x^4$
    d. $135x^3$

Form F Tests

Multiple Choice

Name: _____
Date: _____

1. Let $x \in \{-4, -2, 0, 2\}$. For which values of x is $x < -2$ true?

    a. $\{-4, -2\}$ **b.** $\{0, 2\}$ **c.** $\{-4\}$ **d.** $\{-2, 0, 2\}$

2. Write the set of real numbers less than or equal to three in set-builder notation.

    a. $\{x | x < 3\}$ **b.** $\{x | x \le 3\}$ **c.** $\{x | x > 3\}$ **d.** $\{x | x \ge 3\}$

3. Simplify: $15 - 11 - (-3) - 14$

    a. -7 **b.** -6 **c.** 21 **d.** -13

4. Simplify: $-|-5| - |8|$

    a. -3 **b.** -40 **c.** 3 **d.** -13

5. Simplify: $-156 \div (-13)$

    a. 12 **b.** -12 **c.** 13 **d.** -13

6. Simplify: $|-72 \div (-8)|$

    a. 24 **b.** 9 **c.** -9 **d.** -18

7. Simplify: $-5^2 (-4)^2 (-3)^3$

    a. $-10,800$ **b.** 1200 **c.** -1200 **d.** $10,800$

8. Write $\{x | x \ge -1\}$ in interval notation.

    a. $(-\infty, -1]$ **b.** $[-1, \infty)$ **c.** $(-\infty, -1)$ **d.** $(-1, \infty)$

9. Simplify: $\dfrac{3}{8} - \dfrac{5}{16} + \dfrac{11}{12}$

    a. $\dfrac{37}{48}$ **b.** $\dfrac{17}{16}$ **c.** $\dfrac{2}{3}$ **d.** $\dfrac{47}{48}$

10. Simplify: $-\dfrac{7}{15} \div \dfrac{7}{16}$

    a. $-\dfrac{16}{15}$ **b.** $-\dfrac{7}{15}$ **c.** $-\dfrac{49}{240}$ **d.** $\dfrac{3}{5}$

11. Simplify: $(6.2)(-0.24)(1.5)$

    a. -2.322 **b.** -2.232 **c.** -22.32 **d.** -3.232

12. Simplify: $-12.792 \div (-4.1)$

    a. -3.12 **b.** 3.12 **c.** 0.321 **d.** -0.321

13. Simplify: $4 - 2\left(\dfrac{4-4}{-2+6}\right) \div \dfrac{1}{4}$

    a. 1 **b.** 2 **c.** 4 **d.** 0

14. Simplify: $145 \div (3-8) + 2(5-1)^2$

    a. 496 **b.** -3 **c.** -61 **d.** 3

15. Evaluate $(a - 2c)^2 \div (2b + 1) - a^2$ when $a = 6$, $b = -3$, and $c = -2$.

    a. -56 **b.** -16 **c.** 8 **d.** 16

16. Evaluate $\dfrac{3a + b^3}{c^2 - 1} \div \dfrac{b}{a}$ when $a = 2$, $b = -2$, and $c = 5$.

    a. $-\dfrac{1}{12}$ **b.** $-\dfrac{2}{3}$ **c.** $\dfrac{3}{2}$ **d.** $\dfrac{1}{12}$

17. Identify the property that justifies the statement: $2x + 4y = 2(x + 2y)$

    a. The Commutative Property of Multiplication
    b. The Associative Property of Multiplication
    c. The Distributive Property
    d. The Inverse Property of Multiplication

18. Simplify: $-2(x - y) + 2\left[3x - 2(x + 4y)\right]$

    a. $8x - 14y$ **b.** $8x - 18y$ **c.** $-14y$ **d.** $12x - 14y$

19. Simplify: $-4(b - 2a) - 3\left[2a - 3(a - 2b)\right]$

    a. $-3a - 21b$ **b.** $11a - 22b$ **c.** $9a - 15b$ **d.** $11a + 24b$

20. The length of a rectangle is four more than twice the width. Express the length of the rectangle in terms of the width.

    a. $2w + 4$ **b.** $2(w + 4)$ **c.** $2w - 4$ **d.** $2(w - 4)$

21. Translate and simplify "ten minus one-half of the sum of twice a number and eight."

    a. $6 - n$ **b.** $6 - \dfrac{1}{2}n$ **c.** $10 - \dfrac{1}{2}n$ **d.** $18 - n$

22. Find $A \cap B$, given $A = \{-9, -5, -3, 0\}$ and $B = \{-3, 0, 5, 6\}$.

    a. $\{-3, 0, 3\}$ **b.** $\{-9, -5, -3, 0, 5, 9\}$ **c.** $\{-3, 0\}$ **d.** $\varnothing$

1. Solve: $y + \dfrac{3}{5} = -\dfrac{5}{8}$

   a. $\dfrac{29}{24}$ b. $-\dfrac{11}{24}$ c. $\dfrac{11}{24}$ d. $-\dfrac{49}{40}$

2. Solve: $y - 3.6 = -2.4$

   a. -6 b. 1.2 c. 6 d. -1.2

3. Solve: $-\dfrac{2}{3}x = \dfrac{4}{9}$

   a. $-\dfrac{2}{3}$ b. $-\dfrac{3}{2}$ c. $\dfrac{2}{3}$ d. $\dfrac{8}{27}$

4. Solve: $2x - 5x = 5x - 16$

   a. -2 b. 14 c. 2 d. $-\dfrac{14}{11}$

5. Solve: $3x - 2 + 5x = 6x + 12$

   a. 5 b. 1 c. 7 d. -5

6. Solve: $\dfrac{2}{3}x - 4 = 8$

   a. -18 b. 18 c. 8 d. $\dfrac{3}{2}$

7. Solve: $2\left[x - (3 - 2x)\right] = 5(3 - 7x) - x$

   a. $-\dfrac{10}{3}$ b. $\dfrac{1}{2}$ c. -2 d. $\dfrac{3}{4}$

8. Solve: $\dfrac{x - 6}{3} - 2 = \dfrac{x}{6}$

   a. 24 b. 0 c. 8 d. -24

9. Solve $6 - 7x < 3x - 9$ and write the solution set in interval notation.

   a. $\left(-\infty, \dfrac{3}{2}\right)$ b. $\left(\dfrac{3}{2}, \infty\right)$ c. $\left(\dfrac{3}{10}, \infty\right)$ d. $(3, \infty)$

10. Choose the graph that shows the solution set of $5(2-x)+3x<2(3x-4)$.

a.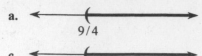
  9/4

b.
  9/4

c.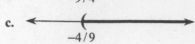
  −4/9

d.
  −2

11. Solve $2(x-3)<9$ and $7 \le 3x-5$ and write the solution set in set-builder notation.

a. $\left\{ x \mid \dfrac{7}{2} \le x < 4 \right\}$

b. $\left\{ x \mid 4 \le x < \dfrac{15}{2} \right\}$

c. $\left\{ x \mid x < \dfrac{3}{2} \text{ and } x \ge 4 \right\}$

d. $\varnothing$

12. Solve $5x-1>9$ or $6-2x<14$ and write the solution set in interval notation.

a. $(-4,2)$

b. $(2,\infty)$

c. $(-4,\infty)$

d. $\varnothing$

13. The length of a rectangle is 3 feet less than five times the width. Express as an integer the maximum width of the rectangle when the perimeter is less than 42 feet.

a. 4 ft

b. 3 ft

c. 5 ft

d. 2 ft

14. Solve: $|5x-4|-2=8$

a. $-\dfrac{14}{5}$ and $-\dfrac{6}{5}$

b. $-\dfrac{14}{5}$ and $\dfrac{6}{5}$

c. $\dfrac{14}{5}$ and $\dfrac{6}{5}$

d. $\dfrac{14}{5}$ and $-\dfrac{6}{5}$

15. Solve $|2-3x|<-4$ and write the solution set in set-builder notation.

a. $\varnothing$

b. $\left\{ x \mid x>2 \text{ or } x<\dfrac{2}{3} \right\}$

c. $\left\{ x \mid -\dfrac{2}{3}<x<2 \right\}$

d. $\left\{ x \mid x>2 \text{ or } x<-\dfrac{2}{3} \right\}$

16. A machinist must make a bushing that has a tolerance of 0.005 in. The diameter of the bushing is 4.32 in. Find the lower and upper limits of the diameter of the bushing.

a. 4.315 in.; 4.325 in.

b. 4.310 in.; 4.330 in.

c. 4.300 in.; 4.400 in.

d. 4.305 in.; 4.331 in.

17. The sum of two integers is fifty-seven. Twice the smaller integer is six less than the larger integer. Find the smaller integer.

a. 21

b. 18

c. 17

d. 25

18. A coin purse contains 19 coins in nickels, dimes, and quarters. There are three times as many quarters as dimes. The total value of all the coins is $2.90. How many nickels are in the coin purse?

    a. 3   **b.** 7   **c.** 14   **d.** 9

19. Cranberry juice that costs $5 per gallon was mixed with 24 gal of apple juice that costs $2 per gallon. How much cranberry juice was used to make cranapple juice to sell for $3.20 per gallon?

    a. 14 gal   **b.** 18 gal   **c.** 16 gal   **d.** 20 gal

20. A cabin cruiser leaves a harbor and travels to a small island at an average speed of 24 mi/h. On the return trip, the cabin cruiser travels at an average speed of 16 mi/h. The total tme for the trip is 4 h. How far is the island from the harbor?

    a. 35 mi   **b.** 38.4 mi   **c.** 40 mi   **d.** 32.8 mi

21. The temperature range for a week is between 50° F and 77° F. Find the temperature range in Celsius degrees.
    $$F = \frac{9}{5}C + 32$$

    a. $-10°C < C < 25°C$ **b.** $10°C < C < 30°C$ **c.** $20°C < C < 25°C$ **d.** $10°C < C < 25°C$

22. A silversmith mixed 50 g of a 60% silver alloy with 100 g of a 20% silver alloy. What is the percent concentration of the resulting alloy?

    a. $33\frac{1}{3}\%$ **b.** 50%   **c.** 3%   **d.** 46%

23. Solve $A = \frac{1}{2}bh$ for b.

    a. $\dfrac{2A}{h}$ **b.** $2A - h$ **c.** $\dfrac{Ah}{2}$ **d.** $2Ah$

1. Which point has coordinates $(3, 2)$?

   a. A
   b. B
   c. C
   d. D

   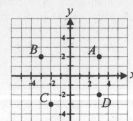

2. Find the ordered-pair solution of $y = -\dfrac{3}{4}x + 2$ when $x = -8$.

   a. $(8, -8)$
   b. $(-8, 6)$
   c. $(-8, -6)$
   d. $(-8, 8)$

3. Which is the graph of $y = -2x + 1$?

   a.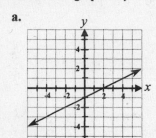
   b.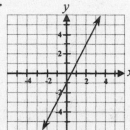
   c.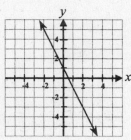
   d.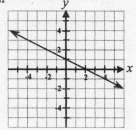

4. Which is the graph of $3x - 5y = 8$?

   a.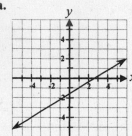
   b.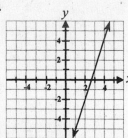
   c.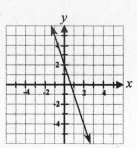
   d.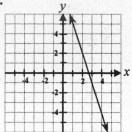

5. Find the slope of the line containing the points $P_1(2, 4)$ and $P_2(-3, 4)$.

   a. undefined
   b. -8
   c. 0
   d. $-\dfrac{1}{5}$

6. Given: $f(x) = 2x^2 - x + 5$, evaluate $f(2)$.

   a. 2
   b. 19
   c. 11
   d. 15

7. Find the *x*-intercept of the line $3x - 2y = -5$.

   a. $\left(\dfrac{5}{3}, 0\right)$ b. $\left(-\dfrac{5}{3}, 0\right)$ c. $\left(\dfrac{1}{2}, 0\right)$ d. $(3, 0)$

8. Which is the graph of the line that passes through the point $(-2, -2)$ and has slope $-\dfrac{2}{3}$?

   a.   b.   c.   d.

   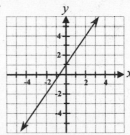   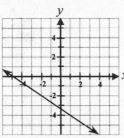   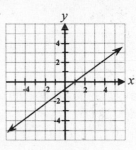   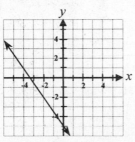

9. Find the equation of the line that contains the point $(1, -7)$ and has slope -2.

   a. $y = -2x + 5$ b. $y = 2x + 5$ c. $y = -2x - 5$ d. $y = -2x - 7$

10. Find the equation of the line that contains the points $P_1(1, 4)$ and $P_2(-3, 2)$.

    a. $y = \dfrac{1}{2}x - \dfrac{7}{2}$ b. $y = \dfrac{1}{2}x + \dfrac{7}{2}$ c. $y = -3x + 11$ d. $y = -\dfrac{3}{2}x - \dfrac{5}{2}$

11. Find the equation of the line that contains the point $(1, -4)$ and is parallel to the line $y = \dfrac{1}{2}x - 12$.

    a. $y = -2x - 2$ b. $y = \dfrac{1}{2}x - \dfrac{9}{2}$ c. $y = \dfrac{1}{2}x + \dfrac{7}{2}$ d. $y = \dfrac{1}{2}x - 12$

12. Find the range of the function $\{(0, 3), (2, 3), (-1, 3), (-2, 3)\}$.

    a. $\{3\}$ b. $\{-2, -1, 0, 2\}$ c. $\{-2, -1, 0, 2, 3\}$ d. This has no range.

13. Which is the graph of the solution set of $x - y \geq 3$?

    a.   b.   c.   d.

    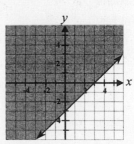   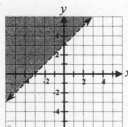   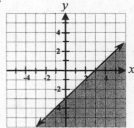   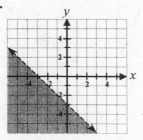

Chapter 3 Test Form F (*continued*)

Name: _____

14. Find the midpoint of the line segment between $P_1(-6,4)$ and $P_2(-3,2)$.

    a. $\left(-\dfrac{3}{2},1\right)$
    b. $\left(-\dfrac{9}{2},3\right)$
    c. $\left(3,-\dfrac{9}{2}\right)$
    d. $\left(1,-\dfrac{3}{2}\right)$

15. Find the length of the line segment between $P_1(2,-2)$ and $P_2(5,2)$.

    a. $\sqrt{5}$
    b. 5
    c. 7
    d. $\sqrt{55}$

16. What values of x are excluded from the domain of $f(x)=x^2-5x-6$?

    a. 6
    b. -1
    c. -1 and 6
    d. None

17. Find the equation for the line that contains the point $(5,-3)$ and has an undefined slope.

    a. $y=-3$
    b. $y=5$
    c. $x=-3$
    d. $x=5$

18. A cyclist begins a training ride at 6:00 A.M. He bikes at a constant pace and at 7:15 A.M. his odometer reads 30.75 miles. Write a linear equation to describe the distance he has traveled, y, in terms of the hours since he began the ride, x.

    a. $y=30.75x$
    b. $y=0.041x$
    c. $y=24.6x$
    d. $y=26.7x$

Problems 19 and 20 both refer to the graph below.

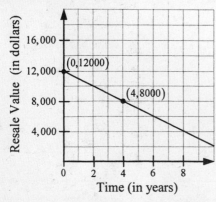

19. The graph to the left shows the relationship between the resale value of a company car and the time since it was purchased. Which of the following statements describes the meaning of the ordered pair $(4,8000)$?

    a. Four cars were purchased for $8,000 each.
    b. 8000 cars were purchased in year four.
    c. The resale value of the car was $8,000 in year four.
    d. 8000 cars were sold in year four.

20. When will the resale value of the car be zero?

    a. 7 years
    b. 12 years
    c. 9 years
    d. 14 years

Name: _____

Date: _____

1. Simplify: $-3^2(-4)(-2)^3$

   a. 36   b. -108 c. -288 d. -72

2. Simplify: $3\left[2-3(1-4)^2 \div 9\right]$

   a. 6   b. -3 c. 9   d. -1

3. Evaluate $a^2b-(c+a)^2$ when $a=-1$, $b=-2$, and $c=5$.

   a. 14   b. -18 c. 18   d. -14

4. Identify the property that justifies the statement: $x \cdot (y \cdot z) = (x \cdot y) \cdot z$

   a. The Associative Property of Multiplication   b. The Commutative Property of Multiplication

   c. The Inverse Property of Multiplication   d. The Distributive Property

5. Simplify: $2x-\left[-2x+3(x-5y)\right]-6y$

   a. $3x+21y$ b. $x+21y$ c. $3x+9y$ d. $x+9y$

6. Translate and simplify "five less than twice the sum of a number and eight."

   a. $2n+11$ b. $2n-11$ c. $2n+3$ d. $n+11$

7. Solve: $y+\dfrac{3}{4}=-\dfrac{5}{6}$

   a. $-\dfrac{1}{12}$ b. $-\dfrac{19}{12}$ c. $\dfrac{19}{12}$ d. $\dfrac{1}{12}$

8. Solve: $\dfrac{4x-3}{2}-2=\dfrac{2+x}{3}$

   a. $-\dfrac{2}{5}$ b. $\dfrac{25}{14}$ c. $\dfrac{5}{2}$ d. -2

9. Solve $2-3x<8$ and $2x-3\geq-9$ and write the solution set in interval notation.

    a. $(-2,-3]$ b. $[-3,2)$ c. $(-2,\infty)$ d. $(-\infty,-2)$

10. Solve: $3+|2x-7|=10$

    a. 10 and −4   b. 0 and 7   c. 0 and −7   d. no solution

11. Three times the sum of the first and third of three consecutive integers is seven more than five times the second integer. Find the third integer.

    a. 6   b. 8   c. 7   d. 9

12. Find the selling price per ounce of a face cream mixture made from 70 oz of face cream that costs $4 per ounce and 30 oz of face cream that costs $15 per ounce.

    a. $6.70   b. $7.05   c. $7.30   d. $8.00

13. Solve: $\dfrac{3}{5}x-2<\dfrac{2}{15}-x$

    a. $\left\{x\,\middle|\,x>-\dfrac{1}{2}\right\}$ b. $\left\{x\,\middle|\,x>\dfrac{3}{2}\right\}$ c. $\left\{x\,\middle|\,x<\dfrac{5}{2}\right\}$ d. $\left\{x\,\middle|\,x<\dfrac{4}{3}\right\}$

14. Which is the graph of $2x+3y=9$?

    a.   b.   c.   d.

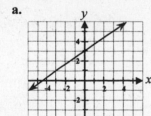   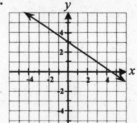   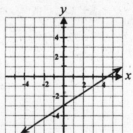   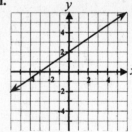

15. Find the slope of the line containing the points $P_1(-1,7)$ and $P_2(-4,-1)$.

    a. $\dfrac{8}{3}$ b. $\dfrac{8}{5}$ c. $-\dfrac{3}{8}$ d. undefined

16. Find the equation of the line that contains the point $(-2, 2)$ and has slope $-\dfrac{4}{3}$.

    a. $y = -\dfrac{4}{3}x - \dfrac{2}{3}$ **b.** $y = -\dfrac{4}{3}x - \dfrac{14}{3}$ **c.** $y = -\dfrac{4}{3}x + \dfrac{2}{3}$ **d.** $y = -\dfrac{4}{3}x + 4$

17. Find the equation of the line that contains the points $(3, -4)$ and is parallel to the line $2x - 3y = 5$.

    a. $y = \dfrac{2}{3}x + 2$ **b.** $y = \dfrac{3}{2}x - \dfrac{17}{2}$ **c.** $y = \dfrac{2}{3}x - 6$ **d.** $y = -\dfrac{3}{2}x + \dfrac{1}{2}$

18. The graph below shows the relationship between the cost of manufacturing radios and the number of radios manufactured. Write the equation that represents the cost of manufacturing the radios.

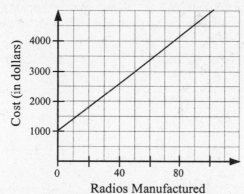

    a. $y = 25x + 1$

    b. $y = 40x + 1000$

    c. $y = -\dfrac{1}{40}x + 100$

    d. $y = 4x + 1$

19. Which is the graph of the solution set of $2x - 3y > 6$?

    a.   **b.**   **c.**   **d.**

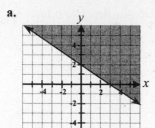 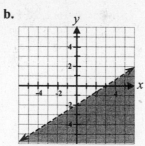 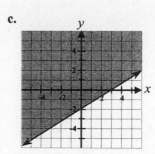 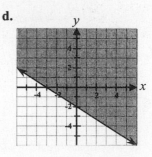

20. Given $f(x) = 3 - 2x^2$, evaluate $f(-3)$.

    a. 39   **b.** 21   **c.** -15 **d.** -33

Name: _____

Date: _____

1. Choose the graph that shows the solution to the following system of equations: $3x - 2y = 10$
$$x + 2y = -5$$

   a.
   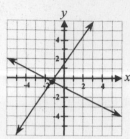

   b.
   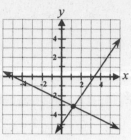

   c.
   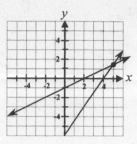

   d.
   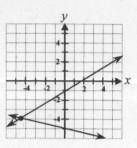

2. Solve by substitution: $2x - 5y = 17$
$$y = 2x + 3$$

   a. $(-4, -5)$ b. $(4, -5)$ c. $(4, 5)$ d. $(-4, 5)$

3. An investment of $5000 is made at an annual simple interest rate of 8.5%. How much additional money must be invested at an annual simple interest rate of 11.8% so that the total interest earned is 9.8% of the total investment?

   a. $2000   b. $3000   c. $3250   d. $2500

4. Solve by the addition method: $6x + 2y = 0$
$$5x - 3y = 14$$

   a. $\left(-1, -\dfrac{19}{3}\right)$ b. $(-1, 3)$ c. $(-3, 9)$ d. $(1, -3)$

5. Solve by the addition method: $x - 2y + z = 6$
$$x + 2z = 3$$
$$-y - 3z = -1$$

   a. $(-1, 2, 2)$ b. $(0, -2, 2)$ c. $(-1, -2, 2)$ d. $(1, -2, 1)$

6. Evaluate the determinant: $\begin{vmatrix} 8 & -2 \\ 5 & -1 \end{vmatrix}$

   a. -2 b. 2 c. -18 d. 18

7. Evaluate the determinant: $\begin{vmatrix} -1 & 3 & -3 \\ 1 & -2 & 2 \\ 3 & -4 & 1 \end{vmatrix}$

   a. 3 b. 14 c. 50 d. -6

8. Solve by using Cramer's Rule: $4x - y = 5$
$$-2x + 3y = -10$$

   a. $(2, 3)$ b. $\left(\dfrac{1}{2}, -3\right)$ c. $(-1, 4)$ d. $(-2, -13)$

Chapter 4 Test Form F (*continued*)

Name: _____

9. Solve by using Cramer's Rule: $x - y + z = 4$
   $2x + y - 3z = -5$
   $x + 3y + 2z = 2$

   a. $(1, 2, 2)$ **b.** $(1, 2, -1)$ **c.** $(1, -1, 2)$ **d.** $(-1, 2, -1)$

10. Flying with the wind, a plane flew 660 mi in 4 hours. Against the wind, the plane could fly only 460 mi in the same amount of time. Find the rate of the plane in calm air.

    a. 25 mi/h   **b.** 120 mi/h   **c.** 165 mi/h   **d.** 140 mi/h

11. A motorboat traveling with the current went 45 mi in 3 hours. Against the current, it took 4.5 hours to travel the same distance. Find the rate of the boat in calm water.

    a. 10 mi/h   **b.** 15 mi/h   **c.** 12.5 mi/h   **d.** 17.5 mi/h

12. A coin bank contains only dimes and quarters. The total value of the 28 coins in the bank is $5.20. Find the number of dimes in the bank.

    a. 7 dimes   **b.** 12 dimes   **c.** 16 dimes   **d.** 22 dimes

13. A carpenter purchased 120 ft of fir and 75 ft of redwood for a total cost of $133.50. A second purchase, at the same prices, included 60 ft of fir and 100 ft of redwood for a total cost of $98. Find the cost per foot of the redwood.

    a. $0.80 /ft   **b.** $0.50 /ft   **c.** $0.60 /ft   **d.** $0.70 /ft

14. Choose the graph that shows the solution set for the system of inequalities: $y \le 5$
   $3x - 4y \le 8$

    a. 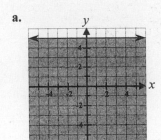   **b.** 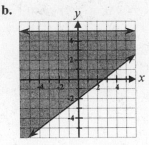   **c.** 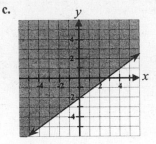   **d.**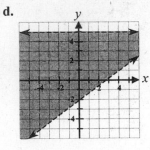

15. Choose the graph that shows the solution set for the system of inequalities: $y \le x - 3$
   $y > -3x + 4$

    a. 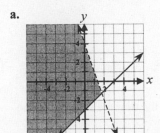   **b.** 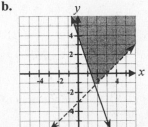   **c.** 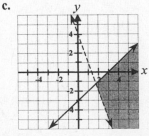   **d.**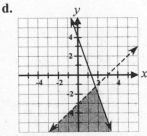

Name: _____
Date: _____

1. Simplify: $\left(5a^3+3a^2-2a-9\right)+\left(2a^3-5a^2-8a+5\right)$

   a. $7a^3-2a^2-10a-4$ **b.** $7a^3-2a^2-5a-14$ **c.** $3a^3-2a^2-9a+5$ **d.** $7a^3-8a^2-10a+4$

2. Simplify: $\left(xz^4\right)\left(x^2y^3z\right)\left(3y^2\right)$

   a. $x^3y^5z^5$ **b.** $3x^3y^5z^5$ **c.** $3x^5y^3z^5$ **d.** $3x^5y^5z^5$

3. Write 0.0063 in scientific notation.

   a. 6.3×10^3 **b.** 6.3×10^{-13} **c.** 6.3×10^{-3} **d.** 6.3×10^{13}

4. A computer can do 7.5×10^9 operations each hour. How many arithmetic operations can the computer perform in one minute?

   a. 1.25×10^6 operations   **b.** 1.25×10^8 operations   **c.** 5×10^8 operations   **d.** 1.25×10^{-8} operations

5. Simplify: $-4a^2b\left(2ab-2a^2+3b\right)$

   a. $-8a^3b^2-2a^2b+12b$ **b.** $-8ab^2+8a^4b+3a^2b^2$

   c. $8a^3b^2+8a^3b-12a^2b^2$ **d.** $-8a^3b^2+8a^4b-12a^2b^2$

6. Simplify: $6y^2-3y\left[3-2y(4-3y)-y^2\right]$

   a. $-18y^3+5y^2+24y-9$ **b.** $-15y^3+24y^2+6y-9$

   c. $-15y^3+30y^2-6y-3$ **d.** $-15y^3+30y^2-9y$

7. Simplify: $\left(2x^n-3\right)\left(5x^n+2\right)$

   a. $10x^n-6$ **b.** $10x^{2n}-11x^n-6$ **c.** $10x^{2n}-19x^n-6$ **d.** $10x^{2n}+11x^n+6$

8. Simplify: $\left(5b-2\right)\left(2b^2-5b+4\right)$

   a. $10b^3-29b^2+30b-8$ **b.** $10b^3-21b^2+10b-8$

   c. $10b^3+21b^2-10b-8$ **d.** $10b^3+29b^2+30b+8$

9. Simplify: $\left(4a-5b\right)\left(4a+5b\right)$

   a. $16a^2+25b^2$ **b.** $16a^2+40ab+25b^2$ **c.** $16a^2-25b^2$ **d.** $16a^2-40ab+25b^2$

10. The base of a triangle is $\left(2x-4\right)$ ft. The height is $\left(x+7\right)$ ft. Find the area of the triangle in terms of the variable x.

    a. $\left(2x^2+10x-42\right)\text{ft}^2$ **b.** $\left(x^2+5x-14\right)\text{ft}^2$ **c.** $\left(x^2+9x-14\right)\text{ft}^2$ **d.** $\left(2x^2+24x-42\right)\text{ft}^2$

11. Given $P(x) = 2x^2 - 3x - 7$, evaluate $P(-2)$.

    a. 15   **b.** -5 **c.** 7   **d.** -7

12. Factor: $x^2 - 2x - 63$

    a. $(x+9)(x-7)$ **b.** $(x-9)(x-7)$ **c.** $(x+9)(x+7)$ **d.** $(x-9)(x+7)$

13. Factor: $14 - 17x - 6x^2$

    a. $(7-2x)^2$ **b.** $(7-2x)(2+3x)$ **c.** $(7+2x)(2-3x)$ **d.** $(7+2x)(2+3x)$

14. Factor: $49x^2 - 4$

    a. Nonfactorable   **b.** $(7x-3)^2$ **c.** $(7x-2)^2$ **d.** $(7x-2)(7x+2)$

15. Factor: $9a^2b^2 - 6ab + 1$

    a. $(3ab+1)^2$ **b.** $(3ab-1)^2$ **c.** $(3ab+1)(3ab-1)$ **d.** Nonfactorable

16. Divide: $\dfrac{6a^2b^2 + 24a^3b^2}{6a^2b^2}$

    a. $ab + 4a$ **b.** 5   **c.** $1 + 4a$ **d.** $4a$

17. Factor: $a^3b^3 - 8$

    a. $(ab-2)(a^2b^2 + 2ab + 4)$ **b.** $(ab-2)(a^2b^2 + 4ab + 4)$

    c. $(ab-8)(a^2b^2 + 2ab + 64)$ **d.** Nonfactorable

18. Factor: $3x^3y^3 + 6x^2y^2 - 45xy$

    a. $xy(3xy-9)(xy+5)$ **b.** $3xy(xy+3)(xy-5)$ **c.** $3xy(xy-3)(xy+5)$ **d.** $3xy(xy-3)(xy-5)$

19. Solve: $2x(x-3) = 140$

    a. 10 and -7 **b.** 0 and 3   **c.** -10 and 7   **d.** 3 and 70

20. Divide by using long division: $\dfrac{3x^3 + 5x^2 + 5x + 14}{x+2}$

    a. $3x^2 - x + 7 - \dfrac{4}{x+2}$ **b.** $3x^2 - x + 7$ **c.** $3x^2 - x + 3 + \dfrac{10}{x+2}$ **d.** $3x^2 + x - 7 + \dfrac{4}{x+2}$

1. Simplify: $\dfrac{x^4 - 4x^2 y^2}{x^4 - 4x^3 y + 4x^2 y^2}$

   a. $\dfrac{x+2y}{x-2y}$ b. $\dfrac{x}{x-2y}$ c. $\dfrac{x-2y}{x+2y}$ d. -1

2. Simplify: $\dfrac{8x^2 + 8x - 6}{8x^2 + 20x - 12}$

   a. $\dfrac{2x+3}{2(x+3)}$ b. $\dfrac{2x-3}{2(x+3)}$ c. 1 d. $\dfrac{2x+3}{2(x-3)}$

3. Simplify: $\dfrac{x^2 - 9x + 20}{2x^2 - 7x - 15} \cdot \dfrac{2x^2 - x - 6}{8 + 2x - x^2}$

   a. $-\dfrac{x-4}{x+4}$ b. $-\dfrac{x-2}{x+2}$ c. -1 d. $-\dfrac{(x-2)(x-4)}{(x+2)(x+4)}$

4. Simplify: $\dfrac{x^2 - 5x + 6}{2x^2 + 2x - 4} \div \dfrac{x^2 - 4}{8x - 8}$

   a. $4(x-3)$ b. $\dfrac{8(x+2)}{x-3}$ c. $\dfrac{4(x-3)}{x+2}$ d. $\dfrac{4(x-3)}{(x+2)^2}$

5. Given $R(x) = \dfrac{x^2 - 3}{x^2 - x + 7}$, find $R(2)$.

   a. 2 b. $-\dfrac{1}{9}$ c. $\dfrac{1}{9}$ d. $\dfrac{1}{13}$

6. Find the domain of $f(x) = \dfrac{3+x}{x^2 - 9}$.

   a. $\{x \,|\, x \neq -3, 3\}$ b. $\{x \,|\, x \neq -9, 9\}$ c. $\{x \,|\, x \neq 9\}$ d. $\{x \,|\, x \neq -9\}$

7. Simplify: $\dfrac{x+1}{x^2 - x - 6} - \dfrac{x-2}{x^2 + 3x + 2}$

   a. $\dfrac{4}{(x+1)(x-3)}$ b. $\dfrac{4}{(x+1)(x+3)}$ c. $\dfrac{8x-3}{(x+1)(x+2)(x-3)}$ d. $\dfrac{7x-5}{(x+1)(x+2)(x-3)}$

8. Simplify: $\dfrac{x-3}{x^2 - 4} - \dfrac{3}{x^2 + 4x + 4}$

   a. $\dfrac{x}{(x-2)(x+2)}$ b. $\dfrac{x-2}{(x+2)^2}$ c. $\dfrac{x(x-2)}{(x+2)^2}$ d. $\dfrac{x(x-4)}{(x-2)(x+2)^2}$

9. Simplify: $\dfrac{\frac{2}{b} - \frac{6}{b-3}}{\frac{5}{b} - \frac{15}{b-3}}$

   a. $-\dfrac{2}{5}$ b. $\dfrac{2(2b+3)}{5(2b-3)}$ c. $-\dfrac{4b-5}{4b+15}$ d. $\dfrac{2}{5}$

10. Simplify: $\dfrac{2 + \frac{5}{x} - \frac{12}{x^2}}{4 - \frac{9}{x^2}}$

    a. $\dfrac{x+4}{2x+3}$ **b.** $\dfrac{x-4}{2x-3}$ **c.** $\dfrac{2x-3}{2x+3}$ **d.** $\dfrac{x-4}{2x+3}$

11. Solve: $\dfrac{x}{2} = \dfrac{x-2}{5}$

    a. $\dfrac{3}{4}$ **b.** $-\dfrac{3}{2}$ **c.** $\dfrac{2}{3}$ **d.** $-\dfrac{4}{3}$

12. Solve: $\dfrac{2}{x-3} = \dfrac{3}{x+1}$

    a. 11   **b.** 3   **c.** $\dfrac{11}{3}$ **d.** -1

13. A quality control inspector found four defective transistors in a shipment of 2000 transistors. At this rate, how many transistors would be defective in a shipment of 74,000 transistors?

    a. 37 transistors   **b.** 74 transistors   **c.** 148 transistors   **d.** 128 transistors

14. Solve: $\dfrac{2}{3x-1} - \dfrac{3}{9x^2-1} = \dfrac{4}{3x+1}$

    a. 2   **b.** $\dfrac{1}{6}$ **c.** $\dfrac{1}{2}$ **d.** -2

15. The distance, s, a ball will roll down an inclined plane is directly proportional to the square of the time, t. If the ball rolls 5 ft in 1 second, how far will it roll in 4 seconds?

    a. 20 ft   **b.** 24 ft   **c.** 36 ft   **d.** 80 ft

16. Solve $L = \dfrac{IW_1 - IW_2}{t}$ for I.

    a. $I = \dfrac{Lt}{W_1 + W_2}$ **b.** $I = \dfrac{L}{t(W_1 + W_2)}$ **c.** $I = Lt - \dfrac{L}{W_1 W_2}$ **d.** $I = \dfrac{Lt}{W_1 - W_2}$

17. An experienced plumber can complete a job twice as fast as an apprentice plumber. Working together, the plumbers can complete the job in 6 hours. How long would it take the apprentice working alone to complete the job?

    a. 4 h   **b.** 18 h   **c.** 9 h   **d.** 12 h

18. A sales executive traveled 72 mi by car and then an additional 840 mi by plane. The rate of the plane was five times greater than the rate of the car. The total time of the trip was 5 hours. Find the rate of the car.

    a. 45 mi/h   **b.** 48 mi/h   **c.** 50 mi/h   **d.** 55 mi/h

19. Find the missing numerator: $\dfrac{3x}{5x-10} = \dfrac{?}{5x^2+10x-40}$

    a. $3x^2 + 12x$ **b.** $3x^2 + 4$ **c.** $3x - 40$ **d.** $13x - 40$

20. Solve: $4 = \dfrac{16}{2x-3}$

    a. $\dfrac{3}{2}$ **b.** $\dfrac{7}{2}$ **c.** 2   **d.** $-\dfrac{3}{2}$

Name: _____
Date: _____

1. Simplify: $\left(-3b^3 - 2b^2 + 4b + 8\right) + \left(2b^3 - 3b^2 + 2b - 12\right)$

   a. $-2b^3 + b^2 + 6b + 20$ b. $-4b^3 - 5b^2 + 6b + 20$ c. $-b^3 - 5b^2 + 6b - 4$ d. $2b^3 - 5b^2 + 6b - 4$

2. Simplify: $\left(-2xy^2\right)\left(-3x^2y\right)\left(4x^2y^4\right)$

   a. $-24x^4y^6$ b. $24x^5y^7$ c. $18x^5y^6$ d. $24x^4y^7$

3. Simplify: $(2xy - 7)(3xy - 4)$

   a. $6x^2y^2 - 13xy + 28$ b. $6x^2y^2 + 13xy + 28$ c. $3x^2y^2 - 29xy - 28$ d. $6x^2y^2 - 29xy + 28$

4. Simplify: $\left(a^2 + 3b\right)^2$

   a. $a^4 + 6a^2b + 9b^2$ b. $a^4 - 9b^2$ c. $a^4 + 9b^2$ d. $a^4 - 6a^2 + 9b^2$

5. Factor: $6a^3b^3 - 9a^3b^4 + 3a^2b^4$

   a. $3a^2b^2\left(2a - 3a^2b + b^2\right)$ b. $3ab\left(2a^3 - 3a^2b^2 + b^2\right)$

   c. $3a^2b^3(2a - 3ab + b)$ d. $3a^2b^3\left(2a - 3ab^2 + b\right)$

6. Factor: $9y^2 + 3xy^2 - 20x^2y^2$

   a. $y^2(3 + 4x)(3 - 5x)$ b. $y^2(3 - 4x)(3 + 5x)$ c. $xy(3 - 4xy)(3 + 5xy)$ d. $y^2(9 - 4x)(1 + 5x)$

7. Solve: $6x^2 = 12x$

   a. 0 and −2   b. 0 and 2   c. 0   d. 2

8. Simplify: $\dfrac{2x^2 - 7x - 4}{x^2 - 7x + 12} \cdot \dfrac{x^2 + x - 12}{2x^2 + 7x + 3}$

   a. $\dfrac{x+4}{x+3}$ b. $\dfrac{x+2}{x-3}$ c. $\dfrac{x-4}{x-2}$ d. $\dfrac{x-4}{2x+1}$

9. Simplify: $\dfrac{16a^5b^7}{11x^2y^2} \div \dfrac{14a^5b^6}{22xy^3}$

   a. $\dfrac{22xy^2}{ab^2}$ b. $\dfrac{16by}{7}$ c. $\dfrac{a^2b}{xy}$ d. $\dfrac{20ab}{x}$

10. Simplify: $-\dfrac{5x}{2x-1} - \dfrac{1+3x}{1-2x}$

   a. $\dfrac{1+2x}{2x-1}$ b. $1 - 2x$ c. 1   d. −1

11. Simplify: $\dfrac{2-\frac{4}{x+2}}{5-\frac{10}{x+2}}$

   a. $\dfrac{2}{5}$ b. $\dfrac{5}{2}$ c. $\dfrac{x}{2}$ d. $\dfrac{2}{x+2}$

12. Solve: $\dfrac{5}{3}=\dfrac{25}{x+3}$

   a. 20   b. 12   c. 25   d. 24

13. Solve: $\dfrac{5}{x-3}-\dfrac{2}{x+3}=\dfrac{12}{x^2-9}$

   a. -4 b. 4   c. -3 d. 8

14. Solve by substitution: $3x-2y=2$
$$x=10-4y$$

   a. $(0,-1)$ b. $(2,2)$ c. $(6,1)$ d. No solution

15. Solve by the addition method: $5x-y=-2$
$$x+3y=-10$$

   a. $(-1,-3)$ b. $(3,-1)$ c. $(3,1)$ d. No solution

16. Solve by using Cramer's Rule: $2x-3y=17$
$$2x+7y=-13$$

   a. $(4,3)$ b. $(4,-3)$ c. $(-3,4)$ d. $\left(\dfrac{1}{4},-\dfrac{11}{2}\right)$

17. Evaluate the determinant: $\begin{vmatrix} 5 & -5 \\ 4 & -4 \end{vmatrix}$

   a. 1   b. 40   c. -40 d. 0

18. A contractor buys 50 yd of nylon carpet and 8 yd of wool carpet for $1656. A second purchase, at the same prices, includes 20 yd of nylon carpet and 18 yd of wool carpet for $1136. Find the cost per yard of the nylon carpet.

   a. $16/yd   b. $29/yd   c. $28/yd   d. $32/yd

19. Simplify: $\dfrac{x^{3n-7}}{x^{2-n}}$

   a. x^{2n-5} b. x^{4n-9} c. $x^{(3n-7)(2-n)}$ d. x^{3n^2-14}

20. Simplify: $(x^3+2x-1)(x-3)$

   a. $x^4-3x^3+2x^2-7x+3$ b. x^4+2x^2-7x+3
   c. x^4-3x^3-7x+3 d. $x^4+3x^3+2x^2+7x-3$

1. Simplify: $\left(x^3 y^{1/2}\right)^{-2} \left(x^{-8} y^4\right)^{1/4}$

    a. $\dfrac{1}{x^8}$
    b. $\dfrac{1}{xy}$
    c. $\dfrac{x}{y^2}$
    d. $\dfrac{y}{x^2}$

2. Simplify: $\left(\dfrac{a^{-1/2} a^{1/5}}{a^{1/10}}\right)^{-10}$

    a. a^2
    b. a^4
    c. 1
    d. $\dfrac{1}{a^4}$

3. Write $(x^2 y)^{3/2}$ as a radical expression.

    a. $\sqrt{x^5 y^3}$
    b. $\sqrt{x^6 y^3}$
    c. $\sqrt[3]{x^4 y^2}$
    d. $\sqrt{x^2 y}$

4. Write $-a \sqrt[4]{b}$ as an exponential expression.

    a. $(-ab)^{1/4}$
    b. $-(ab)^{1/4}$
    c. $-ab^4$
    d. $-ab^{1/4}$

5. Simplify: $\sqrt[3]{54 x^9 y^7}$

    a. $3x^3 y^2$
    b. $3x^3 y \sqrt[3]{2y^2}$
    c. $3x^3 y^2 \sqrt[3]{2y}$
    d. $3x^3 y^2 \sqrt[3]{2}$

6. Simplify: $\sqrt{60 x^8 y}$

    a. $2x^4 \sqrt{15xy}$
    b. $4x^4 \sqrt{15y}$
    c. $2x^4 y \sqrt{15}$
    d. $2x^4 \sqrt{15y}$

7. Simplify: $\sqrt[3]{a^3 b^8 c^{16}}$

    a. $b^2 c^4 \sqrt[3]{a^2 bc}$
    b. $ab^3 c^4 \sqrt[3]{b^2 c}$
    c. $b^2 c^5 \sqrt[3]{abc}$
    d. $ab^2 c^5 \sqrt[3]{b^2 c}$

8. Simplify: $a\sqrt{48ab^4} - 2b\sqrt{75a^3 b^2}$

    a. $-6ab^2 \sqrt{3a}$
    b. $6ab^2 \sqrt{3a}$
    c. $-6ab^2 \sqrt{3ab}$
    d. $-14ab^2 \sqrt{3a}$

9. Simplify: $2\sqrt[3]{64a^5 b^6} - ab\sqrt[3]{125a^2 b^3}$

    a. $21ab^2 \sqrt[3]{a^2}$
    b. $3ab^2 \sqrt[3]{a^2}$
    c. $3ab \sqrt[3]{a^2 b}$
    d. $3ab^2 \sqrt[3]{a^2 b}$

10. Simplify: $\sqrt[3]{6a^3 b^4} \cdot \sqrt[3]{18a^5 b^8}$

    a. $9ab^2 \sqrt[3]{4a^2}$
    b. $3a^2 b^4 \sqrt[3]{2a}$
    c. $3a^2 b^4 \sqrt[3]{4a^2}$
    d. $3a^2 b^3 \sqrt[3]{2ab}$

11. Simplify: $\left(\sqrt{5}-3\right)\left(\sqrt{5}-1\right)$

    a. $5-2\sqrt{5}$ b. $8-4\sqrt{5}$ c. $2-4\sqrt{5}$ d. $8-\sqrt{15}-\sqrt{5}$

12. Simplify: $\dfrac{\sqrt{16a^5b^7}}{\sqrt{32a^7b^3}}$

    a. $\dfrac{b\sqrt{2}}{a}$ b. $\dfrac{b\sqrt{2}}{2a}$ c. $\dfrac{b^2\sqrt{2}}{2a}$ d. $\dfrac{b^2\sqrt{2}}{2a^2}$

13. Simplify: $\dfrac{2+\sqrt{3}}{3\sqrt{3}-4}$

    a. $\dfrac{10\sqrt{3}+17}{11}$ b. $\dfrac{10\sqrt{3}+17}{-4}$ c. $\dfrac{10\sqrt{3}}{11}$ d. $\dfrac{10\sqrt{3}}{-4}$

14. Solve: $\sqrt[4]{2x+5}=3$

    a. -21 b.   38   c.   43   d.   21

15. Solve: $\sqrt{5-2x}-5=2$

    a. -2 b.   22   c. -22 d. -3

16. How far above the water would a submarine periscope have to be to locate a ship 3.5 mi away? The equation for the distance in miles that the lookout can see is $d=1.4\sqrt{h}$, where h is the height in feet above the surface of the water.

    a.   5 ft   b.   6.25 ft   c.   7.5 ft   d.   2.5 ft

17. Simplify: $\sqrt{45}+\sqrt{-98}$

    a. $5\sqrt{3}+7i\sqrt{2}$ b. $3\sqrt{5}-7i\sqrt{2}$ c. $3\sqrt{5}+2i\sqrt{7}$ d. $3\sqrt{5}+7i\sqrt{2}$

18. Simplify: $\left(15-10i\right)-\left(4-3i\right)$

    a. $11+7i$ b. $19+7i$ c. $11-7i$ d. $11-13i$

19. Simplify: $\sqrt{-2}\left(\sqrt{8}-\sqrt{-2}\right)$

    a. $2+4i$ b. $4-2i$ c. $2-4i$ d. $4+2i$

20. Simplify: $\dfrac{3i+1}{2i}$

    a. $\dfrac{3}{2}-\dfrac{1}{2}i$ b. $-\dfrac{3}{2}+\dfrac{1}{2}i$ c. $\dfrac{3}{2}+\dfrac{1}{2}i$ d. $-\dfrac{3}{2}-\dfrac{1}{2}i$

Name: _____

Date: _____

1. Solve by factoring: $16x^2 - 16x = -3$

   a. $\dfrac{1}{4}$ and $\dfrac{3}{4}$

   b. $\dfrac{1}{4}$ and $-\dfrac{3}{4}$

   c. $-\dfrac{1}{4}$ and $-\dfrac{3}{4}$

   d. $-\dfrac{1}{4}$ and $\dfrac{3}{4}$

2. Solve by factoring: $5x(x-4) = 7x - 10$

   a. -5 and $-\dfrac{2}{5}$

   b. 5 and $\dfrac{2}{5}$

   c. -5 and $\dfrac{2}{5}$

   d. 5 and $-\dfrac{2}{5}$

3. Write a quadratic equation that has integer coefficients and has solutions $-\dfrac{2}{5}$ and 2.

   a. $5x^2 - 12x - 4 = 0$

   b. $5x^2 + 8x - 4 = 0$

   c. $5x^2 - 8x - 4 = 0$

   d. $5x^2 - 8x + 4 = 0$

4. Solve by taking square roots: $(3x-4)^2 = 32$

   a. $\dfrac{-4+4\sqrt{2}}{3}$ and $\dfrac{-4-4\sqrt{2}}{3}$

   b. $4+4\sqrt{2}$ and $4-4\sqrt{2}$

   c. $\dfrac{4+2\sqrt{2}}{3}$ and $\dfrac{4-2\sqrt{2}}{3}$

   d. $\dfrac{4+4\sqrt{2}}{3}$ and $\dfrac{4-4\sqrt{2}}{3}$

5. Solve by taking square roots: $x^2 - 32 = 0$

   a. $4\sqrt{2}$

   b. $4\sqrt{2}$ and $-4\sqrt{2}$

   c. $-4\sqrt{2}$

   d. No solution

6. Solve by completing the square: $x^2 - 8x + 24 = 0$

   a. $-4+2i\sqrt{2}$ and $-4-2i\sqrt{2}$

   b. $4+2\sqrt{2}$ and $4-2\sqrt{2}$

   c. $4+2i\sqrt{2}$ and $4-2i\sqrt{2}$

   d. $4+2\sqrt{10}$ and $4-2\sqrt{10}$

7. Solve by completing the square: $2x^2 + 5x + 8 = 0$

   a. $\dfrac{5}{4} + \dfrac{\sqrt{39}}{4}i$ and $\dfrac{5}{4} - \dfrac{\sqrt{39}}{4}i$

   b. $\dfrac{5+\sqrt{39}}{4}$ and $\dfrac{5-\sqrt{39}}{4}$

   c. $-\dfrac{5}{4} + \dfrac{\sqrt{39}}{4}i$ and $-\dfrac{5}{4} - \dfrac{\sqrt{39}}{4}i$

   d. $-\dfrac{5}{2} + \dfrac{\sqrt{39}}{2}i$ and $-\dfrac{5}{2} - \dfrac{\sqrt{39}}{2}i$

8. Solve by using the quadratic formula: $5x^2 = x - 2$

   a. $\dfrac{1+\sqrt{39}}{10}$ and $\dfrac{1-\sqrt{39}}{10}$

   b. $\dfrac{1}{10} + \dfrac{\sqrt{39}}{10}i$ and $\dfrac{1}{10} - \dfrac{\sqrt{39}}{10}i$

   c. $\dfrac{1+\sqrt{39}}{2}$ and $\dfrac{1-\sqrt{39}}{2}$

   d. $\dfrac{1}{2} + \dfrac{\sqrt{39}}{2}i$ and $\dfrac{1}{2} - \dfrac{\sqrt{39}}{2}i$

9. Solve by using the quadratic formula: $2x^2 + 2x + 3 = 0$

   a. $-\dfrac{1}{2} + \dfrac{\sqrt{5}}{2}i$ and $-\dfrac{1}{2} - \dfrac{\sqrt{5}}{2}i$

   b. $-\dfrac{1}{2} + \dfrac{\sqrt{2}}{2}i$ and $-\dfrac{1}{2} - \dfrac{\sqrt{2}}{2}i$

   c. $\dfrac{1}{2} + i\sqrt{5}$ and $\dfrac{1}{2} - i\sqrt{5}$

   d. 2 and $-\dfrac{3}{2}$

10. Use the discriminant to determine whether $3x^2 - 2x - 5 = 0$ has one real number solution, one complex number solution, two real number solutions, or two complex number solutions.

    a. Two real number solutions

    b. Two complex number solutions

    c. One real number solution

    d. None of these

11. Solve: $x^{2/3} - x^{1/3} - 6 = 0$

   a.   −4 and 9   **b.**   9   **c.**   −8 and 27   **d.**   27

12. Solve: $x^4 - 29x^2 + 100 = 0$

   a.   2 and 5   **b.**   −2, 2, −5, and 5   **c.**   −2i, 2i, −5, and 5   **d.**   −2, 2, −5i, and 5i

13. Solve: $\sqrt{3x+1} - 1 = 2x$

   a.   0 and $-\dfrac{1}{4}$ **b.**   0   **c.** $-\dfrac{1}{4}$ **d.**   1 and −4

14. Solve: $\sqrt{2x-6} - 4 = 0$

   a.   −1   **b.**   5   **c.**   11   **d.** $\varnothing$

15. Solve: $\dfrac{4}{x} - \dfrac{3}{2x+1} = 1$

   a. $1+\sqrt{3}$ and $1-\sqrt{3}$ **b.** $1+\sqrt{5}$ and $1-\sqrt{5}$

   c. $-1+\sqrt{5}$ and $-1-\sqrt{5}$ **d.** $\dfrac{2+\sqrt{10}}{2}$ and $\dfrac{2-\sqrt{10}}{2}$

16. Solve: $\dfrac{2x-3}{2x+3} - 1 = x$

   a.   0 and $-\dfrac{3}{2}$ **b.** $-\dfrac{3}{4}+\dfrac{\sqrt{39}}{4}i$ and $-\dfrac{3}{4}-\dfrac{\sqrt{39}}{4}i$

   c. $\dfrac{3}{2}+\dfrac{\sqrt{39}}{2}$ and $\dfrac{3}{2}-\dfrac{\sqrt{39}}{2}i$ **d.** $\dfrac{3+\sqrt{57}}{2}$ and $\dfrac{3-\sqrt{57}}{2}$

17. Solve: $x^2 - 6x + 8 \geq 0$

   a. $\{x \mid 2 < x < 4\}$ **b.** $\{x \mid x < 2 \text{ or } x > 4\}$ **c.** $\{x \mid 2 \leq x \leq 4\}$ **d.** $\{x \mid x \leq 2 \text{ or } x \geq 4\}$

18. Solve: $\dfrac{x-4}{(x+3)(x-1)} < 0$

   a. $\{x \mid x < -3 \text{ or } -1 < x < 4\}$ **b.** $\{x \mid x < -3 \text{ or } -4 < x < 1\}$

   c. $\{x \mid x < -3 \text{ or } 1 < x < 4\}$ **d.** $\{x \mid x > -3 \text{ or } -1 < x < 4\}$

19. A large pipe can fill a tank 10 min faster than it takes a smaller pipe to fill the same tank. Working together, both pipes can fill the tank in 12 min. How long would it take the large pipe working alone to fill the tank?

   a.   18 min   **b.**   30 min   **c.**   32 min   **d.**   20 min

20. The rate of a river's current is 3 mi/h. A boat traveled 24 mi down the river and then returned the same distance. The total time for the round trip was 6 hours. Find the rate of the boat in calm water.

   a.   6 mi/h   **b.**   12 mi/h   **c.**   15 mi/h   **d.**   9 mi/h

1. Find the vertex of the parabola given by $y = x^2 - 8x$.

    a. $(4,16)$　　　　b. $(-8,0)$　　　　c. $(4,-16)$　　　　d. $(0,0)$

2. State the range of the function $y = -2x^2 + 4$.

    a. $\{y \mid y \geq 4\}$　　　b. $\{y \mid y \geq -2\}$　　　c. $\{y \mid y \leq 4\}$　　　d. $\{y \mid y \leq -2\}$

3. Use the discriminant to determine the number of x-intercepts of the graph of $y = x^2 + 5x - 3$.

    a. No x-intercepts　　b. One　　　　c. Three　　　　d. Two

4. Find the x-intercepts of the graph of $y = x^2 - 8x - 20$.

    a. $(2,0),(-10,0)$　　b. $(-2,0),(10,0)$　　c. $(5,0),(-4,0)$　　d. $(-5,0),(4,0)$

5. Find the maximum value of the function $f(x) = -x^2 + 3x - 4$.

    a. -4　　　　b. $-2\frac{3}{4}$　　　　c. $\frac{3}{2}$　　　　d. $2\frac{3}{4}$

6. A rectangle has a perimeter of 64 ft. Find the dimensions of such a rectangle that has the maximum area.

    a. 4 ft by 16 ft　　b. 8 ft by 8 ft　　c. 16 ft by 16 ft　　d. 32 ft by 32 ft

7. Which is the graph of the function $f(x) = 2|x| - 3$?

    a.　　　　　　b.　　　　　　c.　　　　　　d.

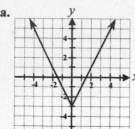 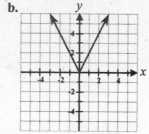 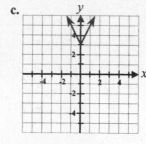 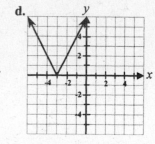

8. Which of the graphs does not represent the graph of a function?

    a.　　　　　　b.　　　　　　c.　　　　　　d.

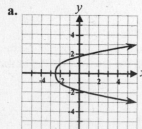 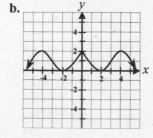 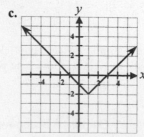 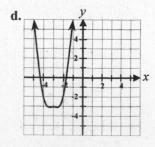

9. For $f(x)=x^2+1$ and $g(x)=x-2$, find $(f \cdot g)(-1)$.

    a. −6   b. 0   c. 4   d. 6

10. For $f(x)=2x-3$ and $g(x)=x^2+1$, find $f(0)-g(0)$.

    a. 0   b. −4   c. −2   d. 4

11. Given $f(x)=5x+1$ and $g(x)=3x^2$, find $g[f(-1)]$.

    a. −16   b. −48   c. 16   d. 48

12. Given $f(x)=4x^2+3x+2$ and $g(x)=x+1$, find $f[g(x)]$.

    a. $-4x^2+11x+7$ b. $4x^2+11x+9$ c. $-4x^2+5x+4$ d. $-x+3$

13. Let $f(x)=\frac{1}{2}x-2$. Find $f^{-1}(x)$.

    a. $f^{-1}(x)=\frac{1}{2}x+4$ b. $f^{-1}(x)=\frac{2}{x-4}$ c. $f^{-1}(x)=2x+2$ d. $f^{-1}(x)=2x+4$

14. Which of the functions are inverses of each other?

    a. $f(x)=3x,\ g(x)=-3x$ b. $f(x)=2x-7,\ g(x)=-2x+7$

    c. $f(x)=4x-1,\ g(x)=\frac{x}{4}+\frac{1}{4}$ d. $f(x)=-2x+1,\ g(x)=-\frac{1}{2}x-1$

15. Find the inverse of the function $\{(2,1),(-3,5),(6,-7)\}$.

    a. $\{(2,1),(3,-5),(6,-7)\}$ b. $\{(1,2),(5,-3),(-7,6)\}$

    c. $\left\{\left(\frac{1}{2},-1\right),\left(-\frac{1}{3},\frac{1}{5}\right),\left(\frac{1}{6},-\frac{1}{7}\right)\right\}$ d. $\{(-2,-1),(3,-5),(-6,7)\}$

1. Simplify: $-\sqrt[3]{x^6 y^9 z^3}$

    a. $-x^2 y^2 z$ b. $x^3 y^3 \sqrt{z}$ c. $-x^2 y^3 z$ d. $x^2 y^3 z$

2. Simplify: $2\sqrt{32x^2 y} - x\sqrt{50y}$

    a. $3x\sqrt{2y}$ b. $2x^2 \sqrt{y}$ c. $8x\sqrt{2y}$ d. $8xy\sqrt{2}$

3. Simplify: $(8i)(-4i)$

    a. $-32i$ b. 32 c. $12i$ d. $4i$

4. Solve: $\sqrt[3]{x-4} + 4 = 2$

    a. -4 b. 4 c. 2 d. -2

5. An object is dropped from a bridge. Find the distance the object has fallen when the speed reaches 56 ft/s. Use the equation $v = \sqrt{64d}$, where v is the speed in feet per second and d is the distance in feet.

    a. 56.25 ft   b. 48.25 ft   c. 49 ft   d. 55.75 ft

6. Write a quadratic equation that has integer coefficients and has solutions $-\dfrac{4}{3}$ and -3.

    a. $3x^2 + 13x + 12 = 0$ b. $3x^2 - 13x - 12 = 0$

    c. $3x^2 + 5x + 12 = 0$ d. $3x^2 + 5x - 12 = 0$

7. Solve by using the quadratic formula: $2x^2 = -2x - 1$

    a. $\dfrac{1}{2} + \dfrac{1}{2}i$ and $\dfrac{1}{2} - \dfrac{1}{2}i$ b. $\dfrac{-1+\sqrt{3}}{2}$ and $\dfrac{-1-\sqrt{3}}{2}$

    c. $-\dfrac{1}{2} + \dfrac{\sqrt{2}}{2}i$ and $-\dfrac{1}{2} - \dfrac{\sqrt{2}}{2}i$ d. $-\dfrac{1}{2} + \dfrac{1}{2}i$ and $-\dfrac{1}{2} - \dfrac{1}{2}i$

8. Solve: $\dfrac{x^2 + 5x}{x+2} + 10x = -24$

    a. -2 and 3 b. -3 and $-\dfrac{16}{11}$ c. -1 and 6 d. -4 and 2

9. Solve: $(3x-2)(x+1)(x-3) \le 0$

    a. $\{x \mid x \le -1 \text{ or } x \ge 3\}$ b. $\left\{x \mid x < -1 \text{ or } \dfrac{2}{3} < x < 3\right\}$

    c. $\left\{x \mid x \le -1 \text{ or } \dfrac{2}{3} \le x \le 3\right\}$ d. $\left\{x \mid -1 \le x \le \dfrac{1}{2} \text{ or } x \ge 3\right\}$

10. An old pump requires 8 h longer to empty a pool than does a new pump. With both pumps operating, the pool can be emptied in 3 h. Find the time required for the new pump working alone to empty the pool.

   a. 5 h   **b.** 8 h   **c.** 12 h   **d.** 4 h

11. Which is the graph of $y = 3 - x^2$?

   a. 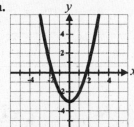   **b.** 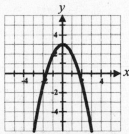   **c.** 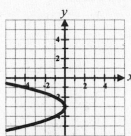   **d.**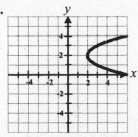

12. Which is the graph of the function $f(x) = |x + 2|$?

   a. 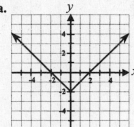   **b.** 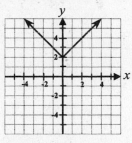   **c.** 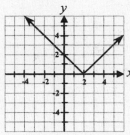   **d.**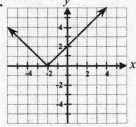

13. Given $f(x) = 3 - x^2$ and $g(x) = 2x^2 - 1$, find $f(3) - g(3)$.

   a. 11   **b.** −23   **c.** −20   **d.** 23

14. Given $f(x) = x^2$ and $g(x) = 3 - x$, find $f[g(-2)]$.

   a. 25   **b.** 36   **c.** −1   **d.** 1

15. Let $f(x) = \frac{2}{3}x - 6$. Find $f^{-1}(x)$.

   a. $f^{-1}(x) = \frac{3}{2}x + 9$ **b.** $f^{-1}(x) = \frac{2}{3}x + 6$ **c.** $f^{-1}(x) = \frac{3}{2}x + 3$ **d.** $f^{-1}(x) = \frac{3}{2x - 12}$

1. Given $f(x) = 2^{x^2}$, evaluate $f(-2)$.

   a. $\dfrac{1}{4}$ b. 16   c. 4   d. 8

2. Given $g(x) = e^{x-2}$, evaluate $g(-1)$.
   Round to the nearest ten-thousandth.

   a. -1.6321 b. 7.3891   c. 0.3679   d. 0.4979

3. Which is the graph of $f(x) = \left(\dfrac{1}{2}\right)^x - 2$?

   a. 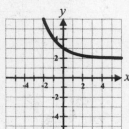   b. 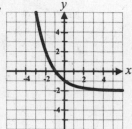   c. 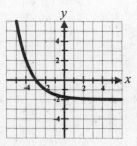   d.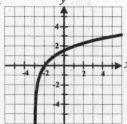

4. Evaluate: $\log_{10} 10{,}000$

   a. 3   b. -3 c. 4   d. 2

5. Solve for x: $\log_{10} x = -3$

   a. $\dfrac{1}{1000}$ b. -1000 c. 1000   d. $-\dfrac{1}{1000}$

6. Write $x^y = S$ in logarithmic form.

   a. $\log_y S = x$ b. $\log_x S = y$ c. $\log_y x = S$ d. $\log_S x = y$

7. Write $\log_2 32 = 5$ in exponential form.

   a. $32^{1/2} = 5$ b. $5^2 = 32$ c. $32^{-1/2} = 5$ d. $2^5 = 32$

8. Write $2\log_4 x - 3\log_4 y - \dfrac{1}{2}\log_4 z$ as a single logarithm with a coefficient of 1.

   a. $\log_4 \dfrac{x^2}{y^3\sqrt{z}}$ b. $\log_4 \dfrac{x^2}{y^3 z^2}$ c. $\log_4 \dfrac{\sqrt{x}}{z\sqrt[3]{y}}$ d. $\dfrac{\log_4 x^2}{\log_4 y \sqrt[3]{z}}$

9. Write $\ln\left(x^2 yz^5\right)$ in expanded form.

    a. $\ln x^2 + \ln y + \ln z^5$ **b.** $2\ln x + \ln y + 5\ln z$ **c.** $2(\ln xyz^3)$ **d.** $2\ln xy + 5\ln z$

10. Write $2\ln x + \dfrac{1}{3}\ln y - 5\ln z$ as a single logarithm with a coefficient of 1.

    a. $\ln \dfrac{x^2 z^5}{\sqrt[3]{y}}$ **b.** $\ln \dfrac{x^2}{\sqrt[3]{y}z^5}$ **c.** $\ln \dfrac{x^2 \sqrt[3]{y}}{z^5}$ **d.** $\ln \dfrac{x^2 y^3}{z^5}$

11. Write $\log_6 \sqrt[3]{xy^2}$ in expanded form.

    a. $\dfrac{1}{2}\log_6 x + \dfrac{3}{2}\log_6 y$ **b.** $\dfrac{1}{3}\log_6 x + \dfrac{2}{3}\log_6 y$ **c.** $3\log_6 x + \dfrac{2}{3}\log_6 y$ **d.** $3\log_6 x - \dfrac{2}{3}\log_6 y$

12. Evaluate: $\log_5 130$
    Round to the nearest ten-thousandth.

    a. 3.4165   **b.** 2.6829   **c.** 3.1224   **d.** 3.0244

13. Evaluate: $\log_5 12$
    Round to the nearest ten-thousandth.

    a. 1.6477   **b.** 0.5440   **c.** 0.6477   **d.** 1.5440

14. Which is the graph of $f(x) = \log_2 x + 3$?

    a.   **b.**   **c.**   **d.**

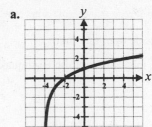 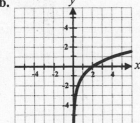 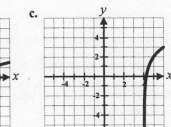 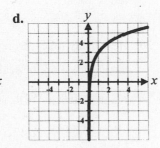

Chapter 10 Test F (*continued*)

Name: _____

15. Solve for x: $2^{x+1} = 16^{x-1}$

   a. 4   b. $\dfrac{5}{3}$ c. 1   d. $\dfrac{3}{5}$

16. Solve for x: $10^x = 80$
Round to the nearest ten-thousandth.

   a. 8.0000   b. 2.0794   c. 0.5255   d. 1.9031

17. Solve for x: $3^x = 21$
Round to the nearest ten-thousandth.

   a. 2.7712   b. 1.946   c. 3.608   d. 3.3447

18. Solve for t: $\log(t-1) = \log(t+2)$

   a. No solution   b. $\dfrac{7}{3}$ c. $-\dfrac{7}{3}$ d. 0

19. Solve for x: $\log_5(x-1) = 2$

   a. 31   b. 24   c. 26   d. 33

20. How many times stronger is an earthquake that has magnitude 6 on the Richter scale than one that has magnitude 4 on the scale? Use the Richter equation $M = \log\dfrac{I}{I_0}$, where M is the magnitude of the earthquake, I is the intensity of its shock waves, I_0 is a constant.

   a. 10 times   b. 50 times   c. 100 times   d. 200 times

Name: _____

Date: _____

1. Which is the graph of $x = y^2 - 2y - 2$?

    a.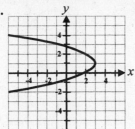
    b.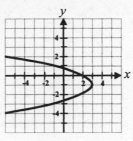
    c.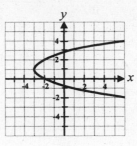
    d.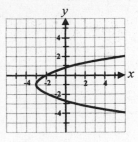

2. Find the axis of symmetry of the parabola $y = -3x^2 + 6x - 1$.

    a. $x = -2$
    b. $x = 1$
    c. $x = \dfrac{1}{3}$
    d. $x = 2$

3. Find the vertex of the parabola given by $y = x^2 - 6x + 1$.

    a. $(-6, 1)$
    b. $(3, 8)$
    c. $(6, 1)$
    d. $(3, -8)$

4. Find the equation of the circle with radius 1 and center $(0, 3)$.

    a. $(x-1)^2 + (y-3)^2 = 1$
    b. $(x-3)^2 + y^2 = 1$
    c. $x^2 + (y+3)^2 = 1$
    d. $x^2 + (y-3)^2 = 1$

5. Find the equation of the circle that passes through the point $(4, 7)$ and whose center is $(-1, 4)$.

    a. $(x+1)^2 + (y-4)^2 = 34$
    b. $(x-1)^2 + (y-4)^2 = 24$
    c. $(x-1)^2 + (y-4)^2 = 34$
    d. $(x-2)^2 + (y+4)^2 = 24$

6. Write $x^2 + y^2 - 4x + 8y + 19 = 0$ in standard form.

    a. $(x-4)^2 + (y+8)^2 = 361$
    b. $(x-2)^2 + (y+4)^2 = 1$
    c. $(x+4)^2 + (y-8)^2 = 361$
    d. $(x+2)^2 + (y-4)^2 = 1$

Name: _____

7. Which is the graph of $x^2 + y^2 + 6x + 6y + 9 = 0$?

a. 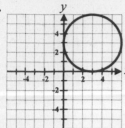   **b.** 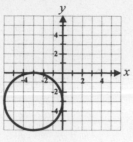   **c.** 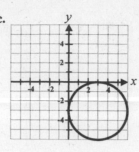   **d.**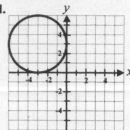

8. Which is the graph of $\dfrac{x^2}{16} + \dfrac{y^2}{1} = 1$?

a. 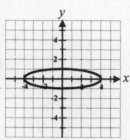   **b.** 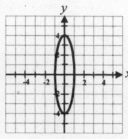   **c.** 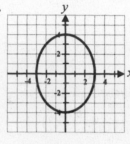   **d.**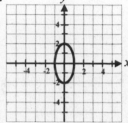

9. Which is the graph of $\dfrac{x^2}{4} - \dfrac{y^2}{25} = 1$?

a. 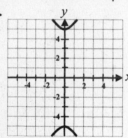   **b.** 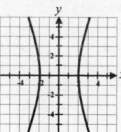   **c.** 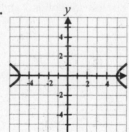   **d.**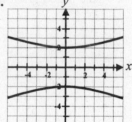

10. Solve: $x^2 + y^2 = 9$
$2x + y^2 = 6$

   a. $(3,0)$ and $(0,3)$

   b. $(3,0), \left(-1, 2\sqrt{2}\right)$, and $\left(-1, -2\sqrt{2}\right)$

   c. $(0,3), \left(-1, 2\sqrt{2}\right)$, and $\left(-1, -2\sqrt{2}\right)$

   d. $\left(-1, 2\sqrt{2}\right)$ and $\left(-1, -2\sqrt{2}\right)$

11. Solve: $y = 2x^2 - 3x - 4$
$y = x^2 + x - 7$

   a. $(-2, 5)$

   b. $(2, -2)$ and $(1, -5)$

   c. $(3, 5)$ and $(1, -5)$

   d. $(3, -1)$ and $(1, -5)$

12. Which is the graph of the solution set of $\dfrac{y^2}{1} - \dfrac{x^2}{4} \le 1$?

    a. 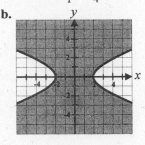   b. 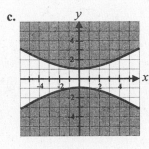   c. 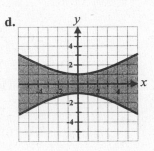   d.

13. Which is the graph of the solution set of $x^2 + (y+1)^2 \le 25$?

    a. 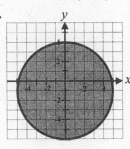   b. 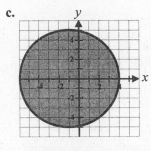   c. 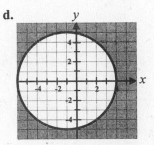   d.

14. Choose the graph that shows the solution set for:
$$y \ge 2x$$
$$x^2 + y^2 > 16$$

    a. 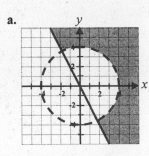   b. 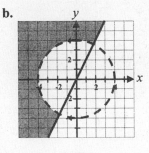   c. 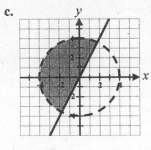   d.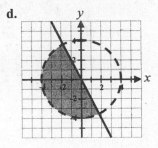

15. Choose the graph that shows the solution set for:
$$x \ge y^2 + 2y - 4$$
$$3x - 4y > 8$$

    a. 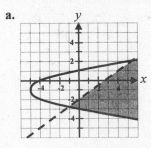   b. 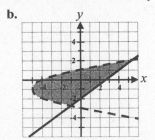   c. 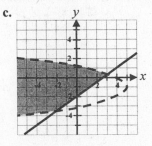   d.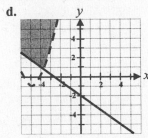

1. Write the 16th term of the sequence whose nth term is given by the formula $a_n = \dfrac{n}{2n+1}$.

   a. $\dfrac{16}{33}$ b. $\dfrac{16}{17}$ c. $\dfrac{1}{16}$ d. $\dfrac{1}{2}$

2. Write the 4th and 8th terms of the sequence whose nth term is given by the formula $a_n = (n+1)(n-5)$.

   a. $-4, 27$ b. $5, -27$ c. $-4, 24$ d. $-5, 27$

3. Evaluate: $\displaystyle\sum_{n=3}^{7} (n-1)^2$

   a. 86   b. 90   c. 91   d. 140

4. Write $\displaystyle\sum_{n=1}^{4} (-1)^{n+1} x^{2n}$ in expanded form.

   a. $-x^2 + x^4 - x^6 + x^8$ b. $x - x^2 + x^3 - x^4$ c. $x^2 - x^4 + x^6 - x^8$ d. $2x^2 - 4x^4 + 6x^6 - 8x^8$

5. Find the 20th term of the arithmetic sequence 2, 4.5, 7, ...

   a. 33   b. 39   c. 49.5   d. 40.5

6. Find the 21st term of the arithmetic sequence whose first term is -12 and whose common difference is 4.

   a. 72   b. -68 c. 68   d. 96

7. Find the formula for the nth term of the arithmetic sequence 7, 2, -3, ...

   a. $a_n = 7 + 5n$ b. $a_n = 12 - 5n$ c. $a_n = 7 - 3n$ d. $a_n = 7 - 5n$

8. Find the sum of the first 30 terms of the arithmetic sequence $-12, -6, 0, ...$

   a. 2500   b. 1995   c. 2250   d. 2155

9. Find the sum of the first 28 terms of the arithmetic sequence whose first term is 5 and whose common difference is -3.

   a. -994 b. 1204   c. -1274 d. -1134

10. A contest offers 12 prizes. The first prize is $8000 and each successive prize is $600 less than the preceding prize. What is the value of the 12th-place prize?

   a. $1400   b. $800   c. $6600   d. $2400

11. Find the sum of the first five terms of the geometric sequence $3, \dfrac{3}{2}, \dfrac{3}{4}, \ldots$

     a. $\dfrac{93}{16}$ **b.** $\dfrac{1}{2}$ **c.** $\dfrac{49}{8}$ **d.** $\dfrac{111}{8}$

12. Find the 5th term of the geometric sequence whose first term is 1 and whose common ratio is 3.

     a. 243   **b.** 27   **c.** 81   **d.** $\dfrac{1}{3}$

13. Find the sum of the first five terms of the geometric sequence $1, 3, 9, \ldots$

     a. -242 **b.** 121   **c.** 242   **d.** $\dfrac{121}{2}$

14. Find the sum of the first six terms of the geometric sequence whose first term is 11 and whose common ratio is 2.

     a. 693   **b.** 346.5   **c.** -693 **d.** 524

15. Find the sum of the infinite geometric sequence $1, \dfrac{1}{3}, \dfrac{1}{9}, \ldots$

     a. 3   **b.** 2   **c.** $\dfrac{2}{3}$ **d.** $\dfrac{3}{2}$

16. Find an equivalent fraction for $0.5\overline{3}$.

     a. $\dfrac{2}{45}$ **b.** $\dfrac{9}{19}$ **c.** $\dfrac{24}{45}$ **d.** $\dfrac{49}{90}$

17. On the first swing, the length of the arc through which a pendulum swings is 16 in. The length of each successive swing is $\dfrac{3}{4}$ of the preceding swing. What is the total distance the pendulum travels before coming to a complete stop?

     a. 64 in.   **b.** 24 in.   **c.** 48 in.   **d.** 54 in.

18. Evaluate: $\dfrac{10!}{6!\,4!}$

     a. 7560   **b.** 1260   **c.** 210   **d.** 5040

19. Evaluate: $\dbinom{9}{6}$

     a. 240   **b.** 126   **c.** 168   **d.** 84

20. Find the 3rd term in the expansion of $(x-3)^{10}$.

     a. $-405x^3$ **b.** $10x^7$ **c.** $405x^8$ **d.** $405x^3$

Name: _____

Date: _____

1. Given $f(x)=3^{-x+2}$, evaluate $f(-1)$.

   a. 27   b. 3   c. 1   d. $\dfrac{1}{9}$

2. Evaluate: $\log_3 729$

   a. 243   b. 4   c. 6   d. 5

3. Write $\log_3 5 + 2\log_3 x - \log_3 y$ as a single logarithm with a coefficient of 1.

   a. $\log_3 \dfrac{5x^2}{y}$ b. $\log_3 5x^2 y$ c. $\log_3 \dfrac{5y}{x^2}$ d. $\log_3 (5x^2 - y)$

4. Solve for x: $2^x = 15$
   Round to the nearest ten-thousandth.

   a. 2.0149   b. 3.9069   c. 0.8751   d. 0.2560

5. Solve for x: $\log_3 x + \log_3 (2x+1) = 1$

   a. -1 b. -1 and $\dfrac{1}{2}$ c. 1 and $-\dfrac{1}{2}$ d. $\dfrac{1}{2}$

6. Find the equation of the circle with center at $(-1,2)$ and radius 3.

   a. $(x-1)^2 + (y+2)^2 = 3$ b. $(x-1)^2 + (y+2)^2 = 9$

   c. $(x+1)^2 + (y-2)^2 = 9$ d. $(x+1)^2 + (y-2)^2 = 3$

7. Which is the graph of $\dfrac{x^2}{9} - \dfrac{y^2}{25} = 1$?

   a. 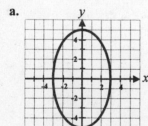   b. 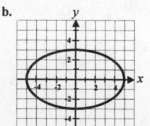   c. 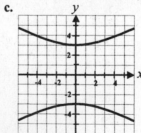   d.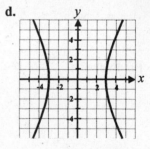

8. Solve: $x^2 + y^2 = 8$
   $\qquad\quad y^2 = 2x$

   a. $(2, 2\sqrt{2})$ and $(2, -2\sqrt{2})$ b. $(-2, 2)$ and $(-2, -2)$

   c. $(2, 2)$ and $(2, -2)$ d. $(-2, 2\sqrt{2})$ and $(-2, -2\sqrt{2})$

9. Which is the graph of $(x+2)^2 + (y-1)^2 \leq 9$?

a.	b.	c.	d.
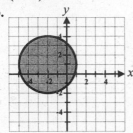	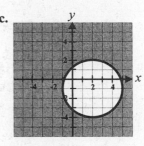	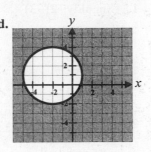	

10. Choose the graph that shows the solution set: $y \geq x^2 - 1$
$$y > x$$

a.	b.	c.	d.
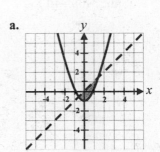	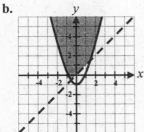	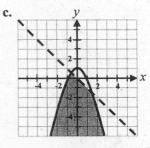	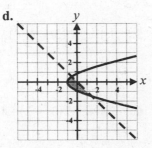

11. Write the 15th term of the sequence whose nth term is given by the formula $a_n = \dfrac{1}{n(n+1)}$.

    a. $\dfrac{1}{255}$ **b.** $\dfrac{1}{240}$ **c.** $\dfrac{1}{210}$ **d.** $\dfrac{1}{220}$

12. Find the sum of the first 25 terms of the arithmetic sequence 16, 20, 24, ...

    a. 1600   **b.** 1650   **c.** 1400   **d.** 1700

13. Find an equivalent fraction for $0.\overline{4}$.

    a. $\dfrac{5}{11}$ **b.** $\dfrac{4}{11}$ **c.** $\dfrac{4}{9}$ **d.** $\dfrac{5}{6}$

14. The temperature of a hot water spa is 72°F. Each hour the temperature is 6% higher than during the previous hour. Find the temperature of the spa after 6 hours. Round to the nearest degree.

    a. 91°F   **b.** 102°F   **c.** 108°F   **d.** 96°F

15. Find the 3rd term in the expression of $(x+2y)^4$.

    a. $16x^3y$ **b.** $24x^2y^2$ **c.** $32xy^3$ **d.** $24x^3y$

Final Exam Form F

1. Simplify: $2(-3)^2 \cdot 5^2$

   a. 900   **b.** -900 **c.** 450   **d.** 300

2. Evaluate $b^2 - 4ac$ when $a = -3$, $b = 2$, and $c = -1$.

   a. -4 **b.** -8 **c.** 16   **d.** -16

3. Simplify: $-3a - 2(3a+1) - 6$

   a. $-9a - 4$ **b.** $-9a - 8$ **c.** $3a - 4$ **d.** $-9a + 8$

4. Translate and simplify "five times the sum of two consecutive odd integers."

   a. 10   **b.** $10n - 2$ **c.** $2n + 2$ **d.** $10n + 10$

5. Solve: $8 - 3t = 2t + 13$

   a. -1 **b.** 5   **c.** $\dfrac{21}{5}$ **d.** -5

6. Solve: $-2(3x - 2) + 4 = 2x - 8$

   a. 4   **b.** 2   **c.** $\dfrac{1}{2}$ **d.** $-\dfrac{1}{2}$

7. A goldsmith combined pure gold that costs \$400 per ounce with an alloy of gold that costs \$150 per ounce. How many ounces of pure gold were used to make 100 oz of gold alloy to sell for \$200 per ounce?

   a. 20 oz   **b.** 25 oz   **c.** 15 oz   **d.** 30 oz

8. An investment of \$4500 is made at an annual simple interest rate of 9%. How much additional money must be invested at an annual simple interest rate of 11.5% so that the total interest earned is \$1325?

   a. \$4500   **b.** \$9000   **c.** \$6000   **d.** \$8000

9. Simplify: $\left(-2a^2b^3\right)\left(-3ab^4\right)^2$

   a. $-18a^4b^{11}$ **b.** $18a^4b^{24}$ **c.** $-18a^3b^9$ **d.** $-6a^3b^7$

10. Simplify: $(3x - y)(2x + 5y)$

    a. $6x^2 - 5y^2$ **b.** $6x^2 + 17xy - 5y^2$ **c.** $6x^2 - 13xy + 5y^2$ **d.** $6x^2 + 13xy - 5y^2$

11. Factor: $x^2 + 6x - 55$

    a. $(x+11)(x-5)$ **b.** $(x-11)(x+5)$ **c.** $(x-5)(x-11)$ **d.** $(x+5)(x+11)$

12. Factor: $-8x^3 - 28x^2 - 24x$

    a. $-4x(2x+3)(x+2)$ **b.** $-4x(2x-3)(x-2)$ **c.** $4x(2x-3)(x-2)$ **d.** $4x(2x+3)(x+2)$

13. Solve by factoring: $2x^2 - 11x = -15$

    a. 3 and $\dfrac{2}{5}$ **b.** -5 and $\dfrac{3}{2}$ **c.** -3 and $\dfrac{5}{2}$ **d.** 3 and $\dfrac{5}{2}$

14. Simplify: $\left(6x^2 - 5x - 8\right) \div (2x + 1)$

    a. $3x - 4 - \dfrac{4}{2x+1}$ **b.** $3x + 4 - \dfrac{4}{2x+1}$ **c.** $3x - 4 + \dfrac{4}{2x+1}$ **d.** $3x - 1 - \dfrac{6}{2x+1}$

15. Simplify: $\dfrac{2x^2 + x - 6}{6x^2 + 12x} \div \dfrac{4x^2 - 12x + 9}{8x^2 - 12x}$

    a. $\dfrac{2x(x+2)}{3(2x-3)}$ **b.** $\dfrac{2(2x-3)^2}{x+2}$ **c.** $\dfrac{2}{3}$ **d.** $\dfrac{2}{3(2x-3)}$

16. Simplify: $\dfrac{8}{2x+8} - \dfrac{2x}{2x^2 + 6x - 8}$

    a. $-\dfrac{1}{x-1}$ **b.** $\dfrac{x-4}{2x^2 + 3x - 8}$ **c.** $\dfrac{6x-4}{x^2 + 3x - 4}$ **d.** $\dfrac{3x-4}{x^2 + 3x - 4}$

17. Solve the proportion: $\dfrac{2}{x+5} = \dfrac{3}{x-1}$

    a. -3 **b.** -17 **c.** 3   **d.** No solution

18. Solve $S = \dfrac{A+L}{2}$ for A.

    a. $2S + L$ **b.** $\dfrac{S-L}{2}$ **c.** $\dfrac{2S}{L}$ **d.** $2S - L$

19. Simplify: $\sqrt{98a^6 b^7}$

    a. $7a^3 b^4 \sqrt{2}$ **b.** $7a^3 b^3 \sqrt{2}$ **c.** $7a^3 b^3 \sqrt{2b}$ **d.** $7a^2 b^4 \sqrt{3a}$

20. Simplify: $a\sqrt[3]{54ab^2} + 2\sqrt[3]{-16a^4 b^2}$

    a. $a\sqrt[3]{2ab^2}$ **b.** $-a\sqrt[3]{2ab^2}$ **c.** $ab\sqrt[3]{2a}$ **d.** $3a\sqrt[3]{ab^2}$

21. Simplify: $\left(2\sqrt{x} - 3\right)^2$

    a. $4x - 9$ **b.** $4x + 9$ **c.** $4x - 12\sqrt{x} + 9$ **d.** $16\sqrt{x} + 9$

22. Simplify: $\dfrac{2+i}{3-i}$

    a. 1   **b.** $\dfrac{5}{8} + \dfrac{5}{8}i$ **c.** $\dfrac{1}{2} + \dfrac{5}{2}i$ **d.** $\dfrac{1}{2} + \dfrac{1}{2}i$

23. Solve: $\sqrt{3x-2} - 4 = 1$

    a. No solution   **b.** $\dfrac{23}{3}$ **c.** 9   **d.** 6

24. Which is the graph of $2x - 3y = -6$?

a.
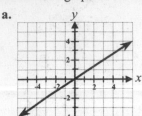

b.
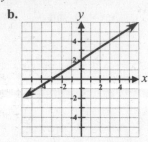

c.
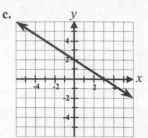

d.
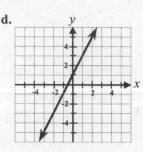

25. Find the slope of the line containing the points $(-3, 4)$ and $(-1, 0)$.

a. 1   b. -1 c. -2 d. $-\dfrac{1}{2}$

26. Find the equation of the line that contains the point $(0, 4)$ and is parallel to the line $3x - 4y = 8$.

a. $y = \dfrac{3}{4}x + 4$ b. $y = \dfrac{2}{3}x + 4$ c. $y = \dfrac{3}{4}x - 4$ d. $y = \dfrac{3}{2}x + 4$

27. Which is the graph of the solution set of $3x - 4y \geq 12$?

a.
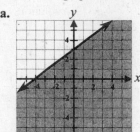

b.
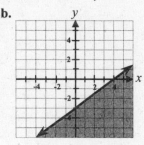

c.
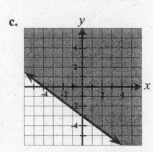

d.
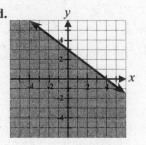

28. Solve: $x^2 - 8x + 4 = 0$

a. 4 and -2 b. $4 + 2\sqrt{3}$ and $4 - 2\sqrt{3}$

c. $4 + \sqrt{3}$ and $4 - \sqrt{3}$ d. $-4 + 2\sqrt{3}$ and $-4 - 2\sqrt{3}$

29. Solve: $x^4 - 7x^2 - 18 = 0$

a. $-3, 3, i\sqrt{2}$, and $-i\sqrt{2}$ b. -3 and 3

c. $-3, 3, 2$, and -2 d. $-3i, 3i, 2i$, and $-2i$

30. Solve: $\dfrac{3x}{x-3} > 2$

a. $\{x \mid x > -6 \text{ and } x > 3\}$ b. $\{x \mid x < -6 \text{ or } x > 3\}$ c. $\{x \mid -6 < x < 3\}$ d. $\{x \mid -3 < x < 6\}$

31. Given $f(x) = 9 - 2x + x^2$, evaluate $f(-1)$.

a. 9   b. 13   c. 10   d. 12

32. Which of the sets of ordered pairs is a function?

    a. $\{(4,0),(0,-4),(0,4),(-4,0)\}$

    b. $\{(3,0),(4,1),(4,-1),(6,2),(6,-2)\}$

    c. $\{(0,0),(1,1),(1,-1),(2,2)(2,-2)\}$

    d. $\left\{(0,0),\left(1,\dfrac{3}{4}\right),(4,3),(8,6)\right\}$

33. Given $f(x)=2x-5$, find $f^{-1}(x)$.

    a. $f^{-1}(x)=x+5$

    b. $f^{-1}(x)=\dfrac{x+5}{2}$

    c. $f^{-1}(x)=x+\dfrac{5}{2}$

    d. $f^{-1}(x)=\dfrac{x}{2}+5$

34. Which is the graph of $y=-x^2+2x+2$?

    a. 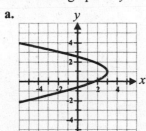   b. 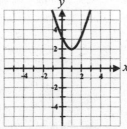   c. 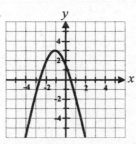   d.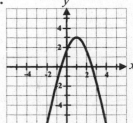

35. Find the minimum value of the function $f(x)=4x^2-12x+5$.

    a. 31   b. 13   c. 4   d. -4

36. Find the distance between the points $(1,-1)$ and $(-2,3)$.

    a. 5   b. $\sqrt{17}$ c. $\sqrt{5}$ d. 25

37. Which is the graph of the circle $x^2+y^2+4x-2y-4=0$?

    a. 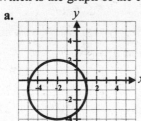   b. 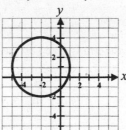   c. 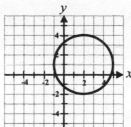   d.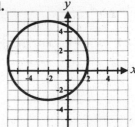

38. Solve: $3x-2y=-7$
    $2x-5y=-12$

    a. $(-1,2)$ b. $(-2,1)$ c. $(1,-2)$ d. $(-2,-1)$

39. Solve: $x-2y+z=5$
    $2x-y+3z=5$
    $3x-3y-5z=1$

    a. $(0,-2,1)$ b. $(-2,-1,1)$ c. $(1,2,-3)$ d. $(1,-2,1)$

40. Evaluate the determinant: $\begin{vmatrix} 5 & 1 \\ 0 & -1 \end{vmatrix}$

    a. 0   **b.** −5   **c.** 5   **d.** −6

41. A crew rowing with the current traveled 15 mi in 2 hours. Against the current, the crew rowed 9 mi in 2 hours. Find the rate of the current.

    a. 1.5 mi/h   **b.** 2 mi/h   **c.** 2.5 mi/h   **d.** 3 mi/h

42. Evaluate: $\log_5 125$

    a. 3   **b.** 5   **c.** 25   **d.** 50

43. Solve for x: $\log_3 x = -2$

    a. −6   **b.** $-\dfrac{2}{3}$ **c.** $\dfrac{1}{9}$ **d.** 8

44. Write $\log_3 \dfrac{x^4}{y^2 z}$ in expanded form.

    a. $4\log_3 x - 2\log_3 y + \log_3 z$ **b.** $4\log_3 x - 2\log_3 yz$

    c. $4\log_3 x - 2\log_3 y - \log_3 z$ **d.** $4\log_3 - 2\left(\log_3 y + \log_3 z\right)$

45. Solve for x: $4^x = 8^{2-x}$

    a. $\dfrac{6}{5}$ **b.** $\dfrac{2}{3}$ **c.** 2   **d.** $-\dfrac{1}{3}$

46. Solve for x: $\log_5 x + \log_5 (2x - 3) = 1$

    a. 1 and $\dfrac{5}{2}$ **b.** −1 and $\dfrac{5}{2}$ **c.** 1   **d.** $\dfrac{5}{2}$

47. Write the 4th and 5th terms of the sequence whose nth term is given by the formula $a_n = \dfrac{n}{2^n}$.

    a. $\dfrac{1}{4}, \dfrac{1}{5}$ **b.** $\dfrac{1}{4}, \dfrac{5}{32}$ **c.** $\dfrac{4}{8}, \dfrac{5}{10}$ **d.** $\dfrac{1}{16}, \dfrac{1}{32}$

48. Find the number of terms in the finite arithmetic sequence −12, −4, 4, ..., 148.

    a. 18   **b.** 19   **c.** 20   **d.** 21

49. Find the sum of the infinite geometric sequence $\dfrac{1}{5}, -\dfrac{2}{15}, \dfrac{4}{45}, \ldots$

    a. $\dfrac{25}{3}$ **b.** 3   **c.** $\dfrac{3}{25}$ **d.** $\dfrac{1}{3}$

50. Find the 3rd term in the expansion of $(x - 3y)^6$.

    a. $18x^5 y$ **b.** $135x^4 y^2$ **c.** $270x^4 y^2$ **d.** $-75x^5 y$

Form G Tests

Multiple Choice

Name: _____

Date: _____

1. Find the additive inverse of $\frac{2}{3}$.

   a. $\frac{3}{2}$ b. $-\frac{2}{3}$ c. $\frac{2}{3}$ d. $-\frac{3}{2}$

2. Write the set of real numbers between -3 and 8, inclusive, in set-builder notation.

   a. $\{x\,|-3 \le x \le 8\}$ b. $\{x\,|-3 < x < 8\}$ c. $\{x\,|-3 < x \le 8\}$ d. $\{x\,|(-3,8]\}$

3. Simplify: $-3-(-8)+24-5$

   a. 7   b. 24   c. 19   d. -5

4. Simplify: $-16(2)(-8)(9)$

   a. -1152 b. 576   c. 2304   d. -2304

5. Simplify: $-104 \div (-8)$

   a. -13 b. 832   c. 31   d. 13

6. Simplify: $-|-4|-|6|$

   a. 2   b. -10 c. -2 d. 10

7. Simplify: $-4(-1)^3(12)$

   a. 48   b. -48 c. 768   d. -768

8. Simplify: $-4(-2)^2(-5)^2$

   a. 200   b. -400 c. 400   d. -200

9. Simplify: $\frac{1}{3}-\frac{11}{24}+\frac{7}{16}$

   a. $\frac{3}{16}$ b. $\frac{11}{48}$ c. $-\frac{11}{48}$ d. $\frac{5}{16}$

10. Simplify: $\left(\frac{7}{8}\right)\left(-\frac{16}{21}\right)\left(-\frac{9}{28}\right)$

   a. $\frac{9}{14}$ b. $\frac{3}{7}$ c. $\frac{3}{14}$ d. $\frac{9}{21}$

11. Simplify: $-3.526+5.421$

   a. 1.895   b. -1.895 c. 8.947   d. -8.947

12. Simplify: 6.023×2.19 (round to the nearest ten-thousandth)

   a. 13.1904   b. 13.19037   c. 13.2   d. 13.19

13. Simplify: $-3-2\left[16\div(-2)^2\right]\cdot3+2\cdot5$

    a. -31 **b.** -17 **c.** 11 **d.** 37

14. Simplify: $\left(-\dfrac{3}{4}\right)^2-\left(\dfrac{3}{4}\div\dfrac{5}{8}\right)+\dfrac{3}{10}$

    a. $-\dfrac{27}{80}$ **b.** $\dfrac{81}{80}$ **c.** $\dfrac{11}{40}$ **d.** $\dfrac{23}{80}$

15. Evaluate $(2a-b)^2\div(2a-b^2)$ when $a=3$ and $b=-2$.

    a. 1 **b.** 32 **c.** 0 **d.** 25

16. Evaluate $3b-a^2-c$ when $a=2$, $b=-2$, and $c=-3$.

    a. -13 **b.** -7 **c.** 7 **d.** -1

17. Identify the property that justifies the statement: $(a+b)x=ax+bx$

    a. The Commutative Property of Addition
    b. The Associative Property of Multiplication
    c. The Commutative Property of Multiplication
    d. The Distributive Property

18. Identify the property that justifies the statement: $2(5)(6)=5(6)(2)$

    a. The Inverse Property of Multiplication
    b. The Associative Property of Multiplication
    c. The Multiplication Property of Zero
    d. The Commutative Property of Multiplication

19. Simplify: $4\left[-2a+3(a+b)\right]-5(a-b)$

    a. $9a-8b$ **b.** $-a+17b$ **c.** $-a+8b$ **d.** $a+8b$

20. Simplify: $5x-2\left[-3x-4(y-3x)\right]-3y$

    a. $-25x+5y$ **b.** $-13x-11y$ **c.** $-13x-5y$ **d.** $-13x+5y$

21. A painter buys twelve gallons of paint to use on two houses. She uses x gallons to paint the first house. Express the amount of paint remaining for the second house in terms of x.

    a. $12+x$ **b.** $x-12$ **c.** $12-2x$ **d.** $12-x$

22. Translate and simplify "a number decreased by the difference between twelve and the number."

    a. 12 **b.** $2n-12$ **c.** -12 **d.** $n-12$

23. Find $A\cup B$, given $A=\{8,10,12,14\}$ and $B=\{10,12,14,16\}$.

    a. $\{8,10,12,14,16\}$ **b.** $\{8,10,12,14\}$ **c.** $\{8,10,12\}$ **d.** $\varnothing$

24. Find $A\cap B$, given $A=\{0,1,2,3,4\}$ and $B=\{-5,-3,0,3,5\}$.

    a. $\{-5,-3,0,1,2,3,4\}$ **b.** $\{-3,0,3\}$ **c.** $\{0,3\}$ **d.** $\varnothing$

Name: _____

Date: _____

1. Solve: $x + 3 = -8$

   a. -6 **b.** 6 **c.** -11 **d.** 11

2. Solve: $-\dfrac{3}{4}y = -9$

   a. -12 **b.** 16 **c.** 12 **d.** $-\dfrac{27}{4}$

3. Solve: $x - \dfrac{3}{5} = \dfrac{2}{7}$

   a. $\dfrac{5}{12}$ **b.** $-\dfrac{11}{35}$ **c.** $-\dfrac{10}{21}$ **d.** $\dfrac{31}{35}$

4. Solve: $3 - 4y = y - 12$

   a. 3 **b.** -3 **c.** $-\dfrac{9}{5}$ **d.** -5

5. Solve: $\dfrac{7}{5}x - 2x = 6$

   a. $-\dfrac{5}{2}$ **b.** $\dfrac{5}{2}$ **c.** 10 **d.** -10

6. Solve: $7x - 12 - 2x = 16 - 2x$

   a. -4 **b.** 4 **c.** $\dfrac{28}{9}$ **d.** $\dfrac{4}{3}$

7. Solve $A = \dfrac{h}{2}(b + B)$ for h.

   a. $\dfrac{A}{2(b + B)}$ **b.** $\dfrac{2A}{B} - b$ **c.** $\dfrac{2A}{(b + B)}$ **d.** $\dfrac{2A}{b} - B$

8. Solve: $\dfrac{3x - 1}{4} - \dfrac{9 - x}{3} = 0$

   a. 3 **b.** $\dfrac{39}{5}$ **c.** $\dfrac{51}{13}$ **d.** 2

9. Solve $1-3(2-4x)<5(3x-4)$ and write the solution set in interval notation.

   a. $(-5,\infty)$ b. $(-\infty,-5)$ c. $\left(-\infty,\dfrac{29}{27}\right)$ d. $(5,\infty)$

10. Choose the graph that shows the solution set of $4-2(3-2x)\geq 7x-2(x-3)$.

   a. 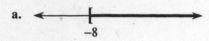 -8

   b. 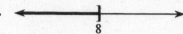 8

   c. $-8/9$

   d. -8

11. Solve $3x-9<-15$ or $2x+1>7$ and write the solution set in interval notation.

   a. $(3,\infty)\cup(-\infty,-2)$ b. $(-2,3)$ c. $(-\infty,3)\cup(-2,\infty)$ d. $(-\infty,-2)\cup(-3,\infty)$

12. Solve $5-8x>-27$ and $3x-7>14$ and write the solution set in set-builder notation.

   a. $\{x\,|\,x<4 \text{ and } x<7\}$ b. $\varnothing$ c. $\{x\,|\,4<x<7\}$ d. $\{x\,|\,x<4 \text{ and } x>7\}$

13. The length of a rectangle is 5 cm less than twice the width. Express as an integer the maximum width of the rectangle when the perimeter is less than 68 cm.

   a. 10 cm   b. 11 cm   c. 12 cm   d. 13 cm

14. Solve: $|7-3b|-12=-3$

   a. $\dfrac{2}{3}$ and $-\dfrac{16}{3}$ b. $-\dfrac{2}{3}$ and $\dfrac{16}{3}$ c. $-\dfrac{2}{3}$ and $-\dfrac{16}{3}$ d. no solution

15. Solve $|2x+5|\leq 4$ and write the solution set in set-builder notation.

   a. $\left\{x\,\middle|\,-\dfrac{9}{2}\leq x\leq -\dfrac{1}{2}\right\}$ b. $\{x\,|\,x\in \text{ real numbers}\}$

   c. $\varnothing$ d. $\left\{x\,\middle|\,-\dfrac{9}{2}<x<\dfrac{1}{2}\right\}$

16. People's Credit Union has two types of checking accounts. One account has a charge of $4 per month plus 3 cents for each check. The second account has a charge of $1 per month plus 9 cents for each check. How many checks can a customer who has the second type of account write if it is to cost the customer less than the first type of account?

    a. Less than 80 checks   **b.** less than 65 checks   **c.** less than 50 checks   **d.** less than 62 checks

17. The sum of two numbers is eighteen. Three times the smaller number is one less than twice the larger number. Find the larger number.

    a. 12   **b.** 7   **c.** 6   **d.** 11

18. A stamp collection consists of 5¢, 8¢, and 13¢ stamps. The number of 13¢ stamps is one more than twice the number of 5¢ stamps. The number of 13¢ stamps is six more than the number of 8¢ stamps. The total face value of all the stamps is $5.37. Find the number of 5¢ stamps.

    a. 5   **b.** 12   **c.** 17   **d.** 24

19. A coffee merchant wants to make 200 lb of a blend of coffee to sell for $5 per pound. The blend is made by using an $8 grade and a $3 grade of coffee. How many pounds of the $8 grade of coffee should be used?

    a. 120 lb   **b.** 80 lb   **c.** 60 lb   **d.** 75 lb

20. A car traveling at 56 mi/h overtakes a cyclist who, riding at 16 mi/h, has a 2-hour head start. How far from the starting point does the car overtake the cyclist?

    a. 52.6 mi   **b.** 44.8 mi   **c.** 40 mi   **d.** 48 mi

21. A piston rod for an automobile is $10\frac{1}{8}$ in. with a tolerance of $\frac{1}{32}$ in. Find the lower and upper limits of the length of the piston rod.

    a. $10\frac{11}{32}$ in.; $10\frac{13}{32}$ in.   **b.** $10\frac{1}{32}$ in.; $10\frac{3}{32}$ in.   **c.** $10\frac{3}{32}$ in.; $10\frac{5}{32}$ in.   **d.** $11\frac{1}{32}$ in.; $11\frac{5}{32}$ in.

22. A butcher has some hamburger that is 24% fat and some that is 12% fat. How many pounds of the hamburger that is 24% fat should be used to make 300 lb of hamburger that is 18% fat?

    a. 150 lb   **b.** 180 lb   **c.** 120 lb   **d.** 50 lb

1. Which point has coordinates $(1, -2)$?

   a. A
   b. B
   c. C
   d. D

   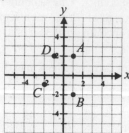

2. Find the ordered-pair solution of $y = 5 + |x|$ when $x = -2$.

   a. $(-2, -1)$ b. $(-2, 3)$ c. $(-2, 7)$ d. $(-2, -3)$

3. Which is the graph of $y = 3x - 2$?

   a. 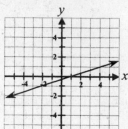   b. 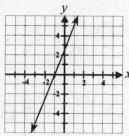   c. 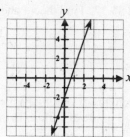   d.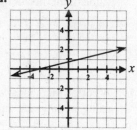

4. Which is the graph of $x + 2y = 8$?

   a. 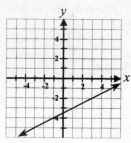   b. 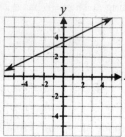   c. 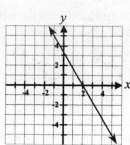   d.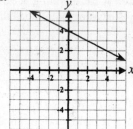

5. Find the slope of the line containing the points $P_1(-4, 2)$ and $P_2(-1, -3)$.

   a. -5 b. $-\dfrac{5}{3}$ c. $-\dfrac{1}{3}$ d. $\dfrac{5}{3}$

6. Given: $S(t) = 3t^2 - 6t$, evaluate $S(2)$.

   a. 0   b. 2   c. 132   d. 24

7. Find the x-intercept of the line $5x - 2y = 20$.

    a. $(0, -10)$ **b.** $(5, 0)$ **c.** $(4, 0)$ **d.** $(0, -2)$

8. Which is the graph of the line that passes through the point $(-2, -2)$ and has slope $\frac{4}{3}$?

  a.   **b.**   **c.**   **d.**

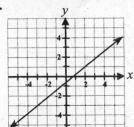 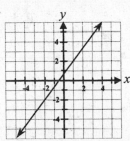 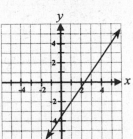 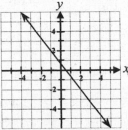

9. Find the equation of the line that contains the point $(-3, 4)$ and has slope $-\frac{4}{3}$.

    a. $y = -\frac{4}{3}x + 8$ **b.** $y = -\frac{4}{3}x - 8$ **c.** $y = -\frac{4}{3}x$ **d.** $y = -\frac{4}{3}x + \frac{8}{3}$

10. Find the equation of the line containing the points $P_1(2, 3)$ and $P_2(5, -1)$.

    a. $y = -\frac{4}{3}x + \frac{17}{3}$ **b.** $y = \frac{4}{3}x + \frac{1}{3}$ **c.** $y = \frac{1}{3}x + \frac{14}{3}$ **d.** $y = \frac{2}{3}x + \frac{5}{3}$

11. Which of the relations below is not a function?

    a. $\{(1, 3), (2, 5), (-2, 0)\}$ **b.** $\{(-2, 0), (-3, 0), (5, 1)\}$

    c. $\{(-3, 4), (-2, 4), (-3, 5)\}$ **d.** $\{(4, 5), (5, 4), (1, 9)\}$

12. Find the equation of the line that contains the point $(-3, 4)$ and is perpendicular to the line $x - 3y = 6$.

    a. $y = 3x - 5$ **b.** $y = \frac{1}{3}x + 5$ **c.** $y = -3x - 5$ **d.** $y = 3x + 13$

13. What values of x are excluded from the domain of $f(x) = \frac{x}{x - 2}$?

    a. $\frac{1}{2}$ **b.** 0 **c.** -2 **d.** 2

14. Which is the graph of the solution set of $3x - 4y < -8$?

a.   b.   c.   d.

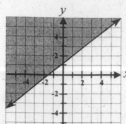   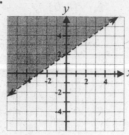   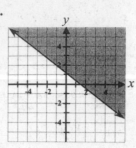   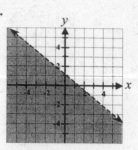

15. Find the midpoint of the line segment between $P_1(6,-5)$ and $P_2(-2,5)$.

   a. $(2,5)$ b. $(2,0)$ c. $(2,-5)$ d. $(4,-5)$

16. Find the length of the line segment between $P_1(6,-1)$ and $P_2(2,1)$.

   a. 7 b. $\sqrt{6}$ c. $2\sqrt{5}$ d. $\sqrt{5}$

17. Find the equation of the line that contains the point $(-2,-1)$ and has undefined slope.

   a. $x = -2$ b. $x = -1$ c. $y = -2$ d. $y = -1$

18. The daily cost to rent a raft includes a paperwork charge of $5 plus $2 per hour. Write a linear equation for the cost of a raft rental in terms of the number of hours it is used. Let y be the cost and x be the number of hours used.

   a. $y = -2x + 5$ b. $y = 2x + 5$ c. $y = 5x + 2$ d. $y = 2x$

Problems 19 and 20 both refer to the graph below.

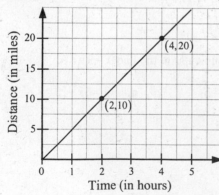

19. The graph to the left shows the relationship between the distance traveled by a cyclist and the time of travel. Which of the following statements describes the meaning of the ordered pair $(4,20)$?

   a. The cyclist has traveled 20 miles in 4 hours.
   b. The cyclist is traveling at a pace of 20mph after 4 hours.
   c. Four cyclists have traveled 20 miles.
   d. The cyclist has traveled 20 miles at a rate of 4mph.

20. How far does the cyclist travel each hour?

   a. 20 mi   b. 4 mi   c. 5 mi   d. 10 mi

Name: _____

Date: _____

1. Simplify: $-\dfrac{7}{16}+\dfrac{3}{8}+\dfrac{5}{6}$

    a. $-\dfrac{1}{6}$
    b. $\dfrac{37}{48}$
    c. $\dfrac{1}{6}$
    d. $\dfrac{49}{48}$

2. Simplify: $\dfrac{5}{14}+\left(\dfrac{4^2-9}{3^2+5}\right)\div\dfrac{7}{8}$

    a. $-\dfrac{3}{14}$
    b. $-\dfrac{13}{14}$
    c. $\dfrac{3}{7}$
    d. $\dfrac{13}{14}$

3. Evaluate $\dfrac{|a-b|}{c^2-ab}$ when $a=-3$, $b=3$, and $c=-2$.

    a. $-\dfrac{6}{5}$
    b. $\dfrac{6}{13}$
    c. 0
    d. 2

4. Identify the property that justifies the statement: $3(x-3)=3x-9$

    a. The Distributive Property
    b. The Commutative Property of Multiplication
    c. The Identity Property of Multiplication
    d. The Inverse Property of Multiplication

5. Simplify: $-20a-2\big[b-3(5a-6b)\big]+25b$

    a. $10a-4b$
    b. $-10a-8b$
    c. $10a-13b$
    d. $-10a-4b$

6. Translate and simplify "seven minus twice the sum of three times a number and five."

    a. $15n+25$
    b. $-6n+12$
    c. $-16n+7$
    d. $-6n-3$

7. Solve: $-\dfrac{5}{7}x=-\dfrac{20}{21}$

    a. $\dfrac{100}{147}$
    b. $\dfrac{4}{3}$
    c. $\dfrac{4}{9}$
    d. $\dfrac{3}{4}$

8. Solve: $\dfrac{1-2x}{3}-\dfrac{2x-3}{4}=\dfrac{4-5x}{6}$

    a. $\dfrac{7}{8}$
    b. $\dfrac{13}{4}$
    c. $\dfrac{5}{4}$
    d. no solution

9. Solve: $|6-3x|=0$

    a.   2 and 0   **b.**   2   **c.**   −2 and 0   **d.**   no solution

10. Solve $|5x-3|<2$ and write the solution set in interval notation.

    a. $\varnothing$ **b.** $\left(-1,-\dfrac{1}{5}\right)$ **c.** $(-\infty,1)$ **d.** $\left(\dfrac{1}{5},1\right)$

11. A drawer contains 15¢ stamps and 20¢ stamps. The number of 15¢ stamps is six more than twice the number of 20¢ stamps. The total value of the stamps is $9.90. Find the number of 15¢ stamps.

    a.   36   **b.**   42   **c.**   18   **d.**   24

12. A goldsmith combined pure gold that costs $380 per ounce with an alloy of gold costing $120 per ounce. How many ounces of pure gold were used to make 40 oz of gold alloy to sell for $185 per ounce.

    a.   15 oz   **b.**   12 oz   **c.**   10 oz   **d.**   30 oz

13. Solve: $3x-5>7x-11$

    a. $\left\{x \mid x<\dfrac{3}{2}\right\}$ **b.** $\left\{x \mid x>\dfrac{3}{2}\right\}$ **c.** $\{x \mid x<-4\}$ **d.** $\{x \mid x>4\}$

14. Which is the graph of $5x-4y=8$?

    a.   **b.**   **c.**   **d.**

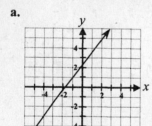 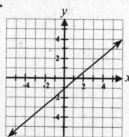 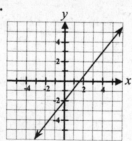 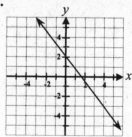

15. Find the x-intercept of the line $2x-3y=-6$.

    a. $(3,0)$ **b.** $(2,0)$ **c.** $(-3,0)$ **d.** $(-2,0)$

16. Find the equation of the line that contains the point $(-4,1)$ and has slope $-\dfrac{1}{2}$.

   a. $y = -\dfrac{1}{2}x - 3$ **b.** $y = -\dfrac{1}{2}x - 1$ **c.** $y = -\dfrac{1}{2}x + 5$ **d.** $y = -\dfrac{1}{2}x + 3$

17. Find the equation of the line that contains the points $P_1(2,3)$ and $P_2(-1,4)$.

   a. $y = -\dfrac{1}{3}x + \dfrac{11}{3}$ **b.** $y = -\dfrac{1}{3}x - \dfrac{13}{3}$ **c.** $y = -\dfrac{2}{3}x + \dfrac{5}{3}$ **d.** $y = -\dfrac{2}{3}x - \dfrac{19}{3}$

18. Find the equation of the line that contains the point $(-1,1)$ and is perpendicular to the line $2x + 3y = 4$.

   a. $y = -\dfrac{3}{2}x + \dfrac{5}{2}$ **b.** $y = \dfrac{3}{2}x + \dfrac{5}{2}$ **c.** $y = 3x + 5$ **d.** $y = -\dfrac{2}{3}x + 5$

19. The relationship between the cost of manufacturing toasters and the number of toasters manufactured is shown in the graph. Write the equation that represents the cost of manufacturing the toasters.

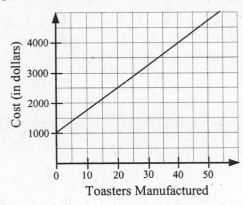

   a. $y = -80x + 1000$

   b. $y = 80x$

   c. $y = -80x$

   d. $y = 80x + 1000$

20. Which is the graph of the solution set of $y \le -\dfrac{3}{5}x - 1$?

   a.   **b.**   **c.**   **d.**

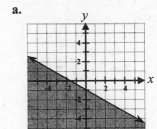 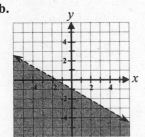 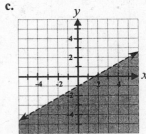 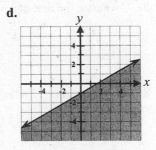

Name: _____

Date: _____

1. Choose the graph that shows the solution to the following system of equations: $3x - y = -2$

$2x + y = -3$

    a. 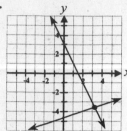   b. 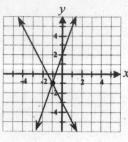   c. 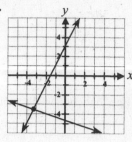   d.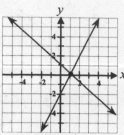

2. Solve by substitution: $5x + 2y = 6$

                              $y = -3 - x$

    a. $(4, -7)$ b. $(3, -6)$ c. $(-2, 7)$ d. $(2, -2)$

3. A small company invested $20,000 by putting part of it into a mutual bond fund that earned 4.5% annual simple interest and the remainder in a corporate bond fund that earned 9.5% annual simple interest. If the company earned $1500 annually from the investments, how much was in the mutual bond fund?

    a. $8000   b. $10,000   c. $9000   d. $7000

4. Solve by the addition method: $4x + 5y = -7$

                                     $-2x - 3y = 3$

    a. $(3, -1)$ b. $(-3, 1)$ c. $(-1, 3)$ d. $(-1, -3)$

5. Solve by the addition method: $x + 3y - 2z = -1$

                                     $2x + 5y + 4z = 7$

                                       $x - 3y - 5z = 2$

    a. $(3, 1, 1)$ b. $(1, -1, 2)$ c. $(-1, 4, 1)$ d. $(4, -1, 1)$

6. Evaluate the determinant: $\begin{vmatrix} -1 & 2 \\ 4 & 3 \end{vmatrix}$

    a. 11   b. 5   c. −11   d. −5

7. Evaluate the determinant: $\begin{vmatrix} -2 & 1 & 3 \\ 0 & -3 & 6 \\ 1 & 1 & -2 \end{vmatrix}$

    a. −30   b. 15   c. −18   d. 12

8. Solve by using Cramer's Rule: $3x - y = 4$

                               $5x - 4y = 16$

    a. $(4, 8)$ b. $(2, 2)$ c. $\left(\frac{4}{3}, 0\right)$ d. $(0, -4)$

9. Solve by using Cramer's Rule:
$$2x - 3y + z = 2$$
$$x + 4y + 2z = -2$$
$$3x - 5y + 3z = 0$$

    a. $(1, 0, -2)$ **b.** $(2, 1, -2)$ **c.** $(2, 0, -2)$ **d.** $(1, 0, -8)$

10. A motorboat traveling with the current went 66 km in 3 hours. Against the current, the boat could go only 36 km in the same amount of time. Find the rate of the boat in calm water.

    a. 12 km/h   **b.** 24 km/h   **c.** 20 km/h   **d.** 17 km/h

11. Flying with the wind, a plane flew 720 mi in 3 hours. Against the wind, the plane required 4.5 hours to fly the same distance. Find the rate of the plane in calm air.

    a. 200 mph   **b.** 400 mph   **c.** 150 mph   **d.** 40 mph

12. A coin bank contains only dimes and quarters. The total value of the coins in the bank is $7.80. If the dimes were quarters and the quarters were dimes, the total value of the coins would be $10.05. Find the number of quarters in the bank.

    a. 18 quarters   **b.** 24 quarters   **c.** 33 quarters   **d.** 15 quarters

13. During one month, a homeowner used 450 units of electricity and 120 units of gas for a total cost of $58.20. The next month, 400 units of electricity and 80 units of gas were used for a total cost of $48.80. Find the cost per unit of gas.

    a. $0.09   **b.** $0.13   **c.** $0.11   **d.** $0.10

14. Choose the graph that shows the solution set for the system of inequalities:
$$2x - y < 4$$
$$x + 3y \geq 6$$

    a. 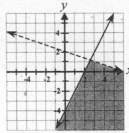   **b.** 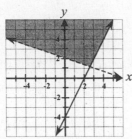   **c.** 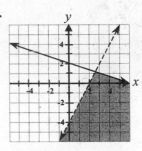   **d.**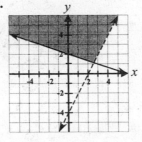

15. Choose the graph that shows the solution set for the system of inequalities:
$$y \leq 3$$
$$x > -3$$

    a. 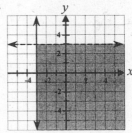   **b.** 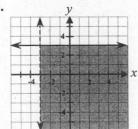   **c.** 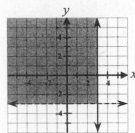   **d.**

Name: _____
Date: _____

1. Simplify: $(-3a^2b)^3(2a^2b^3)^2$

   a. $-108a^{10}b^9$
   b. $-108a^{10}b^{11}$
   c. $54a^9b^{11}$
   d. $-54a^{10}b^9$

2. Simplify: $\left(x^{-3}y\right)^2(xy)^{-3}$

   a. $\dfrac{x^2}{y^2}$
   b. $\dfrac{1}{x^4y}$
   c. $\dfrac{1}{x^9y}$
   d. $\dfrac{x^3}{y^5}$

3. Given $P(x) = -2x^3 + 5x - 3$, evaluate $P(-2)$.

   a. 3
   b. 23
   c. -29
   d. -1

4. Write 63.2 in scientific notation.

   a. 6.32×10^{-1}
   b. 6.32×10^0
   c. 6.32×10^2
   d. 6.32×10^1

5. A high-speed centrifuge makes 6×10^7 revolutions each minute. Find the time in seconds for the centrifuge to make one revolution.

   a. 3×10^8 s
   b. 1×10^{-7} s
   c. 1×10^{-6} s
   d. 2×10^{-7} s

6. Simplify: $\left(3xy^2 + 2xy - 3x^2y\right)\left(-3x^2y^2\right)$

   a. $9x^2y^4 - 6x^2y^3 + 9x^4y^3$
   b. $-9x^3y^4 + 6x^2y^3 + 9x^4y^3$
   c. $-9x^3y^4 - 6x^3y^3 + 9x^4y^3$
   d. $-9x^3y^4 - 6x^3y^3 - 9x^3y^2$

7. Simplify: $4x^2 - x\left[2x - 3(x+2) - 3x^2\right]$

   a. $3x^3 + 7x^2 + 4x$
   b. $3x^3 + 7x^2 - 2x + 6$
   c. $3x^3 - 5x^2 + 2x - 6$
   d. $3x^3 + 5x^2 + 6x$

8. Simplify: $\left(x^n - 4\right)\left(3x^n + 1\right)$

   a. $3x^n + 11x^n + 4$
   b. $3x^{2n} - 11x^n - 4$
   c. $3x^{n^2} - 11x - 4$
   d. $3x^{2n} - 13x^n - 4$

9. Simplify: $(2x + y)\left(x^2 - 3xy + y^2\right)$

   a. $2x^3 - 5x^2y - xy^2 + y^3$
   b. $2x^3 - 7x^2y - 5xy^2 + y^3$
   c. $2x^3 + 7x^2y - 5xy^2 + y^3$
   d. $2x^3 - 5x^2y + xy^2 + y^3$

10. Simplify: $\left(x^2 - 5\right)\left(x^2 + 5\right)$

    a. $x^4 + 25$
    b. $x^4 - 10x^2 + 25$
    c. $x^4 + 10x^2 + 25$
    d. $x^4 - 25$

Chapter 5 Test Form G (*continued*)   Name: _____

11. The length of the side of a cube is $(3x - 2)$ m. Find the volume of the cube in terms of the variable x.

    a. $(27x^3 - 54x^2 + 36x - 8)$ m^3 **b.** $(9x^2 - 6x + 1)$ m^3

    c. $(27x^3 - 9x^2 + 3x - 1)$ m^3 **d.** $(9x^3 - 9x^2 + 9x - 1)$ m^3

12. Factor: $10x^3y - 20x^2y^2 + 5xy^3$

    a. $5xy(2x^2 - 10xy + y^2)$ **b.** $5xy(2x^2 - 4xy + y^2)$

    c. $5xy(2x^2 - 5x + 5y^2)$ **d.** $5x(2x^2y - 5xy + y^2)$

13. Factor: $6ab + 6ay + bx + xy$

    a. $(6a + b)(x + y)$ **b.** $(6a + y)(b + x)$ **c.** $(6a + x)(b + y)$ **d.** Nonfactorable

14. Divide by using long division: $\dfrac{x^3 - 3x^2 + 5x - 2}{x - 3}$

    a. $x^2 - 5x - 15 + \dfrac{13}{x-3}$ **b.** $x^2 + 5 + \dfrac{13}{x-3}$ **c.** $x^2 + 5x + 15 - \dfrac{13}{x-3}$ **d.** $x^2 + 5 - \dfrac{28}{x-3}$

15. Factor: $12a^2 + 11ab + 2b^2$

    a. $(4a - b)(3a - 2b)$ **b.** $(4a + b)(3a - 2b)$ **c.** $(4a - b)(3a + 2b)$ **d.** $(4a + b)(3a + 2b)$

16. Factor: $9a^2 - 121$

    a. $(3a - 11)(3a + 11)$ **b.** $(3a - 11)^2$ **c.** $(3a + 11)^2$ **d.** Nonfactorable

17. Factor: $27 + 8x^3$

    a. $(3 - 2x)(9 + 6x + 4x^2)$ **b.** $(3 + 2x)(9 - 6x + 4x^2)$

    c. $(3 - x)(9 + 2x + 4x^2)$ **d.** Nonfactorable

18. Factor: $a^4b^4 - 7a^3b^3 - 30a^2b^2$

    a. $a^2b^2(ab + 3)(ab - 10)$ **b.** $a^2b^2(ab - 3)(ab + 10)$

    c. $(a^2b^2 + 3)(a^2b^2 - 10)$ **d.** $ab(a^2b^2 + 3)(ab - 10)$

19. Solve: $6x^2 + x = 15$

    a. $\dfrac{5}{2}$ and 15   **b.** $\dfrac{3}{2}$ and $-\dfrac{5}{3}$ **c.** 14 and 15   **d.** $\dfrac{3}{2}$ and -1

20. Solve: $3x(x + 4) + 4 = -4(x + 3)$

    a. -4 and $\dfrac{4}{3}$ **b.** 4 and $-\dfrac{4}{3}$ **c.** 4 and $\dfrac{4}{3}$ **d.** -4 and $-\dfrac{4}{3}$

Name: _____
Date: _____

1. Find the domain of $f(x) = \dfrac{x-5}{x^2 - 2x - 15}$.

   a. $\{x \mid x \neq -3, 5\}$ b. $\{x \mid x \neq -3\}$ c. $\{x \mid x \in \text{real numbers}\}$ d. $\{x \mid x \neq 5\}$

2. Simplify: $\dfrac{x^2 y^2 + xy^3 - 2y^4}{4x^2 y + 10xy^2 + 4y^3}$

   a. $\dfrac{y}{2}$ b. $\dfrac{x-y}{2x-y}$ c. $\dfrac{y(x-y)}{2(2x+y)}$ d. $\dfrac{y(x+y)}{2(2x-y)}$

3. Simplify: $\dfrac{2x^2 - 9x - 18}{x^2 - 2x - 3} \cdot \dfrac{x^2 - 1}{x^2 - 7x + 6}$

   a. $\dfrac{2x-6}{x+1}$ b. $\dfrac{2x+3}{x-3}$ c. $\dfrac{2x+3}{x-1}$ d. $\dfrac{2x+1}{x-6}$

4. Simplify: $\dfrac{2x^2 - 13x - 7}{x^2 - 13x + 42} \div \dfrac{6x^2 + x - 2}{3x^2 - 16x - 12}$

   a. $\dfrac{(2x+1)(x-6)}{(2x-1)(x+6)}$ b. $\dfrac{2x+1}{2x-1}$ c. $\dfrac{2x-1}{2x+1}$ d. 1

5. Given $R(x) = \dfrac{x^2}{3x^2 - 5x}$, find $R(2)$.

   a. $-\dfrac{1}{8}$ b. $\dfrac{1}{2}$ c. -2 d. 2

6. Simplify: $\dfrac{x^5 - 6x^4 - 16x^3}{x^3 - 4x}$

   a. $\dfrac{x^2(x-8)}{x-2}$ b. $\dfrac{x-8}{x-2}$ c. $\dfrac{x^2}{x+2}$ d. $\dfrac{x(x-8)}{x-2}$

7. Find the missing numerator: $\dfrac{2x}{2x-3} = \dfrac{?}{8x^3 - 27}$

   a. $8x^3 + 12x^2 + 18x$ b. $8x^2 - 18x$ c. $8x^2 + 18$ d. $8x^3 - 12x^2 + 18x$

8. Simplify: $\dfrac{3x}{x^2 - 1} - \dfrac{8}{2 - 2x}$

   a. $\dfrac{4-x}{(x+1)(x-1)}$ b. $-\dfrac{x+4}{(x+1)(x-1)}$ c. $7x + 4$ d. $\dfrac{7x+4}{(x+1)(x-1)}$

9. Simplify: $\dfrac{2x+2}{4x^2 - 1} - \dfrac{5}{1 - 2x}$

   a. $\dfrac{-8x-3}{(2x-1)(2x+1)}$ b. $\dfrac{12x+7}{(2x-1)(2x+1)}$ c. $\dfrac{2x-3}{(2x-1)(2x+1)}$ d. $\dfrac{12x+7}{(1-2x)(1+2x)}$

10. Simplify: $\dfrac{3 - \frac{7}{x} - \frac{6}{x^2}}{\frac{3}{x^2} + \frac{5}{x} - 2}$

    a. -1 b. $-\dfrac{2x-1}{2x+1}$ c. $-\dfrac{3x+2}{2x+1}$ d. $\dfrac{3x+2}{2x-1}$

11. Simplify: $\dfrac{x - \frac{6}{x-5}}{1 + \frac{6}{x-5}}$

     a. $\dfrac{x-6}{x+1}$ **b.** $x+6$ **c.** $x-6$ **d.** $\dfrac{x^2-5x+6}{x+6}$

12. Solve: $\dfrac{x}{2} = \dfrac{5-x}{3}$

     a. 2 **b.** -2 **c.** 1 **d.** 3

13. Solve: $\dfrac{2x-7}{5} = \dfrac{x+2}{2}$

     a. -4 **b.** -24 **c.** $\dfrac{4}{9}$ **d.** $-\dfrac{24}{9}$

14. A stock investment of 500 shares pays a dividend of $625. At this rate, how many additional shares are required to earn a dividend of $1200?

     a. 800 shares   **b.** 1000 shares   **c.** 460 shares   **d.** 750 shares

15. Solve: $\dfrac{x}{x-3} = \dfrac{3x-4}{x-3} - x$

     a. $1, 4$ **b.** $-1, \dfrac{4}{3}$ **c.** $\dfrac{1}{3}, -4$ **d.** no solution

16. Solve: $\dfrac{1}{x^2-25} - \dfrac{4}{x-5} = \dfrac{2}{x+5}$

     a. $-\dfrac{3}{2}$ **b.** $\dfrac{3}{2}$ **c.** $-\dfrac{9}{2}$ **d.** $\dfrac{2}{3}$

17. Solve $I = \dfrac{1}{12}mL^2$ for m.

     a. $m = 12IL^2$ **b.** $m = \dfrac{12I}{L^2}$ **c.** $m = \dfrac{I}{12L^2}$ **d.** $m = \dfrac{IL^2}{12}$

18. The stopping distance, s, of a car varies directly as the square of its speed, v. If a car traveling 60 mph requires 220 ft to stop, find the stopping distance for a car traveling 30 mph.

     a. 55 ft   **b.** 75 ft   **c.** 110 ft   **d.** 880 ft

19. One solar heating panel can raise the temperature of water 1° in 16 min. A second solar heating panel can raise the temperature 1° in 24 min. How long will it take to raise the temperature of the water 1° if both panels are operating?

     a. 6 min   **b.** 7.2 min   **c.** 9.6 min   **d.** 9 min

20. An insurance representative traveled 1350 mi by commercial jet and then an additional 135 mi by helicopter. The rate of the jet was five times the rate of the helicopter. The entire trip took 4.5 hours. Find the rate of the jet.

     a. 400 mi/h   **b.** 450 mi/h   **c.** 500 mi/h   **d.** 90 mi/h

Name: _____
Date: _____

1. Simplify: $\left(-4ab^3\right)\left(-a^2b^3\right)\left(-3a^4b\right)$

    a. $12a^6b^7$ **b.** $-12a^7b^7$ **c.** $6a^7b^6$ **d.** $-12a^7b^9$

2. Simplify: $\left(\dfrac{a^{-2}b^2}{ab^{-2}}\right)\left(\dfrac{ab}{a^5b^{-3}}\right)^2$

    a. $\dfrac{1}{a^3}$ **b.** $\dfrac{b^{16}}{a^6}$ **c.** $\dfrac{b^{12}}{a^{11}}$ **d.** $\dfrac{1}{a^{10}}$

3. Factor: $x^2 - x - 12$

    a. $(x+4)(x+3)$ **b.** $(x-4)(x+3)$ **c.** $(x-3)(x+4)$ **d.** $(x-12)(x+1)$

4. Simplify: $\left(2x^{2n} - 4\right)\left(2x^{2n} + 4\right)$

    a. $4x^{4n} + 16$ **b.** $4x^{2n} + 8x^n - 16$ **c.** $4x^{4n} - 8x^n - 16$ **d.** $4x^{4n} - 16$

5. Factor: $4a^4 - 20a^2 + 25$

    a. $\left(2a^2+5\right)\left(2a^2-5\right)$ **b.** $\left(2a^2-5\right)^2$ **c.** $\left(4a^2+1\right)\left(a^2+25\right)$ **d.** $\left(2a^2+5\right)^2$

6. Simplify: $a^{3n} - b^{3n}$

    a. $\left(a^n+b^n\right)\left(a^{2n}+2a^nb^n+b^{2n}\right)$ **b.** Nonfactorable

    c. $\left(a^n-b^n\right)\left(a^{2n}+a^nb^n+b^{2n}\right)$ **d.** $\left(a^n+b^n\right)\left(a^{2n}-a^nb^n+b^{2n}\right)$

7. Factor: $30x^5 + 57x^3 + 18x$

    a. $3x\left(2x^2+3\right)\left(5x^2+2\right)$ **b.** $3x\left(2x^2+3\right)\left(5x^2-2\right)$

    c. $3x(2x+3)(5x+2)$ **d.** $3x\left(x^2+3\right)\left(10x^2+1\right)$

8. Divide: $\dfrac{15x^3 - 9x^2}{3x^2}$

    a. $3x-3$ **b.** $5x-3$ **c.** $5x+3$ **d.** $3x-5$

9. Simplify: $\dfrac{2x-3}{12x} - \dfrac{3x+1}{9x}$

    a. $\dfrac{5x+6}{36x}$ **b.** $\dfrac{-6x-13}{36x}$ **c.** $\dfrac{2x+4}{36x}$ **d.** $\dfrac{6x+13}{36x}$

10. Simplify: $\dfrac{1+\frac{3}{x+3}}{1+\frac{6}{x-1}}$

    a. $\dfrac{(x-1)(x+6)}{(x+3)(x+5)}$ **b.** $\dfrac{x-1}{x+3}$ **c.** $\dfrac{(x-1)(x-6)}{(x-3)(x-5)}$ **d.** $\dfrac{x-6}{x-5}$

11. It takes 190 sec to heat 2 chicken patties in the microwave. At this rate, how many can be heated in 475 sec?

    a. 3 patties   **b.** 4 patties   **c.** 5 patties   **d.** 6 patties

12. Solve: $\dfrac{8}{2x+1} = 5$

    a. $\dfrac{1}{3}$ **b.** $\dfrac{3}{10}$ **c.** $\dfrac{3}{4}$ **d.** $\dfrac{5}{6}$

13. The stopping distance, s, of a car varies directly at the square of its speed, v. If a car traveling 40 mph requires 72 ft to stop, find the stopping distance for a car traveling 55 mph.

    a. 136.125 ft   **b.** 130.175 ft   **c.** 125.78 ft   **d.** 140 ft

14. Solve by substitution: $2x - 7y = -6$

                     $x = 5y - 3$

    a. $\left(0, \dfrac{3}{5}\right)$ **b.** $(-3, 0)$ **c.** $\left(0, \dfrac{6}{7}\right)$ **d.** $(3, 0)$

15. Solve by the addition method: $2x - 3y - 5z = -1$

                          $x + 4y + z = 1$

                          $3x + 6y - z = 1$

    a. $(1, 2, 2)$ **b.** $(3, -1, 2)$ **c.** $(1, -1, 1)$ **d.** $(1, -2, 1)$

16. Solve by using Cramer's Rule: $3x - 5y = 14$

                           $x + 2y = -10$

    a. $(2, -6)$ **b.** $(3, -1)$ **c.** $(-2, -4)$ **d.** $(4, -7)$

17. Flying with wind, a supersonic jet flew 4500 mi in 3 hours. Against the wind, the jet could fly only 4200 mi in the same amount of time. Find the rate of the jet in calm air.

    a. 1500 mph   **b.** 1400 mph   **c.** 1450 mph   **d.** 1550 mph

18. Evaluate the determinant: $\begin{vmatrix} 2 & 3 \\ -5 & 6 \end{vmatrix}$

    a. -3 **b.** 3   **c.** 27   **d.** -27

19. Solve by the addition method: $5x + 2y = 6$

                          $x + y = -3$

    a. $(2, -2)$ **b.** $(0, 3)$ **c.** $(4, -7)$ **d.** $(-2, 8)$

20. Write 0.0000053 in scientific notation.

    a. 5.3×10^{-6} **b.** 5.3×10^{-7} **c.** 5.6×10^{7} **d.** 5.6×10^{6}

Name: _____
Date: _____

1. Simplify: $\left(a^{-2/3}b^2\right)^3\left(a^{-4}b^{12}\right)^{-1/4}$

   a. $\dfrac{b^3}{a}$

   b. $\dfrac{b^3}{a^4}$

   c. ab^3

   d. $\dfrac{b^9}{a^3}$

2. Simplify: $a^{4/3}\left[a^{2/3}-a^{-4/3}\right]$

   a. a^2

   b. a^2-a

   c. $a^2-a^{8/3}$

   d. a^2-1

3. Write $-2x^{2/3}$ as a radical expression.

   a. $\sqrt[3]{-2x^2}$

   b. $\sqrt{-2x^3}$

   c. $-2\sqrt[3]{x^2}$

   d. $-2\sqrt{x^3}$

4. Write $\sqrt[4]{(b-2)^3}$ as an exponential expression.

   a. $b-2$

   b. $(b-2)^{4/3}$

   c. $(b-2)^{3/4}$

   d. $b^{3/4}-2^{3/4}$

5. Simplify: $\sqrt[3]{64a^6b^{15}}$

   a. $4a^3b^{12}$

   b. $16a^2b^5$

   c. $4a^2b^6$

   d. $4a^2b^5$

6. Simplify: $\sqrt[3]{81a^{11}b^7}$

   a. $3a^3b^2\sqrt[3]{3a^2b}$

   b. $3a^2b^2\sqrt[3]{3a^2b}$

   c. $9a^3b^2\sqrt[3]{3a^2b}$

   d. $3a^3b^2\sqrt[3]{3ab}$

7. Simplify: $\sqrt[4]{32x^6y^{10}}$

   a. $2xy\sqrt[4]{2x^2y}$

   b. $4xy^2\sqrt[4]{2x^2y^2}$

   c. $2xy\sqrt[4]{2x^2y}$

   d. $2xy^2\sqrt[4]{2x^2y^2}$

8. Simplify: $5xy^2\sqrt{x^4y^2}+x^2y\sqrt{49x^2y^4}$

   a. $12x^2y^2\sqrt{x^4y^2}$

   b. $12xy^2\sqrt{x}$

   c. $12x^2y\sqrt{x}$

   d. $12x^3y^3$

9. Simplify: $a\sqrt{16b}-\sqrt{32a^2b}+3\sqrt{8a^2b}$

   a. $-4a\sqrt{b}-10\sqrt{2b}$

   b. $4a\sqrt{b}+2a\sqrt{2b}$

   c. $6a\sqrt{b}$

   d. $6a\sqrt{2b}$

10. Simplify: $\sqrt{5a}\left(\sqrt{10a}-\sqrt{5a}\right)$

    a. 0

    b. $5a\sqrt{2}-5a$

    c. $10a\sqrt{2}$

    d. $5a-5\sqrt{2}$

11. Simplify: $\left(\sqrt{y}-2\right)^2$

　　a. $y-\sqrt{2y}-4$　　　　**b.** $y-4$　　　　**c.** $y-2\sqrt{y}+4$　　　　**d.** $y-4\sqrt{y}+4$

12. Simplify: $\dfrac{\sqrt{150a^3b^8}}{\sqrt{3a^7b^2}}$

　　a. $\dfrac{5b^3}{a^2}$　　　　**b.** $\dfrac{25b^3}{a^2}$　　　　**c.** $\dfrac{5b^3\sqrt{2}}{a^2}$　　　　**d.** $\dfrac{50b^4}{a^4}$

13. Simplify: $\dfrac{4}{1+\sqrt{5}}$

　　a. $\sqrt{5}-1$　　　　**b.** $\dfrac{4-4\sqrt{5}}{-5}$　　　　**c.** $1-\sqrt{5}$　　　　**d.** $\dfrac{1-\sqrt{5}}{6}$

14. Solve: $\sqrt{3-5x}+7=9$

　　a. $\dfrac{7}{5}$　　　　**b.** $-\dfrac{7}{5}$　　　　**c.** 5　　　　**d.** $-\dfrac{1}{5}$

15. Solve: $\sqrt[3]{x-3}+5=3$

　　a. No solution　　　　**b.** -1　　　　**c.** 1　　　　**d.** -5

16. Find the distance required for a car to reach a velocity of 64 ft/s when the acceleration is 8 ft/s^2. Use the equation $v=\sqrt{2as}$, where v is the velocity, a is the acceleration, and s is the distance.

　　a. 256 ft　　　　**b.** 128 ft　　　　**c.** 64 ft　　　　**d.** 320 ft

17. Simplify: $\sqrt{108}-\sqrt{-40}$

　　a. $3\sqrt{6}-2i\sqrt{10}$　　　　**b.** $6\sqrt{3}-2i\sqrt{10}$　　　　**c.** $6\sqrt{3}+2i\sqrt{10}$　　　　**d.** $6\sqrt{3}+8i\sqrt{5}$

18. Simplify: $\left(12-\sqrt{-4}\right)+\left(2+13i\right)$

　　a. $10+11i$　　　　**b.** $12+15i$　　　　**c.** $10+15i$　　　　**d.** $14+11i$

19. Simplify: $\sqrt{-8}\cdot\sqrt{-10}$

　　a. $-4i\sqrt{5}$　　　　**b.** $-4\sqrt{5}$　　　　**c.** $4\sqrt{5}$　　　　**d.** $4i\sqrt{5}$

20. Simplify: $\dfrac{5}{3-i}$

　　a. $\dfrac{3}{2}+\dfrac{1}{2}i$　　　　**b.** $3+i$　　　　**c.** $\dfrac{3}{2}-\dfrac{1}{2}i$　　　　**d.** $3-2i$

Name: _____

Date: _____

1. Solve by factoring: $5x^2 + 13x - 6 = 0$

    a. $-\dfrac{2}{5}$ and 3   b. $-\dfrac{2}{5}$ and -3 c. $\dfrac{2}{5}$ and -3 d. $\dfrac{2}{5}$ and 3

2. Solve by factoring: $4x^2 - 8x = 0$

    a. 2 and -2 b. 2   c. 0 and -2 d. 0 and 2

3. Write a quadratic equation that has integer coefficients and has solutions $\dfrac{4}{3}$ and 6.

    a. $3x^2 - 10x + 24 = 0$ b. $3x^2 - 22x + 24 = 0$ c. $4x^2 - 27x + 18 = 0$ d. $4x^2 - 21x - 18 = 0$

4. Solve by taking square roots: $(x-2)^2 + 4 = 0$

    a. $-2 + 2i$ and $-2 - 2i$ b. $2 + \sqrt{2}$ and $2 - \sqrt{2}$
    c. $2 + 2i$ and $2 - 2i$ d. $2 + i\sqrt{2}$ and $2 - i\sqrt{2}$

5. Solve by taking square roots: $\left(x - \dfrac{2}{3}\right)^2 = \dfrac{4}{9}$

    a. 0 and $\dfrac{3}{4}$ b. 0 and $\dfrac{4}{3}$ c. 0 and $\dfrac{3}{2}$ d. 0 and $-\dfrac{4}{3}$

6. Solve by completing the square: $x^2 + 4x + 20 = 0$

    a. $-2 + 4i$ and $-2 - 4i$ b. 2 and -6
    c. $-2 + 2i\sqrt{6}$ and $-2 - 2i\sqrt{6}$ d. $2 + 4i$ and $2 - 4i$

7. Solve by completing the square: $2x^2 + x + 2 = 0$

    a. $-\dfrac{1}{2} + \dfrac{\sqrt{15}}{2}i$ and $-\dfrac{1}{2} - \dfrac{\sqrt{15}}{2}i$ b. $-\dfrac{1}{4} + \dfrac{\sqrt{15}}{4}i$ and $-\dfrac{1}{4} - \dfrac{\sqrt{15}}{4}i$
    c. $\dfrac{1}{2} + \dfrac{\sqrt{15}}{2}i$ and $\dfrac{1}{2} - \dfrac{\sqrt{15}}{2}i$ d. $\dfrac{1 + \sqrt{15}}{4}$ and $\dfrac{1 - \sqrt{15}}{4}$

8. Solve by using the quadratic formula: $5x^2 - 2x + 3 = 0$

    a. $\dfrac{1}{10} + \dfrac{\sqrt{14}}{10}i$ and $\dfrac{1}{10} - \dfrac{\sqrt{14}}{10}i$ b. $\dfrac{1 + \sqrt{14}}{10}$ and $\dfrac{1 - \sqrt{14}}{10}$
    c. $\dfrac{1}{5} + \dfrac{\sqrt{14}}{5}i$ and $\dfrac{1}{5} - \dfrac{\sqrt{14}}{5}i$ d. $\dfrac{1 + \sqrt{14}}{2}$ and $\dfrac{1 - \sqrt{14}}{2}$

9. Solve by using the quadratic formula: $x^2 - 9x + 18 = 0$

    a. $\dfrac{9 + 2\sqrt{2}}{2}$ and $\dfrac{9 - 2\sqrt{2}}{2}$ b. $\dfrac{9}{2} + \sqrt{2}$ and $\dfrac{9}{2} - \sqrt{2}$
    c. -6 and -3 d. 3 and 6

10. Use the discriminant to determine whether $2x^2 - 7x + 8 = 0$ has one real number solution, one complex number solution, two real number solutions, or two complex number solutions.

    a. One real number solution   b. Two real number solutions
    c. One complex number solution   d. Two complex number solutions

11. Solve: $x^4 - 5x^2 + 4 = 0$

    a. $-1, 1, -2,$ and 2 **b.** $-1, 1, -2i,$ and $2i$ **c.** $-i, i, -2i, 2i$ **d.** -1 and -2

12. Solve: $x - x^{1/2} - 12 = 0$

    a. -2 and $i\sqrt{3}$ **b.** 16 and 9 **c.** 16 **d.** 2

13. Solve: $\sqrt{2x - 3} = x - 1$

    a. 6 **b.** 6 and 2 **c.** 2 **d.** -2

14. Solve: $\sqrt{3x - 3} - \sqrt{x} = 1$

    a. 4 **b.** 2 **c.** 1 and 4 **d.** 2 and -1

15. Solve: $\dfrac{x}{3} = \dfrac{3}{x - 8}$

    a. 8 **b.** -1 and -9 **c.** -1 and 9 **d.** 0 and 8

16. Solve: $\dfrac{3x + 2}{x + 2} - 1 = 2x$

    a. 0 and 1 **b.** No solution   **c.** 0 and $-\dfrac{1}{2}$ **d.** 0 and -1

17. Solve: $(x - 2)(x - 4)(x + 1) < 0$

    a. $\{x \mid x < -1 \text{ or } 2 < x < 4\}$ **b.** $\{x \mid x < -1 \text{ or } 2 < x < 4\}$

    c. $\{x \mid x > -1 \text{ or } 2 < x < 4\}$ **d.** $\{x \mid x > -1 \text{ or } -2 < x < 4\}$

18. Solve: $\dfrac{3x}{x - 5} < 5$

    a. $\left\{x \mid -\dfrac{25}{2} < x < 5\right\}$ **b.** $\left\{x \mid -5 < x < \dfrac{25}{2}\right\}$

    c. $\left\{x \mid x < -\dfrac{25}{2} \text{ or } x > 5\right\}$ **d.** $\left\{x \mid x > -\dfrac{25}{2} \text{ and } x > 5\right\}$

19. A small air conditioner requires 5 min longer to cool a room 2° than does a larger air conditioner. Working together, the two air conditioners can cool the room 2° in 6 min. How long would it take the smaller air conditioner working alone to cool the room 2°?

    a. 10 min   **b.** 15 min   **c.** 12 min   **d.** 18 min

20. The length of a rectangle is 5 m more than the width. The area is 336 m². Find the length of the rectangle.

    a. 16 m   **b.** 20 m   **c.** 12 m   **d.** 21 m

1. Find the vertex of the parabola given by $y = 2x^2 - 4x + 3$.

   a. $(1,1)$ b. $(-1,9)$ c. $(-1,1)$ d. $(1,9)$

2. State the range of the function $f(x) = x^2 - 5$.

   a. $\{y \mid y \le -5\}$ b. $\{y \mid y \ge -5\}$ c. $\{y \mid y \le 5\}$ d. $\{y \mid y \ge 5\}$

3. Find the x-intercepts of the graph of $y = 4x^2 + 13x - 12$.

   a. $-2, \dfrac{3}{2}$ b. $2, -\dfrac{3}{2}$ c. $-4, \dfrac{3}{4}$ d. $4, -\dfrac{3}{4}$

4. Find the maximum value of the function $f(x) = -2x^2 + 2x - 3$.

   a. $\dfrac{3}{2}$ b. $-\dfrac{3}{2}$ c. $-\dfrac{5}{2}$ d. -2

5. The height in feet, s, of a ball thrown straight up is given by the function $s(t) = -16t^2 + 56t + 40$, where t is the time in seconds. Find the maximum height reached by the ball.

   a. 89 ft b. 144 ft c. 40 ft d. 128 ft

6. For $f(x) = 3x^2 - 1$ and $g(x) = 3 - 6x$, find $f(2) - g(2)$.

   a. -2 b. 2 c. -20 d. 20

7. Which is the graph of $f(x) = 2|x| + 1$?

   a. 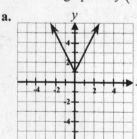 b. 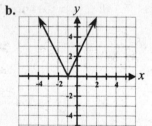 c. 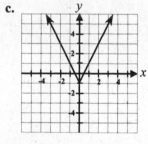 d.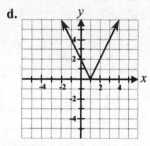

8. Which of the graphs does not represent the graph of a function?

   a. 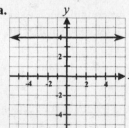 b. 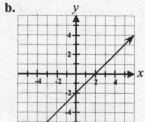 c. 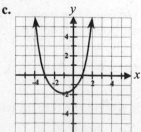 d.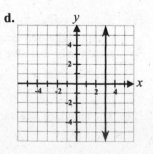

9. For $f(x) = x^2 - 9$ and $g(x) = 4 - x$, find $\left(\dfrac{f}{g}\right)(2)$.

   a. $-\dfrac{2}{5}$ b. $\dfrac{2}{5}$ c. $\dfrac{5}{2}$ d. $-\dfrac{5}{2}$

10. Find $f(x) = 2x^2 - 1$ and $g(x) = x - 3$, find $(f \cdot g)(-1)$.

   a. 4   b. -4 c. -12 d. 12

11. Given $f(x) = 4x + 2$ and $g(x) = 10x - 1$, find $f[g(-1)]$.

   a. 38   b. -42 c. -34 d. 42

12. Given $g(x) = x^2 - 2$ and $h(x) = x + 5$, find $g[h(x)]$.

   a. $x^2 + 10x + 23$ b. $x^2 + x + 3$ c. $x^2 + 3$ d. $x + 23$

13. Let $f(x) = -\dfrac{2}{3}x - 1$. Find $f^{-1}(x)$.

   a. $f^{-1}(x) = -\dfrac{1}{3}x + 2$ b. $f^{-1}(x) = x - \dfrac{3}{2}$ c. $f^{-1}(x) = -\dfrac{3}{2}x - \dfrac{3}{2}$ d. $f^{-1}(x) = -\dfrac{3}{2}x + 1$

14. Which of the functions are inverses of each other?

   a. $f(x) = \dfrac{1}{4}x$ and $g(x) = -4x$ b. $f(x) = 9x$ and $g(x) = -9x$

   c. $f(x) = 2x + 1$ and $g(x) = -2x - 1$ d. $f(x) = -3x$ and $g(x) = -\dfrac{1}{3}x$

15. Find the inverse of the function $\{(2, -1), (3, -2), (8, 7)\}$.

   a. $\left\{\left(\dfrac{1}{2}, -1\right), \left(\dfrac{1}{3}, -\dfrac{1}{2}\right), \left(\dfrac{1}{8}, \dfrac{1}{7}\right)\right\}$ b. $\{(-1, 2), (-2, 3), (7, 8)\}$

   c. $\{(-2, 1), (-3, 2), (-8, -7)\}$ d. $\{(2, -1), (3, -2), (8, 7)\}$

Name: _____

Date: _____

1. Simplify: $\sqrt[3]{-27a^3b^{12}}$

   a. $-3ab$ b. $3ab^3$ c. $-3ab^4$ d. $-9ab^4$

2. Simplify: $4\sqrt[4]{32a^6} - a\sqrt[4]{162a^2}$

   a. $5a\sqrt[4]{2a^2}$ b. $3a^2$ c. $4a\sqrt[4]{2a}$ d. $8a^2\sqrt[4]{2a}$

3. Simplify: $(4-3i)(5+2i)$

   a. $14+7i$ b. $14-7i$ c. $26+7i$ d. $26-7i$

4. Solve: $\sqrt[3]{2x-8} = \sqrt[3]{x+13}$

   a. -7 b. 7 c. 21 d. -21

5. Find the length of a pendulum that makes one swing in 3.5 s. The equation for the time of one swing of a pendulum is given by $T = 2\pi\sqrt{L/32}$, where T is the time in seconds and L is the length in feet. Use 3.14 for π. Round to the nearest hundredth.

   a. 8.53 ft   b. 9.94 ft   c. 7.25 ft   d. 8.10 ft

6. Solve by factoring: $12x^2 + 5x - 2 = 0$

   a. $-\dfrac{3}{2}$ and $\dfrac{1}{4}$ b. $\dfrac{3}{2}$ and 4 c. $-\dfrac{2}{3}$ and $\dfrac{1}{4}$ d. $\dfrac{2}{3}$ and $-\dfrac{1}{4}$

7. Write a quadratic equation that has integer coefficients and has solutions $-\dfrac{1}{4}$ and $\dfrac{2}{3}$.

   a. $12x^2 - 5x - 2 = 0$ b. $12x^2 - 11x + 2 = 0$ c. $12x^2 - 11x - 2 = 0$ d. $12x^2 - 5x + 2 = 0$

8. Solve by completing the square: $x^2 + 2x - 6 = 0$

   a. $-1+\sqrt{5}\,i$ and $-1-\sqrt{5}\,i$ b. $-1+\sqrt{7}$ and $-1-\sqrt{7}$

   c. -8 and 6 d. -4 and 2

9. Solve: $\dfrac{1}{x-1} + \dfrac{x}{x-2} = 2$

   a. $3+i\sqrt{3}$ and $3-i\sqrt{3}$ b. $3+\sqrt{3}$ and $3-\sqrt{3}$

   c. -2 and 1 d. $1+2i$ and $1-2i$

10. Solve: $(x+5)(x-3)x > 0$

    a. $\{x \mid x < -3 \text{ or } -5 < x < 0\}$ **b.** $\{x \mid x < 3 \text{ and } -5 < x < 0\}$

    c. $\{x \mid x > 3 \text{ or } -5 < x < 0\}$ **d.** $\{x \mid x > -3 \text{ or } -5 < x < 0\}$

11. Which is the graph of $y = x^2 + 4x - 1$?

    a. 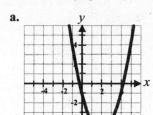   **b.** 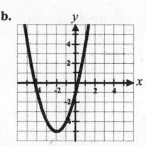   **c.** 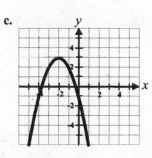   **d.**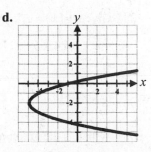

12. Find the zeros of the function $f(x) = 3x^2 + 3x - 18$.

    a. -6 and 1 **b.** -1 and 6 **c.** -2 and 3 **d.** -3 and 2

13. Which of the graphs represents the graph of a function?

    a. 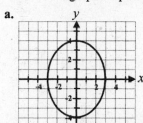   **b.** 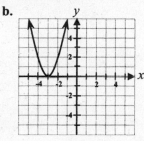   **c.** 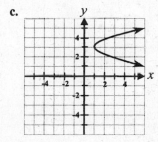   **d.**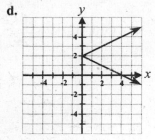

14. Given $f(x) = 2x^2 - 1$ and $g(x) = 5 - 3x$, find $f\left[g(0)\right]$.

    a. 0 **b.** -1 **c.** 51 **d.** 49

15. Let $f(x) = -\dfrac{1}{3}x - 6$. Find $f^{-1}(x)$.

    a. $f^{-1}(x) = 3x - 18$ **b.** $f^{-1}(x) = -3x - 18$ **c.** $f^{-1}(x) = \dfrac{-3}{x - 6}$ **d.** $f^{-1}(x) = 3x + 6$

Name: _____

Date: _____

1. Given $f(x) = \left(\dfrac{3}{4}\right)^{-2x}$, evaluate $f(2)$.

    a. $-\dfrac{16}{9}$ **b.** $\dfrac{9}{16}$ **c.** $-\dfrac{9}{16}$ **d.** $\dfrac{16}{9}$

2. Given $g(x) = e^{-x}$, evaluate $g(2)$. Round to the nearest ten-thousandth.

    a. -5.4366 **b.** 0.1353 **c.** 7.3891 **d.** 0.7183

3. Which is the graph of $f(x) = \left(\dfrac{3}{4}\right)^{x} + 1$?

    a. 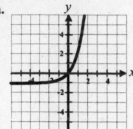   **b.** 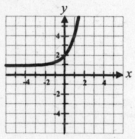   **c.** 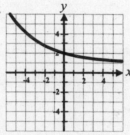   **d.**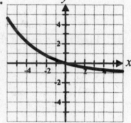

4. Evaluate: $\log_5 \dfrac{1}{125}$

    a. 3 **b.** 6 **c.** -2 **d.** -3

5. Solve for x: $\log_3 x = 5$

    a. 15 **b.** 243 **c.** 81 **d.** 9

6. Write $7^3 = 343$ in logarithm form.

    a. $\log_{343} 7 = 3$ **b.** $\log_7 343 = 3$ **c.** $\log_3 343 = 7$ **d.** $\log_3 7 = 343$

7. Write $\log_{15} 1 = 0$ in exponential form.

    a. $0^{15} = 1$ **b.** $15^{-1} = 0$ **c.** $1^{15} = 0$ **d.** $15^0 = 1$

8. Write $\log_2 \dfrac{\sqrt{x^2 y}}{z^3}$ in expanded form.

   a. $\log_2 x + \dfrac{1}{2}\log_2 y - 3\log_2 z$ **b.** $\dfrac{1}{2}\log_2 x + \dfrac{1}{2}\log_2 y - 3\log_2 z$

   c. $\log_2 x - \dfrac{1}{2}\log_2 y + 3\log_2 z$ **d.** $y^3 \sqrt{\log_2 x^2 y}$

9. Write $\dfrac{1}{3}\left(2\log_2 x - 4\log_2 y\right)$ as a single logarithm with a coefficient of 1.

   a. $\log_2 \sqrt[3]{x^2 y^4}$ **b.** $\log_2 \sqrt[3]{\dfrac{x^2}{y^2}}$ **c.** $\dfrac{\log_2 \sqrt[3]{x^2}}{\log_2 \sqrt[4]{y^2}}$ **d.** $\log_2 \sqrt[3]{\dfrac{x^2}{y^4}}$

10. Write $\ln\left(xy^2 z^3\right)$ in expanded form.

   a. $\ln x - 2\ln - 3z$ **b.** $\ln x + 2\ln - 3\ln z$ **c.** $\ln x \cdot 2\ln y \cdot 3\ln z$ **d.** $\ln x + 2\ln y + 3\ln z$

11. Write $\dfrac{1}{3}\ln x + 2\ln y - \dfrac{1}{2}\ln z$ as a single logarithm with a coefficient of 1.

   a. $\ln \dfrac{x^3}{y^2 z^2}$ **b.** $\ln \dfrac{y^2 \sqrt[3]{x}}{\sqrt{z}}$ **c.** $\ln \dfrac{y^2 \sqrt[3]{x}}{z^2}$ **d.** $\ln \dfrac{\sqrt[3]{x}}{y^2 \sqrt{z}}$

12. Evaluate: $\log_8 60$
   Round to the nearest ten-thousandth.

   a. 2.0476   **b.** 1.0133   **c.** 1.9690   **d.** 0.9640

13. Evaluate: $\log_4 9$
   Round to the nearest ten-thousandth.

   a. 1.5850   **b.** 0.6309   **c.** 0.3522   **d.** −0.3522

14. Which is the graph of $f(x) = 3\log_2 x$?

   a. 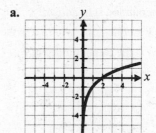   **b.** 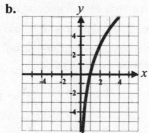   **c.** 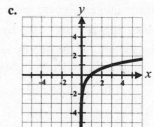   **d.**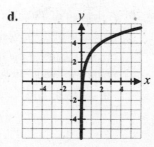

15. Solve for x: $6^x = 23$
    Round to the nearest ten-thousandth.
    a. 0.5714   b. 1.3437   c. 1.7500   d. 5.6181

16. Solve for x: $16^{4x-2} = 64^{x+3}$
    a. $\dfrac{13}{5}$ b. 1   c. $\dfrac{13}{11}$ d. 3

17. Solve for x: $e^x = 5$
    Round to the nearest ten-thousandth.
    a. 1.8394   b. 1.6094   c. 0.6990   d. 148.4132

18. Solve for x: $\log_3 6 + \log_3 x = 4$
    a. $\dfrac{27}{2}$ b. $\dfrac{9}{2}$ c. No solution   d. $\dfrac{2}{27}$

19. Solve for x: $\log_{10}(x-2) + \log_{10}(2x+3) = \log_{10} 9$
    a. 3 and $-\dfrac{5}{2}$ b. -3 and $\dfrac{5}{2}$ c. 5   d. 3

20. A deposit of $8000 is made into an account that earns 10% annual interest compounded semiannually. What is the value of the investment after 5 years? Use the compound interest formula $P = A(1+I)^n$, where a is the original value of the investment, I is the interest rate per compounding period, n is the total number of compounding periods, and p is the value of the investment after n periods.
    a. $13,031.16   b. $20,749.93   c. $12,884.08   d. $14,162.33

Name: _____

Date: _____

1. Which is the graph of $y = x^2 + 6x + 5$?

    a. 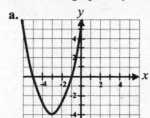   b. 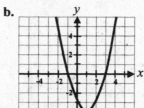   c. 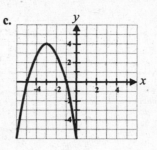   d.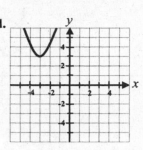

2. Find the axis of symmetry of the parabola $y = -2x^2 + 2x - 3$.

    a. $x = 2$
    b. $x = \dfrac{1}{2}$
    c. $x = -2$
    d. $x = -\dfrac{1}{2}$

3. Find the vertex of the parabola given by $y = x^2 - 4x + 3$.

    a. $(2,1)$
    b. $(-4,39)$
    c. $(2,-1)$
    d. $(4,3)$

4. Find the equation of the circle with radius 6 and center $(-2,-3)$.

    a. $(x+2)^2 + (y+3)^2 = 36$
    b. $(x-2)^2 + (y-3)^2 = 36$
    c. $(x-2)^2 + (y-3)^2 = 6$
    d. $(x+2)^2 + (y+3)^2 = 6$

5. Find the equation of the circle that passes through the point $(4,-5)$ and whose center is $(-1,1)$.

    a. $(x+1)^2 + (y-1)^2 = 25$
    b. $(x-1)^2 + (y+1)^2 = 61$
    c. $(x-1)^2 + (y+1)^2 = 25$
    d. $(x+1)^2 + (y-1)^2 = 61$

6. Write $x^2 + y^2 - 2x - 2y - 2 = 0$ in standard form.

    a. $(x-1)^2 + (y-1)^2 = 4$
    b. $(x-1)^2 + (y-1)^2 = 6$
    c. $(x-2)^2 + (y-2)^2 = 6$
    d. $(x-2)^2 + (y-2)^2 = 16$

7. Which is the graph of $x^2 + y^2 + 4x - 8y + 16 = 0$?

a. 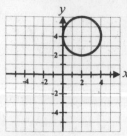   b. 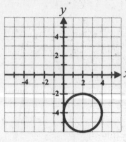   c. 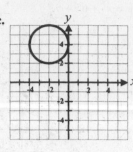   d.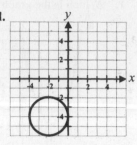

8. Which is the graph of $\dfrac{x^2}{36} + \dfrac{y^2}{4} = 1$?

a. 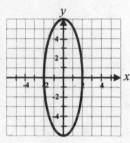   b. 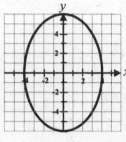   c. 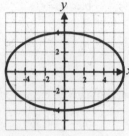   d.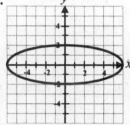

9. Which is the graph of $\dfrac{y^2}{9} - \dfrac{x^2}{4} = 1$?

a. 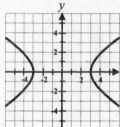   b. 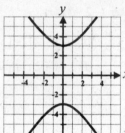   c. 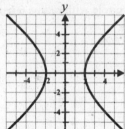   d.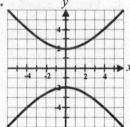

10. Solve: $x^2 + y^2 = 4$
    $4x^2 - y^2 = 16$

a. $(0,2)$ and $(0,-2)$

b. $\left(3, \sqrt{5}\right)$ and $\left(-3, -\sqrt{5}\right)$

c. $\left(1, \sqrt{3}\right)$ and $\left(-1, -\sqrt{3}\right)$

d. $(-2,0)$ and $(2,0)$

11. Solve: $x^2 + 4y^2 = 16$
    $x - y = -2$

a. $(4,0)$ and $(0,2)$

b. $(4,0)$ and $(-4,0)$

c. $\left(-\dfrac{16}{5}, -\dfrac{6}{5}\right)$ and $(0,2)$

d. $(0,2)$ and $(0,-2)$

12. Which is the graph of the solution set of $x^2 + y^2 < 9$?

   a.   **b.**   **c.**   **d.**

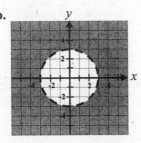 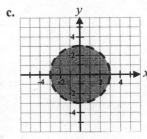 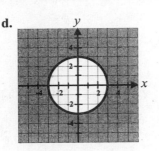

13. Which is the graph of the solution set of $y < x^2 - 5$?

   a.   **b.**   **c.**   **d.**

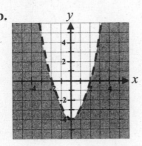 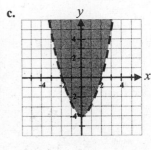 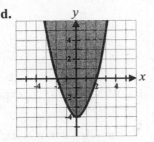

14. Choose the graph that shows the solution set for: $x^2 + y^2 \geq 25$
$$x + 2y \geq 4$$

   a.   **b.**   **c.**   **d.**

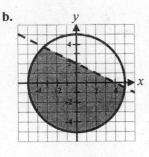 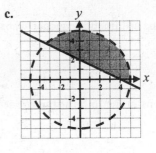 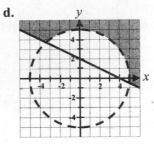

15. Choose the graph that shows the solution set for: $2x^2 - y \geq 4$
$$x + 3y < 6$$

   a.   **b.**   **c.**   **d.**

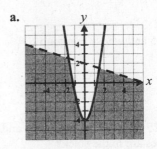 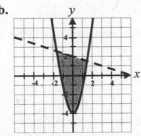 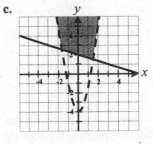

Name: _____
Date: _____

1. Write the 4th term of the sequence whose nth term is given by the formula $a_n = \left(-\dfrac{1}{2}\right)^n$.

   a. $-\dfrac{1}{16}$ b. $\dfrac{1}{16}$ c. $-\dfrac{1}{8}$ d. $\dfrac{1}{8}$

2. Write the 7th and 8th terms of the sequence whose nth term is given by the formula $a_n = n(n-5)$.

   a. 18, 24   b. 14, 18   c. 14, 24   d. 18, 28

3. Evaluate : $\displaystyle\sum_{n=1}^{3} \dfrac{2n}{n+2}$

   a. $\dfrac{43}{15}$ b. $\dfrac{9}{2}$ c. $\dfrac{11}{10}$ d. $\dfrac{43}{10}$

4. Write $\displaystyle\sum_{n=1}^{4} x^{2n-3}$ in expanded form.

   a. $x + x^2 + x^3 + x^5$ b. $\dfrac{1}{x} + x^2 + x^4 + x^6$ c. $\dfrac{1}{x} + x + x^3$ d. $\dfrac{1}{x} + x + x^3 + x^5$

5. Find the 10th term of the arithmetic sequence $-7, -3, 1, \ldots$

   a. 17   b. 29   c. 33   d. -29

6. Find the 44th term of the arithmetic sequence whose first term is -13 and whose common difference is 7.

   a. 314   b. 295   c. 288   d. 260

7. Find the number of terms in the finite arithmetic sequence $-5, -2, 1, \ldots, 88$.

   a. 32   b. 30   c. 26   d. 33

8. Find the sum of the first 28 terms of the arithmetic sequence $12, 4, -4, \ldots$

   a. -2688 b. -3024 c. 2688   d. -2024

9. Find the sum of the first 34 terms of the arithmetic sequence whose first term is 5 and whose common difference is -4.

   a. -2142 b. 2074   c. 2047   d. -2074

10. Boxes are stacked in a warehouse so that there are 28 boxes in the bottom row, 25 boxes in the next row, and so on in an arithmetic sequence. There are 7 boxes in the top row. How many boxes are in the stack?

    a. 72 boxes   b. 140 boxes   c. 120 boxes   d. 280 boxes

11. Find the 5th term of the geometric sequence 81, 54, 36, ...

   a. 16   b. 48   c. $\dfrac{32}{3}$ d. 32

12. Find the 9th term of the geometric sequence whose first term is 8 and whose common ratio is $\sqrt{2}$.

   a. 64   b. 48   c. 128   d. $128\sqrt{2}$

13. Find the sum of the first five terms of the geometric sequence 1, 9, 81, ...

   a. 7381   b. 59,049   c. 6408   d. 12,381

14. Find the sum of the first six terms of the geometric sequence whose first term is 2 and whose common ratio is –2.

   a. –32   b. $\dfrac{130}{3}$ c. –64   d. –42

15. Find the sum of the infinite geometric sequence $\dfrac{1}{2}, \dfrac{1}{4}, \dfrac{1}{8}, \ldots$

   a. $\dfrac{1}{2}$ b. 2   c. 1   d. 4

16. Find an equivalent fraction for $0.6\overline{8}$.

   a. $\dfrac{2}{3}$ b. $\dfrac{7}{11}$ c. $\dfrac{61}{90}$ d. $\dfrac{31}{45}$

17. The temperature of a hot water spa is 44°F. Each hour the temperature is 15% higher than during the previous hour. Find the temperature of the spa after 6 hours. Round to the nearest tenth of a degree.

   a. 101.8°F   b. 92.4°F   c. 102.5·°F   d. 99.1°F

18. Evaluate: $\dfrac{14!}{5!9!}$

   a. 2002   b. 200.2   c. 715   d. 1,153,152

19. Evaluate: $\dbinom{6}{2}$

   a. 56   b. 20,160   c. 15   d. 14

20. Find the 4th term in the expansion of $(2x + y)^8$.

   a. $1792x^5y^3$ b. $28x^6y^2$ c. $28x^7y^3$ d. $448x^3y^5$

1. Given $f(x) = \left(\dfrac{2}{3}\right)^{x-1}$, evaluate $f(-1)$.

   a. $-\dfrac{4}{9}$ b. $\dfrac{9}{4}$ c. $\dfrac{4}{9}$ d. $\dfrac{3}{2}$

2. Solve for x: $\log_2 x = -1$

   a. $\dfrac{1}{2}$ b. -2 c. $-\dfrac{1}{2}$ d. 2

3. Evaluate: $\log_4 24$
   Round to the nearest ten-thousandth.

   a. 0.7782 b. 2.2925 c. 2.2952 d. 6

4. Solve for x: $10^x = 25$
   Round to the nearest ten-thousandth.

   a. 2.5000 b. 0.9163 c. 0.7153 d. 1.3979

5. Solve for x: $\log_3(x+2) - \log_3 x^2 = \log_3 3$

   a. 1 b. 1 and $-\dfrac{2}{3}$ c. -1 d. -1 and $\dfrac{2}{3}$

6. Which is the graph of $y = -x^2 - 4$?

   a. 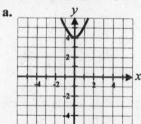   b. 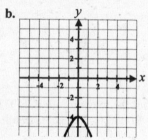   c. 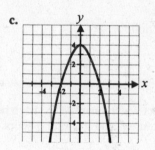   d.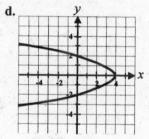

7. Find the equation of the circle with radius 3 and center $(-3, 4)$.

   a. $(x+3)^2 + (y-4)^2 = 3$ b. $(x+3)^2 + (y-4)^2 = 9$

   c. $(x-3)^2 + (y+4)^2 = 3$ d. $(x-3)^2 + (y+4)^2 = 9$

8. Which is the graph of $\dfrac{x^2}{25} + \dfrac{y^2}{4} = 1$?

   a. 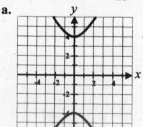   b. 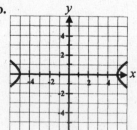   c. 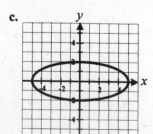   d.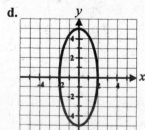

9. Solve: $2x + y = 3$

    $y = 3x^2 - 2x - 9$

    a. $(-2, 7)$ and $(3, 12)$ **b.** $(2, -1)$ and $(-2, 7)$ **c.** $(1, -8)$ and $(2, -1)$ **d.** $(-1, 5)$ and $(2, -1)$

10. Which is the graph of the solution set of $x^2 + y^2 \leq 16$?

    a.   **b.**   **c.**   **d.**

    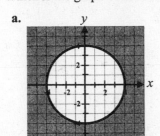   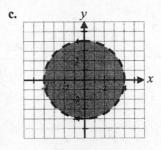   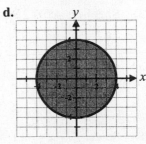

11. Evaluate: $\sum_{n=2}^{4} \dfrac{n^2}{n+2}$

    a. $\dfrac{49}{5}$ **b.** $\dfrac{62}{15}$ **c.** $\dfrac{82}{15}$ **d.** $\dfrac{27}{5}$

12. Find the sum of the first 40 terms of the arithmetic sequence $-3, 1, 5, \ldots$

    a. 3080   **b.** 3120   **c.** 2640   **d.** 3000

13. Find the sum of the infinite geometric sequence $9, 3, 1, \ldots$

    a. $\dfrac{27}{2}$ **b.** 9   **c.** 6   **d.** 12

14. A laboratory ore sample contains 500 mg of a radioactive material with a half-life of 1 day. Find the amount of radioactive material in the sample at the beginning of the second week. Round to the nearest tenth of a milligram.

    a. 7.8 mg   **b.** 3.9 mg   **c.** 12.0 mg   **d.** 2.4 mg

15. Find the 6th term in the expansion of $(x - y)^9$.

    a. $-126x^5 y^4$ **b.** $-42x^4 y^5$ **c.** $-21x^5 y^5$ **d.** $-126x^4 y^5$

Name: _____

Date: _____

1. Simplify: $-2^3(-3)^2(-6)$
   a. -432
   b. 432
   c. 216
   d. -216

2. Simplify: $\left(-\dfrac{1}{2}\right)^3 - \left(\dfrac{3}{4} \div \dfrac{9}{16}\right) + \dfrac{1}{6}$
   a. $\dfrac{11}{8}$
   b. $-\dfrac{11}{8}$
   c. $-\dfrac{31}{24}$
   d. $-\dfrac{17}{24}$

3. Simplify: $-5x + 2(4 - x) + x$
   a. $-5x + 8$
   b. $-6x + 8$
   c. $-5x + 6$
   d. $-4x + 6$

4. Find $A \cap B$, given $A = \{0, 2, 3\}$ and $B = \{-4, -2, 0, 2, 4\}$.
   a. $\{0, 2\}$
   b. $\{-4, -2, 0, 2, 3, 4\}$
   c. $\varnothing$
   d. $\{3\}$

5. Solve: $-\dfrac{11}{13}x = -33$
   a. $\dfrac{3}{11}$
   b. -39
   c. 39
   d. -33

6. Solve: $2y - 5 - 5y = 12 - 2y$
   a. $-\dfrac{17}{5}$
   b. $-\dfrac{7}{5}$
   c. -17
   d. -7

7. Three times the sum of the first two integers of three consecutive even integers is two more four times the third integer. Find the second integer.
   a. 8
   b. 10
   c. 6
   d. 12

8. A passenger train leaves a depot 2.5 hours after a freight train leaves the same depot. The passenger train is traveling 16 mi/h faster than the freight train. Find the rate of the passenger train if the passenger train overtakes the freight train in 6 h 15 min.
   a. 62 mi/h
   b. 56 mi/h
   c. 52 mi/h
   d. 40 mi/h

9. Simplify: $\left(x^{2n-1}\right)\left(x^{3-n}\right)$
   a. x^{n-2}
   b. x^{n-4}
   c. x^{n+2}
   d. x^2

10. Simplify: $\left(2a^n - 3b^n\right)^2$
    a. $4a^{2n} + 12a^n b^n + 9b^{2n}$
    b. $4a^{2n} - 9b^{2n}$
    c. $4a^{2n} + 9b^{2n}$
    d. $4a^{2n} - 12a^n b^n + 9b^{2n}$

11. Factor: $18a^2 + 45ab - 8b^2$
    a. $(6a - b)(3a - 8b)$
    b. $(6a - b)(3a + 8b)$
    c. $(6a + b)(3a + 8b)$
    d. $(6a + b)(3a - 8b)$

12. Factor: $1 - 10x^2 y^2 + 25x^4 y^4$
    a. $\left(1 - 5x^2 y^2\right)^2$
    b. $\left(1 + 5x^2 y^2\right)^2$
    c. $\left(1 + 5x^2 y^2\right)\left(1 - 5x^2 y^2\right)$
    d. Nonfactorable

13. Factor: $2x^4y^2 - 3x^3y^3 - 2x^2y^4$

   a. $x^2y^2(x+2y)(2x-y)$ **b.** $x^2y^2(x-2y)(2x+y)$

   c. $x^2y^2(x-2y)(2x-y)$ **d.** $x^2y^2(x+2y)(2x+y)$

14. Simplify: $\left(2x^3 - 18x + 1\right) \div (2x - 6)$

   a. $x^2 + 3x - \dfrac{1}{2x-6}$ **b.** $x^2 + 3x + \dfrac{1}{2x-6}$ **c.** $x^2 - 3x - \dfrac{1}{2x-6}$ **d.** $x^2 - 3x + 1$

15. Simplify: $\dfrac{x^3 - y^3}{x^2 - 2xy + y^2} \div \dfrac{3x^4y^2 + 3x^3y^3 + 3x^2y^4}{3x^2y - 3xy^2}$

   a. $\dfrac{x-y}{xy(x+y)}$ **b.** $\dfrac{x-y}{xy\left(x^2 + xy + y^2\right)}$ **c.** $\dfrac{1}{xy}$ **d.** $\dfrac{x-y}{3xy}$

16. Find the missing numerator: $\dfrac{2x}{3x-1} = \dfrac{?}{6x^2 + 13x - 5}$

   a. $4x^2 + 10x$ **b.** $4x^2 + 10$ **c.** $4x^2 - 10x$ **d.** $2x^2 + 5x$

17. Three pounds of apples cost $.96. At this rate, how much would 48 pounds of apples cost?

   a. $46.08   **b.** $16.00   **c.** $13.56   **d.** $15.36

18. Solve $a_n = a_1 + (n-1)d$ for n.

   a. $n = \dfrac{a_n a_1}{d}$ **b.** $n = \dfrac{a_n - a_1}{d}$ **c.** $n = \dfrac{a_n - a_1 + d}{d}$ **d.** $n = \dfrac{a_n - a_1 d}{d}$

19. Simplify: $\dfrac{\left(a^{-2/3}b^4\right)^{1/2}}{\left(a^{2/3}b^{-3/4}\right)^{-2}}$

   a. $a^{5/3}b^{1/2}$ **b.** $b^{1/2}$ **c.** $ab^{7/2}$ **d.** $ab^{1/2}$

20. Simplify: $\sqrt[5]{x^{10}y^{25}}$

   a. x^2y^5 **b.** x^5y^{20} **c.** x^2y^2 **d.** x^5y^5

21. Simplify: $\sqrt[3]{192a^{12}b^{11}}$

   a. $4a^4b^4\sqrt[3]{3b}$ **b.** $4a^4b^3\sqrt[3]{3b}$ **c.** $4a^4b^3\sqrt[3]{3b^2}$ **d.** $4a^3b^3\sqrt[3]{3ab^2}$

22. Simplify: $\left(\sqrt{64} - \sqrt{-32}\right) + \left(\sqrt{49} - \sqrt{-98}\right)$

   a. $15 - 3i\sqrt{2}$ **b.** $1 - 11i\sqrt{2}$ **c.** $15 + 11i\sqrt{2}$ **d.** $15 - 11i\sqrt{2}$

23. Simplify: $\dfrac{3}{2+i}$

   a. $2 - i$ **b.** $\dfrac{3}{2} - 3i$ **c.** $\dfrac{6}{5} - \dfrac{3}{5}i$ **d.** $2 - \dfrac{3}{2}i$

24. Which is the graph of $y = -\dfrac{1}{2}x$?

a.
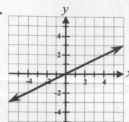

b.
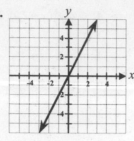

c.
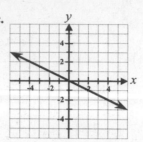

d.
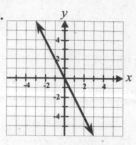

25. Find the slope of the line containing the points $(1,-4)$ and $(-1,2)$.

a. Undefined   b. -2 c. $-\dfrac{1}{2}$ d. -3

26. Find the equation of the line that contains the point $(-4,2)$ and has slope $-\dfrac{3}{2}$.

a. $y = -\dfrac{3}{2}x + 3$ b. $y = -\dfrac{3}{2}x - 4$ c. $y = -\dfrac{3}{2}x + 4$ d. $y = -\dfrac{3}{2}x + 8$

27. Which is the graph of the solution set of $2x - y \le 4$?

a.
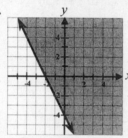

b.
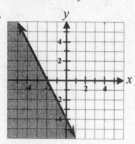

c.
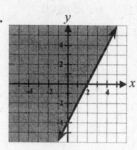

d.
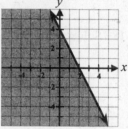

28. Solve: $2x^2 + 3x + 5 = 0$

a. $\dfrac{5}{2}$ and -1

b. $\dfrac{3+\sqrt{31}}{4}$ and $\dfrac{3-\sqrt{31}}{4}$

c. $-\dfrac{3}{4}+\dfrac{\sqrt{31}}{4}i$ and $-\dfrac{3}{4}-\dfrac{\sqrt{31}}{4}i$

d. $\dfrac{-3+\sqrt{31}}{4}$ and $\dfrac{-3-\sqrt{31}}{4}$

29. Solve: $x^2 + 7x + 12 = 0$

a. -4 and -3 b. 3 and 4   c. -6 and -2 d. 2 and 6

30. The sum of the squares of two consecutive positive odd integers is 130. Find the smaller integer.

a. 9   b. 65   c. 7   d. 49

31. For $f(x) = 4x - 3$ and $g(x) = x^2 + 2$, find $f(0) - g(0)$.

a. 0   b. -5 c. -1 d. 6

32. Which of the sets of ordered pairs is a one-to-one function?

a. $\{(0,-3),(1,-1),(2,1),(3,3)\}$ b. $\{(-2,2),(-1,1),(0,0),(1,1),(2,2)\}$

c. $\{(0,0),(1,-3),(2,-4),(3,-3)\}$ d. $\{(-2,0),(0,3),(2,0),(0,-3)\}$

33. Given $f(x) = \frac{1}{2}x - 3$, find $f^{-1}(x)$.

    a. $f^{-1}(x) = \frac{2}{x-6}$ **b.** $f^{-1}(x) = -2x + 3$ **c.** $f^{-1}(x) = 2x - 3$ **d.** $f^{-1}(x) = 2x + 6$

34. Which is the graph of $y = -x^2 - 4x$?

    a. 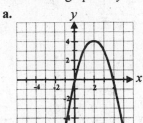   **b.** 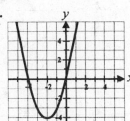   **c.** 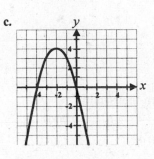   **d.**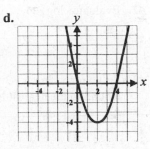

35. The height in feet, s, of a ball thrown straight up is given by the function $s(t) = -16t^2 + 80t$, where t is the time in seconds. Find the maximum height reached by the ball.

    a. 60 ft   **b.** 100 ft   **c.** 80 ft   **d.** 120 ft

36. Find the equation of the circle with radius 7 and center $(-6, 5)$.

    a. $(x-6)^2 + (y+5)^2 = 49$ **b.** $(x+6)^2 + (y-5)^2 = 7$

    c. $(x-6)^2 + (y+5)^2 = 7$ **d.** $(x+6)^2 + (y-5)^2 = 49$

37. Which is the graph of $\frac{x^2}{25} + \frac{y^2}{16} = 1$?

    a. 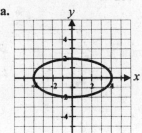   **b.** 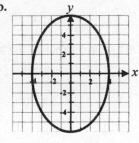   **c.** 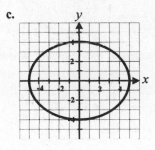   **d.**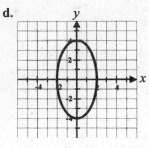

38. Solve: $\begin{aligned} 3x + 2y &= -10 \\ x + 2y &= -2 \end{aligned}$

    a. $(-4, 1)$ **b.** $(2, -2)$ **c.** $(4, -11)$ **d.** $(-2, 2)$

39. Solve: $\begin{aligned} 2x + 3y - z &= 1 \\ x - y + 3z &= -8 \\ 2x + y + 2z &= -6 \end{aligned}$

    a. $(-2, 3, 1)$ **b.** $(-3, 2, -1)$ **c.** $(-1, 2, 0)$ **d.** $(0, 3, -1)$

40. Evaluate the determinant: $\begin{vmatrix} 0 & 2 \\ -11 & 12 \end{vmatrix}$

    a. 0   **b.** 11   **c.** 22   **d.** -22

41. A cabin cruiser traveling with the current went 47.5 mi in 2.5 hours. Against the current, the boat could go only 27.5 mi in the same amount of time. Find the rate of the current.

    a.   3 mph   **b.**   7 mph   **c.**   5 mph   **d.**   4 mph

42. Evaluate: $\log_4 64$

    a.   16   **b.**   8   **c.**   256   **d.**   3

43. Solve for x: $\ln x = -3$
Round to the nearest ten-thousandth.

    a.   −8.1548   **b.**   −0.9061   **c.**   −20.0855   **d.**   0.0498

44. Write $\log_3 \sqrt[5]{x^2 y^3}$ in expanded form.

    a. $\dfrac{2}{5}\log_3 x + \dfrac{3}{5}\log_3 y$ **b.** $\dfrac{5}{2}\log_3 x + \dfrac{5}{3}\log_3 y$ **c.** $2\log_3 x + 3\log_3 y$ **d.** $\dfrac{1}{5}\log_3 x - \dfrac{1}{5}\log_3 y$

45. Solve for x: $6^x = 12$
Round to the nearest ten-thousandth.

    a.   2.1423   **b.**   1.1082   **c.**   1.3869   **d.**   1.567

46. Solve for x: $\log_4\left(x^2 + 2\right) - \log_4\left(2x - 1\right) = \log_4 2$

    a.   −2   **b.**   2 and −3   **c.**   2   **d.**   −2 and 3

47. Write the 7th and 10th terms of the sequence whose nth term is given by the formula $a_n = \dfrac{n-3}{2n-1}$.

    a. $\dfrac{4}{13}, \dfrac{7}{19}$ **b.** $\dfrac{4}{15}, \dfrac{1}{3}$ **c.** $\dfrac{7}{13}, \dfrac{10}{19}$ **d.** $\dfrac{4}{13}, \dfrac{10}{19}$

48. The distance a ball rolls down a ramp each second is given by an arithmetic sequence. The distance in feet traveled by the ball in each of the first three seconds is given by the sequence: 4, 12, 20. Find the total distance traveled during 8 seconds.

    a.   256 ft   **b.**   128 ft   **c.**   60 ft   **d.**   214 ft

49. Find an equivalent fraction for $0.2\overline{46}$

    a. $\dfrac{122}{495}$ **b.** $\dfrac{37}{150}$ **c.** $\dfrac{82}{333}$ **d.** $\dfrac{1109}{4500}$

50. Find the 3rd term in the expansion of $\left(x - 2y\right)^{10}$.

    a. $20x^9 y$ **b.** $180x^2 y^8$ **c.** $960x^7 y^3$ **d.** $180x^8 y^2$

Form H Tests

Multiple Choice

Name: _____

Date: _____

1. Find the additive inverse of $-\dfrac{1}{5}$.

    a. -5 **b.** $\varnothing$ **c.** 5   **d.** $\dfrac{1}{5}$

2. Write the set of real numbers greater than -3 in set-builder notation.

    a. $\{x \mid x \le -3\}$ **b.** $\{x \mid x > -3\}$ **c.** $\{x \mid x < -3\}$ **d.** $\{x \mid x \ge -3\}$

3. Simplify: $2 + (-6) - (-4) + (-3)$

    a. -25 **b.** -19 **c.** -3 **d.** 25

4. Simplify: $-3(-9)(-2)$

    a. -54 **b.** 54   **c.** -33 **d.** 33

5. Simplify: $-117 \div (-9)$

    a. -13 **b.** -11 **c.** 11   **d.** 13

6. Write $\{x \mid x > 3\}$ in interval notation.

    a. $(-\infty, 3)$ **b.** $(3, \infty)$ **c.** $(-\infty, 3]$ **d.** $[3, \infty)$

7. Simplify: $3(-4)^2(-3)^3$

    a. 216   **b.** -1296 **c.** -216 **d.** 864

8. Simplify: $-2^4 \cdot (-3)^2$

    a. 144   **b.** 36   **c.** -144 **d.** -72

9. Simplify: $-\dfrac{1}{4} + \dfrac{5}{24} - \dfrac{5}{8}$

    a. $-\dfrac{2}{3}$ **b.** $\dfrac{3}{8}$ **c.** $-\dfrac{3}{2}$ **d.** $\dfrac{7}{12}$

10. Simplify: $\left(\dfrac{3}{4}\right)\left(-\dfrac{8}{21}\right)\left(\dfrac{7}{15}\right)$

    a. $-\dfrac{1}{4}$ **b.** $-\dfrac{2}{15}$ **c.** $-\dfrac{19}{40}$ **d.** $\dfrac{19}{40}$

11. Simplify: $-1.414 + (-5.1634)$

    a. 3.7494   **b.** -6.5774 **c.** 6.5774   **d.** -3.7494

12. Simplify: $3.06 \times (-5.1)$

    a. -8.16 **b.** -15.606 **c.** -7.04 **d.** 15.606

13. Simplify: $14 - 2\left[15 \div (-5)\right]^2 + 3 \cdot 8 - 5$

    a. -22 b. 54 c. 15 d. -14

14. Simplify: $\dfrac{2}{5} - \left[\dfrac{3}{8} \div \left(-\dfrac{3}{2}\right)\right] - \dfrac{1}{3}$

    a. $-\dfrac{11}{60}$ b. $\dfrac{59}{60}$ c. $\dfrac{19}{60}$ d. $\dfrac{13}{60}$

15. Evaluate $(3a - 2b) \div (a \cdot b)$ when $a = -1$ and $b = -3$.

    a. -1 b. -6 c. 1 d. 6

16. Evaluate $\dfrac{2a - 4c}{ab + b}$ when $a = -3$, $b = -1$, and $c = 2$.

    a. -7 b. $-\dfrac{7}{2}$ c. 1 d. 7

17. Which statement illustrates the Commutative Property of Addition?

    a. $2 \times 8 = 8 \times 2$
    b. $2 + 8 = 8 + 2$
    c. $2x = 2x$
    d. $2 + (3 + 4) = (2 + 3) + 4$

18. Which property justifies the statement: $17x \cdot 1 = 17x$?

    a. The Commutative Property of Multiplication
    b. The Multiplication Property of One
    c. The Distributive Property
    d. The Inverse Property of Multiplication

19. Simplify: $4x - 2\left[5x - 2(x - 2y) - 3y\right]$

    a. $x - 2y$ b. $x + y$ c. $-2x + 4y$ d. $-2x - 2y$

20. Simplify: $2x - 2\left[3x - 3(x - 4y) - 2y\right]$

    a. $14x - 20y$ b. $2x - 14y$ c. $2x - 20y$ d. $5x - 14y$

21. Translate and simplify "a number increased by the sum of the number and 10."

    a. $2n + 10$ b. $n + 10$ c. $n + 20$ d. $12n$

22. The length of a rectangle is the square root of the width. Express the length of the rectangle in terms of the width.

    a. w^2 b. $2w$ c. $\sqrt{w}$ d. $\sqrt{\ell - w}$

23. Find $A \cup B$, given $A = \{-1, 0, 1\}$ and $B = \{0, 1\}$.

    a. $\{-1, 0, 1\}$ b. $\{1\}$ c. $\{0, 1\}$ d. $\varnothing$

24. Find $A \cap B$, given $A = \{-8, -6, -4\}$ and $B = \{4, 6, 8\}$.

    a. $\{-8, -6, -4, 4, 6, 8\}$ b. $\{-6, -4\}$ c. $\varnothing$ d. $\{0\}$

1. Solve: $-\dfrac{8}{15}b = \dfrac{14}{25}$

   a. $\dfrac{21}{20}$ **b.** $-\dfrac{21}{20}$ **c.** $\dfrac{5}{6}$ **d.** $\dfrac{4}{5}$

2. Solve: $x + \dfrac{3}{5} = \dfrac{1}{2}$

   a. $\dfrac{11}{10}$ **b.** $-\dfrac{1}{10}$ **c.** $\dfrac{2}{3}$ **d.** $\dfrac{1}{10}$

3. Solve: $3x + 7 = 5x - 7$

   a. $\dfrac{3}{2}$ **b.** $\dfrac{7}{4}$ **c.** 7 **d.** 0

4. Solve: $13 - 3x = x + 5 - 2x$

   a. 4 **b.** 1 **c.** 0 **d.** no solution

5. Solve $\dfrac{A + 2L}{3} = C$ for L.

   a. $L = \dfrac{3}{2}(C - A)$ **b.** $L = \dfrac{3C}{2} - A$ **c.** $L = \dfrac{1}{3}C - \dfrac{A}{2}$ **d.** $L = \dfrac{3C - A}{2}$

6. Solve: $3x - 4 = 6 - 2(5x - 8)$

   a. 4 **b.** -1 **c.** -3 **d.** 2

7. Solve: $\dfrac{x - 3}{4} = 3 - \dfrac{x}{6}$

   a. 9 **b.** 1 **c.** 3 **d.** 0

8. Solve $6x - 3 > 4x - 5$ and write the solution set in interval notation.

   a. $(1, \infty)$ **b.** $(-\infty, -1)$ **c.** $(-1, \infty)$ **d.** $(-\infty, 1)$

9. Choose the graph that shows the solution set of $3(2-3x)-4 \geq 3(x-4)-8x$.

   a.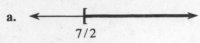

   b.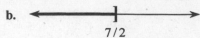

   c.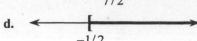

   d.

10. Solve $3x-2>4$ or $5x+1<-4$ and write the solution set in set-builder notation.

    a. $\{x|-1<x\leq 2\}$ b. $\{x|x>2 \text{ or } x<-1\}$ c. $\{x|x<-1 \text{ or } x\leq 2\}$ d. $\{x|x>2 \text{ or } x\leq -1\}$

11. Solve $2x-3\leq 3$ and $2x-7<19$ and write the solution set in interval notation.

    a. $[-3,13)$ b. $(-\infty,-3]\cap(13,\infty)$ c. $(-\infty,3]$ d. $(-\infty,-3]\cap(-\infty,13)$

12. You can rent a car from Hillcrest Agency for $20 a day and 10¢ a mile or from Cushman Rental for $25 a day and 5¢ a mile. You want to rent a car for one week. How many miles can you drive a Hillcrest Agency car during the week if it is to cost you less than a Cushman Rental car?

    a. less than 700 mi   b. less than 600 mi   c. less than 800 mi   d. less than 500 mi

13. Solve: $|2x-1|=5$

    a. 2 and –3   b. –2 and 3   c. $-\frac{2}{5}$ and $-\frac{7}{2}$ d. no solution

14. Solve: $9-|3x-4|=7$

    a. 2   b. 2 and $\frac{2}{3}$ c. 2 and –2   d. no solution

15. Solve $|3x+1|\geq -3$ and write the solution set in set-builder notation.

    a. $\varnothing$ b. $\{x|x<0 \text{ or } x>-1\}$

    c. $\{x|x\in \text{ real numbers}\}$ d. $\{x>2 \text{ or } x<-1\}$

16. Find the lower and upper limits of a 6000-ohm resistor with a 6% tolerance.

    a. 5500 ohms, 6500 ohms   b. 4900 ohms, 5050 ohms

    c. 200 ohms, 300 ohms   d. 5820 ohms, 6180 ohms

17. The sum of three numbers is thirty-one. The second number is twice the first number, and the third number is six more than the second number. Find the second number.

    a. 10   b. 16   c. 8   d. 5

18. Using five-dollar bills, ten-dollar bills, and twenty-dollar bills, a bank teller cashes a check for $185. In all, fourteen bills were handed to the customer. The number of twenty-dollar bills was twice the number of five-dollar bills. Find the number of ten-dollar bills given to the customer.

    a. 10   b. 3   c. 7   d. 5

19. Ninety liters of pure maple syrup that costs $8.00 per liter are mixed with imitation maple syrup that costs $2.80 per liter. How much imitation maple syrup is needed to make a mixture to sell for $5.14 per liter?

    a. 110 L   b. 120 L   c. 130 L   d. 140 L

20. A commuter plane flies to a small town from a major airport. The average speed flying to the small town was 240 mi/h and the average speed returning was 180 mi/h. The total flying time was 7 hours. Find the distance between the two airports.

    a. 720 mi   b. 800 mi   c. 640 mi   d. 460 mi

21. How many ounces of pure water must be added to 75 oz of a 8% salt solution to make a 6% salt solution?

    a. 15 oz   b. 25 oz   c. 50 oz   d. 40 oz

22. A chemist mixed a 40% alcohol solution with a 12% alcohol solution to make a 20% alcohol solution. How many milliliters of the 40% alcohol solution were used to make 245 ml of the 20% solution?

    a. 60 ml   b. 125 ml   c. 70 ml   d. 175 ml

1. Which point has coordinates $(-3, -2)$?

   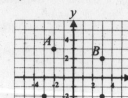

   a. A
   b. B
   c. C
   d. D

2. Find the ordered-pair solution of $y = x^2 - 5$ when $x = -3$.

   a. $(-3, 4)$ b. $(-3, -14)$ c. $(-3, 64)$ d. $(\sqrt{2}, -3)$

3. Which is the graph of $y = -\dfrac{5}{4}x + 2$?

   a. 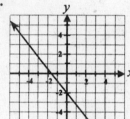   b. 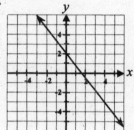   c. 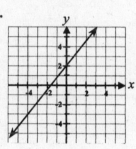   d.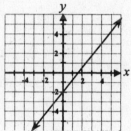

4. Which is the graph of $2x + y = 3$?

   a. 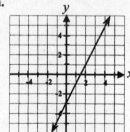   b. 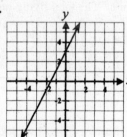   c. 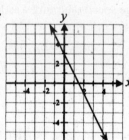   d.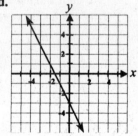

5. Find the slope of the line containing the points $P_1(-5, 1)$ and $P_2(-3, 3)$.

   a. $-\dfrac{1}{4}$ b. $\dfrac{2}{3}$ c. 1 d. -1

6. Given: $f(x) = 2x^2 - x + 6$, evaluate $f(-2)$.

   a. 16 b. 12 c. 0 d. -4

7. Find the x-intercept of the line $2x - y = 5$.

    a. $(0, -4)$　　　　b. $(0, 4)$　　　　c. $\left(\dfrac{5}{2}, 0\right)$　　　　d. $\left(-\dfrac{2}{5}, 0\right)$

8. Which is the graph of the line that passes through the point $(1, -3)$ and has slope $\dfrac{3}{2}$?

    a. 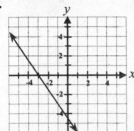　　b. 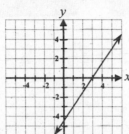　　c. 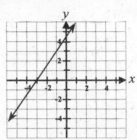　　d.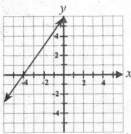

9. Find the equation of the line that contains the point $(3, -3)$ and has slope -2.

    a. $y = \dfrac{1}{2}x + 3$　　b. $y = -2x + 3$　　c. $y = -3x - 2$　　d. $y = 2x - 3$

10. Find the equation of the line containing the points $P_1(1, -4)$ and $P_2(2, 3)$.

    a. $y = -x - 5$　　b. $y = 7x + 17$　　c. $y = x - 5$　　d. $y = 7x - 11$

11. Find the equation of the line that contains the point $(3, -1)$ and is perpendicular to the line $3x - y = 5$.

    a. $y = -\dfrac{1}{3}x$　　b. $y = -\dfrac{1}{3}x - 2$　　c. $y = \dfrac{1}{3}x - 2$　　d. $y = -\dfrac{1}{3}x + 2$

12. Which of the following relations is not a function?

    a. $\{(-1, 3), (3, -1), (-1, 4)\}$　　　　　　b. $\{(0, 1), (1, 1), (2, 1)\}$

    c. $\{(1, 1), (2, 2), (3, 3)\}$　　　　　　d. $\{(-1, 2), (-3, 4), (-2, 2)\}$

13. What values of x are excluded from the domain of $f(x) = \dfrac{x - 1}{x + 7}$?

    a. 1　　　　b. 7　　　　c. -1　　　　d. -7

Name: _____

14. Which is the graph of the solution set of $2x - y < 4$?

a. 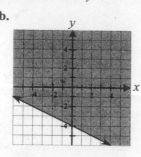   b. 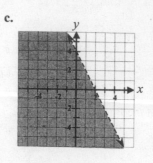   c. 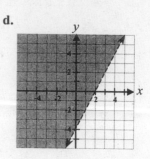   d.

15. Find the midpoint of the line segment between $P_1(3,-1)$ and $P_2(-4,-2)$.

a. $\left(-\dfrac{1}{2}, -\dfrac{3}{2}\right)$ b. $\left(\dfrac{7}{2}, 0\right)$ c. $\left(-\dfrac{1}{2}, 0\right)$ d. $\left(-\dfrac{7}{2}, -\dfrac{1}{2}\right)$

16. Find the length of the line segment between $P_1(4,-3)$ and $P_2(2,5)$.

a. $\sqrt{53}$ b. $2\sqrt{17}$ c. $2\sqrt{2}$ d. $\sqrt{15}$

17. Find the equation of the line that contains the point $(5,-3)$ and has undefined slope.

a. $x = 5$ b. $y = -3$ c. $x = -3$ d. $y = 5$

18. A furniture manufacturer determines that the cost to produce 120 desks is \$10,640. The cost to produce 140 desks is \$12,320. Write a linear equation for the cost, y, to produce x desks.

a. $y = 12x + 9200$ b. $y = 120x + 10640$ c. $y = 20x + 1680$ d. $y = 84x + 560$

Problems 19 and 20 both refer to the graph below.

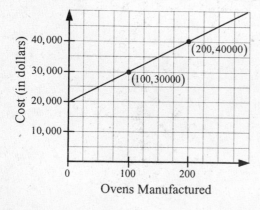

19. The graph to the left shows the relationship between the cost of manufacturing microwave ovens and the number of ovens manufactured. Which of the following statements describes the meaning of the ordered pair $(100, 30000)$?

a. When 100 ovens are manufactured, the cost of each oven is \$30,000.
b. The cost of manufacturing 100 ovens is \$30,000.
c. When 30,000 ovens are manufactured, the cost of each oven is \$100.
d. When 100 ovens are sold, the revenue is \$30,000.

20. Find the number of microwave ovens that were manufactured if the cost of manufacturing was \$45,000.

a. 175 ovens   b. 150 ovens   c. 200 ovens   d. 250 ovens

1. Simplify: $3(-4)^2 \cdot (-1)^3$

       a. −48   **b.** −144   **c.** −36   **d.** 42

2. Simplify: $6 - 2\left[1 - 4(3-7)^2\right]$

       a. −102   **b.** −252   **c.** 132   **d.** −120

3. Evaluate $b^2 - 4ac + a$ when $a = -1$, $b = 2$, and $c = -4$.

       a. 19   **b.** 11   **c.** −13   **d.** −21

4. Simplify: $4x - 2(x - 3y) + 5y$

       a. $2x - 11y$ **b.** $2x - y$ **c.** $6x + 11y$ **d.** $2x + 11y$

5. Translate and simplify "ten added to twice the sum of a number and three."

       a. $2n + 16$ **b.** $2n + 10$ **c.** $2n + 6$ **d.** $2n + 3$

6. Find $A \cap B$, given $A = \{-10, -6, -2, 0\}$ and $B = \{0, 5, 7, 9\}$.

       a. $\{-10, -6, -4, -2, 0, 5, 7, 9\}$ **b.** $\{-10, -6, -2, 0, 5, 7, 9\}$

       c. $\varnothing$ **d.** $\{0\}$

7. Solve: $\dfrac{4}{9}t = -8$

       a. 6   **b.** −18   **c.** $-\dfrac{27}{2}$ **d.** 18

8. Solve: $\dfrac{2x-1}{3} - \dfrac{3x+2}{4} = \dfrac{x-6}{12}$

       a. $-\dfrac{1}{2}$ **b.** 4   **c.** −2   **d.** $\dfrac{1}{4}$

9. Solve $5(x - 2) + 8 > 2(x + 4) - 12$ and write the solution set in interval notation.

       a. $\left(-\dfrac{2}{3}, \infty\right)$ **b.** $\left(-\infty, -\dfrac{2}{3}\right)$ **c.** $\left(\dfrac{2}{3}, \infty\right)$ **d.** $(-2, \infty)$

10. Solve: $|2x-5|+3=7$

    a. no solution   **b.** 2 and 10   **c.** −3 and −2   **d.** $\dfrac{1}{2}$ and $\dfrac{9}{2}$

11. A stamp collection consists of 6¢, 13¢, and 18¢ stamps. There are 26 stamps in the collection and there are twice as many 13¢ stamps as there are 6¢ stamps. The total value of the stamps in the collection is $2.92. Find the number of 18¢ stamps in the collection.

    a. 3   **b.** 8   **c.** 6   **d.** 2

12. How many pounds of an 8% aluminum alloy must be mixed with 2000 lb of a 23% aluminum alloy to make a 20% aluminum alloy?

    a. 800 lb   **b.** 500 lb   **c.** 1200 lb   **d.** 400 lb

13. Given $f(x)=x^2+3x-5$, evaluate $f(-3)$.

    a. 13   **b.** −2   **c.** −5   **d.** 6

14. Solve $\dfrac{Ah-\ell}{p}=k$ for h.

    a. $h=\dfrac{kp}{A}+\ell$ **b.** $h=\dfrac{p(k+\ell)}{A}$ **c.** $h=\dfrac{kp+\ell}{A}$ **d.** $h=\dfrac{k+\ell}{pA}$

15. Which is the graph of $y=-3x-4$?

    a.   **b.**   **c.**   **d.**

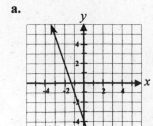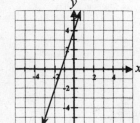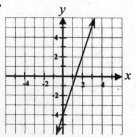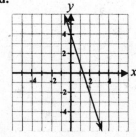

16. Find the slope of the line containing the points $P_1(-3,-4)$ and $P_2(-1,-7)$.

   a. $-\dfrac{3}{2}$ **b.** $\dfrac{3}{2}$ **c.** $-\dfrac{2}{3}$ **d.** $\dfrac{2}{3}$

17. Find the equation of the line that contains the point $(3,-3)$ and has slope $-\dfrac{2}{3}$.

   a. $y=-\dfrac{2}{3}x$ **b.** $y=\dfrac{2}{3}x+1$ **c.** $y=\dfrac{2}{3}x+3$ **d.** $y=-\dfrac{2}{3}x-1$

18. Find the equation of the line that contains the point $(-4,1)$ and is perpendicular to the line $x-2y=6$.

   a. $y=2x-7$ **b.** $y=2x+9$ **c.** $y=-2x-7$ **d.** $y=\dfrac{1}{2}x+3$

19. The graph below shows the relationship between the cost of a van and the depreciation allowed for income tax purposes. Write the equation that represents the depreciated value of the van.

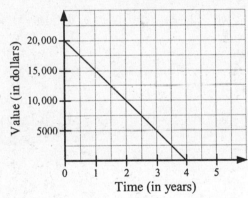

   a. $y=5000x+20000$

   b. $y=-\dfrac{1}{5000}x+20000$

   c. $y=5000x-20000$

   d. $y=-5000x+20000$

20. Which is the graph of the solution set of $3x+y\le 6$?

   a.   **b.**   **c.**   **d.**

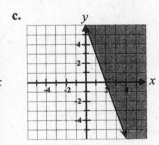

1. Choose the graph that shows the solution to the following system of equations: $3x + 2y = 6$
$$3x - 2y = 6$$

a. 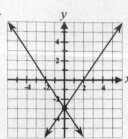   b. 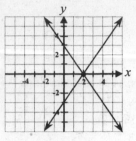   c. 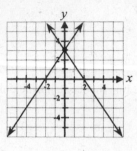   d.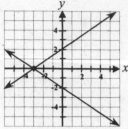

2. Solve by substitution: $y = 6x - 7$
$$y = 2x + 1$$

   a. $(1, -1)$ b. $(-2, -13)$ c. $(-1, -1)$ d. $(2, 5)$

3. An investment of $3200 is made at an annual simple interest rate of 6.2% . How much additional money must be invested at an annual simple interest rate of 8.4% so that the total interest earned is $618.40 ?

   a. $3000   b. $3600   c. $5000   d. $4500

4. Solve by the addition method: $3x + 4y = -2$
$$5x - y = 12$$

   a. $(-4, 2)$ b. $(3, 3)$ c. $(2, -2)$ d. $(6, -5)$

5. Solve by the addition method: $2y - 3z = 10$
$$2x + y = 0$$
$$3x + z = -5$$

   a. $(1, -2, -1)$ b. $(-1, -2, 2)$ c. $(-1, 2, -2)$ d. $(0, 2, -2)$

6. Evaluate the determinant: $\begin{vmatrix} 5 & -5 \\ 1 & -1 \end{vmatrix}$

   a. 0   b. -1 c. -10 d. 10

7. Evaluate the determinant: $\begin{vmatrix} -2 & 1 & -2 \\ 1 & 2 & -1 \\ 4 & 1 & -4 \end{vmatrix}$

   a. 44   b. 8   c. -8 d. 28

8. Solve by using Cramer's Rule: $3x - 2y = 5$
$$x + 3y = 7$$

   a. $\left(\dfrac{3}{7}, -\dfrac{5}{7} \right)$ b. $\left(\dfrac{29}{11}, \dfrac{16}{11} \right)$ c. $(-2, 3)$ d. $(1, 2)$

9. Solve by using Cramer's Rule: $x - 2y + z = -4$
                                     $2x + 4y - 3z = -5$
                                       $-x + y - 5z = -1$

     a. $(1, -3, 1)$ **b.** $(-3, 1, 1)$ **c.** $(1, 1, -3)$ **d.** $(1, -1, -2)$

10. Flying with the wind, a small plane flew 530 mi in 2 hours. Against the wind, the plane flew 645 mi in 3 hours. Find the rate of the plane in calm air.

     a. 240 mph   **b.** 180 mph   **c.** 210 mph   **d.** 220 mph

11. A cabin cruiser traveling with the current went 72 mi in 3 hours. The return trip against the current required 6 hours. Find the rate of the boat in calm water.

     a. 24 mph   **b.** 18 mph   **c.** 12 mph   **d.** 6 mph

12. At a Friday night performance of a play, 120 adult and 75 student tickets were sold. The total receipts were $750. At the Saturday afternoon performance, 80 adult and 110 student tickets were sold for total receipts of $620. Find the cost of a student ticket.

     a. $1.50   **b.** $1.75   **c.** $2.00   **d.** $2.25

13. During one month, a homeowner used 400 units of electricity and 150 units of gas for a total cost of $76.50. The next month, 450 units of electricity and 100 units of gas were used for a total cost of $78.50. Find the cost per unit of gas.

     a. $0.15   **b.** $0.13   **c.** $0.11   **d.** $0.17

14. Choose the graph that shows the solution set for the system of inequalities: $y \le 4$
                                                                           $3x - y > -6$

a. 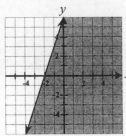   **b.** 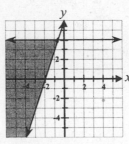   **c.** 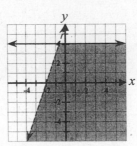   **d.**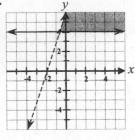

15. Choose the graph that shows the solution set for the system of inequalities: $y \ge -3$
                                                                                $2y < -x + 6$

a. 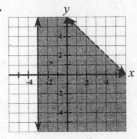   **b.** 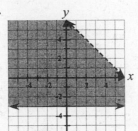   **c.** 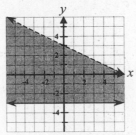   **d.**

Name: _____
Date: _____

1. Simplify: $(5x^2 + 3x - 5) + (-3x^2 - 8x + 1)$

   a. $2x^2 - 5x - 4$ b. $8x^2 + 5x - 6$ c. $-2x^2 + 5x - 4$ d. $2x^2 + 5x + 4$

2. Simplify: $\dfrac{(4a^{-3}b^4)^{-1}}{(a^2b^{-2})^{-2}}$

   a. $\dfrac{a}{4}$ b. $\dfrac{a^7}{4b^8}$ c. $\dfrac{4a^7}{b^8}$ d. $\dfrac{a^7}{4b^4}$

3. Write 0.00000102 in scientific notation.

   a. 1.02×10^6 b. 1.02×10^{-6} c. 1.02×10^{-5} d. 10.2×10^{-6}

4. The distance to the moon is 230,000 mi. A satellite leaves the earth traveling at a constant speed of 30,000 mph. How long does it take the satellite to reach the moon? Round to the nearest hundredth.

   a. 92 h   b. 57.5 h   c. 12 h   d. 7.67 h

5. Simplify: $a^n(5a^{3n} - 2a^{2n} - a^n)$

   a. $5a^{4n} - 2a^{3n} - a^{2n}$ b. $5a^{3n^2} - 2a^{2n^2} - a^{2n^2}$

   c. $5a^{2n} - a^n - 1$ d. $5a^{4n} - 2a^{2n} - a^{n^2}$

6. Simplify: $6b - b[b - 3(2 - 3b) + 4b^2]$

   a. $-4b^3 - 10b^2 + 6b + 6$ b. $-4b^3 - 10b^2 + 12b$

   c. $-4b^3 - 9b^2 + 13b$ d. $-4b^3 - 9b^2 + 7b + 6$

7. Simplify: $(x^n + 4)(2x^n - 5)$

   a. $2x^{2n} - 11x^n - 15$ b. $2x^{2n} - 3x^n - 20$ c. $2x^{n^2} - x^n - 20$ d. $2x^{2n} + 3x^n - 20$

8. Simplify: $(3a - 2b)(a^2 - 3ab + 4b^2)$

   a. $3a^3 - 7a^2b + 6ab^2 - 8b^3$ b. $3a^3 + 7a^2b - 12ab^2 - 8b^3$

   c. $3a^3 - 11a^2b + 18ab^2 - 8b^3$ d. $3a^3 + 11a^2b - 18ab^2 - 8b^3$

9. Simplify: $(4a - 1)^2$

   a. $16a^2 + 1$ b. $16a^2 - 1$ c. $16a^2 - 8a + 1$ d. $16a^2 + 8a + 1$

10. The length of a box is $(x + 5)$ cm. The width is $(x - 5)$ cm, and the height is x cm. Find the volume of the box in terms of the variable x.

    a. $(x^3 - 25x)$ cm³   b. $(x^3 + 10x^2 - 25x)$ cm³

    c. $(x^3 - 10x^2 - 25x)$ cm³   d. $(x^3 + 25x^2)$ cm³

11. Factor: $4a^3b - 4a^2b^2 + 2ab^3$

    a. $2a(2a^2b - 2ab^2 + 2b^3)$ **b.** $ab(4a^2 - 4ab + 2b^2)$

    c. $2ab(2a^2 - 2ab + 1)$ **d.** $2ab(2a^2 - 2ab + b^2)$

12. Factor: $x^2y + 2x^2 - 2y - 4$

    a. $(x^2 + 1)(y - 2)$ **b.** $(x^2 - 2)(y + 1)$ **c.** $(x^2 - 2)(y + 2)$ **d.** $(x^2 + 2 + 2)(y - 1)$

13. Factor: $a^2 + 10ab + 16b^2$

    a. $(a + 2b)(a + 4b)$ **b.** $(a + 2b)(a + 8b)$ **c.** $(a + 4b)(a + 4b)$ **d.** $(a - 8b)(a - 2b)$

14. Factor: $35x^2 - 11xy - 6y^2$

    a. $(5x - 3y)(7x + 2y)$ **b.** $(5x - 3y)(7x - 2y)$ **c.** $(5x + 3y)(7x - 2y)$ **d.** $(5x + 3y)(7x + 2y)$

15. Factor: $16a^2 - 56ab + 49b^2$

    a. $(4a - 7b)^2$ **b.** $(4a + 7b)^2$ **c.** $(4a - 7b)(4a + 7b)$ **d.** nonfactorable

16. Factor: $8a^3 - 27b^3$

    a. $(2a - 3b)(4a^2 - 6ab + 9b^2)$ **b.** $(2a - 3b)(4a^2 + 6ab + 9b^2)$

    c. $(2a + 3b)(4a^2 - 6ab + 9b^2)$ **d.** $(2a + 3b)(4a^2 + 6ab + 9b^2)$

17. Divide by using long division: $\dfrac{x^3 - 2x^2 + 3x + 28}{x + 2}$

    a. $x^2 - 4x + 11 + \dfrac{21}{x + 2}$ **b.** $x^2 - 4x + 12 + \dfrac{3}{x + 2}$ **c.** $x^2 - 4x + 11 + \dfrac{6}{x + 2}$ **d.** $x^2 - 4x + 12 - \dfrac{21}{x + 2}$

18. Factor: $a^4 - 81$

    a. $(a - 3)(a + 3)(a^2 + 9)$ **b.** $(a^2 - 9)(a^2 + 9)$

    c. $(a - 3)(a + 3)(a^2 - 3a + 9)$ **d.** $(a - 3)(a^3 - 27)$

19. Solve: $8x^2 + 29x - 12 = 0$

    a. -8 and $\dfrac{3}{4}$ **b.** -4 and $\dfrac{8}{3}$ **c.** 4 and $-\dfrac{1}{8}$ **d.** -4 and $\dfrac{3}{8}$

20. Solve: $12x^2 = 17x - 6$

    a. $-\dfrac{3}{4}$ and $-\dfrac{2}{3}$ **b.** $-\dfrac{3}{4}$ and $\dfrac{2}{3}$ **c.** $\dfrac{3}{4}$ and $-\dfrac{2}{3}$ **d.** $\dfrac{3}{4}$ and $\dfrac{2}{3}$

1. Simplify: $\dfrac{3x^2y^2 + 4xy - 4}{6x^2y^2 - 19xy + 10}$

    a. $\dfrac{xy+2}{2xy-5}$

    b. $\dfrac{xy-2}{2xy+5}$

    c. $-\dfrac{2}{5}$

    d. $\dfrac{3xy-5}{2xy+5}$

2. Simplify: $\dfrac{x^3 + x^2y - 6xy^2}{x^2 - 2xy}$

    a. $x - 2y$

    b. $x(x+3y)$

    c. $x(x-2y)$

    d. $x + 3y$

3. Simplify: $\dfrac{x^2 - 6x + 8}{x^2 - 16} \cdot \dfrac{9x^2 - 45x - 54}{3x^2 - 24x + 36}$

    a. $\dfrac{x+1}{3(x+4)}$

    b. $\dfrac{3(x+1)}{x+4}$

    c. $-\dfrac{3(x+1)}{x+4}$

    d. 3

4. Simplify: $\dfrac{x^3 - 1}{5x^3 + 5x^2 + 5x} \cdot \dfrac{x^2 + x}{x^2 - 1}$

    a. $\dfrac{1}{5}$

    b. $\dfrac{(x^2 - x + 1)(x - 1)}{(x^2 + x + 1)(x + 1)}$

    c. $\dfrac{x^2 + x + 1}{(x+1)(x+1)}$

    d. $\dfrac{x-1}{x+1}$

5. Simplify: $\dfrac{4x^2 - 9x + 2}{3x^2 - 2x - 8} \div \dfrac{8x^2 + 2x - 1}{6x^2 + 11x + 4}$

    a. $\dfrac{4x-1}{4x+1}$

    b. $\dfrac{2x+1}{2x-1}$

    c. 1

    d. $\dfrac{(x-2)(2x+1)}{(x+2)(2x-1)}$

6. Given $R(x) = \dfrac{x^2 - 1}{5 - 3x^2}$, find $R(-2)$.

    a. $\dfrac{3}{17}$

    b. $-\dfrac{3}{31}$

    c. $-\dfrac{3}{7}$

    d. $\dfrac{3}{7}$

7. Find the domain of $f(x) = \dfrac{x-2}{x^2 - 25}$

    a. $\{x \,|\, x \neq 2\}$

    b. $\{x \,|\, x \neq -5, 2, 5\}$

    c. $\{x \,|\, x \neq -5, 5\}$

    d. $\{x \,|\, x \in \text{real numbers}\}$

8. Find the missing numerator: $\dfrac{5}{3x^2 + 9x} = \dfrac{?}{6x^3 + 15x^2 - 9x}$

    a. $10x^2 - 5x$

    b. $5x^2 - 5x$

    c. $10x + 5$

    d. $10x - 5$

9. Simplify: $\dfrac{2x}{x-2} - \dfrac{7}{x^2 - 8x + 12}$

    a. $\dfrac{(2x-1)(x+7)}{(x-6)(x-2)}$

    b. $\dfrac{2x^2 - 12x - 7}{(x-6)(x-2)}$

    c. $\dfrac{x(2x-5)}{(x-6)(x-2)}$

    d. $\dfrac{2x^2 - 5x}{(x-6)(x-2)}$

10. Simplify: $\dfrac{\frac{3}{y^2} + \frac{7}{y} + 2}{1 + \frac{2}{y} - \frac{3}{y^2}}$

    a. $\dfrac{2y+1}{y-1}$

    b. $\dfrac{2y+1}{2y-3}$

    c. $\dfrac{y-3}{y-5}$

    d. 1

11. Simplify: $\dfrac{2-\frac{4}{x-1}}{6x-18}$

   a. $x-1$ **b.** $\dfrac{x-1}{3}$ **c.** $\dfrac{1}{3(x-1)}$ **d.** $\dfrac{x-1}{x-3}$

12. Solve: $\dfrac{5}{x+2}=\dfrac{3}{x-4}$

   a. 13   **b.** 7   **c.** -7 **d.** no solution

13. Solve: $\dfrac{3}{x+5}=\dfrac{7}{x-3}$

   a. $-\dfrac{29}{4}$ **b.** -11 **c.** 12   **d.** $-\dfrac{7}{4}$

14. Two hundred trout were tagged and then released into a pond. Later 60 trout were caught and examined, and 8 of the 60 trout were found to have tags. Estimate the number of trout in the pond.

   a. 1500 trout   **b.** 750 trout   **c.** 500 trout   **d.** 1000 trout

15. Solve: $\dfrac{-3a}{2a+5}-3=\dfrac{12}{2a+5}$

   a. $-\dfrac{1}{3}$ **b.** -3 **c.** 3   **d.** $\dfrac{1}{3}$

16. Solve: $\dfrac{8}{x^2-16}-\dfrac{2}{x+4}=\dfrac{3}{x-4}$

   a. $\dfrac{5}{6}$ **b.** $\dfrac{4}{5}$ **c.** -6 **d.** 30

17. Solve $S=V_0 t-16t^2$ for V_0.

   a. $V_0=\dfrac{S+16}{t^2}$ **b.** $V_0=\dfrac{S+16t}{t^2}$ **c.** $V_0=\dfrac{S+16t^2}{t}$ **d.** $V_0=\dfrac{S}{16t^2}$

18. The pressure, p, on a diver in the water varies directly as the depth, d. If the pressure is 5.5 lb/in^2 when the depth is 15 ft, what is the pressure when the depth is 18 ft?

   a. 9.9 lb/in^2 **b.** 9.6 lb/in^2 **c.** 12.2 lb/in^2 **d.** 6.6 lb/in^2

19. A mechanic requires 14 hours to do a job. After the mechanic and an apprentice work on a job for 8 hours, the mechanic quits. The apprentice finishes the job in 7 hours. How long would it have taken the apprentice working alone to do the job?

   a. 21 h   **b.** 35 h   **c.** 18 h   **d.** 24 h

20. A jet can fly at a rate of 480 mi/h in calm air. Traveling with the wind, the plane flew 1560 mi in the same amount of time it took to fly 1320 mi against the wind. Find the rate of the wind.

   a. 20 mph   **b.** 60 mph   **c.** 80 mph   **d.** 40 mph

Name: _____
Date: _____

1. Simplify: $5x^{n+2} \cdot x^{3n-1}$

   a. $5x^{-2n+3}$ b. $5x^{4n+1}$ c. 5^{3n^2+4n-2} d. 5^{4n-1}

2. Simplify: $\dfrac{\left(-8a^3b^2c\right)^2}{\left(4a^3bc^2\right)^3}$

   a. $\dfrac{2b}{a^3c^4}$ b. $\dfrac{2b}{a^3c^3}$ c. $\dfrac{b^2}{a^3c^3}$ d. $\dfrac{b}{a^3c^4}$

3. Simplify: $\left(4a^{-3}b^{-7}\right)^2\left(2a^{-2}b^{-3}\right)^{-3}$

   a. $\dfrac{2}{a^{12}b^5}$ b. $\dfrac{2b^{23}}{a^{12}}$ c. $\dfrac{2}{b^5}$ d. $\dfrac{128}{b^5}$

4. Simplify: $a^{n+1}\left(a^n - 3a + 3\right)$

   a. $a^{2n+1} - 3a^{n+1} + 3^{n+1}$

   b. $a^{n^2+n} - 3a^{n+1} + 3^{n+1}$

   c. $a^{n^2+n} - 3a^{n+2} + 3a^{n+1}$

   d. $a^{2n+1} - 3a^{n+2} + 3a^{n+1}$

5. Factor: $x^2 - 13xy + 40y^2$

   a. $(x+5y)(x+8y)$ b. $(x-5y)(x-8y)$ c. $(x-5y)(x+8y)$ d. $(x+5y)(x-8y)$

6. Factor: $x^3 - 27$

   a. $(x-3)(x^2+3x+9)$ b. $(x-3)(x^2-3x+9)$ c. $(x+3)(x^2-3x+9)$ d. $(x-3)(x^2-3x-9)$

7. Factor: $16a^4 - 36a^3 + 20a^2$

   a. $a^2(4a-5)^2$ b. $4a^2(a-1)(4a-5)$ c. $a^2(4a-5)(4a+5)$ d. $a^2(8a-5)(2a+5)$

8. Simplify: $\dfrac{x^3y^3}{2x^2-15x+18} \cdot \dfrac{x^2-5x-6}{x^4y^3}$

   a. $\dfrac{x+2}{x-3}$ b. $\dfrac{x+1}{x(2x-3)}$ c. $\dfrac{x-1}{x+2}$ d. $\dfrac{1}{x}$

9. Simplify: $\dfrac{x^{2n}-9}{5x^n-15} \div \dfrac{x^{n+1}+3x}{15x^3-25x^2}$

   a. $x(3x-5)$ b. $\dfrac{x}{3x-5}$ c. $\dfrac{3x-5}{x}$ d. $x(x^n+3)(3x-5)$

10. Simplify: $\dfrac{3}{4xy} + \dfrac{2}{3x} + \dfrac{5}{6y} - \dfrac{7}{2xy}$

    a. $\dfrac{2y+10x}{y}$ b. $\dfrac{5x-2y}{12xy}$ c. $\dfrac{-33+8y+10x}{12xy}$ d. $\dfrac{10x-8y}{12xy}$

11. Simplify: $\dfrac{1-\frac{2}{x+3}}{1-\frac{1}{x+2}}$

    a. $\dfrac{x+2}{x+3}$

    b. $\dfrac{x+3}{x-2}$

    c. $\dfrac{x-2}{x-3}$

    d. $\dfrac{x}{x-2}$

12. Solve: $\dfrac{10}{2x+3}=\dfrac{6}{x}$

    a. 10

    b. -9

    c. -5

    d. 8

13. Solve: $\dfrac{4}{x+2}+1=\dfrac{3}{x+2}$

    a. -2

    b. 6

    c. -3

    d. -1

14. The rate of a bicyclist is 5 mph faster than the rate of a runner. The bicyclist travels 12 mi in the same amount of time as it takes the runner to travel 8 mi. Find the rate of the runner.

    a. 8 mph

    b. 10 mph

    c. 12 mph

    d. 6 mph

15. Solve by substitution: $x-2y=8$
    $3x-4y=10$

    a. $(2,-4)$

    b. $(-6,-7)$

    c. $(-22,8)$

    d. $(4,-2)$

16. Solve by the addition method: $x-3y+z=12$
    $2x-3z=1$
    $2y+8z=2$

    a. $(2,-3,1)$

    b. $(-3,2,1)$

    c. $(-2,1,-1)$

    d. $(1,-3,1)$

17. Solve by using Cramer's Rule: $x-2y=8$
    $2x+3y=2$

    a. $(2,-3)$

    b. $(-2,3)$

    c. $(4,-2)$

    d. $(-2,4)$

18. Flying with the wind, a plane flew 1170 mi in 4.5 hours. Flying against the wind, the plane could fly only 990 mi in the same amount of time. Find the rate of the plane in calm air.

    a. 210 mph

    b. 360 mph

    c. 200 mph

    d. 240 mph

19. Evaluate the determinant: $\begin{vmatrix} 1 & 0 & -1 \\ 6 & 3 & 5 \\ 0 & 2 & -2 \end{vmatrix}$

    a. -28

    b. -16

    c. -8

    d. 0

20. Simplify: $\left(3x^2+7x-1\right)-\left(x^2-2x+3\right)$

    a. $4x^2-5x+4$

    b. $4x^2+5x+2$

    c. $2x^2+5x+2$

    d. $2x^2+9x-4$

Name: _____
Date: _____

1. Simplify: $\left(x^{2n} \cdot x^{n/2}\right)^4$

   a. $x^{5n/2}$ b. x^{4n} c. x^{9n} d. x^{10n}

2. Simplify: $\dfrac{\left(x^{1/2}y^{-2/3}\right)^6}{\left(x^{-3/4}y^{5/8}\right)^{-8}}$

   a. $\dfrac{x^9}{y}$ b. $\dfrac{x^3}{y}$ c. $\dfrac{y}{x^3}$ d. $x^9 y$

3. Write $5a^{5/3}$ as a radical expression.

   a. $\sqrt[3]{5a^5}$ b. $5\sqrt[5]{5a^3}$ c. $5\sqrt[3]{a}$ d. $5\sqrt[3]{a^5}$

4. Write $3x\sqrt[4]{y^3}$ as an exponential expression.

   a. $3xy^{3/4}$ b. $\left(3xy^3\right)^4$ c. $3xy^{4/3}$ d. $3(xy)^{4/3}$

5. Simplify: $\sqrt[5]{-32a^{10}b^5}$

   a. $-2a^2b$ b. $-2a^2b$ c. $2a^2b$ d. $-2ab$

6. Simplify: $\sqrt[3]{40a^{18}b^8}$

   a. $2a^6b^2\sqrt[3]{5b}$ b. $4a^6b^2\sqrt[3]{5b^2}$ c. $2a^6b^2\sqrt[3]{5b^2}$ d. $2a^5b^2\sqrt[3]{5ab}$

7. Simplify: $\sqrt{45x^8y^{15}}$

   a. $4x^2y^3\sqrt{y^3}$ b. $3x^4y^7\sqrt{5y}$ c. $5x^4y^8\sqrt{3y}$ d. $3x^2y^3\sqrt{5y}$

8. Simplify: $3\sqrt[3]{32x^4y^8} - 5y\sqrt[3]{4x^4y^5}$

   a. $xy\sqrt[3]{4xy}$ b. $11x^2\sqrt[3]{xy^2}$ c. $xy^2\sqrt[3]{4xy^2}$ d. x^2y^4

9. Simplify: $\sqrt{90x^3y} + 4\sqrt{10x^3y} - \sqrt{9x^3y}$

   a. $4x\sqrt{10xy}$ b. $13x\sqrt{xy}$ c. $\sqrt{91x^3y}$ d. $7x\sqrt{10xy} - 3x\sqrt{xy}$

10. Simplify: $2\sqrt{6xy} \cdot \sqrt{9x^2y} \cdot \sqrt{3xy^3}$

   a. $18x^2y^2\sqrt{2y}$ b. $12x^2y^2\sqrt{2y}$ c. $12x^2y\sqrt{3y}$ d. $6xy\sqrt{2xy}$

11. Simplify: $\left(\sqrt{3x}+2\right)\left(\sqrt{3x}-2\right)$

    a. $3x-2$ b. $6x-4$ c. $3x-4\sqrt{3}-4$ d. $3x-4$

12. Simplify: $\dfrac{\sqrt[3]{16ab^4}}{\sqrt[3]{32a^4b}}$

    a. $\dfrac{ab\sqrt[3]{2}}{2}$ b. $\dfrac{b\sqrt[3]{4}}{2a}$ c. $\dfrac{b\sqrt[3]{2}}{2a}$ d. $\dfrac{b\sqrt[3]{4}}{a}$

13. Simplify: $\dfrac{3\sqrt{x}+2}{\sqrt{x}}$

    a. $\dfrac{3+2\sqrt{x}}{x}$ b. $3x+2\sqrt{x}$ c. $\dfrac{3x+2\sqrt{x}}{x}$ d. $\dfrac{1+2\sqrt{x}}{x}$

14. Solve: $\sqrt{4x-3}+1=6$

    a. -7 b. 13 c. 7 d. 25

15. Solve: $\sqrt[3]{6-3x}=-3$

    a. -35 b. 11 c. 35 d. 70

16. Find the length of a rectangle that has a diagonal of 30 ft and a width of 18 ft.

    a.   24 ft   b.   21 ft   c.   27 ft   d.   25 ft

17. Simplify: $\sqrt{60}+\sqrt{-4}$

    a. $3\sqrt{6}$ b. $4\sqrt{15}+4i$ c. $\sqrt{54}$ d. $2\sqrt{15}+2i$

18. Simplify: $\left(7-\sqrt{-12}\right)+\left(5+\sqrt{-27}\right)$

    a. $12+i\sqrt{3}$ b. $12-i\sqrt{3}$ c. $12+i\sqrt{2}$ d. $12+5i\sqrt{3}$

19. Simplify: $\sqrt{-2}\left(\sqrt{6}-\sqrt{-12}\right)$

    a. $2\sqrt{3}-3i\sqrt{2}$ b. $2i\sqrt{3}+2\sqrt{6}$ c. $6+2i\sqrt{3}$ d. $2i\sqrt{3}-2\sqrt{6}$

20. Simplify: $\dfrac{2}{3-i}$

    a. $\dfrac{1}{5}-\dfrac{3}{5}i$ b. $\dfrac{3}{5}-\dfrac{1}{5}i$ c. $\dfrac{2}{3}+2i$ d. $\dfrac{3}{5}+\dfrac{1}{5}i$

Name: _____

Date: _____

1. Solve by factoring: $3x^2 + 2x = 8$

   a. -2 and $\dfrac{4}{3}$ **b.** 2 and $-\dfrac{4}{3}$ **c.** -4 and $\dfrac{2}{3}$ **d.** 4 and $-\dfrac{2}{3}$

2. Solve by factoring: $3x^2 - 20x + 12 = 0$

   a. 2 **b.** 1 and 4 **c.** $\dfrac{4}{3}$ and 3 **d.** $\dfrac{2}{3}$ and 6

3. Write a quadratic equation that has integer coefficients and has solutions -5 and $\dfrac{2}{3}$.

   a. $3x^2 + 13x - 10 = 0$ **b.** $3x^2 - 13x - 10 = 0$ **c.** $2x^2 + 7x - 15 = 0$ **d.** $2x^2 - 7x - 15 = 0$

4. Solve by taking square roots: $2(x-3)^2 = 50$

   a. -8 and 8 **b.** -2 and 8 **c.** -7 and 1 **d.** 0 and 5

5. Solve by taking square roots: $(x+3)^2 + 25 = 0$

   a. $3+5i$ and $3-5i$ **b.** $-3+\sqrt{5}$ and $-3-\sqrt{5}$

   c. $-3+5i$ and $-3-5i$ **d.** 2 and -8

6. Solve by completing the square: $x^2 - 12x + 48 = 0$

   a. $6+2i\sqrt{3}$ and $6-2i\sqrt{3}$ **b.** $6+2\sqrt{3}$ and $6-2\sqrt{3}$

   c. $-6+2i\sqrt{3}$ and $-6-2i\sqrt{3}$ **d.** 6 and -3

7. Solve by completing the square: $x^2 - 14x - 14 = 0$

   a. 7 and -2 **b.** $7+3\sqrt{7}$ and $7-3\sqrt{7}$

   c. $2+3i\sqrt{2}$ and $2-3i\sqrt{2}$ **d.** $-2+3\sqrt{2}$ and $-2-3\sqrt{2}$

8. Solve by using the quadratic formula: $2x^2 - 3x - 2 = 0$

   a. -1 and 4 **b.** -4 and 1 **c.** -2 and $\dfrac{1}{2}$ **d.** $-\dfrac{1}{2}$ and 2

9. Solve by using the quadratic formula: $x^2 - 5x + 7 = 0$

   a. $\dfrac{-5+\sqrt{77}}{2}$ and $\dfrac{-5-\sqrt{77}}{2}$ **b.** $\dfrac{5}{2}+\dfrac{i\sqrt{3}}{2}$ and $\dfrac{5}{2}-\dfrac{i\sqrt{3}}{2}$

   c. $\dfrac{5+\sqrt{77}}{2}$ and $\dfrac{5-\sqrt{77}}{2}$ **d.** $-\dfrac{5}{2}+\dfrac{i\sqrt{3}}{2}$ and $-\dfrac{5}{2}-\dfrac{i\sqrt{3}}{2}$

10. Use the discriminant to determine whether $x^2 - 2x + 5 = 0$ has one real number solution, one complex number solution, two real number solutions, or two complex number solutions.

    a. One complex number solution   **b.** One real number solution

    c. Two real number solutions   **d.** Two complex number solutions

11. Solve: $x^4 - 9 = 0$

    a. $\sqrt{3}, -\sqrt{3}, i\sqrt{3}$, and $-i\sqrt{3}$ **b.** $3, -3, 3i$, and $-3i$

    c. 3 and -3 **d.** $3i$ and $-3i$

12. Solve: $x + 8x^{1/2} - 9 = 0$

    a. 1 **b.** 1 and -3 **c.** 1 and $3i$ **d.** $\varnothing$

13. Solve: $x + \sqrt{x} - 12 = 0$

    a. 9 and -4 **b.** 9 **c.** 9 and 16 **d.** -9

14. Solve: $\sqrt{5 - x} = 2$

    a. 7 **b.** 3 **c.** 1 **d.** $\varnothing$

15. Solve: $\dfrac{2x}{2x + 1} - 3x = -1$

    a. $\dfrac{1}{2}$ **b.** $\dfrac{1}{3}$ **c.** $\dfrac{1}{2}$ and $-\dfrac{1}{3}$ **d.** $-\dfrac{1}{2}$ and $\dfrac{1}{3}$

16. Solve: $\dfrac{4}{x - 2} + \dfrac{4}{x + 2} = 3$

    a. -1 and $\dfrac{1}{3}$ **b.** $\dfrac{2\sqrt{15}}{3}$ and $-\dfrac{2\sqrt{15}}{3}$

    c. $\dfrac{3}{8}$ **d.** $\dfrac{4 + 2\sqrt{13}}{3}$ and $\dfrac{4 - 2\sqrt{13}}{3}$

17. Solve: $\dfrac{x}{x - 4} > 2$

    a. $\{x \mid x < -4 \text{ or } x > 8\}$ **b.** $\{x \mid x > 4 \text{ or } x > 8\}$ **c.** $\{x \mid 4 < x < 8\}$ **d.** $\varnothing$

18. Solve: $(2x - 3)(x + 2)(x - 2) > 0$

    a. $\{x \mid x > -2 \text{ or } x < 2\}$ **b.** $\left\{x \mid x < -2 \text{ or } \dfrac{3}{2} < x < 2\right\}$

    c. $\left\{x \mid -2 < x < \dfrac{3}{2} \text{ or } x > 2\right\}$ **d.** $\left\{x \mid x < -2 \text{ and } x > \dfrac{3}{2}\right\}$

19. The length of a rectangle is 2 ft less than three times the width. The area is 408 ft^2. Find the length of the rectangle.

    a.   12 ft   **b.**   34 ft   **c.**   22 ft   **d.**   30 ft

20. The difference between the squares of two consecutive even integers is 52. Find the smaller integer.

    a.   16   **b.**   10   **c.**   8   **d.**   12

Name: _____

Date: _____

1. Find the axis of symmetry of the parabola given by $y = x^2 - 6x$.

   a. $x = 3$ b. $y = 3$ c. $x = -3$ d. $y = -3$

2. Find the vertex of the parabola given by $y = 3x^2 - 6x + 1$.

   a. $(-2, 25)$ b. $(-1, 10)$ c. $(2, 1)$ d. $(1, -2)$

3. State the range of the function $f(x) = -2x^2 - 3$.

   a. $\{y \mid y \le -3\}$ b. $\{y \mid y \ge -3\}$ c. $\{y \mid y \le 3\}$ d. $\{y \mid y \ge 3\}$

4. Find the x-intercepts of the graph of $y = 4x^2 - 9$.

   a. $(3, 0), (-3, 0)$ b. $\left(\frac{3}{2}, 0\right), \left(-\frac{3}{2}, 0\right)$ c. $(2, 0), (-2, 0)$ d. $\left(0, \frac{3}{2}\right), \left(0, -\frac{3}{2}\right)$

5. Find the maximum value of the function $f(x) = -x^2 - 8x - 22$.

   a. 6 b. 22 c. -6 d. -22

6. Find the maximum area of a rectangle whose perimeter is 40 cm.

   a. 200 cm^2 b. 80 cm^2 c. 300 cm^2 d. 100 cm^2

7. Which is the graph of the function $f(x) = |x - 3|$?

   a. 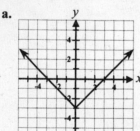 b. 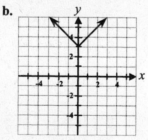 c. 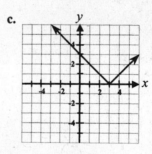 d.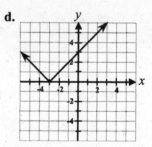

8. For $f(x) = 2 - x$ and $g(x) = x^2 - 1$, find $(f \cdot g)(3)$.

   a. -8 b. -24 c. -6 d. 0

9. For $f(x) = 2x^2 - 3$ and $g(x) = 5 - x$, find $f(3) - g(3)$.

   a. 7 b. 17 c. 13 d. -13

10. Given $f(x) = 3x + 6$ and $g(x) = \frac{1}{3}x + 2$, find $g[f(1)]$.

    a. $\dfrac{16}{3}$ **b.** 5   **c.** 12   **d.** 13

11. Given $g(x) = x^2 + 4$ and $h(x) = x - 1$, find $g[h(0)]$.

    a. 3   **b.** 5   **c.** −3   **d.** −5

12. Which of the graphs represent the graph of a 1-1 function?

   a. 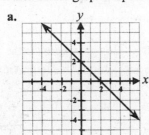   **b.** 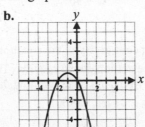   **c.** 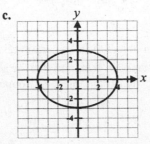   **d.**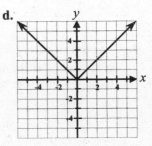

13. Let $f(x) = 3x + 1$. Find $f^{-1}(x)$.

    a. $f^{-1}(x) = \frac{1}{3}x + 1$ **b.** $f^{-1}(x) = \dfrac{1}{3x+1}$ **c.** $f^{-1}(x) = 1 - 3x$ **d.** $f^{-1}(x) = \frac{1}{3}x - \frac{1}{3}$

14. Which of the pairs of functions are inverses of each other?

    a. $f(x) = 2x - 3;\ g(x) = -2x + 3$ **b.** $f(x) = \frac{1}{2}x - 3;\ g(x) = 2x + 3$

    c. $f(x) = \frac{1}{2}x + \frac{3}{2};\ g(x) = 2x + 3$ **d.** $f(x) = 2x - 3;\ g(x) = \frac{1}{2}x + \frac{3}{2}$

15. Find the inverse of the function $\{(3,-1),(2,-2),(1,1)\}$.

    a. $\{(-1,3),(-2,2),(-1,1)\}$ **b.** $\{(3,-1),(2,-2),(1,1)\}$

    c. $\{(-1,3),(-2,2),(1,1)\}$ **d.** $\left\{\left(\frac{1}{3},-1\right),\left(\frac{1}{2},-\frac{1}{2}\right),(1,1)\right\}$

Name: _____

Date: _____

1. Simplify: $\left(64x^3y^{-3}\right)^{2/3}\left(x^{-2/3}y^{1/6}\right)^6$

    a. $\dfrac{4}{xy^2}$

    b. $\dfrac{16}{x^2y}$

    c. $16x^2y$

    d. $\dfrac{16}{xy^2}$

2. Simplify: $\sqrt{16}+\sqrt{-9}$

    a. $12i$

    b. $\sqrt{7}$

    c. $4+3i$

    d. $4-3i$

3. Solve: $\sqrt[3]{x-3}=4$

    a. 58

    b. 60

    c. 46

    d. 67

4. The time it takes for an object to fall a certain distance is given by the equation $t=\sqrt{2d/g}$, where t is the time in seconds, d is the distance in feet, and g is the acceleration due to gravity. The acceleration due to gravity on Earth is 32 feet per second. If an object is dropped from atop a tall building, how far will it fall after 5.5 s?

    a. 470 ft

    b. 484 ft

    c. 88 ft

    d. 968 ft

5. Write a quadratic equation that has integer coefficients and has solutions 3 and $\dfrac{5}{4}$.

    a. $4x^2+17x+15=0$

    b. $4x^2-17x+15=0$

    c. $5x^2+19x+12=0$

    d. $5x^2-19x-12=0$

6. Solve by taking square roots: $2(x-3)^2=32$

    a. -7 and 1

    b. -4 and 4

    c. 0 and 1

    d. 7 and -1

7. Solve: $x^4-13x^2+36=0$

    a. $2i$, $-2i$, 3, and -3

    b. 2, -2, $3i$, and $-3i$

    c. $2i$, $-2i$, $3i$, and $-3i$

    d. 2, -2, 3, and -3

8. Solve: $\dfrac{x}{x-1}-\dfrac{3}{x+2}=3$

    a. $\dfrac{4+\sqrt{22}}{2}$ and $\dfrac{4-\sqrt{22}}{2}$

    b. $1+\dfrac{\sqrt{22}}{2}i$ and $1-\dfrac{\sqrt{22}}{2}i$

    c. $\dfrac{-4+\sqrt{22}}{2}$ and $\dfrac{-4-\sqrt{22}}{2}$

    d. $-1+\dfrac{\sqrt{22}}{2}i$ and $-1-\dfrac{\sqrt{22}}{2}i$

9. Solve: $x^2-3x-10>0$

    a. $\{x\,|\,x<-5 \text{ or } x>2\}$

    b. $\{x\,|\,x>5 \text{ or } x<-2\}$

    c. $\{x\,|\,-2<x<5\}$

    d. $\{x\,|\,-5<x<2\}$

10. A large pipe can fill a tank 24 min faster than it takes a smaller pipe to fill the same tank. Working together, both pipes can fill the tank in 16 min. How long would it take the larger pipe working alone to fill the tank?

    a. 48 min   **b.** 24 min   **c.** 36 min   **d.** 18 min

11. Which is the graph of $y = -x^2 + x - 5$?

    a. 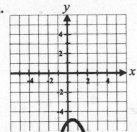   **b.** 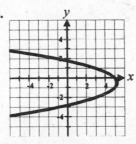   **c.** 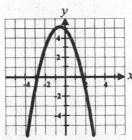   **d.**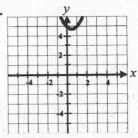

12. Which is the graph of the function $f(x) = 2|x+1|$?

    a. 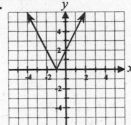   **b.** 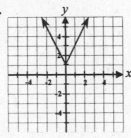   **c.** 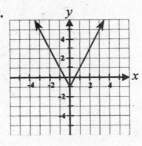   **d.**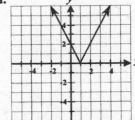

13. Given $f(x) = x^2 - 5$ and $g(x) = x - 2$, find $(f \cdot g)(0)$.

    a. 0   **b.** −1   **c.** −7   **d.** 10

14. Given $f(x) = x - 1$ and $g(x) = \dfrac{1}{2}x + 4$, find $f[g(6)]$.

    a. 8   **b.** $9\dfrac{1}{2}$ **c.** 9   **d.** 6

15. Let $f(x) = 2x - 5$. Find $f^{-1}(x)$.

    a. $f^{-1}(x) = \dfrac{1}{2}x + \dfrac{5}{2}$ **b.** $f^{-1}(x) = 2x - \dfrac{5}{2}$ **c.** $f^{-1}(x) = \dfrac{1}{2x-5}$ **d.** $f^{-1}(x) = \dfrac{1}{2}x - \dfrac{5}{2}$

1. Given $f(x) = \left(\dfrac{1}{3}\right)^{-x+1}$, evaluate $f(3)$.

   a. 9   b. 3   c. $\dfrac{1}{9}$ d. $-\dfrac{1}{9}$

2. Given $F(x) = e^{x-2}$, evaluate $F(-1)$. Round to the nearest ten-thousandth.

   a. 0.3679   b. 2.7183   c. 0.0498   d. 7.3891

3. Which is the graph of $f(x) = 2^{-x} + 1$?

   a. 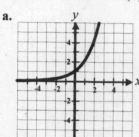   b. 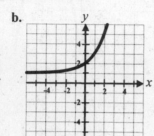   c. 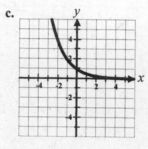   d.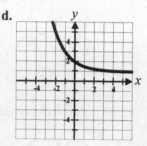

4. Evaluate: $\log_2 16$

   a. 16   b. 6   c. 4   d. 5

5. Solve for x: $\log_5 x = -3$

   a. -125 b. $\dfrac{1}{125}$ c. -15 d. $-\dfrac{1}{15}$

6. Evaluate: $\ln e^3$

   a. 1   b. -3 c. e^3 d. 3

7. Write $\log_4 \sqrt{x^3 y}$ in expanded form.

   a. $\sqrt{(3\log_4 x)(\log_4 y)}$ b. $\sqrt[3]{\log_4 x} + \sqrt{\log_4 y}$ c. $\dfrac{3}{2}\log_4 x + \dfrac{1}{2}\log_4 y$ d. $3\log_4 \sqrt{x} - \log_4 \sqrt{y}$

8. Write $\dfrac{2}{3}\log_7 x - \dfrac{1}{3}\log_7 y$ as a single logarithm with a coefficient of 1.

   a. $\log_7 \sqrt[3]{\dfrac{x^2}{y}}$ b. $\sqrt[3]{\log_7 \dfrac{x^2}{y}}$ c. $\log_7 \sqrt[3]{x^2} - \log_7 \sqrt[3]{y}$ d. $\dfrac{\log_7 x^{2/3}}{\log_7 y^{1/3}}$

9. Evaluate: $\log_{11} 40$
    Round to the nearest ten-thousandth.

    a. 2.5384   b. 1.5743   c. 0.6500   d. 1.5384

10. Evaluate: $\ln 10$
    Round to the nearest ten-thousandth.

    a. 1.000   b. 1.00   c. 2.3026   d. 2.303

11. Which is the graph of $f(x) = \log_2(x-1)$?

    a.   b.   c.   d.

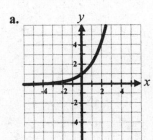 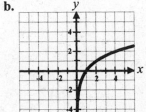 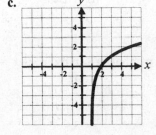 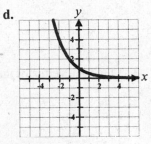

12. Solve for x: $2^{-x} = 5$. Round to the nearest thousandth.

    a. −2.102   b. −2.322   c. −2.556   d. −3.10

13. Solve for x: $5^{3x+1} = 25^{x-4}$

    a. −9   b. 3   c. $-\dfrac{5}{2}$ d. −1

14. Solve for x: $\log_2 x - \log_2 2 = \log_2(x-1)$

    a. −2   b. 0   c. $\dfrac{1}{2}$ d. 2

15. The percent of correct responses that a student can give on a vocabulary test increases with practice and can be approximated by the equation $P = 100(1 - 0.8^t)$, where P is the percent of correct responses and t is the number of days of practice. Find the percent of correct responses a student will make after four days of practice. Round to the nearest percent.

    a. 41%   b. 65%   c. 59%   d. 80%

1. Which is the graph of $y = -x^2 - 2x - 1$?

   a. 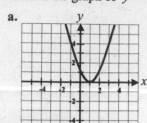 b. 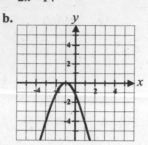 c. 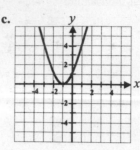 d.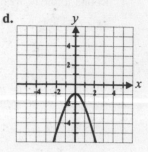

2. Find the axis of symmetry of the parabola $x = y^2 - 6y + 1$.

   a. $x = -8$ b. $y = 3$ c. $y = -8$ d. $x = 3$

3. Find the vertex of the parabola given by $y = -x^2 - 4x + 3$.

   a. $(4, -29)$ b. $(2, -7)$ c. $(4, 3)$ d. $(-2, 7)$

4. Find the equation of the circle with radius 4 and center $(-4, 5)$.

   a. $(x-4)^2 + (y+5)^2 = 4$ b. $(x+4)^2 + (y-5)^2 = 4$
   c. $(x-4)^2 + (y+5)^2 = 16$ d. $(x+4)^2 + (y-5)^2 = 16$

5. Find the equation of the circle that passes through the point $(-2, 2)$ and whose center is $(1, -3)$.

   a. $(x+2)^2 + (y-2)^2 = 34$ b. $(x-1)^2 + (y+3)^2 = 34$
   c. $(x+1)^2 + (y-3)^2 = 34$ d. $(x-2)^2 + (y+2)^2 = 34$

6. Write $x^2 + y^2 + 10x + 8y + 40 = 0$ in standard form.

   a. $(x+5)^2 + (y+4)^2 = 204$ b. $(x+5)^2 + (y+4)^2 = 164$
   c. $(x+5)^2 + (y+4)^2 = 40$ d. $(x+5)^2 + (y+4)^2 = 1$

7. Which is the graph of $x^2 + y^2 - 6x - 8y + 21 = 0$?

a. 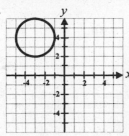   b. 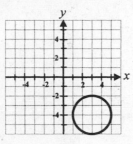   c. 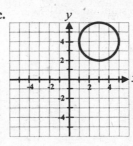   d.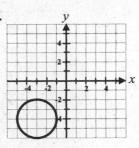

8. Which is the graph of $\dfrac{x^2}{9} + \dfrac{y^2}{16} = 1$?

a. 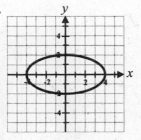   b. 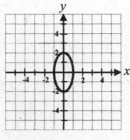   c. 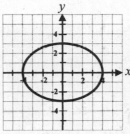   d.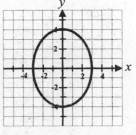

9. Which is the graph of $\dfrac{x^2}{4} - \dfrac{y^2}{9} = 1$?

a. 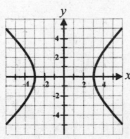   b. 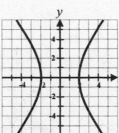   c. 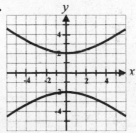   d.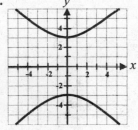

10. Solve: $x^2 + y^2 = 4$
    $y^2 = x - 2$

 a. $(-2,0)$ and $(-3,-5)$ b. $(2,0)$ and $(-2,0)$

 c. $(2,0)$ d. $(2,3)$ and $(2,-3)$

11. Solve: $4x^2 - 3y^2 = 1$
    $x - 2y = 1$

 a. $\left(-\dfrac{7}{13}, -\dfrac{3}{13}\right)$ and $(1,-1)$ b. $(-1,-1)$ and $\left(\dfrac{7}{13}, -\dfrac{3}{13}\right)$

 c. $(3,-1)$ and $(-3,-2)$ d. $\left(2, \dfrac{1}{2}\right)$ and $(-1,-1)$

Name: _____

12. Which is the graph of the solution set of $(x+3)^2 + (y+2)^2 < 1$?

a. 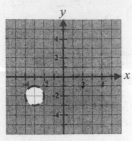　　b. 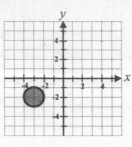　　c. 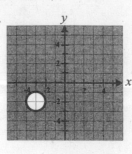　　d.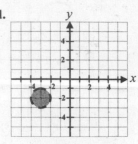

13. Which is the graph of the solution set of $y \geq x^2 + 2x - 3$?

a. 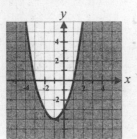　　b. 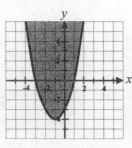　　c. 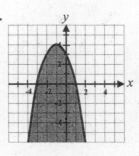　　d.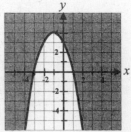

14. Choose the graph that shows the solution set for: $(x-1)^2 + y^2 \geq 9$
$$x - 3y \geq -3$$

a. 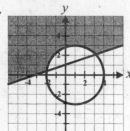　　b. 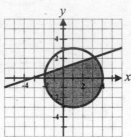　　c. 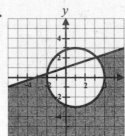　　d.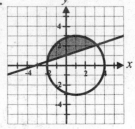

15. Choose the graph that shows the solution set for: $\dfrac{x^2}{9} + \dfrac{y^2}{25} \geq 1$
$$3x - y < -6$$

a. 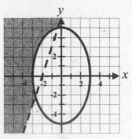　　b. 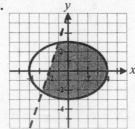　　c. 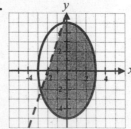　　d.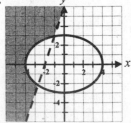

1. Write the 9th term of the sequence whose nth term is given by the formula $a_n = (2n-1)(n+2)$.

   a. 187　　　　　　b. 155　　　　　　c. 228　　　　　　d. 11

2. Write the 10th and 15th terms of the sequence whose nth term is given by the formula $a_n = (n+3)(n+5)$.

   a. 65, 90　　　　　b. 150, 225　　　　c. 130, 225　　　　d. 195, 360

3. Evaluate: $\sum_{n=1}^{4}(-1)^{n+1}(3n)$

   a. 9　　　　　　　b. −9　　　　　　　c. 6　　　　　　　d. −6

4. Write $\sum_{n=1}^{5}(-1)^n x^{2n}$ in expanded form.

   a. $x^2 - x^4 + x^6 - x^8 + x^{10}$　　　　　　b. $-x^2 + x^4 - x^6 + x^8 - x^{10}$

   c. $-x^2 + x^3 - x^4 + x^5 - x^6$　　　　　　d. $x^2 + 2x^4 + 3x^6 + 4x^8 + 5x^{10}$

5. Find the 15th term of the arithmetic sequence −2, 1, 4, ...

   a. 40　　　　　　　b. 50　　　　　　　c. 43　　　　　　　d. 52

6. Find the 35th term of the arithmetic sequence whose first term is −4 and whose common difference is 4.

   a. 136　　　　　　b. 140　　　　　　c. 132　　　　　　d. 144

7. Find the number of terms in the finite arithmetic sequence −8, −5, −2, ... , 148.

   a. 49　　　　　　　b. 51　　　　　　　c. 53　　　　　　　d. 48

8. Find the sum of the first 22 terms of the arithmetic sequence −2, 8, 18, ...

   a. 2376　　　　　　b. 2410　　　　　　c. 2310　　　　　　d. 2266

9. Find the sum of the first 26 terms of the arithmetic sequence whose first term is 10 and whose common difference is −2.

   a. −390　　　　　　b. 650　　　　　　c. 390　　　　　　d. 470

10. The loge seating section in a concert hall consists of 18 rows or chairs. There are 29 seats in the first row, 32 seats in the second row, 35 seats in the third row, and so on in an arithmetic sequence. How many seats are in the loge seating section?

    a. 1008 seats　　　b. 1962 seats　　　c. 1240 seats　　　d. 981 seats

11. Find the 5th term of the geometric sequence $4, -\frac{4}{3}, \frac{4}{9}, \dots$

   a. $-\frac{4}{81}$ **b.** $\frac{4}{81}$ **c.** $-\frac{4}{21}$ **d.** $\frac{4}{21}$

12. Find the 7th term of the geometric sequence whose first term is 3 and whose common ratio is $\sqrt{3}$.

   a. 243   **b.** 81   **c.** 27   **d.** $3\sqrt{3}$

13. Find the sum of the first six terms of the geometric sequence 64, 32, 16, ...

   a. 31.5   **b.** 63   **c.** 126   **d.** 166

14. Find the sum of the first six terms of the geometric sequence whose first term is 2 and whose common ratio is –3.

   a. 364   **b.** 728   **c.** –364   **d.** –424

15. Find the sum of the infinite geometric sequence $12, 4, \frac{4}{3}, \dots$

   a. 26   **b.** 18   **c.** 20   **d.** 24

16. Find an equivalent fraction for $0.3\overline{7}$.

   a. $\frac{4}{9}$ **b.** $\frac{17}{45}$ **c.** $\frac{28}{45}$ **d.** $\frac{37}{99}$

17. On the first swing, the length of the arc through which a pendulum swings is 24 in. The length of each successive swing is $\frac{3}{4}$ of the preceding swing. What is the total distance the pendulum has traveled during four swings? Round to the nearest tenth.

   a. 131.2 in.   **b.** 57.8 in.   **c.** 32.8 in.   **d.** 65.6 in.

18. Evaluate: $\dfrac{12!}{7!\,6!}$

   a. 42   **b.** 132   **c.** 66   **d.** 33

19. Evaluate: $\dbinom{6}{5}$

   a. 3   **b.** 12   **c.** 6   **d.** 24

20. Find the 6th term in the expansion of $(x-2)^8$.

   a. $-896x^4$ **b.** $-1792x^4$ **c.** $-896x^3$ **d.** $-1792x^3$

Name: _____

Date: _____

1. Given $f(x) = 3^x - 5$, evaluate $f(2)$.

   a. 76
   b. 9
   c. $\dfrac{1}{27}$
   d. 4

2. Solve for x: $\log_3 x = -2$

   a. $\dfrac{1}{9}$
   b. 8
   c. $-\dfrac{2}{3}$
   d. $-\dfrac{3}{2}$

3. Write $\log_5 x - 2\log_5 y - 3\log_5 z$ as a single logarithm with a coefficient of 1.

   a. $\log_5 \dfrac{xz^3}{y^2}$
   b. $\log_5 \dfrac{xy^2}{z^3}$
   c. $\log_5 \dfrac{x}{y^2 z^3}$
   d. $\log_5 x y^2 z^3$

4. Solve for x: $\log_5 2x + \log_5 (x-1) = \log_5 12$

   a. 2
   b. 3
   c. -2
   d. 1

5. Radium has a half-life of 1600 years. The amount of radium, A, that remains from a 100-mg sample after t years is given by the equation $A = 100(0.5)^{t/1600}$. Find the amount of radium in the sample after 4800 years.

   a. 33.3 mg
   b. 100 mg
   c. 12.5 mg
   d. 300 mg

6. Which is the graph of $y = -\dfrac{1}{2}x^2 + 2$?

   a.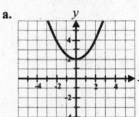
   b.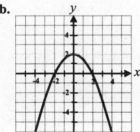
   c.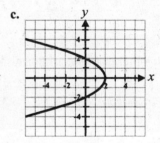
   d.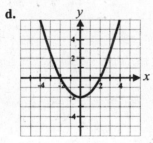

7. Find the equation of the circle with radius 2 and center $(-5, 7)$.

   a. $(x-5)^2 + (y+7)^2 = 2$
   b. $(x+5)^2 + (y-7)^2 = 2$
   c. $(x-5)^2 + (y+7)^2 = 4$
   d. $(x+5)^2 + (y-7)^2 = 4$

8. Which is the graph of $\dfrac{x^2}{4} + \dfrac{y^2}{16} = 1$?

   a.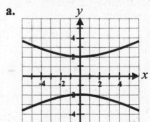
   b.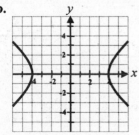
   c.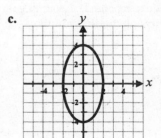
   d.

9. Solve: $y = 3x^2 - 4$
    $y = 5x - 2$

    a. $\left(-\dfrac{1}{3}, -\dfrac{11}{3}\right)$ and $(2,8)$

    b. $\left(\dfrac{4}{3}, -\dfrac{2}{3}\right)$ and $(2,8)$

    c. $\left(\dfrac{1}{3}, 2\right)$ and $\left(\dfrac{1}{3}, 8\right)$

    d. $\left(-\dfrac{1}{3}, \dfrac{11}{3}\right)$ and $(-2,8)$

10. Which is the graph of the solution set of $(x+2)^2 + (y-2)^2 \geq 16$?

    a. 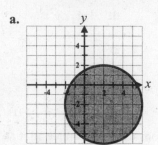   **b.** 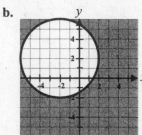   **c.** 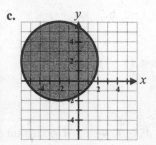   **d.**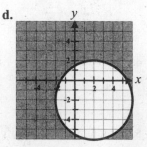

11. Evaluate: $\displaystyle\sum_{n=2}^{5}(-1)^n\left(n^3\right)$

    a. -14 **b.** 80 **c.** -80 **d.** 86

12. Find the sum of the first 44 terms of the arithmetic sequence whose first term is -12 and whose common difference is 4.

    a. 3256 **b.** 4048 **c.** 3648 **d.** 3456

13. Find the sum of the infinite geometric sequence $2, -\dfrac{3}{2}, \dfrac{9}{8}, \ldots$

    a. 8 **b.** $\dfrac{8}{7}$ **c.** $\dfrac{6}{5}$ **d.** $\dfrac{7}{2}$

14. You start a chain letter and send it to eight friends. Each of the eight friends sends the letter to eight other friends and the sequence is repeated. Assuming no one breaks the chain, how many letters will have been mailed from the first through the fifth mailings?

    a. 38,644 letters   **b.** 4096 letters   **c.** 32,768 letters   **d.** 37,448 letters

15. Find the 4th term in the expansion of $(x+y)^7$.

    a. $21x^4y^3$ **b.** $35x^4y^3$ **c.** $35x^3y^4$ **d.** $21x^3y^4$

1. Simplify: $\left(-\dfrac{2}{7}\right)^2 \div \dfrac{3}{14} + \dfrac{4}{21}$

    a. $-\dfrac{4}{21}$ **b.** $\dfrac{4}{7}$ **c.** $\dfrac{66}{343}$ **d.** $\dfrac{11}{21}$

2. Evaluate $\dfrac{b^2 - 4ac}{a+b}$ when $a = -1$, $b = 2$, and $c = -3$.

    a. -16 **b.** -8 **c.** 16 **d.** 8

3. Simplify: $7x - \left[2x - 3(y-x) + 4y\right]$

    a. $12x - 5y$ **b.** $6x - 3y$ **c.** $2x - y$ **d.** $12x - y$

4. Find $A \cap B$, given $A = \{1, 3, 5, 7, 9, 11\}$ and $B = \{-7, 9, 11, 14, 15\}$.

    a. $\{1, 3, 5, 7, 9, 11, 13, 15\}$ **b.** $\varnothing$

    c. $\{9, 11\}$ **d.** $\{0\}$

5. Solve: $\dfrac{x}{3} - \dfrac{3}{5} = \dfrac{x}{6} + \dfrac{11}{15}$

    a. 8 **b.** 7 **c.** -8 **d.** No solution

6. Solve: $4(x+2) + 3(x-4) = 5x$

    a. -2 **b.** 13 **c.** $1/3$ **d.** 2

7. For one performance of a play, 416 tickets were sold. Reserved seat tickets sold for $14 each, and general admission tickets sold for $8 each. Receipts from the sale of the tickets totaled $4840. Find the number of general admission tickets sold.

    a. 245 tickets   **b.** 115 tickets   **c.** 225 tickets   **d.** 164 tickets

8. An investment advisor deposited $50,000 into two simple interest accounts. On the tax-free account the annual simple interest rate is 7%, and on the money market fund the annual simple interest rate is 13%. How much should be invested in the money market fund so that both accounts earn the same interest?

    a. $32,500   **b.** $27,500   **c.** $22,500   **d.** $17,500

9. Simplify: $\dfrac{\left(xy^2\right)^{-2}\left(x^3y\right)}{x^2y^5}$

    a. xy^8 **b.** $\dfrac{x}{y^2}$ **c.** $\dfrac{1}{xy^8}$ **d.** $\dfrac{x}{y^8}$

10. The width of a rectangle is $(3x-5)$ ft and the length is $(5x+2)$ ft. Find the area of the rectangle in terms of the variable x.

    a. $\left(15x^2 + 31x - 10\right)$ ft^2 **b.** $\left(15x^2 - 19x - 10\right)$ ft^2 **c.** $\left(15x^2 - 31x - 10\right)$ ft^2 **d.** $\left(15x^2 - 19x + 10\right)$ ft^2

11. Factor: $6x^{2n} + 7x^n - 20$

    a. $\left(3x^n - 4\right)\left(2x^n - 5\right)$ **b.** $\left(3x^n + 4\right)\left(2x^n + 5\right)$ **c.** $\left(3x^n - 4\right)\left(2x^n + 5\right)$ **d.** $\left(3x^n + 4\right)\left(2x^n - 5\right)$

12. Factor: $64a^3 + 1$

    a. $(4a+3)(16a^2 - 12a + 9)$

                    b. Nonfactorable

    c. $(4a-3)(16a^2 + 12a + 9)$

                    d. $(4a+1)(16a^2 - 4a + 1)$

13. Factor: $2ay + ab - 6xy - 3bx$

    a. $(a+2b)(y-3x)$ **b.** $(a-2b)(y-3x)$ **c.** $(a-3x)(2y+b)$ **d.** $(2a-b)(3x-y)$

14. Simplify: $(2x^3 + 3x^2 + 6) \div (x+2)$

    a. $2x^2 - x + 2 + \dfrac{2}{x+2}$ **b.** $2x - 1 + \dfrac{2}{x+2}$ **c.** $2x^2 + x + 2 - \dfrac{2}{x+2}$ **d.** $2x^2 - x + 2$

15. Simplify: $\dfrac{45x^2 - 60x}{3x^2 + 11x - 20} \cdot \dfrac{2x^2 - 15x + 25}{5x^3 - 25x^2}$

    a. $\dfrac{3(3x+4)}{x(3x-4)}$ **b.** $\dfrac{3(2x-5)}{x(2x+5)}$ **c.** $\dfrac{3(2x-5)}{x(x+5)}$ **d.** $\dfrac{3}{x}$

16. Simplify: $\dfrac{6}{2x-3} + \dfrac{4x}{3-2x}$

    a. $6 + 4x$ **b.** -2 **c.** $\dfrac{6+4x}{3-2x}$ **d.** $\dfrac{6-4x}{2x-3}$

17. Solve: $\dfrac{4}{2x+1} - \dfrac{3}{2x-1} = \dfrac{11}{4x^2 - 1}$

    a. $-\dfrac{1}{2}$ **b.** -9 **c.** 9 **d.** $\dfrac{1}{2}$

18. Solve $A = P + Prt$ for P.

    a. $P = \dfrac{A}{rt}$ **b.** $P = \dfrac{A}{1-rt}$ **c.** $P = Art$ **d.** $P = \dfrac{A}{1+rt}$

19. Simplify: $\left(x^{1/2}y^{1/3}\right)^2 \left(x^{-2}y^4\right)^{1/2}$

    a. $x^2 y^{1/3}$ **b.** $y^{8/3}$ **c.** $x^{3/2} y^{4/3}$ **d.** $\dfrac{1}{xy^3}$

20. Write $(3x-1)^{3/2}$ as a radical expression.

    a. $\sqrt{(3x-1)^3}$ **b.** $(3x)^{3/2} - 1$ **c.** $\sqrt[3]{(3x-1)^2}$ **d.** $\sqrt[3]{(3x)^2} - 1$

21. Simplify: $-\sqrt{81a^{10}b^{20}}$

    a. $-3a^5b^{10}$ **b.** $-9a^5b^{10}$ **c.** $-9a^8b^{18}$ **d.** Not a real number

22. Simplify: $\left(6 - \sqrt{-8}\right) - \left(4 - \sqrt{-32}\right)$

    a. $2 - 6i\sqrt{2}$ **b.** $2 - 2i\sqrt{2}$ **c.** $10 - 6i\sqrt{2}$ **d.** $2 + 2i\sqrt{2}$

Final Exam Form H (*continued*)

Name: _____

23. Solve: $\sqrt[4]{2x-4} = 2$

    a. 10   **b.** -10 **c.** 8   **d.** 4

24. Which is the graph of $y = \dfrac{1}{2}x - 3$?

  a. 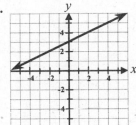   **b.** 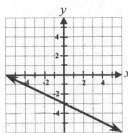   **c.** 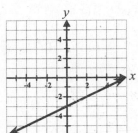   **d.**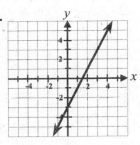

25. Find the slope of the line containing the points $(-2,-4)$ and $(5,-4)$.

    a. $-\dfrac{8}{3}$ **b.** $-\dfrac{3}{8}$ **c.** 0   **d.** Undefined

26. Find the equation of the line that contains the point $(-3,1)$ and has slope $-\dfrac{1}{3}$.

    a. $y = -\dfrac{1}{3}x$ **b.** $y = -3x$ **c.** $y = -\dfrac{1}{3}x + 1$ **d.** $y = \dfrac{1}{3}x$

27. Which is the graph of the solution set of $3x - 2y > 6$?

  a. 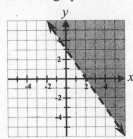   **b.** 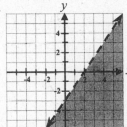   **c.** 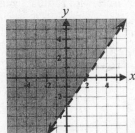   **d.**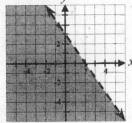

28. Solve: $x^2 + 6x + 4 = 0$

    a. $3 + \sqrt{5}$ and $3 - \sqrt{5}$ **b.** $-3 + \sqrt{5}$ and $-3 - \sqrt{5}$

    c. $3 + \sqrt{14}$ and $3 - \sqrt{14}$ **d.** $-3 + \sqrt{14}$ and $-3 - \sqrt{14}$

29. Solve: $x^2 - 6x + 8 = 0$

    a. -1 and -8 **b.** -1 and 8   **c.** -4 and 2   **d.** 2 and 4

30. Solve: $3x + 14x^{1/2} = 5$

    a. $\dfrac{1}{9}$ and 25   **b.** $\dfrac{1}{9}$ **c.** 25   **d.** $\dfrac{1}{3}$

31. Given $f(x) = x^2 - 2x - 5$, evaluate $f(-2)$.

    a. -3 **b.** 13   **c.** 3   **d.** -13

32. Which of the sets of ordered pairs is a one-to-one function?

    a. $\{(-4,-3),(0,0),(4,3),(8,6)\}$ b. $\{(4,0),(0,4),(-4,0),(0,-4)\}$

    c. $\{(-1,2),(0,1),(1,2),(2,3)\}$ d. $\{(3,0),(-3,0),(0,2),(0,-2)\}$

33. Given $f(x)=2-3x$, find $f^{-1}(x)$.

    a. $f^{-1}(x)=x+\dfrac{2}{3}$ b. $f^{-1}(x)=-3x+2$ c. $f^{-1}(x)=\dfrac{1}{3}x-\dfrac{2}{3}$ d. $f^{-1}(x)=-\dfrac{1}{3}x+\dfrac{2}{3}$

34. Which is the graph of $y=-x^2-4x-1$?

    a.   b.   c.   d.

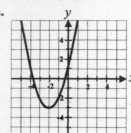

35. Find the minimum value of the function $f(x)=-x^2-6x+5$.

    a. −22   b. 14   c. −3   d. 5

36. Find the equation of the circle with radius 3 and center $(2,6)$.

    a. $(x+2)^2+(y+6)^2=3$ b. $(x+2)^2+(y+6)^2=9$

    c. $(x-2)^2+(y-6^2)=3$ d. $(x-2)^2+(y-6)^2=9$

37. Which is the graph of $\dfrac{x^2}{4}+\dfrac{y^2}{36}=1$?

    a.   b.   c.   d.

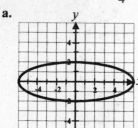

38. Solve: $2x+4y=-3$
              $3x-4y=-2$

    a. $(2,2)$ b. $(2,1)$ c. $(-10,-7)$ d. $\left(-1,-\dfrac{1}{4}\right)$

39. Solve: $x+y+2z=6$
              $2x+y-z=-4$
              $x-2y+z=0$

    a. $(-1,1,3)$ b. $(1,1,2)$ c. $(-1,0,2)$ d. $(1,3,1)$

40. Evaluate the determinant: $\begin{vmatrix} -2 & 1 & 3 \\ 3 & 2 & -1 \\ 4 & 3 & -2 \end{vmatrix}$

    a. -10 **b.** 10 **c.** 7 **d.** -7

41. Solve: $2x^2 + 3y^2 = 18$
$$x^2 + y^2 = 9$$

    a. $(3,-3)$ and $\left(\sqrt{6}, \sqrt{2}\right)$ **b.** $\left(-\sqrt{6}, -\sqrt{2}\right)$ and $(-3,3)$

    c. $\left(1, 2\sqrt{2}\right)$ and $\left(-1, -2\sqrt{2}\right)$ **d.** $(3,0)$ and $(-3,0)$

42. Evaluate: $\log 1000$

    a. 3 **b.** 2 **c.** -2 **d.** 6.9078

43. Solve for x: $\log_4 x = -2$

    a. 16 **b.** $\dfrac{1}{16}$ **c.** $\dfrac{1}{8}$ **d.** 8

44. Write $2\log_6 x - 3\log_6 y + \log_6 z$ as a single logarithm with a coefficient of 1.

    a. $\log_6 \dfrac{x^2 z}{y^3}$ **b.** $\log_6 \dfrac{x^2}{y^3 z}$ **c.** $\log_6 \left(\dfrac{x}{xy}\right)^5$ **d.** $\log_6 \left(\dfrac{x^2 z^2}{y^3}\right)$

45. Solve for x: $2^{3x+3} = 8^{2x-6}$

    a. 3 **b.** -9 **c.** -3 **d.** 7

46. Solve for x: $\log_7 x + \log_7 (x+6) = 1$

    a. -7 and 1 **b.** -1 and 7 **c.** 1 **d.** 7

47. Find the 15th term of the arithmetic sequence whose first term is 20 and whose common difference is -3.

    a. -25 **b.** -22 **c.** -18 **d.** -15

48. Find the sum of the first 30 terms of the arithmetic sequence 2, 4, 6, …

    a. 540 **b.** 990 **c.** 770 **d.** 930

49. Find the sum of the first 5 terms of the geometric sequence $-12,\ 48,\ -192, …$

    a. -7710 **b.** 612 **c.** -2460 **d.** -612

50. Find the 4th term in the expansion of $(x+2)^6$.

    a. $160x^3$ **b.** $240x^3$ **c.** $160x^4$ **d.** $240x$

ANSWERS TO CHAPTER TESTS

Forms A-H

Answers to Chapter Tests: Form A

Chapter 1 Test Form A

1. $-\sqrt{2}$ (1.1A)

2. -2 (1.1A)

3. -7 (1.2A)

4. 84 (1.2A)

5. $\{x \mid x \leq 5\}$ (1.1B)

6. 9 (1.2A)

7. 288 (1.2C)

8. $(-\infty, -2)$ (1.1C)

9. $\dfrac{3}{5}$ (1.2B)

10. $-\dfrac{7}{6}$ (1.2B)

11. -13.42 (1.2B)

12. -5230 (1.2B)

13. 7 (1.2D)

14. 32 (1.2D)

15. 9 (1.3B)

16. 5 (1.3B)

17. The Commutative Property of Addition (1.3A)

18. The Distributive Property (1.3A)

19. $-6x + 7y$ (1.3C)

20. 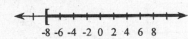 (1.1C)
    -5 -4 -3 -2 -1 0 1 2 3 4 5

21. $2n + 17$ (1.4A)

22. $2w + 4$ (1.4B)

23. $\{0, 2\}$ (1.1C)

24. $\{-4, -3, -2, 0, 1, 2, 3, 4\}$ (1.1C)

25. ⟵ ┼ ┼ ┼ (┼ ┼ ┼ ┼) ┼ ┼ ⟶ (1.1C)
    -5 -4 -3 -2 -1 0 1 2 3 4 5

Chapter 2 Test Form A

1. 17 (2.1A)

2. 36 (2.1A)

3. $\dfrac{1}{24}$ (2.1A)

4. $\dfrac{3}{2}$ (2.1B)

5. $-\dfrac{10}{3}$ (2.1B)

6. $-\dfrac{9}{2}$ (2.1B)

7. $-\dfrac{3}{4}$ (2.1C)

8. $S = C - RT$ (2.1D)

9. $-\dfrac{5}{3}$ (2.1B)

10. $[-8, \infty)$ (2.4A)

    ⟵ ┼[┼┼┼┼┼┼┼┼┼┼┼┼⟶
    -8 -6 -4 -2 0 2 4 6 8

11. $\left\{x \mid x > -7/2\right\}$ (2.4A)

12. $(0, 2)$ (2.4B)

13. $\{x \mid x < 2 \text{ or } x > 4\}$ (2.4B)

14. 1.464 in.; 1.476 in. (2.5C)

15. 5 and -2 (2.5A)

16. $\dfrac{5}{3}$ and 1 (2.5A)

17. $\{x \mid -2 < x < 1\}$ (2.5B)

18. $\left(-\infty, -\dfrac{1}{2}\right) \cup (4, \infty)$ (2.5B)

19. 20 ml (2.3B)

20. 29 (2.2A)

21. 6 (2.2B)

22. 75 oz (2.3A)

23. 140 mi/h (2.3C)

24. 3 ft (2.4C)

Answers to Chapter Tests: Form A

Chapter 3 Test Form A

1.
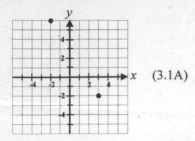
(3.1A)

2.
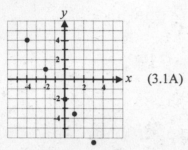
(3.1A)

3. $\left(1, \frac{7}{2}\right)$; 7.81 (3.1B)

4.
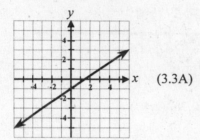
(3.3A)

5.
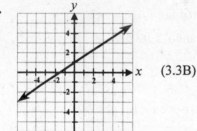
(3.3B)

6. $\frac{2}{3}$ (3.4A)

7. 20 (3.2A)

8. $(2,0)$ (3.3C)

9. $(0,-5)$ (3.3C)

10.
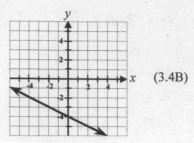
(3.4B)

11.
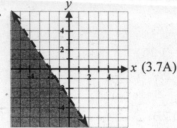
(3.7A)

12. $y = -\frac{2}{3}x + \frac{8}{3}$ (3.5A)

13. $y = 3$ (3.5A)

14. $y = -\frac{1}{2}x - \frac{3}{2}$ (3.5B)

15. $y = -\frac{3}{2}x + 2700$ (3.5C)

16. $y = -\frac{2}{3}x + 19$ (3.6A)

17. D: $\{-1, 1, 2, 3\}$; R: $\{-5, -2, 4, 7\}$ (3.2A)

18. $x = -5$ (3.2A)

19. After four hours, the cyclist has traveled 20 miles. (3.3D)

20. 3 hours (3.1C)

Cumulative Test: Chapters 1-3 Form A

1. 0, 1, 7 (1.1A)

2. $\left\{x \mid x < 3 \text{ or } x > \frac{9}{2}\right\}$ (2.4B)

3.

```
<-+--+--+--+--+--)--+--+--+--+--+->   (1.1C)
 -5 -4 -3 -2 -1  0  1  2  3  4  5
```

4. $\frac{1}{8}$ (1.2B)

5. -20 (1.3B)

6. The Commutative Property of Multiplication (1.3A)

7. $-7x + 10y$ (1.3C)

8. $\frac{3}{16}n$ (1.4A)

9. $-\frac{1}{15}$ (2.1A)

10. $\frac{1}{3}$ (2.1C)

11. $\left[\frac{1}{2},\infty\right)$ (2.4A)

12. -1 and 5 (2.5A)

13. $\left\{x \mid x < -\frac{6}{5} \text{ or } x > 2\right\}$ (2.5B)

14. 9 (2.2A)

15. 28 kg (2.3A)

16. 61.75 ohms, 68.25 ohms (2.4C)

17.
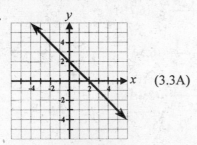
(3.3A)

18.
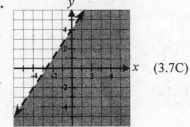
(3.7C)

19. $(0,2)$ (3.3C)

20. $y = -\frac{1}{2}x + 4$ (3.5A)

21. $y = -x - 1$ (3.5B)

22. $y = x - 5$ (3.6A)

23. -2 (3.2A)

24. $-\frac{13}{4}$ (3.4A)

25. $\left(-4, \frac{5}{2}\right)$ (3.1B)

Chapter 4 Test Form A

1.
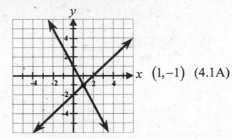
$(1,-1)$ (4.1A)

2.
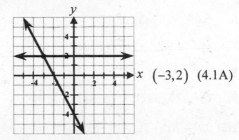
$(-3,2)$ (4.1A)

3. $4320 (4.1C)

4. $(-1,5)$ (4.1B)

5. $(-1,2)$ (4.2A)

6. $(3,-2)$ (4.2A)

7. $(1,-1,2)$ (4.2B)

8. -8 (4.3A)

9. -30 (4.3A)

10. $(-1,2)$ (4.3B)

11. $(1,-2,2)$ (4.3B)

12. 480 mph (4.4A)

13. $6.40 /lb (4.4B)

14.
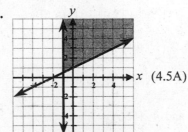
(4.5A)

15.
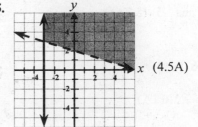
(4.5A)

Answers to Chapter Tests: Form A

Chapter 5 Test Form A

1. $-y^3 - y^2 - 3y + 11$ (5.2B)

2. $16x^5 y^{10}$ (5.1A)

3. $\dfrac{b^3}{2a^2}$ (5.1B)

4. -9 (5.2A)

5. 4.6302×10^{11} (5.1C)

6. 6.696×10^8 mi (5.1D)

7. $-6b^5 + 18b^4 - 9b^3$ (5.3A)

8. $4x^2 + 3x$ (5.3A)

9. $6x^2 - 17xy + 5y^2$ (5.3B)

10. $3a^3 - 2a^2 + 7a + 20$ (5.3B)

11. $16 - 49a^2$ (5.3C)

12. $9x^2 - 24x + 16$ (5.3C)

13. $(2x^2 - 9x + 10)$ ft^2 (5.3D)

14. $x - 5x^2 y$ (5.4A)

15. $x^2 + 2x - 5 + \dfrac{8}{x+2}$ (5.4B)

16. 14 (5.4D)

17. $(x-2)(x-7)$ (5.5C)

18. $(5+y)(3-x^2)$ (5.5B)

19. $(3x-2)^2$ (5.6A)

20. Nonfactorable (5.5D)

21. $(3x-4)(9x^2 + 12x + 16)$ (5.6B)

22. $(x^2 - 2)(x^2 + 9)$ (5.6C)

23. $3x(7x-2)(2x+3)$ (5.6D)

24. $-\dfrac{3}{2}$ and 4 (5.7A)

25. $\dfrac{5}{2}$ and -5 (5.7A)

Chapter 6 Test Form A

1. $\dfrac{x+3}{2}$ (6.1A)

2. $\dfrac{5x+2}{3(x+4)}$ (6.1A)

3. $\dfrac{x-2}{6x}$ (6.1B)

4. $\dfrac{x-4}{2x+1}$ (6.1C)

5. $2x^2 - 2x + 1 - \dfrac{2}{3x-2}$ (6.1C)

6. $\{x \mid x \in \text{real numbers}\}$ (6.1A)

7. $-\dfrac{1}{3}$ (6.1A)

8. $\dfrac{30}{6(3+x)(3-x)}, \dfrac{3x-x^2}{6(3+x)(3-x)}$ (6.2A)

9. $\dfrac{2(x+1)}{x-3}$ (6.2B)

10. $\dfrac{x+1}{2x-1}$ (6.3A)

11. $\dfrac{x+4}{2x+3}$ (6.3A)

12. 8 (6.4A)

13. -1 (6.4A)

14. $14.28 (6.4B)

15. $-\dfrac{5}{2}$ (6.5A)

16. $\dfrac{1}{2}$ (6.5A)

17. $b_1 = \dfrac{2A}{h} - b_2$ (6.5A)

18. 232 ft (6.6A)

19. $10\dfrac{2}{7}$ h (6.5B)

20. 400 mi/h (6.5C)

Cumulative Test: Chapters 4-6 Form A

1. $-32a^5 b^9$ (5.1A)

2. x^{n-3} (5.1B)

3. 28 (5.2A)

4. $-12x^3 + 16x^2 - 28x$ (5.3A)

5. $9b^2 - 4$ (5.3C)

6. $4x^2y^2\left(x^2 - 3xy - y^2\right)$ (5.5A)

7. $(7a + 5b)(a - 2b)$ (5.5D)

8. $\left(4x^3 - 3\right)\left(2x^3 + 5\right)$ (5.6D)

9. $0, 2$ (5.7A)

10. $10b^3x^2$ (6.1B)

11. $\dfrac{23 - 2x}{8x}$ (6.2B)

12. $\dfrac{x - 3}{x + 5}$ (6.3A)

13. $\dfrac{3}{4}$ (6.4A)

14. $-3, -2$ (6.5A)

15. $3x^2y^2 + xy - 10$ (5.3B)

16. $(-15, -29)$ (4.1B)

17. $(-4, 5)$ (4.2A)

18. $(-10, 3)$ (4.3B)

19. -5 (4.3A)

20. $2x + 3$ (5.4B)

21. 20 mi/h (4.4A)

22. 32 ft (6.6A)

23. 2.5 months (6.4B)

24.

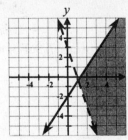

(4.5A)

25.

$(4, 6)$ (4.1A)

Chapter 7 Test Form A

1. $x^{5/2}$ (7.1A)

2. $\dfrac{b^{5/3}}{a^{2/5}}$ (7.1A)

3. $\sqrt[4]{2x - 4}$ (7.1B)

4. $5a^{5/4}$ (7.1B)

5. $x^2y^3\sqrt[4]{x^2}$ (7.1C)

6. $2xy^6\sqrt{2x}$ (7.2A)

7. $3x^4y^2\sqrt[3]{2y}$ (7.2A)

8. $-xy\sqrt{3x}$ (7.2B)

9. $-7ab\sqrt{6b}$ (7.2B)

10. $14xy^4\sqrt{2x}$ (7.2C)

11. $x - 9$ (7.2C)

12. $\dfrac{3}{x}$ (7.2D)

13. $-2\sqrt{3} - 4$ (7.2D)

14. 7 (7.3A)

15. 35 (7.3A)

16. 324 ft (7.3B)

17. $6 - 5i$ (7.4A)

18. $-3 - 11i$ (7.4B)

19. $11 - 10i$ (7.4C)

20. $\dfrac{2}{3} + \dfrac{1}{3}i$ (7.4D)

Chapter 8 Test Form A

1. $-\dfrac{2}{3}$ and 4 (8.1A)

2. $\dfrac{3}{2}$ and $\dfrac{1}{2}$ (8.1A)

3. $3x^2 - 7x - 6 = 0$ (8.1B)

4. $-12\sqrt{2}$ and $12\sqrt{2}$ (8.1C)

5. -1 and 5 (8.1C)

6. $-4 + 3\sqrt{2}$ and $-4 - 3\sqrt{2}$ (8.2A)

Answers to Chapter Tests: Form A

7. $3 - \sqrt{19}$ and $3 + \sqrt{19}$ (8.2A)

8. $\dfrac{-5 + \sqrt{33}}{2}$ and $\dfrac{-5 - \sqrt{33}}{2}$ (8.3A)

9. $\dfrac{3 + \sqrt{7}}{3}$ and $\dfrac{3 - \sqrt{7}}{3}$ (8.3A)

10. Two complex number solutions. (8.3A)

11. $3, -3, 3i,$ and $-3i$ (8.4A)

12. 9 and 25 (8.4A)

13. 5 (8.4B)

14. $\dfrac{2}{3}$ and $\dfrac{4}{3}$ (8.4B)

15. -3 and 4 (8.4C)

16. $\sqrt{10}$ and $-\sqrt{10}$ (8.4C)

17. $\left\{ x \mid -4 < x < \dfrac{3}{2} \right\}$

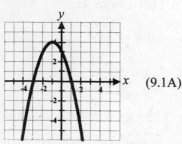 (8.5A)

18. $\left\{ x \mid 2 < x < 3 \right\}$

(8.5A)

19. 40 mi/h (8.6A)

20. 25 m (8.6A)

Chapter 9 Test Form A

1. $\left(\dfrac{5}{4}, -\dfrac{1}{8} \right); \ x = \dfrac{5}{4}$ (9.1A)

2. Domain: $\left\{ x \mid x \in \text{real numbers} \right\}$
   Range: $\left\{ y \mid y \geq -3 \right\}$ (9.1A)

3. (9.1A)

4. 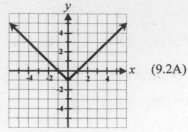 (9.2A)

5. $(3,0), \left(\dfrac{2}{3}, 0 \right)$ (9.1B)

6. $\left(-3 + \sqrt{7}, 0 \right), \left(-3 - \sqrt{7}, 0 \right)$ (9.1B)

7. Two (9.1B)

8. -11 (9.1C)

9. 20 and 20 (9.1D)

10. 100 ft^2 (9.1D)

11. No (9.2A)

12. Yes (9.4A)

13. 3 (9.3A)

14. 15 (9.3A)

15. $-\dfrac{2}{3}$ (9.3A)

16. 33 (9.3B)

17. $x^2 - 4x + 5$ (9.3B)

18. $f^{-1}(x) = 3x - 1$ (9.4B)

19. No (9.4B)

20. $\left\{ (3,1), (5,2), (7,6) \right\}$ (9.4B)

Cumulative Test: Chapters 7-9 Form A

1. $4a^4 b^4$ (7.2A)

2. $\sqrt{2x^2 + 7}$ (7.1B)

3. $4\sqrt{y} - 2x\sqrt{5y}$ (7.2B)

4. $\sqrt{3} + 7i\sqrt{3}$ (7.4B)

5. 4 (7.3A)

6. $3x^2 + 5x - 2$ (8.1B)

7. -2 and 2 (8.1C)

8. $3 + \sqrt{5}$ and $3 - \sqrt{5}$ (8.2A)

9. $\sqrt{3}, -\sqrt{3}, i\sqrt{2}, -i\sqrt{2}$ (8.4A)

10. −3 and −2 (8.4B)

11. $\{x \mid x < -2 \text{ or } x > 7\}$ (8.5A)

12. 25 ft (8.6A)

13. Domain: $\{x \mid x \in \text{real numbers}\}$

Range: $\left\{ y \mid y \le \dfrac{13}{4} \right\}$ (9.1A)

14. 8 (9.1C)

15.
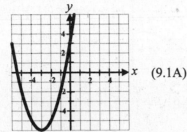
(9.1A)

16.
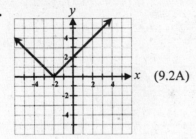
(9.2A)

17. $f^{-1}(x) = \dfrac{1}{3}x + 3$ (9.4B)

18. $-\dfrac{3}{4}$ (9.3A)

19. −6 (9.3A)

20. 23 (9.3B)

Chapter 10 Test Form A

1. 0.0498 (10.1A)

2. 2 (10.1A)

3.
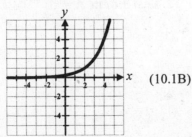
(10.1B)

4. 4 (10.2A)

5. 81 (10.2A)

6. $\log_2 8 = 3$ (10.2A)

7. $5^3 = 125$ (10.2A)

8. $2\log_3 x + \dfrac{1}{2}\log_3 y + 4\log_3 z$ (10.2B)

9. $\log_2 \dfrac{x^2}{y^5 z}$ (10.2B)

10. 1.5850 (10.2C)

11. $\dfrac{1}{2}\ln x - \ln 2y$ (10.2B)

12. $\ln \dfrac{y^2}{x\sqrt[3]{z}}$ (10.2B)

13. 3.9069 (10.2C)

14.
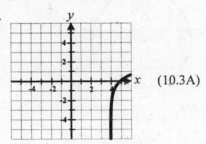
(10.3A)

15. 1.8614 (10.4A)

16. 7 (10.4A)

17. $\dfrac{11}{2}$ (10.4A)

18. 2 (10.4B)

19. 41 (10.4B)

20. 6 years (10.5A)

Chapter 11 Test Form A

1.
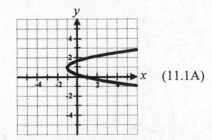
(11.1A)

Answers to Chapter Tests: Form A

2.

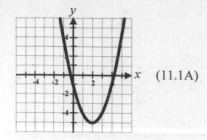 (11.1A)

3. $\left(\dfrac{1}{3}, \dfrac{2}{3}\right);\ x = \dfrac{1}{3}$ (11.1A)

4. $(x-3)^2 + (y+2)^2 = 25$ (11.2A)

5. $(x+1)^2 + (y-4)^2 = 34$ (11.2A)

6. $x^2 + (y+1)^2 = 25$

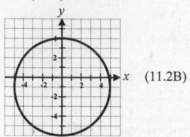 (11.2B)

7. $(x-3)^2 + (y+2)^2 = 9$

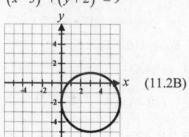 (11.2B)

8.

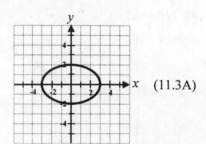 (11.3A)

9.

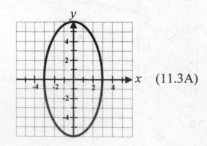 (11.3A)

10.

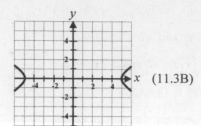 (11.3B)

11.

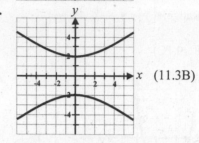 (11.3B)

12. $(4,6)$ and $\left(-\dfrac{1}{2}, \dfrac{15}{4}\right)$ (11.4A)

13. $\left(2\sqrt{2}, \sqrt{2}\right),\ \left(-2\sqrt{2}, \sqrt{2}\right),\ \left(2\sqrt{2}, -\sqrt{2}\right),$ and $\left(-2\sqrt{2}, -\sqrt{2}\right)$ (11.4A)

14.

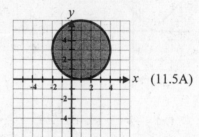 (11.5A)

15.

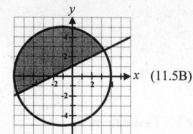 (11.5B)

Chapter 12 Test Form A

1. $\dfrac{3}{5}$ (12.1A)

2. $\dfrac{1}{2},\ \dfrac{11}{15}$ (12.1A)

3. 5 (12.1B)

4. $\frac{1}{2}x + x^2 + \frac{3}{2}x^3 + 2x^4$ (12.1B)

5. 73 (12.2A)

6. $a_n = 5n - 3$ (12.2A)

7. 43 (12.2A)

8. −168 (12.2B)

9. 684 (12.2B)

10. $\frac{\sqrt{3}}{9}$ (12.3A)

11. 96 (12.3A)

12. $-\frac{43}{8}$ (12.3B)

13. $\frac{31}{4}$ (12.3B)

14. $\frac{16}{3}$ (12.3C)

15. $\frac{13}{30}$ (12.3C)

16. $15x^8 y^4$ (12.4A)

17. 72 (12.4A)

18. 495 (12.4A)

19. $56,400 (12.2C)

20. $129,687.12 (12.3D)

Cumulative Test: Chapters 10-12 Form A

1. 9 (10.1A)

2. $\frac{1}{9}$ (10.2A)

3.

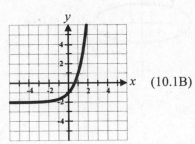

x (10.1B)

4.

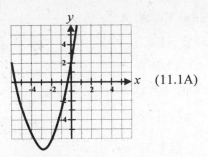

x (11.1A)

5. 5 (10.2A)

6. $3\log_2 x - \log_2 y - 4\log_2 z$ (10.2B)

7. 2 (10.4A)

8. 6 (10.4B)

9. 74% (10.5A)

10. 144 boxes (12.2C)

11.

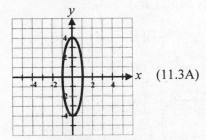

x (11.3A)

12.

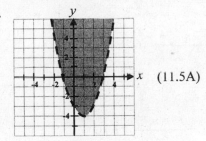

x (11.5A)

13. $(x+1)^2 + y^2 = 16$ (11.2A)

14. $(2,0)$ and $(-1,6)$ (11.4A)

15. $2\frac{38}{105}$ (12.1B)

16. 825 (12.2B)

17. $\frac{1}{5}$ (12.1A)

18. 2439 (12.3A)

19. 4 (12.3C)

20. $560x^3 y^4$ (12.4A)

Answers to Chapter Tests: Form A

Final Exam Form A

1. 2352 (1.2C)

2. −11 (1.3B)

3. $-11y+8x$ (1.3C)

4. $3n-2$ (1.4A)

5. $-\dfrac{2}{5}$ (2.1C)

6. 10 (2.1B)

7. 110 (2.2B)

8. 25% (2.3B)

9. $-432a^5b^{13}$ (5.1A)

10. $x^{3n+3}-3x^{n+4}-5x^{n+3}$ (5.3A)

11. $(x-10)(x+3)$ (5.5C)

12. $(2x^2y^2-3)(x^2y^2+4)$ (5.6C)

13. 0 and −3 (5.7A)

14. $\dfrac{2x-y}{5xy}$ (6.1A)

15. $\dfrac{x+2}{x-2}$ (6.1B)

16. $\dfrac{-2x-26}{x^2+x-6}$ (6.2B)

17. $\dfrac{2}{x+3}$ (6.5A)

18. $V_1=\dfrac{Ft+mV_2}{m}$ (2.1D)

19. $5a^2b^3\sqrt{2b}$ (7.2A)

20. $-5x^2\sqrt{3y}$ (7.2B)

21. $-8+4\sqrt{5}$ (7.2D)

22. $2\sqrt{13}+5i\sqrt{5}$ (7.4A)

23.

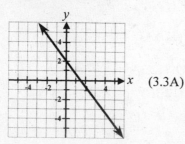 (3.3A)

24.

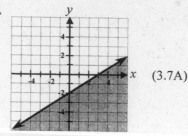 (3.7A)

25. $-\dfrac{1}{3}$ (3.4A)

26. $y=\dfrac{3}{8}x+\dfrac{17}{8}$ (3.5A)

27. $7+i$ (7.4C)

28. $3+3\sqrt{6}$ and $3-3\sqrt{6}$ (8.1C)

29. $-3+2i$ and $-3-2i$ (8.3A)

30. $\dfrac{3}{2}$ and 2 (8.4C)

31. $8-2h-h^2$ (3.2A)

32. $\sqrt{17}$ (3.1B)

33. 27 (9.3B)

34. 64 ft^2 (8.6A)

35.

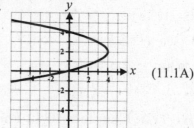 (11.1A)

36.

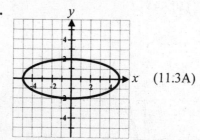 (11.3A)

37. $x^2+(y+4)^2=49$ (11.2A)

38. $\dfrac{1}{3}\log_2 x-\dfrac{2}{3}\log_2 y-\dfrac{1}{3}\log_2 z$ (10.2B)

39. $(-2,2)$ (4.1B)

40. $(2,-2,-1)$ (4.2B)

41. −6 (4.3A)

42. (2,1) and (−2,1) (11.4A)

43. 3 (10.2A)

44. 81 (10.4B)

45. −6 (10.4A)

46. 4 (10.4B)

47. 1 (12.1A)

48. 2415 (12.2B)

49. $\frac{1}{3}$ (12.3A)

50. $x^5 + 10x^4 + 40x^3 + 80x^2 + 80x + 32$ (12.4A)

Answers to Chapter Tests: Form B

Chapter 1 Test Form B

1. -401 (1.1A)

2. $\{-8\}$ (1.1A)

3. -6 (1.2A)

4. $\{x \mid -1 < x < 3\}$ (1.1B)

5. 15 (1.2A)

6. 8 (1.2A)

7. 288 (1.2C)

8. (1.1C)

9. $\dfrac{5}{6}$ (1.2B)

10. 1 (1.2B)

11. -1.06 (1.2B)

12. -4.31 (1.2B)

13. 90 (1.2D)

14. 10 (1.2D)

15. -31 (1.3B)

16. $\dfrac{3}{4}$ (1.3B)

17. The Commutative Property of Addition (1.3A)

18. The Commutative Property of Multiplication (1.3A)

19. $7a + b$ (1.3C)

20. (1.1C)

21. $2n - 2$ (1.4A)

22. $12 - L$ (1.4B)

23. $\{2,3,4,5,6,8\}$ (1.1C)

24. $\{-2,0,2\}$ (1.1C)

25. (1.1C)

Chapter 2 Test Form B

1. -18 (2.1A)

2. $-\dfrac{12}{5}$ (2.1A)

3. $-\dfrac{1}{2}$ (2.1A)

4. No solution (2.1B)

5. $-\dfrac{5}{3}$ (2.1B)

6. 21 (2.1B)

7. $-\dfrac{1}{2}$ (2.1C)

8. $\dfrac{PV}{nR} = T$ (2.1D)

9. 1 (2.1C)

10. $\{x \mid x \geq 4\}$ (2.4A)

11. $(-\infty, 5]$ (2.4A)

12. $\{x \mid x < -1\}$ (2.4B)

13. $(-1, \infty)$ (2.4B)

14. 5 ft (2.4C)

15. 2 and 5 (2.5A)

16. 0 and 6 (2.5A)

17. $[2,5]$ (2.5B)

18. $\left\{x \mid x < -\dfrac{9}{5} \text{ or } x > 1\right\}$ (2.5B)

19. Less than 140 mi (2.4C)

20. 3 (2.2A)

21. 12 (2.2B)

22. $\$1.90$ per pound (2.3A)

23. 405 mph (2.3C)

24. 190 volts; 250 volts (2.5C)

25. 6 oz (2.3B)

Chapter 3 Test Form B

1.

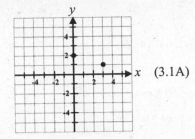 (3.1A)

2.

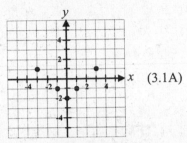 (3.1A)

3. $(4,1)$; $\sqrt{20}$ (3.1B)

4.

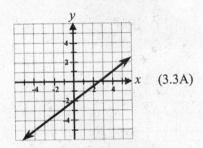 (3.3A)

5.

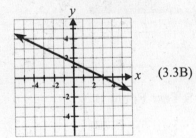 (3.3B)

6. $-\dfrac{1}{3}$ (3.4A)

7. 8 (3.2A)

8. $(4,0)$ (3.3C)

9. $(0,-4)$ (3.3C)

10.

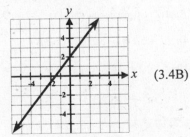 (3.4B)

11.

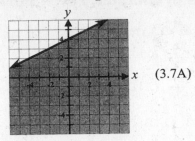 (3.7A)

12. $y = \dfrac{1}{6}x + \dfrac{5}{2}$ (3.5A)

13. $y = 0.10x + 24$ (3.5C)

14. $y = \dfrac{7}{2}x - \dfrac{13}{2}$ (3.5B)

15. $x = 3$ (3.5A)

16. $y = \dfrac{4}{3}x - \dfrac{10}{3}$ (3.6A)

17. $\{-1,1,3,5\}$ (3.2A)

18. $x = -3$ (3.2A)

19. The cost of manufacturing 100 microwave ovens is $30,000. (3.3D)

20. 250 ovens (3.1C)

Cumulative Test: Chapters 1-3 Form B

1. 4 (1.2A)

2. $\left\{ x \mid x < -6 \text{ or } x > \dfrac{5}{3} \right\}$ (2.4B)

3. -56 (1.2C)

4. 2 (1.2D)

5. $-3/5$ (1.3B)

6. $13x - 75y - 20$ (1.3C)

7. $\dfrac{11}{8}n$ (1.4A)

8. $\{0,2\}$ (1.1C)

9. -3 (2.1B)

10. -6 (2.1C)

11. $[6,\infty)$ (2.4A)

12. -1 and 4 (2.5A)

13. $\{x \mid x \le -2 \text{ or } x \ge 6\}$ (2.5B)

14. 5 and 9 (2.2A)

15. 20 oz (2.3A)

16. $94 \le x \le 100$ (2.4C)

17. $h = \dfrac{2A}{b}$ (2.1D)

18. $\sqrt{13}$ (3.1B)

19. $-7/3$ (3.4A)

20. $(2,0)$ (3.3C)

21. $y = \dfrac{3}{2}x + 6$ (3.5A)

22. $y = \dfrac{4}{3}x + \dfrac{13}{3}$ (3.5B)

23. $y = -\dfrac{3}{2}x$ (3.6A)

24.

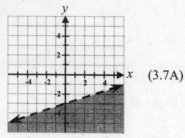 (3.7A)

25. 24 (3.2A)

Chapter 4 Test Form B

1.

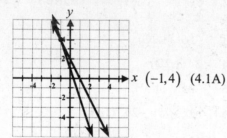 $(-1,4)$ (4.1A)

2.

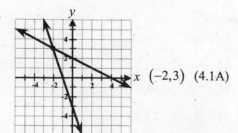 $(-2,3)$ (4.1A)

3. $5750 at 3.5%; $4250 at 7.5% (4.1C)

4. $(-3,-4)$ (4.1B)

5. No solution (4.2A)

6. $\left(\dfrac{1}{3}, \dfrac{2}{9}\right)$ (4.2A)

7. $(4,-1,0)$ (4.2B)

8. 24 (4.3A)

9. -7 (4.3A)

10. $(3,4)$ (4.3B)

11. $\left(\dfrac{41}{31}, \dfrac{25}{31}, \dfrac{2}{31}\right)$ (4.3B)

12. 14 mph (4.4A)

13. 17 ft (4.4B)

14.

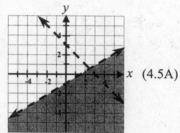 (4.5A)

15.

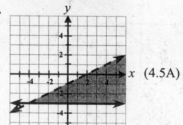 (4.5A)

Chapter 5 Test Form B

1. $y^3 - 3y^2 + 5y$ (5.2B)

2. $36x^4 y^{12} z^4$ (5.1A)

3. $-\dfrac{b^7}{2a^7}$ (5.1B)

4. 30 (5.2A)

5. 2.32×10^{-7} (5.1C)

6. 7.5×10^6 operations (5.1D)

7. $-4a^3 b^3 + 6a^2 b^3 - 8a^2 b^4$ (5.3A)

8. $-13y^2 + 12y$ (5.3A) $(3x-y)^2$

9. $2a^{2n} + 5a^n - 3$ (5.3B)

10. $6x^3 - 17x^2 + 8x - 1$ (5.3B)

11. $16x^2-1$ (5.3C)

12. $25x^2-30x+9$ (5.3C)

13. $\left(6x^2-11x-7\right)$ ft^2 (5.3D)

14. a^2-3a+8 (5.4A)

15. $3x+1+\dfrac{8}{x-2}$ (5.4B)

16. 23 (5.4D)

17. $(5-2x)(3+2y)$ (5.5B)

18. $(x-13)(x-1)$ (5.5C)

19. $(4a-1)(2a+3)$ (5.5D)

20. $(8-3y)(8+3y)$ (5.6A)

21. $(3x-y)^2$ (5.6A)

22. $(2x+3)\left(4x^2-6x+9\right)$ (5.6B)

23. $x^n\left(x^n+4\right)\left(3x^n-2\right)$ (5.6D)

24. 1 and 4/5 (5.7A)

25. −2 and 1/3 (5.7A)

Chapter 6 Test Form B

1. $\dfrac{5}{a-2}$ (6.1A)

2. $\dfrac{x^n+1}{x^n-1}$ (6.1A)

3. $-\dfrac{(x+4)(x+2)}{3(x-4)}$ (6.1B)

4. $\dfrac{x^n+6}{x^n-3}$ (6.1C)

5. −1/3 (6.1A)

6. $\left\{x\,\middle|\,x\neq-2,5\right\}$ (6.1A)

7. $\dfrac{3x^2+5x-12}{(x-6)(x+2)(x+3)}$,

$\dfrac{2x^2-11x-6}{(x-6)(x+2)(x+3)}$ (6.2A)

8. $\dfrac{78x^2+33x-50}{(2x-1)(3x-2)(3x+2)}$ (6.2B)

9. $\dfrac{3x^2-x-7}{x(x-1)}$ (6.2B)

10. $\dfrac{x+2}{5}$ (6.3A)

11. $\dfrac{x+4}{x+1}$ (6.3A)

12. 12 (6.4A)

13. 5 (6.4A)

14. 15 (6.5A)

15. 6 (6.5A)

16. $R=\dfrac{V}{I}$ (6.5A)

17. 24 teaspoons (6.4B)

18. 30.72 foot candles (6.6A)

19. 24 min (6.5B)

20. 2 mph (6.5C)

Cumulative Test: Chapters 4-6 Form B

1. $a^{18}b^6$ (5.1A)

2. $3a$ (5.1B)

3. 4.5×10^{10} (5.1D)

4. $x^4-2x^3+4x^2-2x+3$ (5.3B)

5. $4a^2+12ab+9b^2$ (5.3C)

6. $(x-3)(x-2)$ (5.5C)

7. $\left(2x^n-7\right)\left(x^n+1\right)$ (5.6C)

8. $(x-2)\left(x^2+2x+4\right)$ (5.6B)

9. −1/2 and 2 (5.7A)

10. $\dfrac{x^2+4}{x^2+3}$ (6.1A)

11. $\dfrac{x^2+2}{(x-1)\left(x^2+x+1\right)}$, $\dfrac{3x-3}{(x-1)\left(x^2+x+1\right)}$ (6.2A)

12. $\dfrac{3x+12}{x+2}$ (6.2B)

Answers to Chapter Tests: Form B

13. $2/5$ (6.3A)

14. 36 (6.4A)

15. 9.5 ft by 15 ft (6.4B)

16. 8 hours (6.5B)

17. 8 lb/in^2 (6.6A)

18.

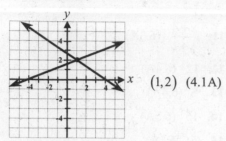

(1, 2) (4.1A)

19.

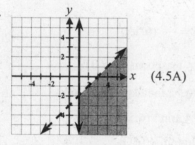

(4.5A)

20. $(-2, 1)$ (4.1B)

21. $(4, 3)$ (4.2A)

22. $(0, 2, 3)$ (4.2B)

23. $\left(-2, -\dfrac{2}{3}\right)$ (4.3B)

24. 16 (4.3A)

25. $0.15 (4.4B)

Chapter 7 Test Form B

1. $1/3$ (7.1A)

2. $\dfrac{1}{a^{10}}$ (7.1A)

3. $\sqrt[3]{4x-1}$ (7.1B)

4. $x^{5/2}$ (7.1B)

5. $-7x^3y^8$ (7.1C)

6. $x^2y^3\sqrt[4]{xy^2}$ (7.2A)

7. $xy^2z^2\sqrt[4]{x^2z^2}$ (7.2A)

8. $5\sqrt{6}$ (7.2B)

9. $-2x^2\sqrt{3xy}$ (7.2B)

10. 40 (7.2C)

11. $x-4y^2$ (7.2C)

12. $5x\sqrt{x}$ (7.2D)

13. $\dfrac{12\sqrt{x}+12\sqrt{7}}{x-7}$ (7.2D)

14. -24 (7.3A)

15. 1 (7.3A)

16. 12 in. (7.3B)

17. $6-5i$ (7.4A)

18. $2+4i$ (7.4B)

19. 13 (7.4C)

20. $i-1$ (7.4D)

Chapter 8 Test Form B

1. $-1/3$ and $2/5$ (8.1A)

2. 1 and -5 (8.1A)

3. $x^2-9=0$ (8.1B)

4. $-5/6$ and $5/6$ (8.1C)

5. $1-2\sqrt{3}$ and $1+2\sqrt{3}$ (8.1C)

6. $4+3\sqrt{2}$ and $4-3\sqrt{2}$ (8.2A)

7. 1 and -2 (8.2A)

8. $-1/2$ and -2 (8.3A)

9. $\dfrac{1}{3}+\dfrac{\sqrt{11}}{3}i$ and $\dfrac{1}{3}-\dfrac{\sqrt{11}}{3}i$ (8.3A)

10. Two complex number solutions (8.3A)

11. $-3, -\dfrac{\sqrt{3}}{3}, \dfrac{\sqrt{3}}{3}$, and 3 (8.4A)

12. 9 (8.4A)

13. 9 (8.4B)

14. 1 (8.4B)

15. 1 and 3 (8.4C)

16. $1+\sqrt{3}$ and $1-\sqrt{3}$ (8.4C)

17. $\{x \mid 4 < x \le 5\}$

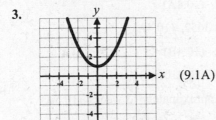

(8.5A)

18. $\{x \mid x < -2 \text{ or } 2 < x < 3\}$

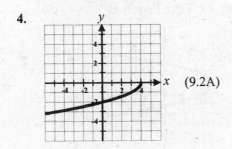

(8.5A)

19. 9 and 13 (8.6A)

20. 45 mph and 60 mph (8.6A)

Chapter 9 Test Form B

1. $(3, -6)$; $x = 3$ (9.1A)

2. Domain: $\{x \mid x \in \text{real numbers}\}$

   Range: $\{y \mid y \ge 5\}$ (9.1A)

3. 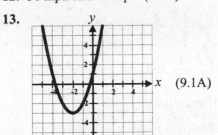 (9.1A)

4. 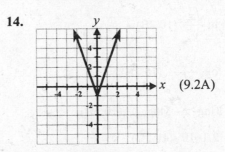 (9.2A)

5. $(0,0), (-3,0)$ (9.1B)

6. $7/2, 4$ (9.1B)

7. None (9.1B)

8. 14 (9.1C)

9. 8 ft by 8 ft (9.1D)

10. 1764 (9.1D)

11. No (9.2A)

12. Yes (9.4A)

13. 2 (9.3A)

14. -45 (9.3A)

15. $2/5$ (9.3A)

16. -1 (9.3B)

17. $2x^2 + 8x + 5$ (9.3B)

18. $f^{-1}(x) = \dfrac{1}{4}x + \dfrac{3}{2}$ (9.4B)

19. No (9.4B)

20. $\{(3,-1),(5,2),(11,7)\}$ (9.4B)

Cumulative Test: Chapters 7-9 Form B

1. $\dfrac{4n^2}{m}$ (7.1A)

2. $\sqrt{5 - x^2}$ (7.1B)

3. $x + 6\sqrt{x} + 9$ (7.2C)

4. $-2\sqrt{2} + 8i\sqrt{2}$ (7.4B)

5. 3 (7.3A)

6. $3x^2 - 7x - 6 = 0$ (8.1B)

7. -1 and 9 (8.1C)

8. $-\dfrac{1 - \sqrt{7}}{2}$ and $-\dfrac{1 + \sqrt{7}}{2}$ (8.2A)

9. 25 and 9 (8.4A)

10. $-16/3$ and 5 (8.4C)

11. $\{x \mid x < -2 \text{ or } x > 2\}$ (8.5A)

12. 30 mph and 40 mph (8.6A)

13. 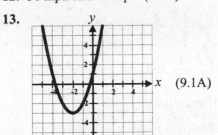 (9.1A)

14. 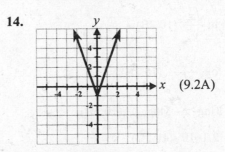 (9.2A)

15. $-4, 6$ (9.1B)

Answers to Chapter Tests: Form B

16. 1 (9.1C)

17. 29 (9.3A)

18. 324 (9.3B)

19. No (9.4A)

20. $f^{-1}(x) = \dfrac{1}{2}x - \dfrac{3}{2}$ (9.4B)

Chapter 10 Test Form B

1. 3.7183 (10.1A)

2. 1/16 (10.1A)

3. 3 (10.2A)

4.
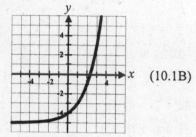
(10.1B)

5.
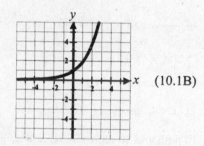
(10.1B)

6. $\log_2 \dfrac{1}{8} = -3$ (10.2A)

7. $8^{-1} = \dfrac{1}{8}$ (10.2A)

8. 1/36 (10.2A)

9. $2\ln x - \ln y - 3\ln z$ (10.2B)

10. $\ln \dfrac{\sqrt{x}}{y}$ (10.2B)

11. $\log_5 \dfrac{x^3 z^2}{\sqrt{y}}$ (10.2B)

12. $3\log_4 x + 3\log_4 y$ (10.2B)

13. 2.1610 (10.2C)

14.
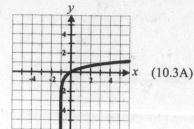
(10.3A)

15.
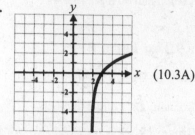
(10.3A)

16. 2 (10.4A)

17. 2.3652 (10.4A)

18. 2 (10.4B)

19. 0.008 (10.5A)

20. Approximately 13 weeks (10.5A)

Chapter 11 Test Form B

1.
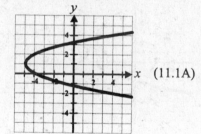
(11.1A)

2.
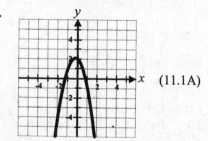
(11.1A)

3. $(-1,1)$; $y = 1$ (11.1A)

4. $(x+1)^2 + (y-4)^2 = 25$ (11.2A)

5. $(x-1)^2 + (y+2)^2 = 41$ (11.2A)

6. $(x-3)^2 + (y-3)^2 = 4$

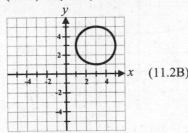

(11.2B)

7. $(x-3)^2 + y^2 = 9$

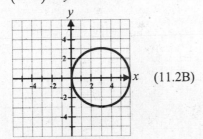

(11.2B)

8.

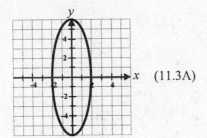

(11.3A)

9.

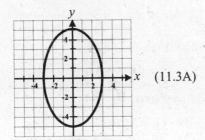

(11.3A)

10.

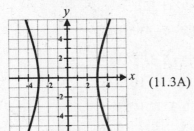

(11.3A)

11.

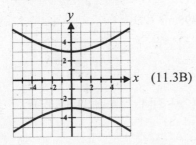

(11.3B)

12. $(-1,-2)$ and $(7,22)$ (11.4A)

13. $(5,0)$ and $(0,5)$ (11.4A)

14.

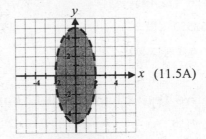

(11.5A)

15.

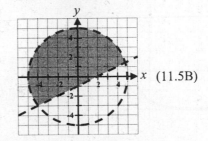

(11.5B)

Chapter 12 Test Form B

1. -8 (12.1A)

2. $\dfrac{50}{9}$ (12.1A)

3. $2\dfrac{43}{60}$ (12.1B)

4. $1 + \dfrac{x}{4} + \dfrac{x^2}{9} + \dfrac{x^3}{16} + \dfrac{x^4}{25}$ (12.1B)

5. $-1/2$ (12.2A)

6. $a_n = 7n - 1$ (12.2A)

7. 50 (12.2A)

8. 625 (12.2B)

9. 145 (12.2B)

10. 2048 (12.3A)

11. 729 (12.3A)

12. 4920 (12.3B)

13. -96 (12.3B)

14. $\dfrac{3}{5}$ (12.3C)

15. $\dfrac{29}{90}$ (12.3C)

Answers to Chapter Tests: Form B

16. $-216x$ (12.4A)

17. 182 (12.4A)

18. 126 (12.4A)

19. \$2550 (12.2C)

20. 6.6 ft (12.3D)

12.

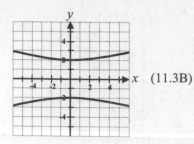 (11.3B)

Cumulative Test: Chapters 10-12 Form B

1. 9 (10.1A)

2.

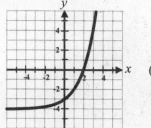 (10.1B)

3. 4 (10.2A)

4. $\log_5 \dfrac{x^3}{y^2 \sqrt{z}}$ (10.2B)

5. 0.8009 (10.2C)

6. 403.4288 (10.2A)

7. 3 (10.4A)

8. 1 (10.4B)

9.

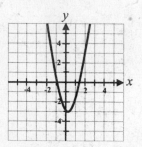 (11.1A)

10. $(x+1)^2 + (y-4)^2 = 64$ (11.2A)

11.

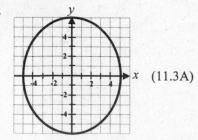 (11.3A)

13. $\left(\dfrac{1}{2}, -\dfrac{7}{2}\right)$ and $(2, -2)$ (11.4A)

14.

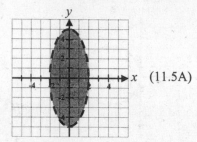 (11.5A)

15. $\dfrac{26}{9}$ (12.1A)

16. 18 (12.1B)

17. -245 (12.2B)

18. $\dfrac{9}{4}$ (12.3C)

19. $\dfrac{11}{45}$ (12.3C)

20. $15360x^3y^7$ (12.4A)

Final Exam Form B

1. -108 (1.2C)

2. 49 (1.3B)

3. $9x - 6 - 4y$ (1.3C)

4. $4n + 8$ (1.4A)

5. 35/3 (2.1B)

6. 10/3 (2.1C)

7. 4¢ stamps: 16; 9¢ stamps: 7 (2.2B)

8. 495 mi (2.3C)

9. $-32x^3y^4$ (5.1A)

10. $a^3 + 2a^2 - 9a + 2$ (5.3B)

11. $(2x-3)(4x^2 + 6x + 9)$ (5.6B)

12. $(2x+3)(x-6)$ (5.5D)

13. $3x(2x-1)(x+3)$ (5.6D)

14. $\dfrac{x-3}{x+2}$ (6.1A)

15. $\dfrac{x}{3(x+5)}$ (6.1B)

16. $\dfrac{x+5}{x+4}$ (6.2B)

17. $-\dfrac{3(a+2)}{2(a+3)}$ (6.3A)

18. 3 and 5 (6.5A)

19. $-ab\sqrt{3a}$ (7.2B)

20. $\dfrac{2x+2\sqrt{xy}}{x-y}$ (7.2D)

21. $3\sqrt{2}+4i$ (7.4C)

22. 7 (7.3A)

23.
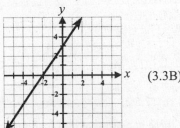
(3.3B)

24.
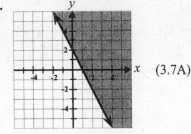
(3.7A)

25. Undefined (3.4A)

26. $y-\dfrac{2}{3}x-\dfrac{11}{3}$ (3.5B)

27. $\dfrac{1}{3}+\dfrac{\sqrt{2}}{3}i$ and $\dfrac{1}{3}-\dfrac{\sqrt{2}}{3}i$ (8.3A)

28. $\dfrac{11+\sqrt{73}}{2}$ and $\dfrac{11-\sqrt{73}}{2}$ (8.2A)

29. 4 (8.4B)

30. 18 (3.2A)

31. $\sqrt{40}$ (3.1B)

32. $f^{-1}(x)=\dfrac{3}{2}x+6$ (9.4B)

33. 12 ft (7.4B)

34.
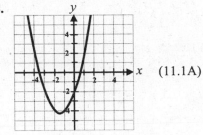
(11.1A)

35. $\left(-\dfrac{1}{2},0\right)$ and $(4,0)$ (9.1B)

36. $(x+2)^2+(y-3)^2=20$ (11.2A)

37.
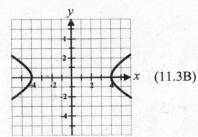
(11.3B)

38. $\left(\dfrac{1}{2},-3\right)$ (4.2A)

39. $(1,-2,-1)$ (4.2B)

40. $\left(\dfrac{1}{2},-\dfrac{3}{4}\right)$ and $(-3,1)$ (11.4A)

41. $\dfrac{1}{32}$ (10.2A)

42. 2 (10.4B)

43. 5 (10.1A)

44. $\dfrac{1}{2}\log_5 x+\dfrac{3}{2}\log_4 z-4\log_5 x$ (10.2B)

45. 4 (10.4A)

46. $54x^2y^2$ (12.4A)

47. 31/15 (12.1A)

48. 3820 (12.2B)

49. 525 mph (4.4A)

50. 31.25 mg (12.3D)

Answers to Chapter Tests: Form C

Chapter 1 Test Form C

1. -16 (1.1A)

2. $\{x \mid -4 \le x < -2\}$ (1.1C)

3. 6 (1.2A)

4. -30 (1.2A)

5. 8 (1.2A)

6. -19 (1.2A)

7. 72 (1.2C)

8. [number line with point at -3] (1.1C)
   -5 -4 -3 -2 -1 0 1 2 3 4 5

9. $-\dfrac{7}{6}$ (1.2B)

10. $\dfrac{1}{15}$ (1.2B)

11. $\{x \mid x < -3\}$ (1.1B)

12. 44.2 (1.2B)

13. 12 (1.2D)

14. $\dfrac{22}{5}$ (1.2D)

15. -19 (1.3B)

16. -20 (1.3B)

17. The Distributive Property (1.3A)

18. The Division Property of Zero (1.3A)

19. $15x - 64y$ (1.3C)

20. [number line with point at -2] (1.1C)
   -5 -4 -3 -2 -1 0 1 2 3 4 5

21. $2n + 7$ (1.4A)

22. $\dfrac{1}{4}L$ (1.4B)

23. $\{-2, -1, 0, 1, 2, 3\}$ (1.1C)

24. $\varnothing$ (1.1C)

25. [number line open at -3, closed at 4] (1.1C)
   -5 -4 -3 -2 -1 0 1 2 3 4 5

Chapter 2 Test Form C

1. 1 (2.1B)

2. 7 (2.1A)

3. $-3/20$ (2.1A)

4. $\dfrac{8}{5}$ (2.1B)

5. 34 (2.1B)

6. -3 (2.1B)

7. 8 (2.1C)

8. $a = 2s - b - c$ (2.1D)

9. -1 (2.1C)

10. $\{x \mid x > -5\}$ (2.4A)
   [number line open at -5 extending right]
   -5 -4 -3 -2 -1 0 1 2 3 4 5

11. $\left[\dfrac{16}{13}, \infty\right)$ (2.4A)

12. $\{x \mid -1 < x < 3\}$ (2.4B)

13. $(-\infty, -5) \cup (-3, \infty)$ (2.4B)

14. \$80,000 or more (2.4C)

15. $-3/2$ and $5/2$ (2.5A)

16. $-8/5$ (2.5A)

17. $\{x \mid x \in \text{real numbers}\}$ (2.5B)

18. $\left(-\dfrac{2}{3}, \dfrac{4}{3}\right)$ (2.5B)

19. 4.25 cc (2.5C)

20. Any three consecutive odd integers (2.2A)

21. 5 (2.2B)

22. \$4.25 per ounce (2.3A)

23. 50.4 mi (2.3C)

24. $9\dfrac{14}{25}$ in., $9\dfrac{16}{25}$ in. (2.5C)

25. 30 oz (2.3B)

Chapter 3 Test Form C

1. 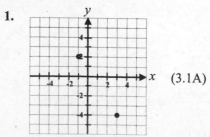 (3.1A)

2.

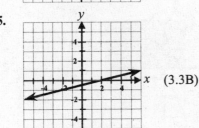 (3.1A)

3. $\left(1, \dfrac{1}{2}\right);\ \sqrt{73}$ (3.1B)

4.

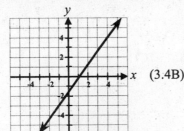 (3.3A)

5.

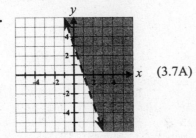 (3.3B)

6. $-\dfrac{1}{6}$ (3.4A)

7. 19 (3.2A)

8. $(2,0)$ (3.3C)

9. $(0,2)$ (3.3C)

10.

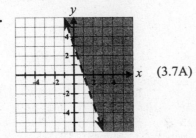 (3.4B)

11.

(3.7A)

12. $y = -\dfrac{5}{2}x + 1$ (3.5A)

13. $y = -1$ (3.5A)

14. $y = \dfrac{4}{5}x + \dfrac{13}{5}$ (3.5B)

15. $y = 3.8x$ (3.5C)

16. $y = \dfrac{4}{3}x - \dfrac{16}{3}$ (3.6A)

17. D: $\{-3, -2, 0, 2\}$; R: $\{0, 1, 3, 4\}$ (3.2A)

18. $x = 0$ (3.2A)

19. The cost of manufacturing zero dryers is $4,000 (the overhead cost is $4,000). (3.3D)

20. $8,200 (3.1C)

Cumulative Test: Chapters 1-3 Form C

1. -3 (1.1A)

2. 48 (1.2C)

3. $\{x \mid x < -3 \text{ or } x > 8\}$ (2.4B)

4. $-\dfrac{71}{6}$ (1.2D)

5. $\dfrac{49}{2}$ (1.3B)

6. The Associative Property of Multiplication (1.3A)

7. $5x - 4$ (1.3C)

8. $2n + 7$ (1.4A)

9. $\dfrac{2}{3}$ (2.1A)

10. 3 (2.1B)

11. $[-3, \infty)$ (2.4A)

12. $\dfrac{2}{3}$ and $-\dfrac{1}{3}$ (2.5A)

13. $\{x \mid x \le 1 \text{ or } x \ge 2\}$ (2.5B)

14. 5 and 7 (2.2A)

15. 125 lb (2.3A)

16. Less than 70 minutes (2.4C)

17. $b = 2s - a - c$ (2.1D)

Answers to Chapter Tests: Form C

18. $\left(-5, \dfrac{1}{2}\right)$ (3.1B)

19. $-\dfrac{2}{7}$ (3.4A)

20. $(1, 0)$ (3.3C)

21. $y = -\dfrac{3}{2}x + 6$ (3.5A)

22. $y = 2x - 8$ (3.5B)

23. $y = 3x + 2$ (3.6A)

24.

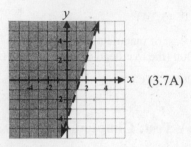 (3.7A)

25. 0 (3.2A)

Chapter 4 Test Form C

1.

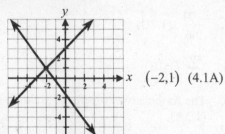 $(-2, 1)$ (4.1A)

2.

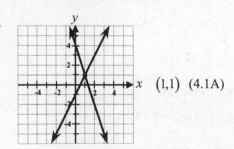 $(1, 1)$ (4.1A)

3. $10,000 (4.1C)

4. $(-3, -4)$ (4.1B)

5. $(4, -1)$ (4.2A)

6. $(-2, -3)$ (4.2A)

7. $(2, -1, -2)$ (4.2B)

8. -2 (4.3A)

9. 2 (4.3A)

10. $(2, -1)$ (4.3B)

11. $(1, 3, 4)$ (4.3B)

12. 575 mi/h (4.4A)

13. Redwood: $0.28 per foot;

Fir: $0.32 per foot (4.4B)

14.

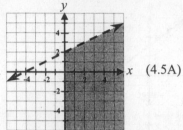 (4.5A)

15.

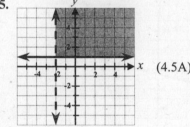 (4.5A)

Chapter 5 Test Form C

1. $2x^2 - 7x - 3$ (5.2B)

2. y^{6n-3} (5.1A)

3. $-\dfrac{x^3}{3yz^3}$ (5.1B)

4. -26 (5.2A)

5. 1656 (5.1C)

6. $\left(27x^3 - 27x^2 + 9x - 1\right)\text{ft}^3$ (5.3D)

7. $a^{n+2} - 3a^2 + 4a^{2-n}$ (5.3A)

8. $6x^2 - 16x$ (5.3A)

9. $x^{3n+1} - 3x^{2n} - x^{n+2} + 3x$ (5.3B)

10. $x^4 + 3x^3 - 23x^2 - 29x + 6$ (5.3B)

11. $9 - x^2$ (5.3C)

12. $25x^{2n} - 10x^n y^n + y^{2n}$ (5.3C)

13. $1.\overline{09} \times 10^{21}$ horsepower (5.1D)

14. $2+4y^2$ (5.4A)

15. $x+4+\dfrac{13}{x-3}$ (5.4B)

16. -37 (5.4D)

17. $(x-3)(a-4)$ (5.5B)

18. $(x+9)(x+8)$ (5.5C)

19. $(5x+2)(x-3)$ (5.5D)

20. $\left(3+a^{2n}\right)\left(3-a^{2n}\right)$ (5.6A)

21. $(7x-2)^2$ (5.6A)

22. $(2x-1)\left(4x^2+2x+1\right)$ (5.6B)

23. $3ab(a-b)\left(a^2+ab+b^2\right)$ (5.6D)

24. $\dfrac{7}{5}$ and $-\dfrac{9}{2}$ (5.7A)

25. $0, 7,$ and -3 (5.7A)

Chapter 6 Test Form C

1. $-\dfrac{x+4}{x(x+2)}$ (6.1A)

2. 5 (6.1A)

3. 1 (6.1B)

4. $3-x$ (6.1C)

5. $\dfrac{2}{3}$ (6.1A)

6. $\{x\,|\,x\neq-7,2\}$ (6.1A)

7. $\dfrac{7x^n+14}{\left(x^n-3\right)\left(x^n+2\right)},\ \dfrac{6x^n-18}{\left(x^n-3\right)\left(x^n+2\right)}$ (6.2A)

8. $\dfrac{7x-10}{4(x-2)(x+2)}$ (6.2B)

9. $\dfrac{x+8}{x+5}$ (6.2B)

10. $\dfrac{x-5}{x+4}$ (6.3A)

11. $\dfrac{x+3}{x+2}$ (6.3A)

12. -16 (6.4A)

13. $\dfrac{17}{4}$ (6.4A)

14. 5 and -3 (6.5A)

15. $-1/2$ (6.5A)

16. $f=\dfrac{T+gm}{m}$ (6.5A)

17. $6\dfrac{2}{3}$ tanks (6.4B)

18. 13.5 lb (6.6A)

19. 4 h (6.5B)

20. 45 mph (6.5C)

Cumulative Test: Chapters 4-6 Form C

1. $-3a^3-2a^2-a+3$ (5.2A)

2. $\dfrac{a^6}{b^2}$ (5.1B)

3. $-72x^7y^{12}$ (5.1A)

4. $2a^2-13ab+20b^2$ (5.3B)

5. $81x^2-y^4$ (5.3C)

6. $2x^2\left(2y^2-3y+6\right)$ (5.5A)

7. $(x-3)(a+b)$ (5.5B)

8. $(5x-2)(x+4)$ (5.5D)

9. $(x+1)(x-1)(x+2)(x-2)$ (5.6C)

10. $\dfrac{2xy+1}{3xy-1}$ (6.1A)

11. $\dfrac{3x-24y+4xy}{6x^2y^2}$ (6.2B)

12. $\dfrac{3-2a}{1+4a}$ (6.3A)

13. $\dfrac{10}{11}$ (6.4A)

14. 3 (6.5A)

15. -6 (4.3A)

16. $a=\dfrac{fb}{b-f}$ (6.5A)

Answers to Chapter Tests: Form C

17. 96 min (6.5B)

18. 180 mph (4.4A)

19.
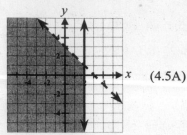
(4.5A)

20.
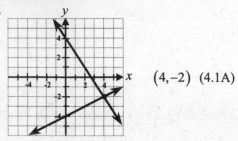
$(4,-2)$ (4.1A)

21. $(-2,4)$ (4.2A)

22. $(2,1,-1)$ (4.2B)

23. $(-1,1,3)$ (4.3B)

24. $(-2,5)$ (4.1B)

25. 12 gallons (6.4B)

Chapter 7 Test Form C

1. a^3 (7.1A)

2. $\dfrac{y^3}{x}$ (7.1A)

3. $-3\sqrt[4]{a^3}$ (7.1B)

4. $5(x-2)^{1/4}$ (7.1B)

5. $xy^4\sqrt[3]{x}$ (7.1C)

6. $5ab^2\sqrt{2a}$ (7.2A)

7. $4ab^2\sqrt[3]{a^2b^2}$ (7.2A)

8. $9\sqrt{2a}$ (7.2B)

9. $6xy\sqrt{x}$ (7.2B)

10. $4x^2y^3$ (7.2C)

11. $4-\sqrt{5}$ (7.2C)

12. $\dfrac{4x\sqrt{y}}{y}$ (7.2D)

13. $\dfrac{\sqrt{x}-2\sqrt{xy}+y}{x-y}$ (7.2D)

14. 8 (7.3A)

15. -7 (7.3A)

16. 160 ft (7.3B)

17. $10i$ (7.4A)

18. $14+2i$ (7.4B)

19. -16 (7.4C)

20. $6i$ (7.4D)

Chapter 8 Test Form C

1. 4 and $\dfrac{2}{3}$ (8.1A)

2. -2 and 7 (8.1A)

3. $2x^2-x-15=0$ (8.1B)

4. 4 and -2 (8.1C)

5. $1-\sqrt{2}$ and $1+\sqrt{2}$ (8.1A)

6. $2-\sqrt{11}$ and $2+\sqrt{11}$ (8.2A)

7. $1-2i\sqrt{2}$ and $1+2i\sqrt{2}$ (8.2A)

8. $-\dfrac{1}{2}$ and 1 (8.3A)

9. -2 and $\dfrac{9}{2}$ (8.3A)

10. Two complex number solutions (8.3A)

11. $4, -4, 4i,$ and $-4i$ (8.4A)

12. 64 (8.4A)

13. 1 (8.4B)

14. 4 (8.4B)

15. 3 and 9 (8.4C)

16. 0 and 3 (8.4C)

17. $\{x \mid x < -4 \text{ or } x > 2\}$

(8.5A)

18. $\left\{x \mid x < 1 \text{ or } x > \dfrac{3}{2}\right\}$

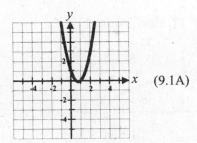

(8.5A)

19. 9 and 11, or −11 and −9 (8.6A)

20. 16 m (8.6A)

Chapter 9 Test Form C

1. Domain: $\left\{x \mid x \in \text{real numbers}\right\}$
   Range: $\left\{y \mid y \geq 4\right\}$ (9.1A)

2. $(2,-2)$; $x = 2$ (9.1A)

3.

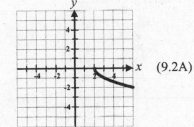

(9.1A)

4.

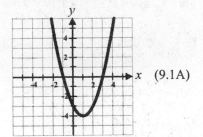

(9.2A)

5. $(-8,0), (3,0)$ (9.1B)

6. $\left(\dfrac{1}{2}, 0\right), (-3, 0)$ (9.1B)

7. 2 (9.1B)

8. 3 (9.1C)

9. −144 (9.1D)

10. 15 ft by 15 ft (9.1D)

11. Yes (9.2A)

12. No (9.4A)

13. 6 (9.3A)

14. −3 (9.3A)

15. $-\dfrac{1}{9}$ (9.3A)

16. −31 (9.3B)

17. $x^2 + 1$ (9.3B)

18. $f^{-1}(x) = \dfrac{1}{5}x + \dfrac{2}{5}$ (9.4B)

19. $f^{-1}(x) = 2x - 6$ (9.4B)

20. Yes (9.4B)

Cumulative Test: Chapters 7-9 Form C

1. $x^{13/4}$ (7.1A)

2. $-2a^2 b^3$ (7.1C)

3. $2 - i$ (7.3B)

4. $-6 + 4i$ (7.4C)

5. 50 (7.3A)

6. 0 and 3 (8.1A)

7. 8 and −4 (8.1C)

8. 6 (8.2A)

9. $\sqrt{2}, -\sqrt{2}, \sqrt{3}$, and $-\sqrt{3}$ (8.4A)

10. 4 (8.4C)

11. $\left[-\dfrac{5}{4}, \dfrac{3}{2}\right]$ (8.5A)

12. 8 min and 24 min (8.6A)

13.

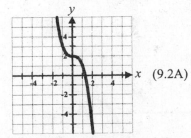

(9.1A)

14.

(9.2A)

15. 12 ft by 12 ft (9.1D)

16. No (9.4A)

17. −1 (9.3A)

Answers to Chapter Tests: Form C

18. -8 (9.3B)

19. $f^{-1}(x) = 3x + 18$ (9.4B)

20. $(7,0)$, $(2,0)$ (9.1B)

Chapter 10 Test Form C

1. 1.0183 (10.1A)

2. $\dfrac{1}{4}$ (10.1A)

3. 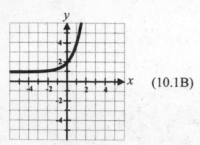 (10.1B)

4. 3.3201 (10.2A)

5. $\log_5 \dfrac{1}{125} = -3$ (10.2A)

6. $10^0 = 1$ (10.2A)

7. 8 (10.2A)

8. $\log_b x + 2\log_b y + \dfrac{1}{2}\log_b z$ (10.2B)

9. $5\ln x + 2\ln y + \ln z$ (10.2B)

10. $\ln \dfrac{x^2}{y^5}$ (10.2B)

11. $\log_a \dfrac{x^3}{y^2 z}$ (10.2B)

12. -0.4055 (10.2C)

13. 2.0868 (10.2C)

14. -7 (10.4A)

15. 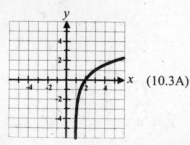 (10.3A)

16. 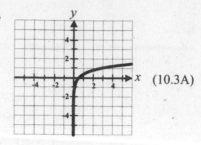 (10.3A)

17. 2 (10.4A)

18. -4 (10.4B)

19. 45.1 days (10.5A)

20. Approximately 87 decibels (10.5A)

Chapter 11 Test Form C

1. 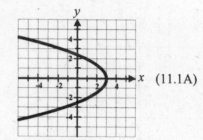 (11.1A)

2. 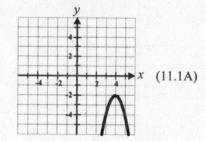 (11.1A)

3. $(6,2)$; $y = 2$ (11.1A)

4. $(x+1)^2 + (y-2)^2 = 5$ (11.2A)

5. $(x+1)^2 + (y-1)^2 = 9$ (11.2A)

6. $(x-2)^2 + (y-2)^2 = 9$

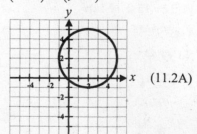 (11.2A)

7. $(x-1)^2 + (y-2)^2 = 4$

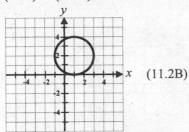

(11.2B)

8.

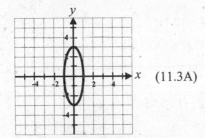

(11.3A)

9.

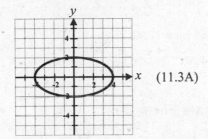

(11.3A)

10.

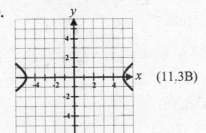

(11.3B)

11.

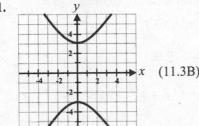

(11.3B)

12. $\left(2, -2\sqrt{2}\right)$, $\left(2, 2\sqrt{2}\right)$, $\left(-2, 2\sqrt{2}\right)$, and $\left(-2, -2\sqrt{2}\right)$ (11.4A)

13. $(-5, -3)$ and $(3, 5)$ (11.4A)

14.

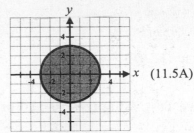

(11.5A)

15.

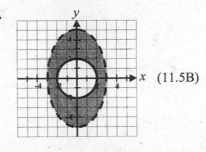

(11.5B)

Chapter 12 Test Form C

1. -8 (12.1A)

2. $\dfrac{1}{56}$ and $\dfrac{1}{110}$ (12.1A)

3. 14 (12.1B)

4. $\dfrac{x^2}{2} + \dfrac{x^3}{3} + \dfrac{x^4}{4} + \dfrac{x^5}{5}$ (12.1B)

5. 103 (12.2A)

6. -37 (12.2A)

7. $a_n = 5n - 4$ (12.2A)

8. 18 (12.2A)

9. 1800 (12.2B)

10. -64 (12.3A)

11. $\dfrac{1}{81}$ (12.3A)

12. 605 (12.3B)

13. $\dfrac{85}{64}$ (12.3B)

14. $\dfrac{25}{3}$ (12.3C)

15. $\dfrac{4}{33}$ (12.3C)

16. $-1080x^2$ (12.4A)

17. 120 (12.4A)

Answers to Chapter Tests: Form C

18. 36 (12.4A)

19. 25 ft (12.2C)

20. 3.9 ft (12.3D)

Cumulative Test: Chapters 10-12 Form C

1. 3 (10.1A)

2.

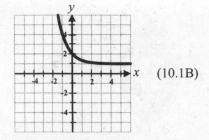 (10.1B)

3. 3 (10.2A)

4. 81 (10.2A)

5. $2\log_3 x + \log_3 y$ (10.2B)

6.

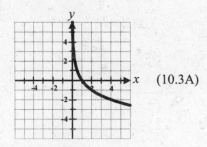 (10.3A)

7. −4 (10.4A)

8. 1 (10.4B)

9.

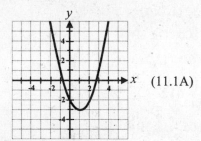 (11.1A)

10. $x^2 + (y+4)^2 = 81$

11.

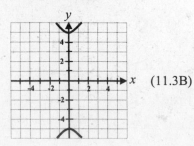 (11.3B)

12. $\left(2, 2\sqrt{3}\right)$ and $\left(2, -2\sqrt{3}\right)$ (11.4A)

13.

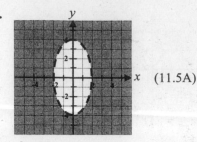 (11.5A)

14. 18 (12.1B)

15. 53 (12.2A)

16. 5 (12.1A)

17. $\dfrac{1}{64}$ (12.3A)

18. $\dfrac{31}{90}$ (12.3C)

19. 165 cans (12.2C)

20. $1120x^4$ (12.4A)

Final Exam Form C

1. 8 (1.2C)

2. $\dfrac{3}{2}$ (1.2C)

3. $8x + y$ (1.3C)

4. $2n - 5$ (1.4A)

5. 4 (2.1B)

6. −4 (2.1C)

7. 8 nickels and 14 quarters (2.2B)

8. 48 ml (2.3B)

9. $\dfrac{1}{2y^5}$ (5.1B)

10. $2x^2 - 5xy - 3y^2$ (5.3B)

11. $y\left(2x^2 - x - 21y\right)$ (5.5A)

12. $(8+x)(1-x)$ (5.5C)

13. $x(4x-1)\left(16x^2 + 4x + 1\right)$ (5.6D)

14. $a + b$ (6.1A)

15. $\dfrac{5}{x-3}$ (6.1C)

16. $\dfrac{3(x+2)}{(x+3)(x-3)}$ (6.2B)

17. $-\dfrac{5(6x-5)}{4(3x-1)}$ (6.3A)

18. $h=\dfrac{V-\pi r^2}{\pi r}$ (2.1D)

19. $2xy^2\sqrt[5]{x^3}$ (7.2A)

20. $-3x\sqrt{x}$ (7.2B)

21. $\dfrac{x+\sqrt{5x}}{x-5}$ (7.2D)

22. -20 (7.4C)

23. $-6+3i$ (7.4C)

24. -2 (3.2A)

25.

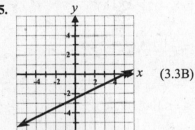 (3.3B)

26.

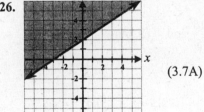 (3.7A)

27. $\dfrac{5}{3}$ (3.4A)

28. $y=\dfrac{2}{3}x+\dfrac{14}{3}$ (3.5A)

29. -2 and 1 (8.1A)

30. -6 and $\dfrac{3}{8}$ (8.1A)

31. Length: 25 cm; Width: 15 cm (8.6A)

32.

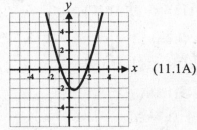 (11.1A)

33. No (3.2A)

34. $f^{-1}(x)=\dfrac{1}{3}x+\dfrac{2}{3}$ (9.4B)

35. $(6,0)$ and $(-3,0)$ (9.1B)

36. $(x+2)^2+(y-4)^2=64$ (11.2A)

37. $(-4,3)$ (4.1B)

38. $(2,3),\ (-2,3),\ (-2,-3),\ (2,-3)$ (11.4A)

39.

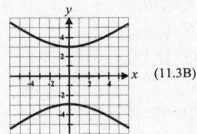 (11.3B)

40. $(1,2,3)$ (4.2B)

41. 3 (4.3A)

42. 81 (10.1A)

43. $\dfrac{1}{16}$ (10.2A)

44. 3.7210 (10.2C)

45. 9 (10.4A)

46. 2 (10.4B)

47. -4 (12.1B)

48. 12 (12.2A)

49. $\dfrac{3}{4}$ (12.3C)

50. $54x^2$ (12.4A)

Answers to Chapter Tests: Form D

Chapter 1 Test Form D

1. π (1.1A)

2. $\{x \mid 2 \leq x < 7\}$ (1.1C)

3. 1 (1.2A)

4. $\{x \mid 1 \leq x \leq 3\}$ (1.1B)

5. -4 (1.2A)

6. -4 (1.2A)

7. 144 (1.2C)

8. (1.1C)

9. $-\dfrac{1}{2}$ (1.2B)

10. $\dfrac{13}{9}$ (1.2B)

11. 1.225 (1.2B)

12. -1.7 (1.2B)

13. 73 (1.2D)

14. $-\dfrac{7}{24}$ (1.2D)

15. $\dfrac{11}{6}$ (1.3B)

16. 5 (1.3B)

17. 1 (1.3A)

18. The Multiplication Property of Zero (1.3A)

19. (1.1C)

20. $-11y + 4x - 4$ (1.3C)

21. $n^2 + n + 3$ (1.4A)

22. $1000 - x$ (1.4B)

23. $\{-10, -5, 0, 10, 20\}$ (1.1C)

24. $\{0, 2\}$ (1.1C)

25. (1.1C)

Chapter 2 Test Form D

1. -15 (2.1A)

2. 4 (2.1A)

3. $\dfrac{3}{2}$ (2.1A)

4. -4 (2.1B)

5. -28 (2.1B)

6. 4 (2.1B)

7. 1 (2.1C)

8. $c = \dfrac{100m}{I}$ (2.1D)

9. 2 (2.1C)

10. $\left[\dfrac{3}{2}, \infty\right)$ (2.4A)

11. $\{x \mid x > -32\}$ (2.4A)

12. $\left(-\infty, \dfrac{6}{5}\right) \cup (5, \infty)$ (2.4B)

13. $\varnothing$ (2.4B)

14. $72 \leq x \leq 100$ (2.4C)

15. $\dfrac{7}{4}$ (2.5A)

16. $-\dfrac{16}{5}$ and 4 (2.5A)

17. $\varnothing$ (2.5B)

18. $\left\{x \mid -1 \leq x \leq \dfrac{7}{3}\right\}$ (2.5B)

19. $80,000 (2.4C)

20. 29, 31, 33 (2.2A)

21. 5¢ stamps: 7; 12¢ stamps: 23 (2.2B)

22. 40 lb (2.3A)

23. 180 mi/h (2.3C)

24. 1.693 in.; 1.707 in. (2.5C)

25. 76.8% (2.3B)

Chapter 3 Test Form D

1. 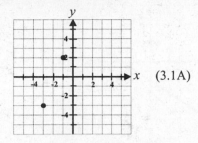 (3.1A)

2. 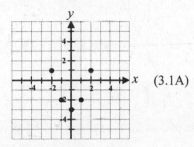 (3.1A)

3. $\left(\frac{7}{2},\frac{1}{2}\right)$; 7.62 (3.1B)

4. 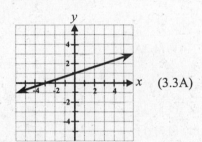 (3.3A)

5. 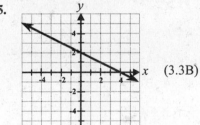 (3.3B)

6. $\frac{1}{5}$ (3.4A)

7. $-\frac{3}{2}$ (3.2A)

8. $(3,0)$ (3.3C)

9. $\left(0,\frac{2}{3}\right)$ (3.3C)

10. 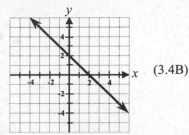 (3.4B)

11. 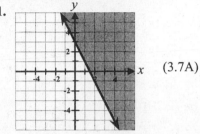 (3.7A)

12. $y=-\frac{3}{2}x-\frac{5}{2}$ (3.5A)

13. $y=3.2x+400$ (3.5C)

14. $y=x-3$ (3.5B)

15. $y=3$ (3.5A)

16. $y=\frac{2}{3}x-\frac{16}{3}$ (3.6A)

17. D: $\{-7,-1,1,3\}$; R: $\{2\}$ (3.2A)

18. none (3.2A)

19. The resale value of the printing press is $40,000 after 2.5 years. (3.3D)

20. 3.75 years (3.1C)

Cumulative Test: Chapters 1-3 Form D

1. 9 (1.2A)

2. −72 (1.2C)

3. $-\frac{7}{12}$ (1.2B)

4. $\frac{1}{3}$ (1.2D)

5. −4 (1.3B)

6. The Distributive Property (1.3A)

7. $-9x-14$ (1.3C)

Answers to Chapter Tests: Form D

8. $\{1,2,3,4,5,6\}$ (1.1C)

9. $-\dfrac{2}{3}$ (2.1A)

10. 60 (2.1B)

11. $\left[\dfrac{2}{3},\infty\right)$ (2.4B)

12. 2 and −1 (2.5A)

13. $\left\{x \mid x > 3 \text{ or } x < -\dfrac{3}{2}\right\}$ (2.5B)

14. −1 (2.2A)

15. 12 mi (2.3C)

16. 32 oz (2.3B)

17. $h = 2A - b$ (2.1D)

18. 15 (3.2A)

19. 0 , horizontal (3.4A)

20. $(0,-3)$ (3.3C)

21. $y = -3x + 16$ (3.5A)

22. $y = -\dfrac{1}{2}x + \dfrac{7}{2}$ (3.5B)

23. $y = \dfrac{4}{3}x - \dfrac{19}{3}$ (3.6A)

24.

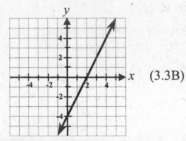 (3.3B)

25.

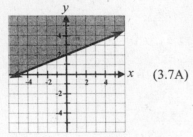 (3.7A)

Chapter 4 Test Form D

1.

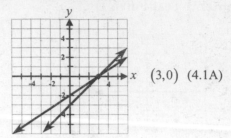 $(3,0)$ (4.1A)

2.

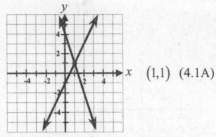 $(1,1)$ (4.1A)

3. $35,000 at 3.9%; $15,000 at 10.5% (4.1C)

4. $\left(-\dfrac{1}{2},\dfrac{1}{2}\right)$ (4.1B)

5. $(-2,1)$ (4.2A)

6. $(5,-4)$ (4.2A)

7. $(1,1,2)$ (4.2B)

8. −11 (4.3A)

9. −11 (4.3A)

10. $(-3,2)$ (4.3B)

11. $(1,2,-2)$ (4.3B)

12. 2 mi/h (4.4A)

13. $3.00 (4.4B)

14.

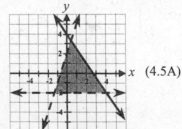 (4.5A)

15.

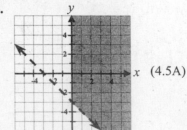 (4.5A)

Chapter 5 Test Form D

1. $3y^3 - 9y^2 + 8y + 10$ (5.2B)

2. a^{3n+6} (5.1A)

3. $\dfrac{xy}{40z^4}$ (5.1B)

4. -72 (5.2A)

5. 7.3×10^{-4} (5.1C)

6. 4.32×10^{12} m (5.1D)

7. $-12a^6 + 8a^5 - 14a^4$ (5.3A)

8. $y^{n+3} - 3y^{n+2} + y^{n+1}$ (5.3A)

9. $6x^2 + 7xy - 3y^2$ (5.3B)

10. $x^3 + 2x^2 - 17x + 6$ (5.3B)

11. $9x^2 - 6x + 1$ (5.3C)

12. $x^2 - 6x + 3$ (5.2B)

13. $\left(4x^3 + 15x^2 - 4x\right)$ in^3 (5.3D)

14. $2x - 4$ (5.4A)

15. $x^2 + 4x - 1 + \dfrac{3}{x-4}$ (5.4B)

16. 8 (5.4D)

17. $(y-3)(x-4)$ (5.5B)

18. $(x-7)(x-9)$ (5.5C)

19. $(7x-2)(x+3)$ (5.5D)

20. $(8x-y)(8x+y)$ (5.6A)

21. $\left(x^n - 3\right)^2$ (5.6A)

22. $(3d-c)\left(9d^2 + 3cd + c^2\right)$ (5.6B)

23. $3ab(a-b)\left(a^2 + ab + b^2\right)$ (5.6D)

24. $\dfrac{1}{3}$ and $\dfrac{7}{4}$ (5.7A)

25. Base: 9 ft; height: 14 ft (5.7B)

Chapter 6 Test Form D

1. $\left\{x \,\middle|\, x \neq \dfrac{10}{3}\right\}$ (6.1A)

2. $\dfrac{a+2b}{2a-b}$ (6.1A)

3. $\dfrac{a^{n+1}}{a^n - 1}$ (6.1B)

4. 1 (6.1C)

5. $-\dfrac{8}{3}$ (6.1A)

6. $\dfrac{x^2 - 3x - 1}{(x-2)(x-4)}$ (6.2B)

7. $\dfrac{x^2 + x - 2}{x(x-1)}, \ \dfrac{5x}{x(x-1)}$ (6.2A)

8. $\dfrac{4}{3x-1}$ (6.2B)

9. $\dfrac{x+4}{2x}$ (6.2B)

10. $-\dfrac{1}{y+1}$ (6.3A)

11. $\dfrac{2x+5}{-5x-11}$ (6.3A)

12. 17 (6.4A)

13. 22 (6.4A)

14. $\dfrac{1}{2}$ (6.5A)

15. $\dfrac{2}{5}$ (6.5A)

16. $R = \dfrac{E - Ir}{I}$ (6.5A)

17. 100 (6.4B)

18. 1188 (6.6A)

19. 60 h (6.5B)

20. 25 mph (6.5C)

Answers to Chapter Tests: Form D

Cumulative Test: Chapters 4-6 Form D

1. $3x^3 - 7x^2 - x + 1$ (5.2B)

2. $-108x^8y^7z^{11}$ (5.1A)

3. $-\dfrac{z^2}{4x^2y}$ (5.1B)

4. $2b^{2n} - 13b^n + 15$ (5.3B)

5. $9a^4 + 6a^2b + 4b^2$ (5.3C)

6. $x^2\left(5x^{n+3} + x^{n+2} + 4\right)$ (5.5A)

7. $\left(y^2 - 2\right)\left(x^2 + 4\right)$ (5.5B)

8. $a(a+1)(a-1)\left(a^2+1\right)$ (5.6D)

9. $2x - 1$ (6.1A)

10. $\dfrac{10x^2y^2}{7}$ (6.1C)

11. $\dfrac{8y - 5x + 9y^2}{6xy^2}$ (6.2B)

12. $-\dfrac{1}{y(x+y)}$ (6.3A)

13. -2 (6.4A)

14. 0 (6.5A)

15. 60 minutes (6.5B)

16. $\dfrac{3}{11}$ (6.5A)

17. $R = \dfrac{R_1 R_2}{R_1 + R_2}$ (6.5A)

18.
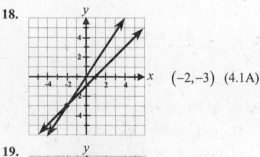 $(-2,-3)$ (4.1A)

19.
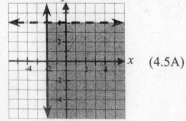 (4.5A)

20. $(0,6)$ (4.1B)

21. $\left(\dfrac{4}{3}, \dfrac{1}{15}\right)$ (4.2A)

22. no solution (4.2B)

23. $(-2,7)$ (4.3B)

24. 180 mph (4.4A)

25. 15 (4.3A)

Chapter 7 Test Form D

1. $a^{18}b^{34}$ (7.1A)

2. $\dfrac{b^{5/12}}{a^3}$ (7.1A)

3. $4\sqrt[3]{3z}$ (7.1B)

4. $\left(a^2 - 2\right)^{1/3}$ (7.1B)

5. $2a^3b^4$ (7.1C)

6. $-3xy^3\sqrt[3]{x^2y^2}$ (7.2A)

7. $5x^2y\sqrt{2y}$ (7.2A)

8. $4x\sqrt{3x}$ (7.2B)

9. $x\sqrt[3]{2} + 2x\sqrt[3]{4}$ (7.2B)

10. $4x^2y^3$ (7.2C)

11. $16x + 24\sqrt{x} + 9$ (7.2B)

12. $\dfrac{\sqrt{15}}{5x}$ (7.2C)

13. $1 + 2x\sqrt{5}$ (7.2C)

14. 19 (7.3A)

15. 29 (7.3A)

16. 2500 ft (7.3B)

17. $10\sqrt{2} + 2i\sqrt{3}$ (7.4A)

18. $3 - 2i$ (7.4B)

19. $4 + 3i$ (7.4C)

20. $\dfrac{6}{5} - \dfrac{2}{5}i$ (7.4D)

Chapter 8 Test Form D

1. $-\dfrac{3}{4}$ and -2 (8.1A)

2. $-\dfrac{1}{2}$ and 1 (8.1A)

3. $2x^2 - 5x - 3 = 0$ (8.1B)

4. -2 and 6 (8.1C)

5. 3 and -3 (8.1C)

6. $-\dfrac{1}{2}$ and 2 (8.2A)

7. -4 and $\dfrac{3}{2}$ (8.2A)

8. $3 + \sqrt{6}$ and $3 - \sqrt{6}$ (8.3A)

9. $\dfrac{7 + \sqrt{37}}{2}$ and $\dfrac{7 - \sqrt{37}}{2}$ (8.3A)

10. One real number solution (8.3A)

11. $-2\sqrt{2}, -2i\sqrt{2}, 2i\sqrt{2}, 2\sqrt{2}$ (8.4A)

12. 36 and 9 (8.4A)

13. $5 + \sqrt{5}$ (8.4B)

14. $1 + \dfrac{\sqrt{6}}{2}$ (8.4B)

15. 3 and -2 (8.4C)

16. 0 and -1 (8.4C)

17. $\{x \mid x \le -4 \text{ or } x \ge 2\}$

(8.5A)

18. $\left\{x \mid -5 < x < -2 \text{ or } x > \dfrac{3}{2}\right\}$

(8.5A)

19. 24 m (8.6A)

20. 11 (8.6A)

Chapter 9 Test Form D

1. Domain: $\{x \mid x \in \text{real numbers}\}$
   Range: $\{y \mid y \ge 0\}$ (9.1A)

2. $(5, -23); x = 5$ (9.1A)

3. 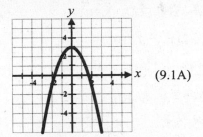 (9.1A)

4. 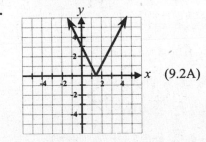 (9.2A)

5. $\left(\dfrac{1}{2}, 0\right), (1, 0)$ (9.1B)

6. $-\dfrac{7}{2}, \dfrac{5}{2}$ (9.1B)

7. 0 (9.1B)

8. 5 (9.1C)

9. 16 and -16 (9.1D)

10. $225\ \text{ft}^2$ (9.1D)

11. 7 (9.3A)

12. -6 (9.3A)

13. $\dfrac{1}{2}$ (9.3A)

14. -22 (9.3B)

15. $x^2 + 6x + 8$ (9.3B)

16. $f^{-1}(x) = 3 - \tfrac{1}{2}x$ (9.4B)

17. Yes (9.4A)

18. No (9.2A)

19. $f^{-1}(x) = \dfrac{1}{5}x - \dfrac{1}{5}$ (9.4B)

20. No (9.4B)

Answers to Chapter Tests: Form D

Cumulative Test: Chapters 7-9 Form D

1. $x^2 - x^{3/4}$ (7.1A)

2. $(x-1)^{4/3}$ (7.1B)

3. $7 + 8i$ (7.4B)

4. $3\sqrt{2} - 3i$ (7.4C)

5. 22 (7.3A)

6. $2x^2 - 5x - 12 = 0$ (8.1B)

7. $2 + 2\sqrt{6}$ and $2 - 2\sqrt{6}$ (8.1C)

8. $4 - \sqrt{10},\ 4 + \sqrt{10}$ (8.2A)

9. $-2, -1, 1,$ and 2 (8.4A)

10. $5 + 2\sqrt{2}$ (8.4B)

11. $2 + 4\sqrt{2}$ and $2 - 4\sqrt{2}$ (8.4C)

12. $\{x \mid x < -4 \text{ or } x > 4\}$ (8.5A)

13. 45 ft (8.6A)

14. $(5,0), (-4,0)$ (9.1B)

15. 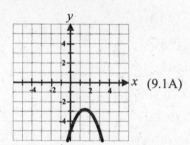 (9.1A)

16. 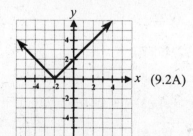 (9.2A)

17. 1 (9.1C)

18. -4 (9.3A)

19. 49 (9.3B)

20. $f^{-1}(x) = \dfrac{1}{2}x - \dfrac{3}{2}$ (9.4B)

Chapter 10 Test Form D

1. 7.3891 (10.1A)

2. 16 (10.1A)

3. 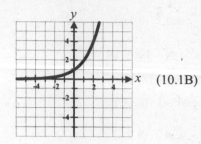 (10.1B)

4. 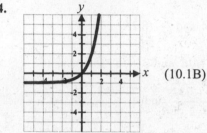 (10.1B)

5. $\log_5 \dfrac{1}{25} = -2$ (10.2A)

6. $7^{-2} = \dfrac{1}{49}$ (10.2A)

7. -6 (10.2A)

8. 55.9017 (10.2A)

9. $\dfrac{1}{3}\left(2\log x + 4\log y\right)$ (10.2B)

10. $\log_2 \dfrac{\sqrt{x}}{y\,z}$ (10.2B)

11. $3\ln x - \dfrac{1}{2}\ln y$ (10.2B)

12. $\ln \dfrac{x^2 z^3}{\sqrt{y}}$ (10.2B)

13. -0.2877

14. 0.1133 (10.2C)

15. 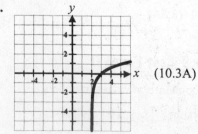 (10.3A)

16.

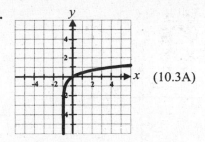

(10.3A)

17. 7 (10.4A)

18. $\dfrac{3}{8}$ (10.4A)

19. 5 (10.4B)

20. \$9646.86 (10.5A)

Chapter 11 Test Form D

1.

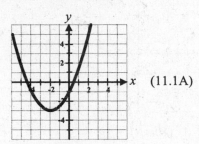

(11.1A)

2.

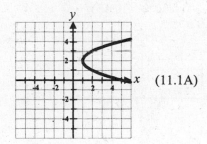

(11.1A)

3. $(2,-3)$; $x=2$ (11.1A)

4. $x^2 + (y+2)^2 = 9$ (11.2A)

5. $(x+3)^2 + (y-4)^2 = 25$ (11.2A)

6.

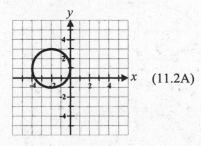

(11.2A)

7. $(x+3)^2 + (y-2)^2 = 9$

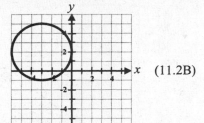

(11.2B)

8.

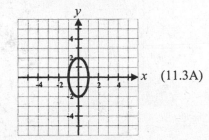

(11.3A)

9.

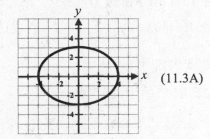

(11.3A)

10.

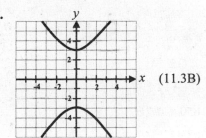

(11.3B)

11.

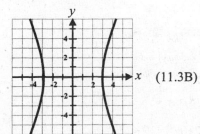

(11.3B)

12. $(3,3)$ (11.4A)

13. $(4,28)$ and $(-7,83)$ (11.4A)

Answers to Chapter Tests: Form D

14.

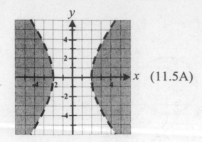 x (11.5A)

15.

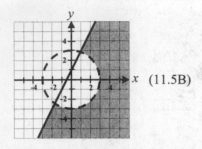 x (11.5B)

Chapter 12 Test Form D

1. 7/10 (12.1A)

2. $\dfrac{5}{6}$ and $\dfrac{9}{10}$ (12.1A)

3. 225 (12.1B)

4. $\dfrac{2}{x} + \dfrac{2}{x^2} + \dfrac{2}{x^3} + \dfrac{2}{x^4}$ (12.1B)

5. 106 (12.2A)

6. $a_n = 4n - 2$ (12.2A)

7. 27 (12.2A)

8. -72 (12.2B)

9. 1650 (12.2B)

10. 768 (12.3A)

11. 3 (12.3A)

12. 2188 (12.3B)

13. 47.25 (12.3B)

14. 27/2 (12.3C)

15. 19/30 (12.3C)

16. $216x^2$ (12.4A)

17. 4896 (12.4A)

18. 56 (12.4A)

19. 3960 seats (12.2C)

20. 94.3°F (12.3D)

Cumulative Test: Chapters 10-12 Form D

1. 3 (10.1A)

2.

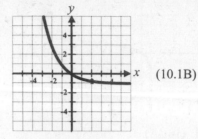 x (10.1B)

3. 2 (10.2A)

4. $\dfrac{1}{9}$ (10.2A)

5. $\log_2 \dfrac{x^3 z^2}{y^4}$ (10.2B)

6.

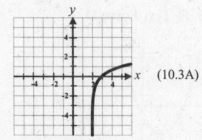 x (10.3A)

7. -1 (10.4A)

8. -1 and 9 (10.4B)

9.

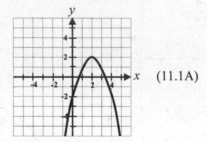 x (11.1A)

10. $(x+3)^2 + (y-3)^2 = 49$ (11.2A)

11.

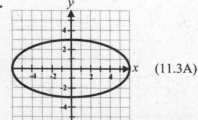 x (11.3A)

12. $(3,4)$ and $(-5,0)$ (11.4A)

13.

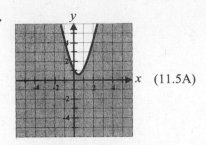 (11.5A)

14. −5 (12.1B)

15. −34 (12.1A)

16. 15 (12.2A)

17. 2380 (12.2B)

18. $-\dfrac{3}{16}$ (12.3A)

19. 4 (12.3C)

20. $1080x^2$ (12.4A)

Final Exam Form D

1. 31 (1.2D)

2. −74 (1.2C)

3. $45x - 72y$ (1.3C)

4. $\{2, 3, 4\}$ (1.1C)

5. 10 (2.1B)

6. 1 (2.1C)

7. There are thirty-two 3¢ coins and ten 2¢ coins. (2.2B)

8. 250 mi/h (2.3C)

9. $-24x^5y^4$ (5.1A)

10. $a^3 + 2a^2 - 4a - 3$ (5.3B)

11. $(4x+1)(3x-2)$ (5.5D)

12. $(y-3)(y^2+3y+9)$ (5.6B)

13. $5x^2(x-6)(x+4)$ (5.6D)

14. $\dfrac{3x+4}{x+4}$ (6.1A)

15. $\dfrac{x-5}{4}$ (6.1B)

16. $\dfrac{x+5}{x-5}$ (6.3A)

17. $180,000 (6.4B)

18. 24 ft up on the building (6.4B)

19. 3/2 (6.5A)

20. $4xy\sqrt{2}$ (7.2B)

21. $2+\sqrt{2}$ (7.2D)

22. $-2+4i\sqrt{3}$ (7.4C)

23. 11 (7.3A)

24. 4 and $-\dfrac{2}{3}$ (8.1A)

25.

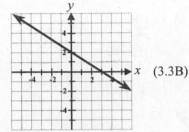 (3.3B)

26.

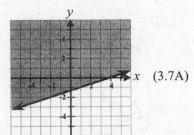 (3.7A)

27. $y = -\dfrac{3}{4}x + \dfrac{15}{4}$ (3.5A)

28. $y = 2x + 3$ (3.6A)

29. $\dfrac{3+\sqrt{37}}{2}$ and $\dfrac{3-\sqrt{37}}{2}$ (8.3A)

30. $\dfrac{5+\sqrt{73}}{4}$ and $\dfrac{5-\sqrt{73}}{4}$ (8.4C)

31. $2h^2 + 7h + 12$ (3.2A)

32. Yes (3.2A)

33.

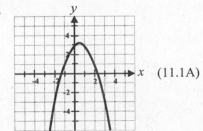 (11.1A)

371

Answers to Chapter Tests: Form D

34.

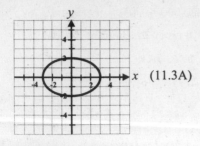 (11.3A)

35. $(3,0)$ and $(4,0)$ (9.1B)

36. $(x-3)^2+(y+2)^2=25$ (11.2A)

37. 9 (9.3B)

38. $(8,30)$ (4.1B)

39. $(1,-1,-2)$ (4.2B)

40. $\left(2\sqrt{3},0\right)$ and $\left(-2\sqrt{3},0\right)$ (11.4A)

41. 33 (4.3A)

42. 5 (10.2A)

43. 64 (10.2A)

44. $\dfrac{5}{2}\log_2 x+\dfrac{3}{2}\log_2 y$ (10.2B)

45. 0 (10.4A)

46. 2 (10.4B)

47. -68 (12.2A)

48. 3940 (12.2B)

49. $31\dfrac{31}{125}$ (12.3B)

50. $-60x^2$ (12.4A)

Chapter 1 Test Form E

1. c (1.1A)
2. a (1.1B)
3. b (1.2A)
4. d (1.2A)
5. b (1.2A)
6. d (1.2A)
7. a (1.2C)
8. c (1.1C)
9. b (1.2B)
10. b (1.2B)
11. a (1.2B)
12. c (1.2B)
13. b (1.2D)
14. a (1.2D)
15. b (1.3B)
16. a (1.3B)
17. a (1.3A)
18. a (1.3A)
19. b (1.3C)
20. a (1.3C)
21. d (1.4A)
22. c (1.4B)
23. a (1.1C)
24. d (1.1C)

Chapter 2 Test Form E

1. b (2.1A)
2. a (2.1A)
3. d (2.1A)
4. a (2.1B)
5. c (2.1B)
6. a (2.1B)
7. c (2.1C)
8. a (2.1D)
9. c (2.1C)
10. d (2.4A)
11. b (2.4A)
12. b (2.4B)
13. d (2.4B)
14. c (2.4C)
15. a (2.5A)
16. d (2.5A)
17. a (2.5B)
18. d (2.5B)
19. d (2.4C)
20. b (2.2A)
21. b (2.2B)
22. a (2.3A)
23. d (2.3C)
24. a (2.5C)
25. c (2.3B)

Chapter 3 Test Form E

1. b (3.1A)
2. c (3.1A)
3. b (3.1B)
4. a (3.3A)
5. c (3.3B)
6. b (3.4A)
7. c (3.2A)
8. c (3.3C)
9. b (3.4B)
10. d (3.5A)
11. a (3.5A)
12. c (3.5B)
13. b (3.5C)
14. c (3.6A)
15. d (3.2A)
16. b (3.7A)
17. a (3.1B)
18. b (3.2A)
19. d (3.3D)
20. a (3.1C)

Cumulative Test: Chapters 1–3 Form E

1. b (1.2A)
2. c (1.2C)
3. a (1.2B)
4. b (1.2D)
5. d (1.3B)
6. b (1.1C)
7. d (1.3C)
8. a (1.4A)
9. d (2.1A)
10. c (2.1C)
11. c (2.4A)
12. a (2.5A)
13. b (2.5B)
14. a (2.2B)
15. a (2.3C)
16. c (2.3B)
17. b (3.2A)
18. a (3.3B)
19. b (3.4A)
20. a (3.3C)
21. b (3.5A)
22. d (3.5B)
23. c (3.6A)
24. c (3.5C)
25. c (3.7A)

Chapter 4 Test Form E

1. a (4.1A)
2. b (4.1B)
3. d (4.1C)
4. d (4.2A)
5. b (4.2B)
6. d (4.3A)
7. c (4.3A)
8. c (4.3B)
9. d (4.3B)

Answers to Chapter Tests: Form E

10. c (4.4A)
11. d (4.4A)
12. d (4.4B)
13. c (4.4B)
14. c (4.5A)
15. d (4.5A)

Chapter 5 Test Form E

1. b (5.2B)
2. a (5.1A)
3. d (5.1B)
4. d (5.2A)
5. c (5.1C)
6. a (5.1D)
7. b (5.3A)
8. a (5.3B)
9. d (5.3C)
10. a (5.3D)
11. b (5.5A)
12. b (5.5B)
13. c (5.5C)
14. d (5.5D)
15. b (5.4A)
16. c (5.4B)
17. b (5.6A)
18. a (5.6B)
19. c (5.6C)
20. b (5.7A)

Chapter 6 Test Form E

1. c (6.1A)
2. b (6.1A)
3. d (6.1B)
4. a (6.1C)
5. b (6.1A)
6. d (6.1A)
7. c (6.2A)
8. a (6.2B)

9. c (6.2B)
10. d (6.3A)
11. a (6.3A)
12. b (6.4A)
13. c (6.4A)
14. a (6.4B)
15. d (6.5A)
16. d (6.5A)
17. c (6.6A)
18. a (6.5A)
19. c (6.5B)
20. c (6.5C)

Cumulative Test: Chapters 4-6 Form E

1. a (5.1A)
2. a (5.1B)
3. c (5.1C)
4. d (5.3B)
5. b (5.3C)
6. b (5.5C)
7. c (5.5D)
8. d (5.6D)
9. b (5.7A)
10. c (6.1A)
11. a (6.2B)
12. c (6.4A)
13. b (6.3A)
14. d (6.5A)
15. a (6.5B)
16. b (6.5C)
17. a (6.6A)
18. b (4.1B)
19. c (4.2A)
20. b (4.3B)

Chapter 7 Test Form E

1. b (7.1A)
2. a (7.1A)
3. d (7.1B)
4. c (7.1B)
5. d (7.1C)
6. b (7.2A)
7. a (7.2A)
8. c (7.2B)
9. d (7.2B)
10. a (7.2C)
11. a (7.2C)
12. b (7.2D)
13. d (7.2D)
14. c (7.3A)
15. b (7.3A)
16. c (7.3B)
17. d (7.4A)
18. c (7.4B)
19. b (7.4C)
20. d (7.4D)

Chapter 8 Test Form E

1. a (8.1A)
2. a (8.1A)
3. c (8.1B)
4. a (8.1C)
5. a (8.1C)
6. b (8.2A)
7. c (8.2A)
8. a (8.3A)
9. c (8.3A)
10. a (8.3A)
11. d (8.4A)
12. c (8.4A)
13. a (8.4B)
14. b (8.4B)
15. a (8.4C)

16. d (8.4C)

17. b (8.5A)

18. c (8.5A)

19. c (8.6A)

20. d (8.6A)

Chapter 9 Test Form E

1. d (9.1A)

2. b (9.1B)

3. b (9.1C)

4. c (9.1D)

5. b (9.2A)

6. a (9.2A)

7. d (9.3A)

8. c (9.3A)

9. c (9.3A)

10. b (9.3B)

11. d (9.3B)

12. b (9.4A)

13. c (9.4B)

14. d (9.4B)

15. d (9.4B)

Cumulative Test: Chapters 7-9 Form E

1. b (7.1A)

2. d (7.2A)

3. a (7.4C)

4. a (7.3A)

5. b (8.1B)

6. a (8.1C)

7. c (8.4B)

8. c (8.4C)

9. a (8.5A)

10. b (8.6A)

11. c (9.1A)

12. d (9.2A)

13. b (9.3A)

14. a (9.3B)

15. a (9.4B)

Chapter 10 Test Form E

1. b (10.1A)

2. d (10.1A)

3. c (10.1B)

4. c (10.2A)

5. a (10.2A)

6. b (10.2A)

7. d (10.2A)

8. b (10.2B)

9. d (10.2B)

10. c (10.2B)

11. d (10.2B)

12. a (10.2C)

13. c (10.2C)

14. a (10.3A)

15. a (10.4A)

16. d (10.4A)

17. c (10.4A)

18. a (10.4B)

19. b (10.4B)

20. c (10.5A)

Chapter 11 Test Form E

1. c (11.1A)

2. b (11.1A)

3. d (11.1A)

4. b (11.2A)

5. c (11.2A)

6. a (11.2B)

7. c (11.2B)

8. b (11.3A)

9. d (11.3B)

10. b (11.4A)

11. d (11.4A)

12. a (11.5A)

13. a (11.5A)

14. d (11.5B)

15. b (11.5B)

Chapter 12 Test Form E

1. c (12.1A)

2. c (12.1A)

3. b (12.1B)

4. a (12.1B)

5. d (12.2A)

6. b (12.2A)

7. b (12.2A)

8. c (12.2B)

9. a (12.2B)

10. c (12.2C)

11. c (12.3A)

12. d (12.3A)

13. d (12.3B)

14. a (12.3B)

15. c (12.3C)

16. b (12.3C)

17. c (12.3D)

18. a (12.4A)

19. d (12.4A)

20. a (12.4A)

Cumulative Test: Chapters 10-12 Form E

1. c (10.1A)

2. a (10.2A)

3. a (10.2B)

4. d (10.4B)

5. a (10.5A)

6. b (11.1A)

7. d (11.2A)

8. c (11.3B)

9. a (11.4A)

10. d (11.5A)

Answers to Chapter Tests: Form E

11. b (12.1A)
12. c (12.2A)
13. d (12.3C)
14. d (12.2C)
15. b (12.4A)

Final Exam Form E

1. b (1.2C)
2. b (1.3B)
3. c (1.3C)
4. d (1.4A)
5. b (2.1B)
6. a (2.1C)
7. b (2.2A)
8. c (2.3C)
9. a (5.1B)
10. b (5.3B)
11. b (5.5A)
12. c (5.5D)
13. d (5.7A)
14. a (5.4B)
15. d (6.1C)
16. a (6.2B)
17. b (6.3A)
18. a (6.5A)
19. b (7.1C)
20. c (7.2B)
21. a (7.2C)
22. d (7.4B)
23. b (7.4D)
24. c (3.3A)
25. b (3.4A)
26. c (3.5B)
27. a (3.7A)
28. a (8.3A)
29. d (8.4A)
30. b (8.4B)
31. c (3.2A)

32. c (9.2A)
33. b (9.3B)
34. a (11.1A)
35. a (9.1C)
36. c (3.1B)
37. d (11.2A)
38. c (4.2A)
39. a (4.2B)
40. d (4.3A)
41. c (4.4A)
42. b (10.1A)
43. d (10.2A)
44. a (10.2B)
45. c (10.4A)
46. c (10.4B)
47. d (12.1B)
48. a (12.2A)
49. d (12.3B)
50. a (12.4A)

Chapter 1 Test Form F

1. c (1.1A)
2. b (1.1B)
3. a (1.2A)
4. d (1.2A)
5. a (1.2A)
6. b (1.2A)
7. d (1.2C)
8. b (1.1C)
9. d (1.2B)
10. a (1.2B)
11. b (1.2B)
12. b (1.2B)
13. c (1.2D)
14. d (1.2D)
15. a (1.3B)
16. d (1.3B)
17. c (1.3A)
18. c (1.3C)
19. b (1.3C)
20. a (1.4B)
21. a (1.4A)
22. c (1.1C)

Chapter 2 Test Form F

1. d (2.1A)
2. b (2.1A)
3. a (2.1A)
4. c (2.1B)
5. c (2.1B)
6. b (2.1B)
7. b (2.1C)
8. a (2.1C)
9. b (2.4A)
10. a (2.4A)
11. b (2.4B)
12. c (2.4B)
13. b (2.4C)
14. d (2.5A)
15. a (2.5B)
16. a (2.5C)
17. c (2.2A)
18. b (2.2B)
19. c (2.3A)
20. b (2.3C)
21. d (2.4C)
22. a (2.3B)
23. a (2.1D)

Chapter 3 Test Form F

1. a (3.1A)
2. d (3.1A)
3. c (3.3A)
4. a (3.3B)
5. c (3.4A)
6. c (3.2A)
7. b (3.3C)
8. b (3.4B)
9. c (3.5A)
10. b (3.5B)
11. b (3.6A)
12. a (3.2A)
13. c (3.7A)
14. b (3.1B)
15. b (3.1B)
16. d (3.2A)
17. d (3.5A)
18. c (3.5C)
19. c (3.3D)
20. b (3.1C)

Cumulative Test: Chapters 1-3 Form F

1. c (1.2C)
2. b (1.2D)
3. b (1.3B)
4. a (1.3A)
5. d (1.3C)
6. a (1.4A)
7. b (2.1A)
8. c (2.1C)
9. c (2.4B)
10. b (2.5A)
11. b (2.2A)
12. c (2.3A)
13. d (2.4A)
14. b (3.3B)
15. a (3.4A)
16. a (3.5A)
17. c (3.6A)
18. b (3.5C)
19. b (3.7A)
20. c (3.2A)

Chapter 4 Test Form F

1. b (4.1A)
2. a (4.1B)
3. c (4.1C)
4. d (4.2A)
5. d (4.2B)
6. b (4.3A)
7. a (4.3A)
8. b (4.3B)
9. c (4.3B)
10. d (4.4A)
11. c (4.4A)
12. b (4.4B)
13. b (4.4B)
14. b (4.5A)
15. c (4.5A)

Answers to Chapter Tests: Form F

Chapter 5 Test Form F

1. a (5.2B)
2. b (5.1A)
3. c (5.1C)
4. b (5.1D)
5. d (5.3A)
6. d (5.3A)
7. b (5.3B)
8. a (5.3B)
9. c (5.3C)
10. b (5.3D)
11. c (5.2A)
12. d (5.5C)
13. c (5.5D)
14. d (5.6A)
15. b (5.6A)
16. c (5.4A)
17. a (5.6B)
18. c (5.6D)
19. a (5.7A)
20. b (5.4B)

Chapter 6 Test Form F

1. a (6.1A)
2. a (6.1A)
3. b (6.1B)
4. d (6.1C)
5. c (6.1A)
6. a (6.1A)
7. d (6.2B)
8. d (6.2B)
9. d (6.3A)
10. a (6.3A)
11. d (6.4A)
12. a (6.4A)
13. c (6.4B)
14. c (6.5A)
15. d (6.6A)

16. d (6.5A)
17. b (6.5B)
18. b (6.5C)
19. a (6.2A)
20. b (6.5A)

Cumulative Test: Chapters 4-6 Form F

1. c (5.2B)
2. b (5.1A)
3. d (5.3B)
4. a (5.3C)
5. c (5.5A)
6. b (5.6D)
7. b (5.7A)
8. a (6.1B)
9. b (6.1C)
10. d (6.2B)
11. a (6.3A)
12. b (6.4A)
13. c (6.5A)
14. b (4.1B)
15. a (4.2A)
16. b (4.3B)
17. d (4.3A)
18. c (4.4B)
19. b (5.1B)
20. a (5.3B)

Chapter 7 Test Form F

1. a (7.1A)
2. b (7.1A)
3. b (7.1B)
4. d (7.1B)
5. c (7.1C)
6. d (7.2A)
7. d (7.2A)
8. a (7.2B)

9. b (7.2B)
10. c (7.2C)
11. b (7.2C)
12. c (7.2D)
13. a (7.2D)
14. b (7.3A)
15. c (7.3A)
16. b (7.3B)
17. d (7.4A)
18. c (7.4B)
19. a (7.4C)
20. a (7.4D)

Chapter 8 Test Form F

1. a (8.1A)
2. b (8.1A)
3. c (8.1B)
4. d (8.1C)
5. b (8.1C)
6. c (8.2A)
7. c (8.2A)
8. b (8.3A)
9. a (8.3A)
10. a (8.3A)
11. c (8.4A)
12. b (8.4A)
13. a (8.4B)
14. c (8.4B)
15. a (8.4C)
16. b (8.4C)
17. d (8.5A)
18. c (8.5A)
19. d (8.6A)
20. d (8.6A)

Chapter 9 Test Form F

1. c (9.1A)
2. c (9.1C)

3. d (9.1B)

4. b (9.1B)

5. b (9.1C)

6. c (9.1D)

7. a (9.2A)

8. a (9.2A)

9. a (9.3A)

10. b (9.3A)

11. d (9.3B)

12. b (9.3B)

13. d (9.4B)

14. c (9.4B)

15. b (9.4B)

Cumulative Test: Chapters 7-9 Form F

1. c (7.1C)

2. a (7.2B)

3. b (7.4C)

4. a (7.3A)

5. c (7.4B)

6. a (8.1B)

7. d (8.3A)

8. b (8.4C)

9. c (8.5A)

10. d (8.6A)

11. b (9.1A)

12. d (9.2A)

13. b (9.3A)

14. a (9.3B)

15. a (9.4B)

Chapter 10 Test Form F

1. b (10.1A)

2. d (10.1A)

3. b (10.1B)

4. c (10.2A)

5. a (10.2A)

6. b (10.2A)

7. d (10.2A)

8. a (10.2B)

9. b (10.2B)

10. c (10.2B)

11. b (10.2B)

12. d (10.2C)

13. d (10.2C)

14. d (10.3A)

15. b (10.4A)

16. d (10.4A)

17. a (10.4A)

18. a (10.4B)

19. c (10.4B)

20. c (10.5A)

Chapter 11 Test Form F

1. c (11.1A)

2. b (11.1A)

3. d (11.1A)

4. d (11.2A)

5. a (11.2A)

6. b (11.2B)

7. b (11.2B)

8. a (11.3A)

9. b (11.3B)

10. b (11.4A)

11. c (11.4A)

12. d (11.5A)

13. b (11.5A)

14. b (11.5B)

15. a (11.5B)

Chapter 12 Test Form F

1. a (12.1A)

2. d (12.1A)

3. b (12.1B)

4. c (12.1B)

5. c (12.2A)

6. c (12.2A)

7. b (12.2A)

8. c (12.2B)

9. a (12.2B)

10. a (12.2C)

11. a (12.3B)

12. c (12.3A)

13. b (12.3B)

14. a (12.3B)

15. d (12.3C)

16. c (12.3C)

17. a (12.3D)

18. c (12.4A)

19. d (12.4A)

20. c (12.4A)

Cumulative Test: Chapters 10-12 Form F

1. a (10.1A)

2. c (10.2A)

3. a (10.2B)

4. b (10.4A)

5. d (10.4B)

6. c (11.2A)

7. d (11.3A)

8. c (11.4A)

9. b (11.5A)

10. b (11.5B)

11. b (12.1A)

12. a (12.2B)

13. c (12.3C)

14. b (12.2C)

15. b (12.4A)

Answers to Chapter Tests: Form F

Final Exam Form F

1. c (1.2C)
2. b (1.3B)
3. b (1.3C)
4. d (1.4A)
5. a (2.1B)
6. b (2.1C)
7. a (2.3A)
8. d (4.1C)
9. a (5.1A)
10. d (5.3B)
11. a (5.5C)
12. a (5.6D)
13. d (5.7A)
14. a (5.4B)
15. c (6.1C)
16. d (6.2B)
17. b (6.4A)
18. d (2.1D)
19. c (7.2A)
20. b (7.2B)
21. c (7.2C)
22. d (7.4D)
23. c (7.3A)
24. b (3.3B)
25. c (3.4A)
26. a (3.6A)
27. b (3.7A)
28. b (8.2A)
29. a (8.4A)
30. b (2.4A)
31. d (3.2A)
32. d (9.2A)
33. b (9.4B)
34. d (9.1A)
35. d (9.1C)
36. a (3.1B)
37. b (11.2A)

38. a (4.2A)
39. a (4.2B)
40. b (4.3A)
41. a (4.4A)
42. a (10.2A)
43. c (10.2A)
44. c (10.2B)
45. a (10.4A)
46. d (10.4B)
47. b (12.1A)
48. d (12.2A)
49. c (12.3C)
50. b (12.4A)

Chapter 1 Test Form G

1. b (1.1A)
2. a (1.1B)
3. b (1.2A)
4. c (1.2A)
5. d (1.2A)
6. b (1.2A)
7. a (1.2C)
8. b (1.2C)
9. d (1.2B)
10. c (1.2B)
11. a (1.2B)
12. a (1.2B)
13. b (1.2D)
14. a (1.2D)
15. b (1.3B)
16. b (1.3B)
17. d (1.3A)
18. d (1.3A)
19. b (1.3C)
20. d (1.3C)
21. d (1.4B)
22. b (1.4A)
23. a (1.1C)
24. c (1.1C)

Chapter 2 Test Form G

1. c (2.1A)
2. c (2.1A)
3. d (2.1A)
4. a (2.1B)
5. d (2.1B)
6. b (2.1B)
7. c (2.1D)
8. a (2.1C)
9. d (2.4A)
10. d (2.4A)
11. b (2.4B)
12. b (2.4B)
13. c (2.4C)
14. b (2.5A)
15. a (2.5B)
16. c (2.4C)
17. d (2.2A)
18. b (2.2B)
19. b (2.3A)
20. b (2.3C)
21. c (2.5C)
22. a (2.3B)

Chapter 3 Test Form G

1. b (3.1A)
2. c (3.1A)
3. c (3.3A)
4. d (3.3B)
5. b (3.4A)
6. a (3.2A)
7. c (3.3C)
8. b (3.4B)
9. c (3.5A)
10. a (3.5B)
11. c (3.2A)
12. c (3.6A)
13. d (3.2A)
14. b (3.7A)
15. b (3.1B)
16. c (3.1B)
17. a (3.5A)
18. b (3.5C)
19. a (3.3D)
20. c (3.1C)

Cumulative Test:
Chapters 1-3 Form G

1. b (1.2B)
2. d (1.2D)

3. b (1.3B)
4. a (1.3A)
5. c (1.3C)
6. d (1.4A)
7. b (2.1A)
8. c (2.1C)
9. b (2.5A)
10. d (2.5B)
11. b (2.2B)
12. c (2.3A)
13. a (2.4A)
14. c (3.3B)
15. c (3.3C)
16. b (3.5A)
17. a (3.5B)
18. b (3.6A)
19. d (3.5C)
20. d (3.7A)

Chapter 4 Test Form G

1. b (4.1A)
2. a (4.1B)
3. a (4.1C)
4. b (4.2A)
5. d (4.2B)
6. c (4.3A)
7. b (4.3A)
8. d (4.3B)
9. c (4.3B)
10. d (4.4A)
11. a (4.4A)
12. a (4.4B)
13. c (4.4B)
14. d (4.5A)
15. b (4.5A)

Answers to Chapter Tests: Form G

Chapter 5 Test Form G

1. a (5.1A)
2. c (5.1B)
3. a (5.2A)
4. d (5.1C)
5. c (5.1D)
6. c (5.3A)
7. d (5.3A)
8. b (5.3B)
9. a (5.3B)
10. d (5.3C)
11. a (5.3D)
12. b (5.5A)
13. c (5.5B)
14. b (5.4B)
15. d (5.5D)
16. a (5.6A)
17. b (5.6B)
18. a (5.6D)
19. b (5.7A)
20. d (5.7A)

Chapter 6 Test Form G

1. a (6.1A)
2. c (6.1A)
3. b (6.1B)
4. b (6.1C)
5. d (6.1A)
6. a (6.1A)
7. a (6.2A)
8. d (6.2B)
9. b (6.2B)
10. c (6.3A)
11. c (6.3A)
12. a (6.4A)
13. b (6.4A)
14. c (6.4B)

15. a (6.5A)
16. a (6.5A)
17. b (6.5A)
18. a (6.6A)
19. c (6.5B)
20. b (6.5C)

Cumulative Test: Chapters 4–6 Form G

1. b (5.1A)
2. c (5.1B)
3. b (5.5C)
4. d (5.3C)
5. b (5.6A)
6. c (5.6B)
7. a (5.6D)
8. b (5.4A)
9. b (6.2B)
10. a (6.3A)
11. c (6.4B)
12. b (6.5A)
13. a (6.6A)
14. b (4.1B)
15. b (4.2B)
16. c (4.3B)
17. c (4.4A)
18. c (4.3A)
19. c (4.2A)
20. a (5.1C)

Chapter 7 Test Form G

1. a (7.1A)
2. d (7.1A)
3. c (7.1B)
4. c (7.1B)
5. d (7.1C)
6. a (7.2A)

7. d (7.2A)
8. d (7.2B)
9. b (7.2B)
10. b (7.2C)
11. d (7.2C)
12. c (7.2D)
13. a (7.2D)
14. d (7.3A)
15. d (7.3A)
16. a (7.3B)
17. b (7.4A)
18. d (7.4B)
19. b (7.4C)
20. a (7.4D)

Chapter 8 Test Form G

1. c (8.1A)
2. d (8.1A)
3. b (8.1B)
4. c (8.1C)
5. b (8.1C)
6. a (8.2A)
7. b (8.2A)
8. c (8.3A)
9. d (8.3A)
10. d (8.3A)
11. a (8.4A)
12. c (8.4A)
13. c (8.4B)
14. a (8.4B)
15. c (8.4C)
16. d (8.4C)
17. a (8.5A)
18. a (8.5A)
19. b (8.6A)
20. d (8.6A)

Chapter 9 Test Form G

1. a (9.1A)
2. b (9.1A)
3. c (9.1B)
4. c (9.1C)
5. a (9.1D)
6. d (9.3A)
7. a (9.2A)
8. d (9.2A)
9. d (9.3A)
10. c (9.3A)
11. b (9.3B)
12. a (9.3B)
13. c (9.4B)
14. d (9.4B)
15. b (9.4B)

Cumulative Test: Chapters 7-9 Form G

1. c (7.1C)
2. a (7.2B)
3. d (7.4C)
4. c (7.3A)
5. b (7.3B)
6. c (8.1A)
7. a (8.1B)
8. b (8.2A)
9. b (8.4C)
10. c (8.5A)
11. b (9.1A)
12. d (9.1B)
13. b (9.2A)
14. d (9.3B)
15. b (9.4B)

Chapter 10 Test Form G

1. d (10.1A)
2. b (10.1A)
3. c (10.1B)
4. d (10.2A)
5. b (10.2A)
6. b (10.2A)
7. d (10.2A)
8. a (10.2B)
9. d (10.2B)
10. d (10.2B)
11. b (10.2B)
12. c (10.2C)
13. a (10.2C)
14. b (10.3A)
15. c (10.4A)
16. a (10.4A)
17. b (10.4A)
18. a (10.4B)
19. d (10.4B)
20. a (10.5A)

Chapter 11 Test Form G

1. a (11.1A)
2. b (11.1A)
3. c (11.1A)
4. a (11.2A)
5. d (11.2A)
6. a (11.2B)
7. c (11.2B)
8. d (11.3A)
9. b (11.3B)
10. d (11.4A)
11. c (11.4A)
12. c (11.5A)
13. b (11.5A)
14. a (11.5B)
15. a (11.5B)

Chapter 12 Test Form G

1. b (12.1A)
2. c (12.1A)
3. a (12.1B)
4. d (12.1B)
5. b (12.2A)
6. c (12.2A)
7. a (12.2A)
8. a (12.2B)
9. d (12.2B)
10. b (12.2C)
11. a (12.3A)
12. c (12.3A)
13. a (12.3B)
14. d (12.3B)
15. c (12.3C)
16. d (12.3C)
17. a (12.3D)
18. a (12.4A)
19. c (12.4A)
20. a (12.4A)

Cumulative Test: Chapters 10-12 Form G

1. b (10.1A)
2. a (10.2A)
3. b (10.2C)
4. d (10.4A)
5. b (10.4B)
6. b (11.1A)
7. b (11.2A)
8. c (11.3A)
9. b (11.4A)
10. d (11.5A)
11. c (12.1B)
12. d (12.2B)
13. a (12.3C)
14. b (12.3D)

Answers to Chapter Tests: Form G

15. d (12.4A)

Final Exam Form G

1. b (1.2C)
2. c (1.2D)
3. b (1.3C)
4. a (1.1C)
5. c (2.1A)
6. c (2.1B)
7. a (2.2A)
8. b (2.3C)
9. c (5.1A)
10. d (5.3C)
11. b (5.5D)
12. a (5.6C)
13. b (5.6D)
14. b (5.4B)
15. c (6.1C)
16. a (6.2A)
17. d (6.4B)
18. c (2.1D)
19. d (7.1A)
20. a (7.1C)
21. c (7.2A)
22. d (7.4B)
23. c (7.4D)
24. c (3.3A)
25. d (3.4A)
26. b (3.5A)
27. c (3.7A)
28. c (8.3A)
29. a (8.1A)
30. c (8.6A)
31. b (9.3A)
32. a (9.4A)
33. d (9.4B)
34. c (11.1A)
35. b (9.1D)

36. d (11.2B)
37. c (11.3A)
38. a (4.2A)
39. b (4.2B)
40. c (4.3A)
41. d (4.4A)
42. d (10.2A)
43. d (10.2A)
44. a (10.2B)
45. c (10.4A)
46. c (10.4B)
47. a (12.1A)
48. a (12.2C)
49. a (12.3C)
50. d (12.4A)

Chapter 1 Test Form H

1. d (1.1A)
2. b (1.1B)
3. c (1.2A)
4. a (1.2A)
5. d (1.2A)
6. b (1.1C)
7. b (1.2C)
8. c (1.2C)
9. a (1.2B)
10. b (1.2B)
11. b (1.2B)
12. b (1.2B)
13. c (1.2D)
14. c (1.2D)
15. c (1.3B)
16. a (1.3B)
17. b (1.3A)
18. b (1.3A)
19. d (1.3C)
20. c (1.3C)
21. a (1.4A)
22. c (1.4B)
23. a (1.1C)
24. c (1.1C)

Chapter 2 Test Form H

1. b (2.1A)
2. b (2.1A)
3. c (2.1B)
4. a (2.1B)
5. d (2.1D)
6. d (2.1C)
7. a (2.1C)
8. c (2.4A)
9. b (2.4A)
10. d (2.4B)
11. c (2.4B)

12. a (2.4C)
13. b (2.5A)
14. b (2.5A)
15. c (2.5B)
16. d (2.5C)
17. a (2.2A)
18. d (2.2B)
19. a (2.3A)
20. a (2.3C)
21. b (2.3B)
22. c (2.3B)

Chapter 3 Test Form H

1. d (3.1A)
2. a (3.1A)
3. b (3.3A)
4. c (3.3B)
5. c (3.4A)
6. a (3.2A)
7. c (3.3C)
8. b (3.4B)
9. b (3.5A)
10. d (3.5B)
11. a (3.6A)
12. a (3.2A)
13. d (3.2A)
14. d (3.7A)
15. a (3.1B)
16. b (3.1B)
17. a (3.5A)
18. d (3.5C)
19. b (3.3D)
20. d (3.1C)

**Cumulative Test:
Chapters 1-3 Form H**

1. a (1.2C)
2. c (1.2D)

3. c (1.3B)
4. d (1.3C)
5. a (1.4A)
6. d (1.1C)
7. b (2.1A)
8. c (2.1C)
9. a (2.4A)
10. d (2.5A)
11. d (2.2B)
12. b (2.3B)
13. c (3.2A)
14. c (2.1D)
15. a (3.3A)
16. a (3.4A)
17. d (3.5A)
18. c (3.6A)
19. d (3.5C)
20. d (3.7A)

Chapter 4 Test Form H

1. b (4.1A)
2. d (4.1B)
3. c (4.1C)
4. c (4.2A)
5. c (4.2B)
6. a (4.3A)
7. d (4.3A)
8. b (4.3B)
9. b (4.3B)
10. a (4.4A)
11. b (4.4A)
12. c (4.4B)
13. c (4.4B)
14. c (4.5A)
15. c (4.5A)

Answers to Chapter Tests: Form H

Chapter 5 Test Form H

1. a (5.2B)
2. b (5.1B)
3. b (5.1C)
4. d (5.1D)
5. a (5.3A)
6. b (5.3A)
7. d (5.3B)
8. c (5.3B)
9. c (5.3C)
10. a (5.3D)
11. d (5.5A)
12. c (5.5B)
13. b (5.5C)
14. a (5.5D)
15. a (5.6A)
16. b (5.6B)
17. c (5.4B)
18. a (5.6D)
19. d (5.7A)
20. d (5.7A)

Chapter 6 Test Form H

1. a (6.1A)
2. d (6.1A)
3. b (6.1B)
4. a (6.1B)
5. c (6.1C)
6. c (6.1A)
7. c (6.1A)
8. d (6.2A)
9. b (6.2B)
10. a (6.3A)
11. c (6.3A)
12. a (6.4A)
13. b (6.4A)
14. a (6.4B)

15. b (6.5A)
16. b (6.5A)
17. c (6.5A)
18. d (6.6A)
19. b (6.5B)
20. d (6.5C)

Cumulative Test: Chapters 4–6 Form H

1. b (5.1A)
2. d (5.1B)
3. c (5.1B)
4. d (5.3A)
5. b (5.5D)
6. a (5.6A)
7. b (5.6D)
8. b (6.1B)
9. a (6.1C)
10. c (6.2B)
11. a (6.3A)
12. b (6.4A)
13. c (6.5A)
14. b (6.5C)
15. b (4.1B)
16. a (4.2B)
17. c (4.3B)
18. d (4.4A)
19. a (4.3A)
20. d (5.2B)

Chapter 7 Test Form H

1. d (7.1A)
2. c (7.1A)
3. d (7.1B)
4. a (7.1B)
5. b (7.1C)
6. c (7.2A)

7. b (7.2A)
8. c (7.2B)
9. d (7.2B)
10. a (7.2C)
11. d (7.2C)
12. b (7.2D)
13. c (7.2D)
14. c (7.3A)
15. b (7.3A)
16. a (7.3B)
17. d (7.4A)
18. a (7.4B)
19. b (7.4C)
20. d (7.4D)

Chapter 8 Test Form H

1. a (8.1A)
2. d (8.1A)
3. a (8.1B)
4. b (8.1C)
5. c (8.1C)
6. a (8.2A)
7. b (8.2A)
8. d (8.3A)
9. b (8.3A)
10. d (8.3A)
11. a (8.4A)
12. a (8.4A)
13. b (8.4B)
14. c (8.4B)
15. c (8.4C)
16. d (8.4C)
17. c (8.5A)
18. c (8.5A)
19. b (8.6A)
20. d (8.6A)

Chapter 9 Test Form H

1. a (9.1A)
2. d (9.1A)
3. a (9.1C)
4. b (9.1B)
5. c (9.1C)
6. d (9.1D)
7. c (9.2A)
8. a (9.3A)
9. c (9.3A)
10. b (9.3B)
11. b (9.3B)
12. a (9.4A)
13. d (9.4B)
14. d (9.4B)
15. c (9.4B)

Cumulative Test:
Chapters 7-9 Form H

1. b (7.1A)
2. c (7.4A)
3. d (7.3A)
4. b (7.3B)
5. b (8.1B)
6. d (8.1C)
7. d (8.4A)
8. c (8.4C)
9. b (8.5A)
10. b (8.6A)
11. a (9.1A)
12. a (9.2A)
13. d (9.3A)
14. d (9.3B)
15. a (9.4B)

Chapter 10 Test Form H

1. a (10.1A)
2. c (10.1A)
3. d (10.1B)
4. c (10.2A)
5. b (10.2A)
6. d (10.2A)
7. c (10.2B)
8. a (10.2B)
9. d (10.2C)
10. c (10.2C)
11. c (10.3A)
12. b (10.4A)
13. a (10.4A)
14. d (10.4B)
15. c (10.5A)

Chapter 11 Test Form H

1. b (11.1A)
2. b (11.1A)
3. d (11.1A)
4. d (11.2A)
5. c (11.2A)
6. d (11.2B)
7. c (11.2B)
8. d (11.3A)
9. b (11.3B)
10. c (11.4A)
11. b (11.4A)
12. d (11.5A)
13. b (11.5A)
14. c (11.5B)
15. a (11.5B)

Chapter 12 Test Form H

1. a (12.1A)
2. d (12.1A)
3. d (12.1B)
4. b (12.1B)
5. a (12.2A)
6. c (12.2A)
7. c (12.2A)
8. d (12.2B)
9. a (12.2B)
10. d (12.2C)
11. b (12.3A)
12. b (12.3A)
13. c (12.3B)
14. c (12.3B)
15. b (12.3C)
16. b (12.3C)
17. d (12.3D)
18. b (12.4A)
19. c (12.4A)
20. d (12.4A)

Cumulative Test:
Chapters 10-12 Form H

1. d (10.1A)
2. a (10.2A)
3. c (10.2B)
4. b (10.4B)
5. c (10.5A)
6. b (11.1A)
7. d (11.2A)
8. c (11.3A)
9. a (11.4A)
10. b (11.5A)
11. c (12.1B)
12. a (12.2B)
13. b (12.3C)
14. d (12.3D)
15. b (12.4A)

Answers to Chapter Tests: Form H

Final Exam Form H

1. b (1.2D)
2. b (1.3B)
3. c (1.3C)
4. c (1.1C)
5. a (2.1B)
6. d (2.1C)
7. d (2.2A)
8. d (4.1C)
9. c (5.1B)
10. b (5.3D)
11. c (5.5D)
12. d (5.6B)
13. c (5.5B)
14. a (5.4B)
15. c (6.1B)
16. b (6.2B)
17. c (6.5A)
18. d (2.1D)
19. b (7.1A)
20. a (7.1B)
21. b (7.1C)
22. d (7.4B)
23. a (7.3A)
24. c (3.3A)
25. c (3.4A)
26. a (3.5A)
27. b (3.7A)
28. b (8.3A)
29. d (8.1A)
30. b (8.4A)
31. c (3.2A)
32. a (9.4A)
33. d (9.4B)
34. b (9.1A)
35. b (9.1C)
36. d (11.2B)
37. d (11.3A)
38. d (4.2A)
39. a (4.2B)
40. c (4.3A)
41. d (8.5A)
42. a (10.2A)
43. b (10.2A)
44. a (10.2B)
45. d (10.4A)
46. c (10.4B)
47. b (12.2A)
48. d (12.2B)
49. c (12.3B)
50. a (12.4A)

SELECTED TEXT TABLES

Table of Common Logarithms

Decimal approximations have been rounded to the nearest thousandth.

Number	Square Root	Cube Root	Number	Square Root	Cube Root
1	1	1	51	7.141	3.708
2	1.414	1.260	52	7.211	3.733
3	1.732	1.442	53	7.280	3.756
4	2	1.587	54	7.348	3.780
5	2.236	1.710	55	7.416	3.803
6	2.449	1.817	56	7.483	3.826
7	2.646	1.913	57	7.550	3.849
8	2.828	2	58	7.616	3.871
9	3	2.080	59	7.681	3.893
10	3.162	2.154	60	7.746	3.915
11	3.317	2.224	61	7.810	3.936
12	3.464	2.289	62	7.874	3.958
13	3.606	2.351	63	7.937	3.979
14	3.742	2.410	64	8	4
15	3.873	2.466	65	8.062	4.021
16	4	2.520	66	8.124	4.041
17	4.123	2.571	67	8.185	4.062
18	4.243	2.621	68	8.246	4.082
19	4.359	2.668	69	8.307	4.102
20	4.472	2.714	70	8.367	4.121
21	4.583	2.759	71	8.426	4.141
22	4.690	2.802	72	8.485	4.160
23	4.796	2.844	73	8.544	4.179
24	4.899	2.884	74	8.602	4.198
25	5	2.924	75	8.660	4.217
26	5.099	2.962	76	8.718	4.236
27	5.196	3	77	8.775	4.254
28	5.292	3.037	78	8.832	4.273
29	5.385	3.072	79	8.888	4.291
30	5.477	3.107	80	8.944	4.309
31	5.568	3.141	81	9	4.327
32	5.657	3.175	82	9.055	4.344
33	5.745	3.208	83	9.110	4.362
34	5.831	3.240	84	9.165	4.380
35	5.916	3.271	85	9.220	4.397
36	6	3.302	86	9.274	4.414
37	6.083	3.332	87	9.327	4.431
38	6.164	3.362	88	9.381	4.448
39	6.245	3.391	89	9.434	4.465
40	6.325	3.420	90	9.487	4.481
41	6.403	3.448	91	9.539	4.498
42	6.481	3.476	92	9.592	4.514
43	6.557	3.503	93	9.644	4.531
44	6.633	3.530	94	9.695	4.547
45	6.708	3.557	95	9.747	4.563
46	6.782	3.583	96	9.798	4.579
47	6.856	3.609	97	9.849	4.595
48	6.928	3.634	98	9.899	4.610
49	7	3.659	99	9.950	4.626
50	7.071	3.684	100	10	4.642

Table of Common Logarithms

Decimal approximations have been rounded to the nearest ten-thousandth.

x	0	1	2	3	4	5	6	7	8	9
1.0	.0000	.0043	.0086	.0128	.0170	.0212	.0253	.0294	.0334	.0374
1.1	.0414	.0453	.0492	.0531	.0569	.0607	.0645	.0682	.0719	.0755
1.2	.0792	.0828	.0864	.0899	.0934	.0969	.1004	.1038	.1072	.1106
1.3	.1139	.1173	.1206	.1239	.1271	.1303	.1335	.1367	.1399	.1430
1.4	.1461	.1492	.1523	.1553	.1584	.1614	.1644	.1673	.1703	.1732
1.5	.1761	.1790	.1818	.1847	.1875	.1903	.1931	.1959	.1987	.2014
1.6	.2041	.2068	.2095	.2122	.2148	.2175	.2201	.2227	.2253	.2279
1.7	.2304	.2330	.2355	.2380	.2405	.2430	.2455	.2480	.2504	.2529
1.8	.2553	.2577	.2601	.2625	.2648	.2672	.2695	.2718	.2742	.2765
1.9	.2788	.2810	.2833	.2856	.2878	.2900	.2923	.2945	.2967	.2989
2.0	.3010	.3032	.3054	.3075	.3096	.3118	.3139	.3160	.3181	.3201
2.1	.3222	.3243	.3263	.3284	.3304	.3324	.3345	.3365	.3385	.3404
2.2	.3424	.3444	.3464	.3483	.3502	.3522	.3541	.3560	.3579	.3598
2.3	.3617	.3636	.3655	.3674	.3692	.3711	.3729	.3747	.3766	.3784
2.4	.3802	.3820	.3838	.3856	.3874	.3892	.3909	.3927	.3945	.3962
2.5	.3979	.3997	.4014	.4031	.4048	.4065	.4082	.4099	.4116	.4133
2.6	.4150	.4166	.4183	.4200	.4216	.4232	.4249	.4265	.4281	.4298
2.7	.4314	.4330	.4346	.4362	.4378	.4393	.4409	.4425	.4440	.4456
2.8	.4472	.4487	.4502	.4518	.4533	.4548	.4564	.4579	.4594	.4609
2.9	.4624	.4639	.4654	.4669	.4683	.4698	.4713	.4728	.4742	.4757
3.0	.4771	.4786	.4800	.4814	.4829	.4843	.4857	.4871	.4886	.4900
3.1	.4914	.4928	.4942	.4955	.4969	.4983	.4997	.5011	.5024	.5038
3.2	.5051	.5065	.5079	.5092	.5105	.5119	.5132	.5145	.5159	.5172
3.3	.5185	.5198	.5211	.5224	.5237	.5250	.5263	.5276	.5289	.5302
3.4	.5315	.5328	.5340	.5353	.5366	.5378	.5391	.5403	.5416	.5428
3.5	.5441	.5453	.5465	.5478	.5490	.5502	.5514	.5527	.5539	.5551
3.6	.5563	.5575	.5587	.5599	.5611	.5623	.5635	.5647	.5658	.5670
3.7	.5682	.5694	.5705	.5717	.5729	.5740	.5752	.5763	.5775	.5786
3.8	.5798	.5809	.5821	.5832	.5843	.5855	.5866	.5877	.5888	.5899
3.9	.5911	.5922	.5933	.5944	.5955	.5966	.5977	.5988	.5999	.6010
4.0	.6021	.6031	.6042	.6053	.6064	.6075	.6085	.6096	.6107	.6117
4.1	.6128	.6138	.6149	.6160	.6170	.6180	.6191	.6201	.6212	.6222
4.2	.6232	.6243	.6253	.6263	.6274	.6284	.6294	.6304	.6314	.6325
4.3	.6335	.6345	.6355	.6365	.6375	.6385	.6395	.6405	.6415	.6425
4.4	.6435	.6444	.6454	.6464	.6474	.6484	.6493	.6503	.6513	.6522
4.5	.6532	.6542	.6551	.6561	.6571	.6580	.6590	.6599	.6609	.6618
4.6	.6628	.6637	.6646	.6656	.6665	.6675	.6684	.6693	.6702	.6712
4.7	.6721	.6730	.6739	.6749	.6758	.6767	.6776	.6785	.6794	.6803
4.8	.6812	.6821	.6830	.6839	.6848	.6857	.6866	.6875	.6884	.6893
4.9	.6902	.6911	.6920	.6928	.6937	.6946	.6955	.6964	.6972	.6981
5.0	.6990	.6998	.7007	.7016	.7024	.7033	.7042	.7050	.7059	.7067
5.1	.7076	.7084	.7093	.7101	.7110	.7118	.7126	.7135	.7143	.7152
5.2	.7160	.7168	.7177	.7185	.7193	.7202	.7210	.7218	.7226	.7235
5.3	.7243	.7251	.7259	.7267	.7275	.7284	.7292	.7300	.7308	.7316
5.4	.7324	.7332	.7340	.7348	.7356	.7364	.7372	.7380	.7388	.7396

Table of Common Logarithms

x	0	1	2	3	4	5	6	7	8	9
5.5	.7404	.7412	.7419	.7427	.7435	.7443	.7451	.7459	.7466	.7474
5.6	.7482	.7490	.7497	.7505	.7513	.7520	.7528	.7536	.7543	.7551
5.7	.7559	.7566	.7574	.7582	.7489	.7597	.7604	.7612	.7619	.7627
5.8	.7634	.7642	.7649	.7657	.7664	.7672	.7679	.7686	.7694	.7701
5.9	.7709	.7716	.7723	.7731	.7738	.7745	.7752	.7760	.7767	.7774
6.0	.7782	.7789	.7796	.7803	.7810	.7818	.7825	.7832	.7839	.7846
6.1	.7853	.7860	.7868	.7875	.7882	.7889	.7896	.7903	.7910	.7917
6.2	.7924	.7931	.7938	.7945	.7952	.7959	.7966	.7973	.7980	.7987
6.3	.7993	.8000	.8007	.8014	.8021	.8028	.8035	.8041	.8048	.8055
6.4	.8062	.8069	.8075	.8082	.8089	.8096	.8102	.8109	.8116	.8122
6.5	.8129	.8136	.8142	.8149	.8156	.8162	.8169	.8176	.8182	.8189
6.6	.8195	.8202	.8209	.8215	.8222	.8228	.8235	.8241	.8248	.8254
6.7	.8261	.8267	.8274	.8280	.8287	.8293	.8299	.8306	.8312	.8319
6.8	.8325	.8331	.8338	.8344	.8351	.8357	.8363	.8370	.8376	.8382
6.9	.8388	.8395	.8401	.8407	.8414	.8420	.8426	.8432	.8439	.8445
7.0	.8451	.8457	.8463	.8470	.8476	.8482	.8488	.8494	.8500	.8506
7.1	.8513	.8519	.8525	.8531	.8537	.8543	.8549	.8555	.8561	.8567
7.2	.8573	.8579	.8585	.8591	.8597	.8603	.8609	.8615	.8621	.8627
7.3	.8633	.8639	.8645	.8651	.8657	.8663	.8669	.8675	.8681	.8686
7.4	.8692	.8698	.8704	.8710	.8716	.8722	.8727	.8733	.8739	.8745
7.5	.8751	.8756	.8762	.8768	.8774	.8779	.8785	.8791	.8797	.8802
7.6	.8808	.8814	.8820	.8825	.8831	.8837	.8842	.8848	.8854	.8859
7.7	.8865	.8871	.8876	.8882	.8887	.8893	.8899	.8904	.8910	.8915
7.8	.8921	.8927	.8932	.8938	.8943	.8949	.8954	.8960	.8965	.8971
7.9	.8976	.8982	.8987	.8993	.8998	.9004	.9009	.9015	.9020	.9025
8.0	.9031	.9036	.9042	.9047	.9053	.9058	.9063	.9069	.9074	.9079
8.1	.9085	.9090	.9096	.9101	.9106	.9112	.9117	.9122	.9128	.9133
8.2	.9138	.9143	.9149	.9154	.9159	.9165	.9170	.9175	.9180	.9186
8.3	.9191	.9196	.9201	.9206	.9212	.9217	.9222	.9227	.9232	.9238
8.4	.9243	.9248	.9253	.9258	.9263	.9269	.9274	.9279	.9284	.9289
8.5	.9294	.9299	.9304	.9309	.9315	.9320	.9325	.9330	.9335	.9340
8.6	.9345	.9350	.9355	.9360	.9365	.9370	.9375	.9380	.9385	.9390
8.7	.9395	.9400	.9405	.9410	.9415	.9420	.9425	.9430	.9435	.9440
8.8	.9445	.9450	.9455	.9460	.9465	.9469	.9474	.9479	.9484	.9489
8.9	.9494	.9499	.9504	.9509	.9513	.9518	.9523	.9528	.9533	.9538
9.0	.9542	.9547	.9552	.9557	.9562	.9566	.9571	.9576	.9581	.9586
9.1	.9590	.9595	.9600	.9605	.9609	.9614	.9619	.9624	.9628	.9633
9.2	.9638	.9643	.9647	.9652	.9657	.9661	.9666	.9671	.9675	.9680
9.3	.9685	.9689	.9694	.9699	.9703	.9708	.9713	.9717	.9722	.9727
9.4	.9731	.9736	.9741	.9745	.9750	.9754	.9759	.9763	.9768	.9773
9.5	.9777	.9782	.9786	.9791	.9795	.9800	.9805	.9809	.9814	.9818
9.6	.9823	.9827	.9832	.9836	.9841	.9845	.9850	.9854	.9859	.9863
9.7	.9868	.9872	.9877	.9881	.9886	.9890	.9894	.9899	.9903	.9908
9.8	.9912	.9917	.9921	.9926	.9930	.9934	.9939	.9943	.9948	.9952
9.9	.9956	.9961	.9965	.9969	.9974	.9978	.9983	.9987	.9991	.9996

AIM for Success

Motivation

- Prepare to succeed.

  - Be motivated!

  - Actively pursue success!

- List two reasons you are taking this course.

- Are the reasons you listed sufficient motivation for you to succeed?

Commitment

- List one or two current activities (sports, hobbies, music, dance, art, etc.) in which you would like to improve.

- Next to each activity, put the number of hours per week you spend doing that activity.

- You must commit at least the same amount of time to math.

Develop a "Can Do" Attitude

- Be an active learner.

- Take responsibility for studying.

- Attend class.

- Participate in class discussions.

- Math is not a spectator sport.

- Do the homework—**regularly!**

- Create good study habits.

Strategies for Success

- Know the course requirements.
- Manage your time effectively.
- Take complete notes in class.
- Ask a question when you are confused.

Study Strategies

- Use flash cards for important definitions and formulas.

- Set aside time for study and homework.

- Form a study group.

- Keep up to date.

Text Features that Promote Success

- Prep Tests
- Annotated examples
- "You Try It" problems
- Chapter Reviews
- Chapter Tests
- Cumulative Reviews

Word Problems

- Read the problem.

- Make a list of known and unknown quantities.

- Develop a strategy.

- Solve the problem.

- Check your answer.

Preparing for a Test

- Start at least three days before the test.
- Read the Chapter Summary.
- Review every section.
- Do the Chapter Review Exercises.
- Do the Chapter Test.

Stay Focused!

- Do not fall behind.

- Remind yourself why you are taking this course.

- Success demands effort.

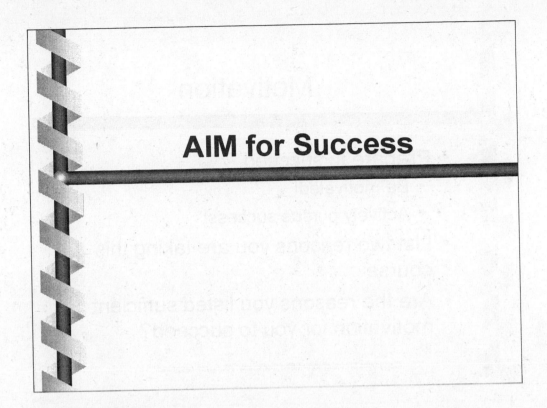

Explain to students that the purpose of this lesson is to suggest to them successful strategies that will help them succeed in your class. The most important aspect of success is consistent practice.

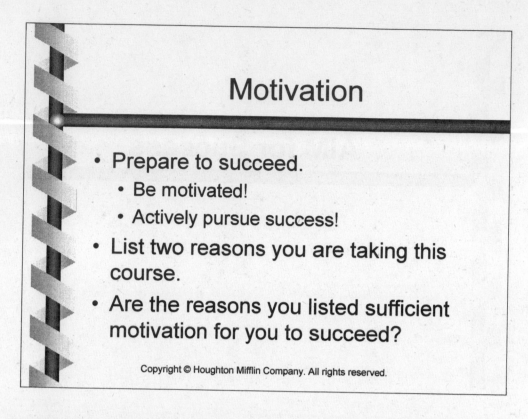

Motivation

- Prepare to succeed.
  - Be motivated!
  - Actively pursue success!
- List two reasons you are taking this course.
- Are the reasons you listed sufficient motivation for you to succeed?

It is easy for students to be motivated during the first week of class. An important key to success is to revitalize that motivation throughout the term. Have students list reasons they are taking this class. A reason does not have to be, "to learn math." Whatever reasons students mention, suggest they reflect on those reasons when their enthusiasm wanes.

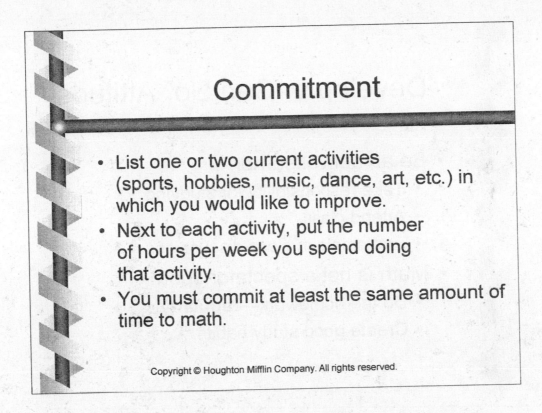

Commitment

- List one or two current activities (sports, hobbies, music, dance, art, etc.) in which you would like to improve.
- Next to each activity, put the number of hours per week you spend doing that activity.
- You must commit at least the same amount of time to math.

Having students list activities they currently pursue and the amount of time they spend doing those activities will help them understand that success in math requires devoting a lot of time to studying it.

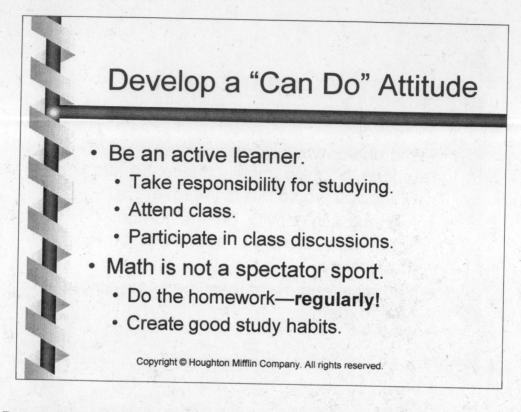

Develop a "Can Do" Attitude

- Be an active learner.
  - Take responsibility for studying.
  - Attend class.
  - Participate in class discussions.
- Math is not a spectator sport.
  - Do the homework—**regularly!**
  - Create good study habits.

People who feel part of a community are generally active in the community. This activity is rewarding to the participant and it benefits the community. The same is true for the community of the classroom. Students who participate in class become active learners who take responsibility for learning.

Encourage students to consistently study math. Studying a half-hour every day (which is probably not enough for most students) is better than spending three and one-half hours once a week.

Learning math is much like learning to play the guitar, piano, or any other musical instrument. It cannot be achieved by watching. The student must practice.

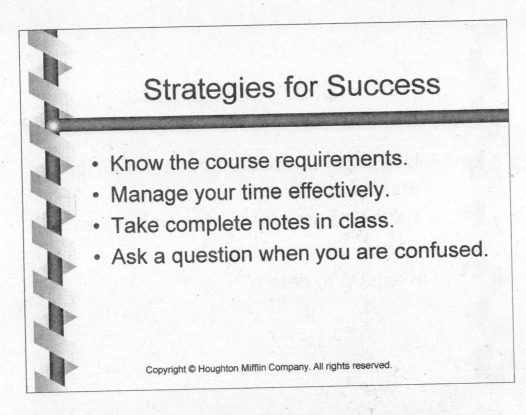

Strategies for Success

- Know the course requirements.
- Manage your time effectively.
- Take complete notes in class.
- Ask a question when you are confused.

Give students a course syllabus and go over it with them. Besides the course requirements, let students know where they can go for help. Encourage them to seek help immediately upon having difficulty.

There is a sample time management form in the AIM for Success portion of the text. Many people have unrealistic expectations of how much time is available to meet personal, work, and educational demands. Encourage students to complete the form. It may help them in becoming more realistic about how much time they have available to study.

Students should take complete notes that include all steps to the solution of a problem. These notes can then be used as additional models for doing homework.

Encourage students to ask questions but to stay away from "I don't understand anything." First, it is not true, and second, it does not help in finding the root of the confusion.

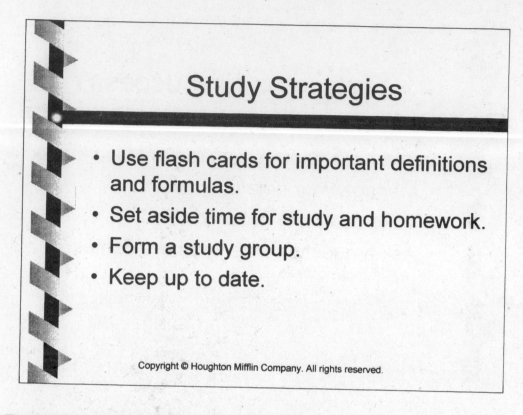

Study Strategies

- Use flash cards for important definitions and formulas.
- Set aside time for study and homework.
- Form a study group.
- Keep up to date.

Encourage students to keep flash cards with them. Any time they have a few minutes (waiting for a friend, on the subway), they should take them out and review them.

It is an advantage for students to arrange their schedules so they have a free hour right after class. This is the perfect time to review the class material. Also suggest that they rework the examples in their notes before starting on the homework.

Urge students to form a study group. These groups should meet at the same time each week.

To be a successful math student requires constant practice. The best time to start homework is right after class when the topic is fresh. This will help solidify new knowledge. Another learning aid is to review the homework before class.

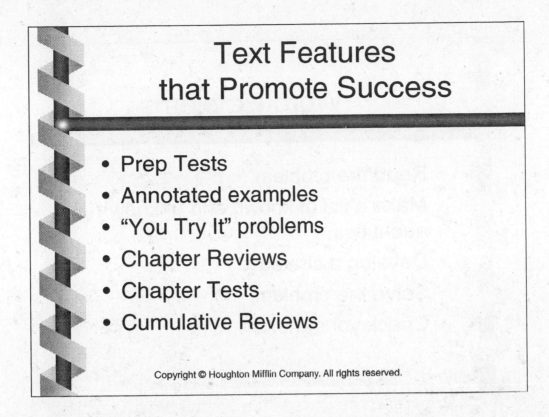

Text Features
that Promote Success

- • Prep Tests
- • Annotated examples
- • "You Try It" problems
- • Chapter Reviews
- • Chapter Tests
- • Cumulative Reviews

Guide students through the features of the text that will help them succeed. Students should turn to the pages mentioned below.

•Prep Tests – These tests (see page 200) focus on skills that are required for the upcoming chapter. The answers to the Prep Test are in the Answer Section (see page A12). Next to each answer, there is a reference (except in Chapter 1) to the objective from which that question was taken. Students should review the lesson material corresponding to any question that was missed.

•Annotated examples are designated by the HOW TO feature (see page 85). After reading through an annotated example, the student should cover up the solution and try to solve the problem without looking at it.

•You Try It – Next to each Example (see page 86), there is a corresponding You Try It. Students should study the solution to the Example and then attempt the You Try It. A complete solution to the You Try It can be found in the Appendix (see page S5).

•Chapter Reviews Exercises (see page 251) and Chapter Tests (see page 253) help students prepare for a test. As with the Prep Tests, the Chapter Review Exercises and Chapter Test have objective references listed with the answers in the Answer Section so that students can focus on the objectives associated with questions they missed.

•The Cumulative Reviews (see page 255) allow students to refresh skills learned in earlier chapters. The answers to all Cumulative Review exercises are in the Answer Section along with an objective reference.

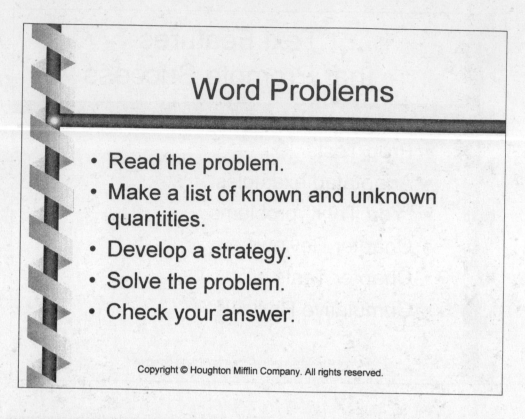

Urge students to take a disciplined approach to solving word problems. The most fundamental part of solving word problems is to identify what must be found. Have students turn to page 88 and look at Example 6. Without asking students to solve the problem, have them write a <u>sentence</u> that states what must be found.

Each of the word problem examples in the text shows both a strategy and the solution for solving the problem. For the You Try It problems, students are given a place to write their own strategies (see page 88).

Encourage students to check their answers.

412

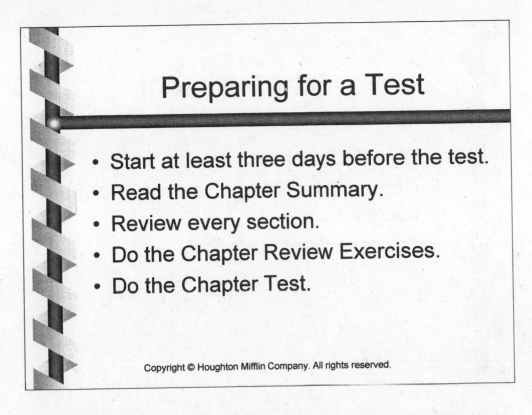

Preparing for a Test

- Start at least three days before the test.
- Read the Chapter Summary.
- Review every section.
- Do the Chapter Review Exercises.
- Do the Chapter Test.

Preparing for a test should start well before the actual date. Remind students that if they keep up with class assignments, preparing for a test will be much easier.

At least 3 days before the test, students should:

•Read the Chapter Summary.

•Review every section, paying close attention to items mentioned in the Chapter Summary. Attempt a few problems from each objective in the exercise sets.

•Do the Chapter Review Exercises. Remind students that the objective reference next to each answer in the Answer Section indicates the objective from which the exercise was taken.

•Do the Chapter Test. Set aside the amount of time allotted for the actual test, making sure there are no interruptions.

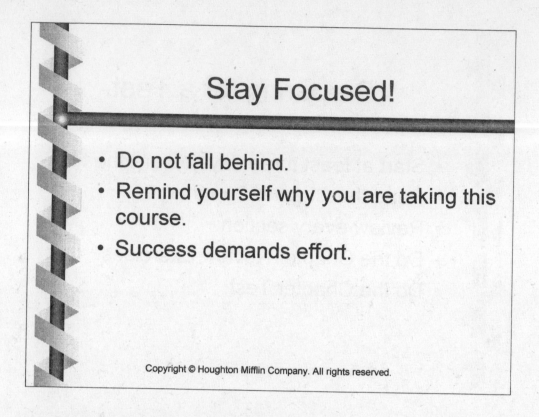

Stay Focused!

- Do not fall behind.
- Remind yourself why you are taking this course.
- Success demands effort.

Remind students that the most important factor that leads to success in math is to keep up—they must not fall behind.

Encourage students to review the reasons why they are taking this course. Even if it is to complete a degree requirement and they hate math, completing this course is a necessary prerequisite to reaching that goal. Urge them to complete the class so that math is not an obstacle to success.

Remind students that all successful endeavors require effort.